PUBLISHED ON THE FOUNDATION

ESTABLISHED IN MEMORY OF

PHILIP HAMILTON McMILLAN

OF THE CLASS OF 1894

YALE COLLEGE

NET IMPRESSIONS

BY

A. G. KELLER

WILLIAM GRAHAM SUMNER PROFESSOR OF
THE SCIENCE OF SOCIETY, EMERITUS,
YALE UNIVERSITY

NEW HAVEN
YALE UNIVERSITY PRESS
LONDON · HUMPHREY MILFORD · OXFORD UNIVERSITY PRESS
1942

To

Maurice Rea Davie *and* William Ewart Lawrence

*With Enduring Appreciation
and Affection*

PREFACE

Ceteros pudeat, si qui ita se litteris abdiderunt, ut nihil possint ex eis neque ad communem adferre fructum neque in aspectum lucemque proferre. M. T. Cicero, Pro Archia, 12. (Which is to say, that it is nothing to be proud of, if one spends time and energy upon studies that are inconsequential to human living.)
If we could first know where we are and whither we are tending, we could better judge what to do and how to do it. A. Lincoln, opening Freeport Debates, quoted by Sandburg, C., *Lincoln, Prairie Years,* II, 103.

A "NET IMPRESSION" is a kind of precipitate or residue. It is like a composite photograph. The evidence it rests upon is largely incapable of documentation because it is an accumulation of experience or of reading whose significance was not realized at the time, often long ago, so that it is now irrecoverable, so far as source identification goes. The pieces that make up this volume represent the way certain matters look to one man, especially in their contemporary aspects, after years of concern with their earlier phases. They are opinions and inferences rather than demonstrations. Learned apparatus is renounced, and not without a sigh of relief.

As these reflections were set down on often widely separated occasions during the last ten years or so, there is bound to be some repetitiousness. When detected, it has not always been eliminated, for what is repeated has seemed repeatable, particularly when the angle of approach has varied. In a general way, what follows is a set of corollaries or extensions upon principles arrived at during forty-odd years of study and teaching. I have tried to set the tone of this collection through the citation of the two quotations which head this preface.

A. G. KELLER

West Boothbay Harbor, Maine,
September 1, 1942.

CONTENTS

NET IMPRESSIONS

I

THE SCIENTIFIC STUDY OF SOCIETY.

As long ago as 1874 Herbert Spencer set forth convincingly the need of a science of society. That need is more vital now than ever before. Issues involving the life of human society are wider, deeper, more complicated, and more threatening than at any time in the past. Maladjustments in any one part of the world are no longer purely local in their effects, for the earth's peoples have been drawn together into such close interrelations that no one of them can live unto itself alone. Not so long ago, the assassination at Sarajevo would not have been heard of outside a circle of short radius. Shrinkage of distance has brought societies into a proximity by reason of which their interests are the more likely to overlap, chafe, and generate heat. The need of a science upon which to develop an art of dealing with social issues of the present and future is no less than imperative.

That an urgent need exists is, however, no evidence at all that it is about to be satisfied. No competent science of society is now in being, nor is there any clear prospect that it will be evoked within any predictable period of the future. It is even debatable whether there can ever be a science of society deserving of the name. All one needs to do to envisage the case is to make some kind of comparison between what is now called social science and any one of the physical sciences that we live by. Such a comparison can be made by imagining the race bereft, over night, of a real or working science—chemistry, for instance. Suppose all the manuals and other chemical documents were entirely to disappear; and, to make the case extreme, that those who had been familiar with the lost knowledge could rescue none of it by writing down promptly what they had been carrying in their heads. What would happen to the very apparatus of living, all along the line, beginning with the food-supply itself? Of course the loss would be irreparable, in the sense, at least, that the race would have to go back and then face about to encounter the prospect of centuries on centuries of effort in the re-doing of what had already been once done, tested, accepted, and stored away as an asset of mankind.

Imagine, on the other hand, that all the writings on social science were to be swept away. How much poorer would the race be? To what degree would it be crippled in facing the future? There are some who assert that the only thing to be learned from history is that there is nothing to be learned from history. We are being adjured, nowadays, even by self-styled economists, not to pay any attention to the "old" economics. Adam Smith and Mill are alluded to much as a modern astronomer or chemist might refer to the astrologer or alchemist. (But fancy a chemist who would reject the finding of his predecessors that water is H_2O and assert that, under some new dispensation, it will be H_3O, or even, in noble simplicity, HO: that the H_2O phase is all old and superseded stuff!)

The fact is that no one would be much terrified by the prospect of losing what social science we have. It might be deplorable in some academic way, though the practical men might insist that mankind would be better off to be rid of a mass of academic nonsense. Few would mourn because men must now, else they were lost, do all that work over again. Thousands of volumes on social themes could be spared, to the economy of shelf-space in libraries and of burdensome and unprofitable research. The only reason for reading a large percentage of books on social subjects is to find out how not to view or study society.

The degree of misgiving felt at the prospective loss of a physical science as contrasted with that of social science is a good enough measure of the scientific character accorded the two types respectively.

One further comparison: suppose that a science comparable to chemistry were available within the social realm—a science with laws and an art based upon them, accepted as a matter of course by everyone, whether or not understood by them. Suppose that defective social machinery could be taken to some expert with half the confidence reposed as a matter of course in the ordinary automobile mechanic; suppose, even, that there were the justified confidence in social doctors that there is in a good physician or surgeon; then would not this life of ours on earth become an infinitely less hazardous and blind existence?

The question is a rhetorical one, carrying its own answer.

Any competent student of society is clear enough as to the impossibility of developing a science of society comparable in exactitude to the laboratory sciences and outfitted with laws as definite and cogent as theirs. To hope for such success is futile. Hopes and procedures must take account of the nature of the materials upon which a proposed science of society must work. We have to do the best we can with things as they are, under the conditions imposed by the nature of society and of social phenomena. The conviction is re-stated here, not re-argued, that the student of society had better develop a method approaching, as closely as conditions within the societal range allow, to that of the natural sciences—which we trust enough to live by them, however foolishly we may rail at them in our loftier moods. We can at least work, instead of dreaming and chattering. We can at least begin by observing how things are, and facing them as they are, instead of imagining them to be as they are not and then erecting futile utopian structures upon phantasms so agreeable that we are autohypnotized into believing them real.

We can begin by rejecting, once and for all, and then absolutely barring the doors against, the natural and favorite delusions of the past, which have manifestly profited us nothing to speak of. The common characteristics of them all is their origin in deduction from emotionally adopted major premises. Their originators have been the "Builders of Delusion," whom Mr. Henshaw Ward has sufficiently identified.

There is no need to expend much space upon the non-scientific writers of the past any more than to devote much time and effort to reading them. There is admittedly an historical value in the record of men's thinking, however unscientific it may have been; but that does not mean that their conclusions are of any validity whatever. Scattered through the poetry and philosophy of even the remote past are stray bits of genuine insight which it is a pleasure to encounter; even in so early and unpremeditated a piece of artistic narrative as Homer's, occur keen observations upon life as lived by men; but they are at most no more than materials for a science, not science at all. Utterances that sound true and profound may turn out to be so, or they may not; they carry no guarantee or authority in themselves but only as they are found, perhaps long subsequently, to fall in with conclusions drawn by induction from accumulated and organized experience.

In *The Origin of Species,* Darwin scrupulously accords recognition to everyone he has heard of who has in any measure anticipated the evolution theory. The classic case of an obscure contributor to a volume on naval timber is probably the most striking as an illustration of Darwin's honesty of character. Among the rest he cites Goethe, a man of insight, if there ever was one, and of no small scientific attainment. But most of these forerunners had done no more than set down a happy thought; the citation of Lucretius, for instance, as an "anticipator of evolution" is evidence only of Darwin's scrupulosity. Wallace himself, though called a co-discoverer of the evolution theory, maintained all his life that Darwin alone had established the theory, declaring at the Darwin centenary, in 1909, that his own share in that exploit was to Darwin's as two weeks to twenty-one years—and he entitled his own work on evolution "Darwinism." Only Darwin carried the guns, in his huge collection of classified and organized materials, to win the campaign. He could demonstrate; the rest could not, not even Lamarck or Wallace, much less Mathews, or Goethe, or Lucretius. Evolutionists have ever since drawn upon the Darwinian materials to an astonishing degree, not to mention their imitation of and reverence for the Darwinian methods.

The case is not utterly dissimilar, in the range of social evolution, with Spencer.[1] However much of a philosopher, as distinguished from a scientist, Spencer was, when he came to his *Principles of Sociology* he was forced away from his "diabolical dialectics" into the collection of materials. For once, at least, he was obliged to renounce the juggling of theories and get down to the laborious accumulation and comparison of original data. Presumably, if he had been built that way, he too might have compiled a list of "anticipators," to include every antecedent writer upon social topics back at least to Confucius, or Plato, or even to Job. Later sociologists have won prestige by supplying learnedly irrelevant lists of such forerunners: Plato, Aristotle, Cicero, Seneca, Vico, Machiavelli, and other writers whom the recorder has happened to have read, heard about, and consulted *ad hoc*. These enterprises seem to have been pursued upon the theory that anyone who has relieved himself of any thoughts upon human social arrangements is a "sociologist," whereas, despite Comte's invention of "sociologie," the first man who has a genuine claim to the fathering of sociology as a science is the man who did the first inductive, systematic, scientific job, however defective, upon the evolution and life of human society as a whole—the first man to demonstrate that society is a whole and to indicate the articulation of its several major institutions—and that

1. See essay on "Outstanding Sociologists and Others," below.

man is Spencer. After Spencer, once remarked Dr. George B. Adams, history could no longer be written as it had been before.

Up to Spencer's time, treatises upon society as a whole did not bear the characteristic mark of science: universality as to place and time, together with the free employment of the comparative method. Comte rested his often acute inferences upon evidence that must be called contemporary and local. And there was in the preceding treatises upon society another defect much more serious than this, one which Comte too shared, and which Spencer, indeed, never outgrew, namely, the above-mentioned approach by way of deduction from grand major premises adopted under the spell of "logical," wishful thinking. This kind of intellectual exercise, as the unsophisticated forerunner of science, is natural enough in any field; all the sciences grew out of such soil; and the record of that growth is of high historical importance. There can be no fault to find with the study of it, as of other false starts; but when that earlier procedure is prolonged into the present, or when it is conceded any weight of authority out of the past, the result is superstition and not science. As well stage a really thoroughgoing comedy, or farce, or tragedy by resurrecting the methods and authority of the shaman.

The construction of utopias is self-confessed wishfulness; yet the somewhat unlearned H. G. Wells is on record that utopia-making is, and should be, the prime occupation of "sociologists." One of the world's most prominent utopia-dreamers was Plato. He acquired far-reaching authority, though it was of a type unrecognized and unconferred by science, and succeeded in muddling the thinking of generations. He is one of the pre-scientists to whom certain sociologists lay vaunting claim as a lineal progenitor; to them, I repeat, anyone, especially any prominent person, who has emitted striking opinions, no matter how they have been formed, about any human society, is a sociologist—all the way from Moses to Joseph Smith, Jr., from the witch of Endor to Mother Jones. No wonder, therefore, that the philosophers acclaimed as "authorities"—no matter how consistently laid low, domino-fashion, by their own successors—have continued, especially in the social realm, to enjoy a species of ancestor-worship.

This untoward result has been contributed unto by the common and unscientific habit of seeking agency rather than cause. How did the French Revolution come about? Through the philosophy of Rousseau and others! And did not these same profound thinkers exercise a "creative" function in the New World? And so on. Then ensues a dithyrambic eulogy on the power of ideas (which no one denies), with the implication, at least, that ideas pop up, full-blown and without antecedents, in the inspired minds of great men. This is a fancy derived straight from primitive daimonism. It would be an insult to any enlightened historian to assume that he knew no better than to ignore the causal antecedents of any revolution. He knows that the Rousseaus do no more than vocalize for the inarticulate at the apt time, and that the apt time is when the inarticulate are miserable enough (because they are in a state, automatically evolved, of protracted maladjustment) to rally to any battlecry, however vague—in fact, the vaguer the better—into which they can read a promise of relief. Hence the slogans: "Rights of Man," "Natural Rights," "Égalité," "Fraternité."

Wishful or wistful thinkers, as the term implies, take counsel of emotion. They are idealists in the plain sense of that word and, as such, are to be ruled out of science. It ought not to be necessary to qualify this statement, either to avoid abuse or to guard against misconception. With the latter object alone in view, I call attention to the fact of common experience that no ideal, strictly speaking, has even been realized on earth. Ideas have been realized; but the antithesis between "idealist" and "realist," or "materialist," or "pragmatist," betrays clearly enough that ideals by common usage are figments of fancy, generally arrived at by self-persuasion that things are not as they are in experience, but are, or may be, what one wishes, even yearns, that they were or might be. A yearning used to be regarded, and still is among juveniles of whatever age in years, as proof positive of the existence of the object of yearning—say, of immortality; but for the chastened or the discreet that proof exists no more. I am aware that the noun "ideal" is used by a metaphorical shift and an understatement to mean less than an "unrealizable vision," just as "infinite" or "immeasurable" is invoked as a colorful overstatement for "very long" or "very numerous"; but to execute a verbal shift (and then to oscillate according to the demands of the argument between makeshift and original) seems to me as tricky as to make "religious" mean "moral" or, more vulgarly, unostentatiously to alter the figures on a bank note in common circulation.

To bring the issue to a practical head: pure science is realistic, and nothing else, and in it emotion is out of order; in applied science, while idealism is irrelevant and emotion a good servant but a bad master, amelioration through readjustment is always in order, as is also any kind of realistic betterment-program that takes account of things as they are. I know that programs have been brought off in the social realm that the opposition has branded, partisan-fashion, as idle dreams; the most realistic social scientist may not be bold enough to assert of any program, perhaps, that it is impossible, as perpetual motion is impossible. That is because the science of society lacks the exactitude of the laboratory. But any person of sense, whether or not he is a professional student of society, must look with deep suspicion upon every social scheme which involves, let us say, the "alteration of human nature." Such a scheme, and plenty of them have been proposed, is idealistic enough; it well illustrates the need of ruling idealism—and, naturally, "ideology"—out of science. So do all social programs that propose to effect within a short time a radical change in long-established and repeatedly tested mores and institutions. Whoever coined the saying that "Rome was not built in a day" knew that. Popular wisdom gleaned out of ordinary experience confirms him. And yet even the honest prophet of reform—who yearns with pure heart, and not because there is something in it for himself—is all ready to cast such truisms overboard, and the crowd is entirely likely to applaud him until such time as, in disillusionment, they force him to enact the star rôle in some Jonah episode.

The gist of the matter is that if we want a science of society, we must rule all the builders of delusion, ancient and reverend, or modern and mænadic, out of the enterprise.

Also all the philosophers and metaphysicians. No scientist has any confidence in the belief that ultimate truth is lodged somewhere in the constitution of human minds, to be extracted and assembled by logic or dialectics of any description. All the sciences have had to extricate themselves from metaphysics before they could go their proper way, just as they were obliged to grow out of the daimonistic phase—as Comte expressed it, out of the religious and the metaphysical stages into the positive.

Whoever has insight knows that life is surrounded by mystery; that every avenue of positive knowledge debouches upon the inexplicable. Where verifiable facts are lacking, science must stop; that is where every scientist, in his quality of scientist, must become agnostic, as he repeats an honest: "I do not know." Besides the Knowable Unknown, there is to science an endless Unknowable; whether or not one believes that it can be known by religion or metaphysics is irrelevant to him as

a scientist. The alignment of scientific expectation, based upon anticipated recurrence, with religious or philosophical faith, as being even
of the same species or genus, is due to inexcusable carelessness of
analysis, if to nothing worse.

Although science must needs have developed out of the correction
of original fumblings, it can get no profit from the attempt to settle
metaphysical issues as a prerequisite to its actual labors. Such issues—
say that of free will versus determinism—never have been settled, and
in all probability never will be; and then, again, it does not matter
much or at all to science whether they are settled or not. Nor does it
concern science whether or not its findings issue, when fastened upon
by philosophers, in this or that theory about God and His relation to
the universe. In these days we are always hearing from the orthodox
religionists that Eddington or someone else has found his way back to
God; or that the order of the universe is not order at all because there
is, at bottom, only chance; or that the very foundations of physics or
chemistry have been discovered to be crumbling, so that the whole
structure is shaky.

None of these assertions is competent to dismay the genuine scientist; each is a speculative coruscation, sure presently to fade away, that
plays about that solid body of verified experience by which, in the
traditional way, we continue to live. I have great sympathy with the
gentleman who, desiring to know something about elasticity, had to
go back to 1896 to find a manual on physics that treated of matters
less sublime than the nature of God; and who expressed the wish that
physicists would stick to physics, since he knew where to go to inform
himself on theology, should he so desire. And the case of the social
sciences is far more parlous than that of physics because it still lacks
that dense core of verified facts possessed by physicists, its own collection of data being of a loose and spongy texture conducive to gaseous
absorption and emanation.

There is no profit to be gained from hanging over the bottomless
abysses of mystery that surround life. It merely causes vertigo. If the
race had confined itself to such peerings and attempted fathomings,
it could not have persisted; and though it is academically debatable
whether or not its persistence is a good thing, that issue is not worth
considering in view of the "instinct of self-preservation" and its projection into practice. There is no object in fancying what *Hamlet* might
have been without Hamlet. Nor is there anything to be gained by
allowing the metaphysically inclined to stir up sediment by smartly

requiring a definition of "fact" or "reality" or any other term whose signification to all practical intents and purposes is well enough known by everybody. There are always gadflies in cap and gown with plenty of time to spare for logical or dialectical alightings and ticklings, buzzing around any realistic worker. You say, when they ask your creed: "I believe in facts." "Yes, but what do you *mean* by 'I'?" they drone; "What do you *mean* by 'believe'? What do you *mean* by 'in'?" And your only safe and time-saving reply is: "Any normal human being knows what I mean. Quit your fooling!"

If it is regarded as superficial to live and move upon that thin skin of sense-perceived actuality that separates us from grisly depths, without thinking about those underlying mysteries too much—not thinking of them at all while there is anything actual, and human, and possibly helpful, to do—then science is superficial. At the same time, no other person, whether poet or even philosopher, gets so realizing a sense of those depths as does the delver who has actually worked through, possibly broken through, to them. In any case, as I have already asserted, the way the race has lived on and has developed the adjustments to life-conditions upon which it prides itself is by operating upon the aforesaid thin skin in a wholly realistic manner. By such operation mankind has food, clothing, and shelter, machines, trade, medicines— yes, social institutions—in a word, civilization. Thus has it won leisure for some to spin fantasies: imaginings recognized as such, and also insubstantial meditations conceived to have an import demanding their imposition upon all others.

It is futile to enlarge upon the deceptiveness of the senses: sight, hearing, and the rest. Defective as they are, there has been nothing else comparable to them in dependability, judging by the experience of the race in actual self-preservation and in the development of defense against the savage sweep of nature-forces. But for them we should not be here at all to repudiate them in our magnificence. Those who do that are singularly like the grossly infatuated Ajax just before his rock was split and he perished, "when he had drunk of the brine."

It is impossible to see how a bath in metaphysics helps in any way toward the professional conditioning of any student whose ambition is to help construct a science of any sort. I do not deny, I repeat, that the history of human thought, including all its vagaries, yields materials for the social scientist; what I deny is that philosophy equips him with anything that he needs prior to dealing with materials. It does not give him point of view, bearings, or method. Rather does it diffuse his attention by directing it toward word-churning, concept-juggling, and reverence for authority, where he should be concentrating on facts and their verification, recognizing no ipse-dixit authority whatsoever.

What has been said of the unreliability of the senses suggests the asserted relationship between a science of society and psychology. Spencer, in his *Study of Sociology* devotes a chapter to "the preparation [for a science of society] in psychology." However disposed one might be to follow Spencer's lead in this direction, he hesitates rather soberly when he realizes that what Spencer regarded as psychology is relegated by the psychologists of the day to an unregarded top shelf. The writer has always regarded Spencer's *Principles of Psychology* as at least understandable, non-freakish, and related to actualities; he can readily understand that if Freud is a psychologist, then Spencer is not. And, fresh from the perusal of a volume entitled *Psychology, Science or Superstition?,* he finds confirmed his own layman's impressions that to seek out psychology as a guide for a science of society would be to select the blind to lead the blind, or, perhaps, to pick out one infant as mentor or pedagogue to another. The domino-motif, where each knocks his neighbor over, so characteristic of philosophy, would seem to be characteristic of the psychological stage as well. To say the least, the rigorous methods and the general acceptance of verified fact that are characteristic of the genuine sciences do not yet stand forth within the psychological establishment. Therein, perhaps, is psychology recognizable as a true child of philosophy, even though handled stepmotherwise by its parent.

Nobody is to blame for being an ordinary infant instead of an Athena struck in full maturity out of some godlike skull. Least of all. could a reasonable-minded "sociologist" cast up infantilism against a fellow-discipline. But when it comes to selecting a tutor to prepare one for future exigencies, even the sub-Freshman knows enough not to lay too much stress upon a candidate's own self-recommendations or those of his relatives. The prospective tutor must have demonstrated himself at least able to pass the tests for which he undertakes to prepare his pupil. Herein lies the reluctance of a cautious social scientist to accept Spencer's "preparation in psychology," though he is quite willing to concede the advisability of the "preparation in biology" advocated in Spencer's preceding chapter—of which more later on.

There is another reason, in addition to the bewildered immaturity of psychology, that gives the social scientist pause. And this hesitation has nothing to do with the insistence of psychology upon becoming his tutor, whether or no; or upon its claim to his territory by a kind of gratuitous eminent domain—though such a disposition does not pre-dispose the encroached-upon in favor of the encroacher. I may return briefly to this trespass matter; but it does not enter into the present phase of the issue between psychology and the science of society. The added reason that gives pause is that the doings of psychology, even when they shall have begun to appear as a body of positive knowledge agreed upon by psychologists after the manner and with a degree of unanimity resembling that of the physical scientists, will still be no more than remotely relevant to a science of society. For the latter has a range of its own, namely, human society. If it had not such a range, there would be no reason for erecting or distinguishing it as a special discipline.

This point is of considerable importance. Most of the aforesaid encroachment of psychology is natural and venial so long as the science of society fails to stake off its own range and then stay within it. Sociologists are by no means free of the tendency to megalomania; indeed, that is in good part what has confused their minds and diffused their energies, so that they have lodged claims indefinite and absurd, all-inclusive and contradictory, to which no one has felt it necessary or possible to pay any attention.

The contention here is that the science of society is a discipline that has to do with human society. The trouble with the term "sociology" is that, in its etymology as well as in usage, it has come to mean "the science of the social" (*socius,* the adjective) or "the science of the social being" (*socius,* the noun). It was to avoid that connotation that Sumner tried for some years to introduce the Latin-Greek monstrosity, "societology" and that some have toyed with the possibility of the etymologically purer modern Greek term, "koinoniology." "Science of society" would be exact enough, provided it were practical, as it is not by reason of its lack of an adjectival form. Presumably there is nothing to do but try to redeem "sociology" from its sinful state of ambiguity, through inducing a conviction of sin followed by reformation—a con-siderable feat, if accomplished.

If the science of society has to do with human society, then it pos-sesses a definite range. The only basis upon which psychology can then lay claim to its territory is on the ground that, as a society is composed of individuals (which, as nobody denies it, calls for no debate at all, much less a rabid one), then there is a "social mind" understandable only through investigation of the individual psyche.

But this conception of a "crowd mind" is no more than a metaphor or analogy, belonging in the same spurious and insidious category as "the social organism." There are those who admit that psychology is necessarily concerned with the individual, but at the same time assert that society cannot be surveyed apart from an antecedent study of its constituent elements. Here is a proposition that will not bear generalization; for, if generalized, it would hold that no aggregate could be studied in and for itself, so that the body must be studied in the cell, and anatomy and physiology must be reduced to histology—indeed, to get down to bedrock, to organic chemistry. However logical such a contention might be, its acceptance would remove all the categories into which men have usefully and necessarily classified phenomena— necessarily, because the mind could not deal with the welter of phenomena otherwise.

New categories, or disciplines, have been established and recognized wherever valid distinctions could be drawn, whether or not these distinctions have been obvious. The final criterion has been, in the event, practical convenience. Pure logic and dialectics have had nothing to do with this classification-process except to confuse it for a season. In the present case, the distinction lies in the fact that a science of society is concerned with mass-phenomena, and that that type of phenomena is *sui generis*. To the science of society, which studies mores and institutions, what goes on in the mind of the individual is pretty much a matter of indifference; what enchains its interest is not guesses as to what individual men *think* but knowledge of what societies of men *do*.

Naturally, the question of the individual motive arises from time to time in relation to anything human; but common sense operating upon common experience is quite capable of furnishing all that the student of societal phenomena needs to know. Men sacrifice to their gods because they are scared. They say so. What need of psychology here? It is the fashion nowadays to call the sheerest truisms derived out of experience with the working of the human mind "psychological"; things concerning which there is no need of a ghost risen from the grave to give us instruction are elaborately explained by the credulous clientèle of some new psychology that discards all former psychologies with scorn. It is one thing to elaborate the obvious; quite another to beplaster it with pretentious terms and gratuitous technicalities. To accept and base one's work in the science of society upon any one of the rapidly displaced and replaced psychologies is wholly hazardous as well as unnecessary.

What enlists the interest and contributes to productive study within the societal range is preoccupation with what associated human beings *have done*. That can be known, while human states of mind can be no more than inferred—and inferred solely from what men do. Elaborate demonstration on the bases of Oedipus complexes, or even of commonplace knowledge bedight in high-sounding terminology, is capable of befogging the clearest of issues.

The science of society accords the individual an indispensable function in the evolution of the mores, namely, variation. Without variation, no adjustment-process can even start. But, variation once started (and it is of no social consequence as to just what train of thought suggests it to the individual), the rest of the process of societal adjustment is almost if not quite impersonal. Under a condition of maladjustment, the several individuals—who alone suffer or rejoice, love or hate—try to squirm out of their uncomfortable predicament. Some one or few of them are a little ahead of the rest in hitting upon the more expedient ways of avoiding pain and attaining comfort or pleasure. Many tentatives may be launched under a great variety of impulses. In the absence of causal connection between purposes and consequences, the same purposes or calculations may issue in unlike consequences. Most commonly, probably, the element of chance (the unpredictable) decides, entirely apart from any identifiable psychological states or movements of individuals. At any rate, the objective results are all that count, so far as the science of society is concerned: the mother-family passes into the father-family, bride-price into dowry, and so on. What specific individuals, even if they could be identified, have thought, is of curious interest only. Even if tangible and accepted results of the study of the mind existed, as distinguished from lay knowledge of the way men think, they would be of small utility within the range of a science that concerns itself with mass-phenomena: mores and institutions. Hence the givings of psychology, whatever their degree of accuracy as respects the individual, do not constitute a *sine qua non* for the operations of a science of society.

This should dispose of terms like "psychological sociology." As for other hybrids, such as "educational sociology," "Christian sociology," and the like, they are to be deprecated on general principles as contributing to the muddlement over the conception of what a science is.

They are much more baneful than similar compounds, e.g., agricultural chemistry, structural geology, because they are so much more indefinite and because they can therefore conceal so much more irrelevancy. As for "social psychology," insofar as it is a study of the individual mind in a social milieu, that is defensible enough, though all minds, with few and abnormal exceptions, exist in an environment of fellow-men; but if the term means, as it sometimes does, merely the study of society from the standpoint of psychology, it is no more than another name for "psychological sociology," as considered above.

Spencer, as stated, wrote a chapter in his *Study of Sociology,* entitled "Preparation in Biology." As is well known, he seems, before he was done with his "biological analogy," to have got, if not himself, certainly his disciples, pretty well entangled in what is called "reasoning from analogy." He himself, despite his self-warnings and his definite reservations, let the title "Society Is an Organism" stand at the head of a chapter in the *Principles of Sociology.*[2] I do not intend to give further space or attention here either to this "biological analogy" or, more generally, to the fallacy of "reasoning from analogy." That manner of reasoning is sufficiently characterized elsewhere.[3]

Biology is nearer to the range of a science of society than any other of the disciplines accepted as sciences. It has not the rigor of physics; mathematics cannot be employed very extensively or profitably within its range; but controlled experimentation is possible there, and not so many biases have to be identified and repressed as in dealing with social phenomena. Also no science of society can ignore the body of verified fact established by biology. It is significant of the closeness of relation between the social and the organic that both Darwin and Wallace caught up suggestion vital to the evolution theory from Malthus's *Essay on the Principles of Population.* Incidentally, that fact disposes of the captious objection to Darwinism, based upon the sentimental conviction that it is demeaning to man to have applied to his loftiness a set of conclusions originating in the study of lower forms of life. What happened was that Darwin took certain unpopular truths out of Malthus's *Essay,* carried them over to the plant and animal world, proved them there, and then, having developed them toward universalization, brought them back to man.

The science of society can profit much by reversing that process: by taking suggestion from biology, even though it cannot carry it back

2. Vol. I, Pt. II, chap. ii.
3. Sumner, W. G., and Keller, A. G., *The Science of Society,* III, 2179–2180.

ultimately to its source. I have said that the science of society should derive all it can apply in the way of method from the firmly established disciplines, including all the physical sciences; but, being nearer to biology, it can derive more than method from that science. It can get suggestion from the great biological generalization, the evolution theory. I am interested to explain why the adoption of such suggestion is not "reasoning from analogy," that is, to explain to those who are open to reason; others will not care to read further, for my conception of a science of society is built squarely upon an evolutionary, adjustment-theory.

I may perhaps be allowed to become a little autobiographical in this connection. For some years, while making an acquaintance with the data of my subject, evolution lingered only vaguely upon my horizon, accepted in a general sort of way but not impressing me as particularly vital to my enlightenment. But I had acquired the conviction that mores and institutions were adaptations to the conditions of their places and times. I knew, for example, that slavery had once been an unquestioned expedient among all civilized nations and that it remained so in the tropics and sub-tropics after it had become anathema in other regions. I knew also that it was correlative with tillage rather than with hunting or herding, and I could see why. It was, in short, an adjustment or a maladjustment, according to circumstances. But the *how* of that process did not reveal itself until I chanced one day upon a remark of Romanes[4] that the evolutionary theory was a theory of adjustment, and only secondarily or incidentally a theory about species. I should have seen that for myself but had not.

It then occurred to me that Darwin had explained to the general satisfaction of scientists the process of adjustment or adaptation in the organic field, and I asked myself whether his demonstration might not afford suggestion as to the adjustment-process in a neighboring range. The factors in the organic process, I had learned from Wallace's chart of the evolutionary process, where they were brought together and condensed—almost tabulated—were variation, selection, and heredity. Meanwhile Sumner's *Folkways* had become known to me, and I had been convinced that the mores have been and are the lowest terms, so to speak, of all of society's institutions. It seemed to me that it might be enlightening to try out the Darwinian factors upon the mores.

That there were ever-arising differences in the mores, that is, varia-

4. *Darwin and after Darwin*, II, 161.

tion as that term was understood when Darwin adopted it, seemed obvious; also that selective elimination took place among them. Being acquired characteristics, the mores were not, it is true, transmitted by heredity, through the germ-plasm; but they were passed on just the same, when they had weathered selection. It made no difference to me then, when I had very slowly come to these conclusions, nor does it now, that the variation, selection, and transmission of the mores are not secured by the specific biological processes; I should not object, except for the needlessness of it and also the clumsiness of the terms and their adjectival forms, to replacing variation, selection, and transmission by "difference," "elimination," and "likeness."[5] Here is no illegitimate use whatever of the analogy. I have never conceded it a particle of argumentative weight. I have merely accepted its suggestion, which is no uncommon procedure in science or in life and seems not to be reprehensible, any more than adapting the principles of flight, as observed in birds, to aviation.

The only convincing "proof" of anything is that it works. There are not a few beside myself who think the adjustment-process basic in the societal range as in the organic. Some think it too obvious to need explanation. Once I thought that, too, and wrote on societal evolution in forgetfulness of Huxley's maxim: "Take nothing for granted." Years of experience with students have altered my judgment in the matter, and I have come to harbor an ever-heightened respect for the "elaboration of the obvious." The adjustment-theory, to which a succeeding essay is devoted, clarifies a good many things within the societal range. I know of no other that explains more. Pending the arrival of a better, more widely explanatory basis for a science of society, I am cleaving to this one. And, as for the charge of "reasoning from analogy," it does not touch me any more than if it were an accusation of having committed mayhem. I have a clear conscience as to either crime.

There is an impersonality about the adjustment-process on the organic level which, over eighty years ago, roused much resentment in the hearts of those who were reading the recently published *Origin of Species*. Nowadays that sentiment has been greatly weakened. Even the most orthodox seem to have concluded that it takes a far more exalted Person to create an impersonal process than personally to fashion a number of products, singly, one after the other. Similarly,

5. As in Keller, A. G., *Starting Points in Social Science,* chap. ii.

it is to be hoped, contemporary resentment of the view that the adjustment-process on the societal level likewise is impersonal and automatic may evaporate away.

There has been considerable ground-clearing in the foregoing. Much of it has been negative: how not to study society. There is sense in the remark that you have to "find where it isn't before you can find where it is." The next essay is of a more positive character.

II

COMMON SENSE: ITS TRAINING AND ORGANIZATION.

COMMON SENSE has been present in untrained and unorganized guise from the earliest times. If it had not been, we should not be here to worry over its apparent absence in the present. All human beings who are better than half-wits, and even some of the moronic, have a modicum of that quality available, if they care to use it. The child, even the animal, once burned, avoids the fire. To the savage, with whom science began in the rueful, unpremeditated accumulation of respect for hard facts, not understood but painfully experienced, it was plain common sense to give hornets' nests a wide berth instead of masterfully wading through them. They were a feature of the environment that did not, as the result of yearnings and protestations, turn into some variety of heart's desire. Hornet-habits and hornet-nature were recognized as permanent facts which had to be accepted, learned about, and adjusted to upon the basis of experience. Common sense consisted in knowing all you could find out about Nature's ways and then looking to it that you did not cross Her.

Also the veriest savage values the experience of others. To him, "one man's opinion is as good as another's" would have been rank nonsense; and so would it be to us except when common sense is in eclipse. You do not summon the first chance passer-by to come in and counsel you on matters of import. You want an adviser to whom you can concede a right to an opinion because he knows something about the matter in hand. Tearful sympathy is not enough.

Positive knowledge, meaning knowledge based upon repeated and re-verified experience, is the variety of wisdom that all men depend on at a pinch; it is that by which the race has lived and continues to be able to live, the while considerable sections of it have been, and still are, playing with various phantasms. If men have been dragged back to firm earth, out of the quagmires in which they have stuck while pursuing divers will-o'-the-wisps of heated imagination, it has been by the hand of prosaic Experience. Experience is what we all come down to in the end as a qualification of trustworthiness, as constituting the only safe approach to some newly encountered situation. To do so is only common sense. All of which leads straight to Science, the very priestess of Experience, never absent from Her shrine.

Science is plain common sense, when "trained and organized." It is the highest refinement of that adjustment-to-environment-process which is imposed upon life as a condition of its persistence. By it experience has been deliberately gathered; and out of such accumulation has been distilled a very different type of knowledge from that set of alleged certainties provided by hunches, yearnings, dreams, and revelations. For the accumulations of experience made by science have been subjected to the most rigorous scrutiny and test before being accepted at all. Scientific truth is not embraced because it is pleasing; the great scientist who struck off the definition of science as common sense has recorded the fact that he always demanded stricter proof of what he wanted to believe than of what he rebelled against believing —an attitude exactly opposite to that of the wishful thinker.

Untrained and unorganized common sense, heeding day-to-day experience, was from the outset, then, enough to disclose the nearest-lying barriers to the realization of humanity's desires. Thereafter came the training and organization. Facts of experience have been recorded, compared, classified, and organized. From them have been extracted dependable regularities, so that men could anticipate repetitions or recurrences of events under like conditions. An advance was at length made to the deliberate setting of a stage for experience to manifest itself upon. That was called experimentation. Out of all this experience, spontaneously offered in practical living or artfully brought to pass in a laboratory, were derived sequences and laws in accordance with which human beings might discreetly adapt their conduct. Thus were mapped for man the stone walls against which he needed no longer, in ignorance of their tough resistance, to butt his poll bloody.

A homely bit of history may serve to illustrate the use of common sense and the subsequent training thereof. A young soldier, escaping the enemy, was passing through an open forest. He was in great distress from hunger. About him he noted hundredweights of fungi. He had heard that some were edible, though others were speedy death. He ardently desired the knowledge which would enable him to distinguish between them, so as to stay his stomach. Not having the knowledge available, he consulted common sense and stayed off fungi altogether. He did not say to himself: "They must be all right because my need of food is so great"; nor yet, "Yonder toadstool is too beautiful not to be nutritious"; and hurry to cook up a plateful. He did not make a potpourri out of a little of everything fungoid in the vicinity. No. Because he had "ordinary common sense," he let the fungi alone and tightened his belt instead. Then, when he got home where he could get knowledge, he went for it. He had made a vow, there in the woods, that he would not stop till he knew about the edible qualities of a potential, large food-supply.

There was very little knowledge to be found in books, so he set to experimentation, eventually publishing a big volume entitled *One Thousand American Fungi*. His method was as follows. He chewed up a small piece of any strange variety, swallowing a minute portion of the pulp. On some occasions even this cautious tasting resulted in racking nausea and even in temporary prostration. That is what experience is wont to cost. But he gradually accumulated trustworthy, because verified, information, especially about what to avoid; and there is now, as the result of his investigations and those of others, no reason why anybody who does not reject recorded experience as futile, need become a victim of fungus-poisoning. Persons of sense do not have to experiment with any of the fungi which the original experimenter had examined and listed but only with new ones—and even then they have a method, a training of common sense, to follow. Moreover, even the newly encountered specimens are likely enough to resemble the investigated ones, so that later experimenters have had at least a hint or two to go by.

This is a homely and humble instance, but its method is the same as that of better-known, even world-renowned, scientists. Two illustrations out of many available may bring out the point that all truly scientific experimentation is one: the same simple, cautious, toilsome process of gathering and analyzing experience.

When Edison experimented, he started by ransacking the literature of the subject and always began, as he said, "where the other fellow left off." The testing which he gave his results was ruthlessly thorough. His take-off was always from a solid body of recorded experience, upon which he meant to pile his own.

When Darwin tackled the species-question, he began by gathering facts out of the literature of geology, zoölogy, ornithology—in short, out of "natural history" of all description. He subscribed to agricultural journals; he joined pigeon-fanciers' associations. In particular, he refused to draw any conclusions from his assembled data for five years, for he had no thesis to prove and no petty vanity to serve, but merely an inquiry, in the prosecution of which he wanted to learn from the facts of experience. Then he set up his own carefully guarded and controlled experiments with plants and animals, thus sowing and culling his own experience. In particular was he eager for criticism; he carried a small notebook about with him in which to record, not tributes and flattery, but every last fact or objection that seemed to oppose the conclusions gradually forming in his mind as a kind of precipitate of his broodings over his facts. He wrote many letters of appreciation to obscure persons who had furnished him with additional facts or, on the basis of their special information, questioned his conclusions. In short, as one of his adversaries admiringly commented: "Mr. Darwin cares for nothing whatever except the truth."

Science thus develops out of a cultivated bed of experience. The deeper the bed and the more highly it is cultivated within any range of living, the more confidently can men forecast the future, in the sense of anticipating recurrences of similar results under like situations. This kind of forecasting is something very different from the delphic emissions of a medicine-man in the throes of prophetic ecstasy, for if he is thought to know anything and everything, that is because he is possessed or inspired, so that he is merely the mouthpiece of some Mumbo Jumbo. It is Mumbo who knows; the medicine-man knows solely because he stands in with Mumbo, who tells him. That is not the same as knowing on one's own hook.

The object of science's being is to handle experience. Its distinguishing maxim holds that the only safe way to determine how things are, or are to be, is to know how they have been and have become; that there are no great cataclysms but only the steady interaction of changeless forces—so that the best that men can do is to identify the given factors and forces, with their qualities and modes of action, and then to adapt to them as permanent life-conditions. Having kept its eye singly upon this course of action, science has developed a proved technique—proved, because it verifies in living. This is genuine experimentation, not some slapdash empirical process. Science has, in the laboratory, a device by which it can, so to speak, breed experience. It can cause the same event to happen over and over and under varied and controlled conditions, so that it can sort out the factors which enter into the situation, eliminate some and retain others, until it is possible to discriminate the influence of each. There is no need, in these days, to enlarge upon laboratory experimentation; it is enough to note that its results can be, and are, tested immediately at any other laboratory, no matter in what country, and as many times as may be desirable.

Science exhibits both a characteristic method and a characteristic attitude. Essential to its method is that the searcher shall start with verified facts, a large body of them, out of his own experience or the recorded results of others, letting the facts tell their own story and lead him where they will. Thus, and not from some swelling major premise adopted under intuition and emotion, does he rise to generalization; and his theory is always carried back, over and over again, to his ever-increasing collection of data, to be altered as the facts dictate. Selection of comfortable instances in support of some grand theory, or a Procrustean mutilation of facts so that they can be forced under it, betrays at once the lurking cuckoo that is trying to sneak alien eggs into the nest of science.

The perfected technique and method of the scientific experimenter is the projection of an attitude that is wholly characteristic. A good part of it is the exclusion of emotion. The laboratory is quiet and passionless; it is no place for heated bias, fervid oratory, tearful threnody, or partisan denunciation. In it, one neither points with pride nor views with alarm. It always invites criticism. If anyone can find defects in its apparatus or methods, he is not a Doubting Thomas nor a Tory but a benefactor. It is the magician or prophet, with a heaven-sent revelation, who begins to get red of neck and growl about heresy when he encounters objection; who scents plots wherever he overhears "grumblers," and who finally swoops bloodily down upon them. One can readily and safely use the attitude toward criticism as a criterion to distinguish the young or old who dream dreams or see visions from the scientists who do neither.

The genuine scientist has a single-track, Darwinian mind in that he too cares for nothing whatever save the truth. He is Honesty Personified.

Science comes at the end of a long series of devices for securing adjustment by men to their life-conditions. An instrumentality of such efficiency, demanding so copious a stock of hard-won and arduously recorded knowledge and so high a degree of self-discipline in the gathering, storage, and handling of it, was as hopelessly out of the ken of earlier ages as it is now beyond the grasp of a child. The mode of thought throughout human history, and of the masses of mankind today, especially outside the range of material things, is far from scientific—no matter how sedulously, now that science, though ill-understood, has become something of a fad, the older modes of thought have tried to bedeck themselves with scientific terminology.

A certain saving common sense, or direct reliance upon experience, was, as has been pointed out, a prime endowment of the most primitive of mankind; but there were obstacles to its training and organization that for long ages stunted its development; naïve beliefs, some of which we loftily and contemptuously call "superstition," others of which we still cherish, to the detriment of future development. These have served, and still serve, as a kind of cocoon out of which science must break before it can discharge its service to mankind.[1]

No charge of folly or stupidity can be held against mankind for not acting in the light of knowledge not yet possessed; and it is hardly blameworthy in any modern man, when he is at his wit's end, that he backslides into the old morass out of which the race has partially pried itself. It is condonable enough that a distraught husband or father, having seen the best of available scientific knowledge focused in vain upon a suffering or dying loved one, should take despairing recourse to any kind of quackery. That is what distracted and agonized mankind has done and is almost sure to do. It explains why the mountebank flourishes best in an environment of misery, physical or social, and why his wild ideas are taken at his own valuation. For the moment, at least, his benumbed victims know no better. They have lost what heads they had. Emotion has overpowered and rides them. Nevertheless, the fact that no one can justly blame the panic-stricken does not mean that they have done well. There is a sensible way for people to act, particularly when an emergency lies outside the range of existing positive knowledge, that does not involve a falling back upon the methods of magic. The emergency is precisely the time not to lose one's head. The sensible, scientific way to act, when we face an issue that lies beyond the realm of available knowledge, is *as if* that outer region were still within the sphere of influence of knowledge, even if as yet unconquered. This is not a dark saying. It is a piece of common sense.

Nor are the aberrations of the "thinkers" of past ages to be censured. They could know no better. To them, the mind was an original source of truth and power, and all that was needed was to work out of it, logically and "creatively," what was in it already. This readily came to mean that the head was reserved to spin plausible reason for thinking as one wanted to. The head served the hunch. Tuition from experience

1. Essay on "Science and 'Superstition,' " below.

being sour, not to say hard to get and to appropriate, men were, and are, readily persuaded that intuition, "free meditation," and other gossamer forms of revelation are, "after all," the nobler and more revealing movements of the human spirit. There is about them an unearthly iridescence. Throughout the melodrama of history, and despite the dismal proverbial injunction that "all is not gold that glitters," the gold brick of unearthbound speculation has remained a stock, ever-appealing stage property.

In the past, such obstacles to the development of science, however deplorable, were inevitable. If we had been there, we should have been just as credulous of phantasms as anybody else. We should have known no better. We should have fallen for the astrology and alchemy and magic in general out of which astronomy and chemistry and medicine have painfully emerged. Now that we do know better, we rightly name all those "pseudo-sciences," as they last on into our day, plain superstition.

Our lack of a developed and recognized science of society is some excuse for our ignorance and credulity within the societal range; but the likeness of present-day "social experimentation" to the procedure of science is far more remote than it need be.

That resemblance is, in the main, superficial and scarcely more than verbal—"in the main," I say, because there have been, here and there, sound attempts to secure a take-off from experience, which contrast glaringly with the favorite method of starting with a wish fortified by a contemptuous dismissal of experience. Nevertheless, it is perhaps something in the nature of thin and cold comfort that scientific terminology is used at all, even though the idea in employing it is merely to convey the false impression that the "experimenters" are not pursuing either a vision or some ulterior purpose or blindly stabbing around in the dark. Here is at least a sketchy gesture of deference to science, whereas once all the salutes were for metaphysics and philosophy. It is significant, at its worst, of a somewhat altered attitude, verging, however slightly or hypocritically, toward rather than away from that of science.

There is no longer any excuse whatever for the failure of honest men either themselves to take the scientific, common sense attitude or to be hoodwinked by a spurious scientific pose in others. If serious students of the social sciences cannot hope as yet for a full scientific technique, they can face social issues in a scientific frame of mind, taking on at the same time whatever scientific technique they may be able to appropriate. Social science can concern itself with the accumulation and verification of facts out of experience, which it can then analyze, compare, and synthesize. It can face toward induction, turning resolutely away from deduction out of pretentious but shaky major premises. It can strive to be objective, dispassionate, unbiassed, and unevangelical, seeking only for the truth. If it cannot have a laboratory, it can seek to generate the atmosphere of a laboratory; it can renounce forensics, dialectics, adjurations to open-mindedness, resentment of criticism, name-calling, and other futile air-churning, and get down to actual work. It can quit spawning the bright idea whose originator has not stopped to verify it, lest he lose acclaim for originality—rather does he hurry on to hatch out another before the newness of its predecessor can evaporate away, along with the moisture behind its ears. It can cease its efforts to astonish simpletons by its "daring" and "revolutionary" proposals and try to win the confidence of the discerning by having been right according to the retrospective light of experience.

There are only the two ways of getting to know: either out of experience or out of revelation vouchsafed to piety by Authority or to intuition or to philosophic meditation under autohypnosis. The trouble with revelation is that it sees facts through a medium of emotion. Thinking, thus rendered emotional, attains no conclusions admitting of unremitting verification. Also, while a laboratory experiment can be stopped instantly, it is not so with an "experiment" that includes emotional elements, as does a Plan within the social range, which becomes forthwith encased and insulated in a sheath of vested interest, precedent, and uncriticizable authority. Once launched, as an accomplished deed, it cannot be shored up on the ways again. Consider dollar-devaluation, with its consequences soon so numerous that the Supreme Court could hardly consider it upon its merits.[2] Such "experiments" are like an eel-trap: easy to get into, hard to get out of. Reform through relaxation is prone to be a one-way street. Once launched, such social "experiments" must take a course ordained by uncontrollable, automatically acting forces whose very entrance into the situation cannot, in many a case, be foreseen—not even by him who knows and values the experience of mankind, much less by the versatile and volatile taster of the Pierian spring. All the more reason, then, for initiating all reforms in a spirit of seriousness and caution.

2. Noyes, A. D. and Weil, C. A., *New York Times,* January 16, 1935, January 14, 1935.

All the more danger in evangelism. One marvels at the feather-headedness of even the fuzzy-pates, when he realizes the damage that light-hearted, light-minded Planning can do.

Social experimentation, so-called, is a slippery and hazardous undertaking at best. No one knows enough to envisage its field, or to foresee its reach, as a whole. The only way to view it at all is from the top of the small pile of experience, the heaping up and mounting of which, low as it is, involves much and protracted effort. The only way to get a better view is to add to the pile instead of capering around it, chattering and jeering at its modest proportions, and then rushing off on some Children's Crusade after the nearest plausible illusion revealed to credulous impulsiveness.

Many citizens have felt for some time that they were lost in a fog. There has occurred before them a dimming of the lights by which they had thought confidently to steer their courses. In the misty atmosphere, vision is refracted, mirages generated, and bearings easily lost. When in a fog, the safe course is to stand still for a while where you are, for motion, however earnestly enjoined upon you, is more than likely to bring you around circularly to the same old place, discouraged, tired, and lacerated. When the experienced seaman does not know where he is, it is commonsenseless to lend credence to self-proclaimed pilots who rush about shouting: "Lo, here! Lo, there!"

The old, reliable lights have not gone out. It is the mist that deceives. nothing will dispel the mist that befogs half-seen issues presented for adjudication except to insist upon viewing them in the manner described heretofore as scientific. That word need no longer seem formidable, for it means simply "commonsensible." A novelty may be correctly presented as noble, high-minded, humanitarian, or even Christian, and one may agree that it is all of that; but the final question—and no emergency should ever induce us to answer it precipitately, for time is never gained by getting into a panic—must always be, not "Do I like it?" or "Ought it to be?" but "Can it be?" "Can the cost of it be paid?" "Who is to pay?" These are simple questions, requiring no technical equipment for their answering. There is yet another: "What qualifications, aside from enthusiasm and a command of rhetoric and a carrying voice, have those who are urging these enterprises upon us?" The replies to these crucial queries must come out of what available experience we possess, coolly and unemotionally applied. That is the way of both plain and refined common sense.

III

THE POPULARIZATION OF SOCIAL SCIENCE.

No MATTER how valid the conclusions of science may be, they must get out of the laboratory or study into the life of the people before they can have social effect. For the seat of all social power resides in the masses. As regards the findings of social science, there are those who maintain that the dissemination of them among the masses is impossible; that the process of popularization has always so denatured scientific truth that, by the time it reaches the masses, it is not truth at all. Such perversion in transit is not the fate of social truth alone; consider how the evolution theory has been transformed into the banal formula: "Man is descended from the monkey."

"The masses" is not a very good term. It is indefinite, and it has acquired a fringe of disfiguring attachments. There is a whiff of snobbery in the jingle, "the classes and the masses." It lurks also in the phrase, "the common people" (as contrasted with Us, the uncommon), or, once more, in the adjectives "upper" and "lower," as applied to population "strata." To avoid any such subjective taint, one might, quite objectively, distinguish three groups: the privileged (well-to-do, well-educated); the defective; and, between these two, the average. The first are relatively few; the second fall out of present account, as hopeless; the third comprise the great bulk of humanity. They are the common people, whom, said Lincoln, God must love because He made so many of them. For the sake of brevity, and also to promote objectivity, the privileged group is to be designated by *"X"* and the average group by *"Y."* The question here proposed is as to the dissemination of social truth in Y.

Comparison often offers a good take-off. As everyone knows, physical or laboratory science has penetrated into Y and enjoys there a high and unquestioned repute. Nobody jeers at a chemist. When it comes to bodily ills, nobody thinks that one man's opinion is just as good as another's. Nobody derides a Pasteur or an Edison. Experts are recognized. That is not at all, however, because the average man understands about the germ-theory or the nature of electricity. The mechanic who attends to the storage battery could not pass an examination on what was in the head of its inventor, any more than the stretcher of bridge-cables upon the calculations of the bridge designer. All that the garageman knows is that if the battery is as the inventor meant it to be, it works. Similarly with the bridge. Thus arrives confidence, albeit with little or no understanding, in the laboratory scientist and his science.

That kind of scientist does not need to bother much with popularization. His results do that for him. There is an automatic popularization of laboratory science by way of the practical daily and hourly assessments of its tangible results. The advertising that is done is of scientific products; it has little or nothing to do with scientific theory. It is confined really to the promotion of rival methods of applying the same scientific principles upon which as a common basis rest, as a matter of course and of common knowledge, all the variations in application. It is the promotion of this or that detail of technique, not of science as against something else. Science stands, solid and unquestioned, as the trunk from which spring all the results, smaller or greater. And, along with this, goes a kind of perception of the scientific, realistic attitude: a respect for facts and for cool dispassion in the deft dealing with them, a skepticism as regards miracles or magic.

It seems to me [remarks a character in a recent novel,[1]] we're all mixed up in something that's too big for us and that we don't understand. There isn't one person in a hundred who has any clear idea what it is that makes a contraption of steel and tin travel sixty miles an hour without horses, or why a light goes on in the middle of the room when you push a button in the wall. Remove the spark plugs and cut the wires and practically everybody is reduced to a state of immobility and darkness. The average man has sense enough to know that it's all beyond him and that he'd best not monkey with it, and so he lets it strictly alone.

Laboratory science needs no defense. Its assailants are negligible as carrying no real weapons at all, and as writing themselves down in character through living by that of which, as crawling and materialistic, they are fastidiously scornful. The common conviction, reaching far into Y, is settled in favor of the sciences that deal with things that actually work; indeed, their givings can be made to work by anyone who puts his mind and heart to it; and that lends them an abiding interest. Up to a certain point, also, even the amateur can gain understanding of how, if not why, they work. There is a real satisfaction in

1. Rice, E., *Imperial City*, p. 226.

making things work: the boy experiences it when his homemade Leyden jar gives out a spark and a snap; the breeder feels it when he develops a plant or animal strain; the physician, when he has evolved some new treatment by modification of an older one.

This rough sketch of the manner in which the physical sciences popularize themselves, largely automatically and without campaigning, is enough to establish the contrast between their enviable estate and the unpromising plight of the social sciences. With the case of the successful sciences as a kind of yardstick, let us consider the possibility of developing a similar awareness of and respect for the social sciences. Is there any automatic process in sight that is operating in like manner to their interest? If not, is that because their givings do not work, or even because they have no givings to offer to the test of workability? Are the so-called social sciences different in kind—in nature, not in degree of development—from those others that have something to offer for test and that do work?

An offhand answer is that there is no social science, anyway. But that retort is too easy. As Cardozo remarked: "Exactness may be impossible, but it is not enough to cause the mind to acquiesce in incoherence." There may not be any body of social laws, but there are some facts and distinctions that are not controversial: for instance, the expediency of division of labor. There is a modest accumulation of experience-derived knowledge. There is something to be passed on to those who can profit by it. It is that passing-on that is in question here, rather than the amount available to transmit. There is something to offer to whatever agency of transmission there may be. The discussion is not closed before it is opened by an utter lack of matter.

"But where are the interpreters with the training and the willingness to think their way through this knowledge and translate it into the language of the street? I raise the recruiting trumpet for the interpreters."[2]

For some time there have been some enlightening college courses in the social sciences, and even several sound elementary text-books for lower schools. Some students have learned a good deal from certain superior teachers. But those who have profited by such instruction, all of them in *X,* are relatively few; and the costly process of teaching them what little or much they have learned has scarcely scratched the population surface. The average man has not been reached, so as to

---

2. Frank, Glenn, *Salesmen of Knowledge.* Reprint by Customer Research Staff, General Motors Corp.

become science-minded as regards social matters as he is when it comes
to chemicals, batteries, bridges, and other items of material culture.
Yet, be it underscored, no science can have much result or influence
until it gets out of the laboratory or study and into the life of the
people. It must somehow be popularized. How can what is known
about social life be disseminated? That is the topic here presented.

Let *E*—Edison, for instance—be an eminent investigator and inventor in the laboratory range, and *S* an equally able, serious, and
industrious student of human society. *E's* results, we know, are
speedily transmitted, so as to be known, and his knowledge respected,
not only in *X*, but also in *Y*. This happens without much or deliberate
campaigning. But how about *S*? He encounters only the *X's*, the relatively few privileged hundreds or thousands who come into direct
contact with him or who are readers of serious books, magazines, or
newspapers. Even a Huxley cannot penetrate far into *Y*. *S*, even
though he influences his students and others in *X*, so that they continue,
even after he is long dead, to disseminate his teachings, can scarcely
reach beyond *X*. For, if his findings are so popularized as to win a
wide appeal, they are almost certain to be stripped of all the genuine-
ness there is in them. They may be debased into a travesty of science
—into triviality, misrepresentation, half-truth, emotionalism, idealism,
or even propaganda. Many an eminent *S* has prayed to be delivered
from his devoted but half-understanding adherents, who pant to
spread the gospel according to *S*—getting it all wrong by importing
into it what is not there or by distorting it into a shape more suited to
their own slight comprehension or to what they know or conceive to
be the intelligence of the public.

Within the social range, it is only the final outcome of investigation,
anyway, that can be popularized; and that is a generalization, not a
physical product. It is also and necessarily so simplified as to be
readily perverted and misapprehended, unless the laborious process
has been followed by which it has been arrived at. But that process is
not susceptible of popularization. An Edison's end-result is not so
threatened. There it is, in tangible form: an electric bulb or a gramo-
phone, ready to be handled without losing contour or character, capable of undergoing concrete test anywhere, at any time, and over and
over again. There is insulin, similarly verifiable; and you do not need
to know anything about the process by which its discoverer reached
it. You do not have to understand it. There is nothing to misunderstand. Yet, if anything can be misunderstood, it will be misunder-

stood. Such has been the fate of many a hard-won truth about society, for there is always plenty of chance to misunderstand, when demonstrations are matters of words, not of tangible, palpable things.

The scientist within the social range has at most a sadly chastened hope that if he finds some truth and teaches it to a member of the X-group, it will, by way of him, gradually percolate even into Y. But he has no real evidence out of human history to shore up that hope. Mankind seems always ready to jettison social truths thought to have been demonstrated, once and for all, and pelt off on a wild-goose chase after some prancing Pied Piper. It can scarcely be questioned that the alleged general respect for science does not really extend beyond physical science.

Maybe this attitude will change if the social sciences take on a genuinely scientific attitude and try at least to approximate to scientific method instead of quacking, dabbling about and up-ending noisily, pretentiously, and shamelessly in various pools of wishfulness; but that millennium is too far off as yet for anything better than prayerfulness. The outlook for the popularization of the results of social studies—actual studies—is at present rather dismal.

Let us take another tack. There are certain boasted instrumentalities of knowledge-dissemination: the church, the public school, the press, the screen, the radio. What are they doing, or what can they do, as agents for the popularization of science in the social realm? Do they reach Y? If so, what gifts do they bear?

Consider these agencies in reverse order—the press, the school, the church—setting aside the others for the moment. The best and most responsible newspapers and magazines do not reach far into Y. There are probably more good local sheets than is realized: country newspapers, for instance, that purvey sound sense to a small clientage. In the aggregate, they may exert more educative influence than one might think. If they no more than harp upon the stock social virtues, that is something. But neither they, nor the responsible metropolitan dailies, reach more than a fraction of the circulation in Y attained by a press that appeals to emotion and passion, in cynical indifference to the truth. The masses read, says Mencken,[3] only "the most imbecile parts of the newspapers." Maybe the people are getting what they want, but the fact remains that scientific knowledge about society is not being disseminated by the press beyond X.

The public school actually transmits, or used to, certain types of

3. *Prejudices* (3d series), p. 257.

practical knowledge: it makes the masses literate; it is supposed to teach arithmetic, geography, and other elementary subjects. It has done so to millions. But that is about all it is competent to do, not only because its beneficiaries are juvenile but also because its teachers are not competent to go much farther. When a clear and simple elementary text on English Composition is found "too hard," so that teachers clamor for a key to its exercises in punctuation, there is not much hope that they can disseminate much sound social science. When boys and girls are not taught to spell, there is not much prospect of their being taught to "think"—that is to say, to think scientifically, for there is no doubt that they can be, and are, taught plenty of wishful thinking.

In short, the chance that the public schools can or will disseminate the elements of social science as they have the elements of arithmetic, language, or what used to be called "natural history," is a vanishing one. "Discussion" of the social order by children becomes at best a juggling of parental preconceptions and at worst mere propaganda. The making of debating-points, even if clever and plausible, is not science at all. For any real enlightenment as regards the life of society, I repeat, the pupil is too young and the teacher too ignorant. That is nothing against either one of them. Neither can be expected to be otherwise. It is probable that a skillful teacher, once clear in his own mind, could make understandable, even to small boys, the law of supply and demand or possibly the nature of money; but no advocate of infant economics or politics is willing to engage in such small business. He wants to "discuss" large matters, such as Communism, Capitalism, Fascism, or reforms of one kind or another that have appealed to his emotions. He wants the children to debate the tariff, war, the State. They, and he, might as well center on Einstein.

The schools pay some attention to the inculcation of the current folkways. That is their unconscious contribution to the dissemination of essential truths, perhaps. I shall return to that matter.

The church has taught a great deal to the Y-group. Religious instruction, being bound to be propagandist, is, however, never deliberately scientific. Religion is alleged, quite reasonably, to be "over" and "above" science. Its teachings are not presented as generalizations out of human experience. Nevertheless, the scriptures of all religions contain sound inferences from the observation of life, for instance, in the Proverbs, the Parables, the Commandments and Taboos. The fact that such realistic injunctions are referred to a supernatural source does not detract from their practical validity. The church has sanctioned and disseminated many expedient folkways, as has the school; but it has not inculcated, any more than has the school, either the scientific attitude or the scientific method and technique. Both have contributed to the elevation of members of Y into membership in X, where science can get at them more readily; but, even in so doing, they have not seldom so deeply infected their pupils with utopianism, and so saturated them with preconceptions, as to render them immune for life to science and all its works.

There is another school of great influence: the home. Those who propose lightly to abolish it ought to realize that fact. The home teaches the folkways and mores. They are not, of course, the results of the findings of any science; but they are, as will soon appear, materials for scientific study. They have been inculcated within the family, unconsciously or deliberately, since the beginning of things social, in Y as well as in X. And one thing is certain: nothing can be taught the masses, by any agency, that runs counter to the code unwittingly appropriated in early years.

The radio and the screen have been saved over to point the fact that all the agencies mentioned may disseminate error as well as truth. Take the "talkie" as a kind of combination of the two. It may easily fix a wrong tradition about, for instance, some historic figure like Napoleon or Zola. It may represent social situations with any degree of distortion—and through the eye, the shortest road to the brain. Its interpretation may not be actuated in the least by a consuming passion for the truth, but with an eye ever acock to the box office. Thus might history be perverted to a purpose scientifically irrelevant, or worse. And it is probable that the screen is relatively innocuous, in this respect, compared with the incessantly intrusive radio. What can be done to discipline these new agencies into the service of society remains to be seen. They have great potentialities for good or ill. They have done much good and not a little ill. They are not singled out for condemnation, for, in their degree, all the other agencies of dissemination have their sinister aspect.

The upshot of the foregoing is something like this: there is something that has actually been transmitted throughout both X and Y, no matter what mankind has tried to do about it, namely, a body of custom—of folkways upon which not much stress is laid, so that departure from them is not very heavily penalized; of mores, upon which much more stress is laid and departure from which is regarded as much more serious, because they are regarded as vital to collective welfare.

These folkways and mores are not the findings of social science. In one sense, they fall outside the present topic. From another angle they are the very nub of it. They are not the findings of science, but they are its elemental materials and data. There are findings to be got out of them. Science can do with them what men have always done with elemental objects and forces: learn their nature and ways, and then apply that knowledge. It can assess the mores on their record of expediency or inexpediency for society's welfare, as the zoölogist can assess animal qualities. It can try to relieve those of the mores that have been found sound and expedient of the clutter of irrelevance or nonsense under which they are at times suffocating. This contention may look vague and sound academic and cryptic. It needs some development. But this postern door seems to be the only entrance into Y available to what social science there is in the present. As intimated, it has been used rather habitually, though not premeditatedly, by church, school, and home.

Though it is not to be expected that social-scientific conclusions, or respect for social-scientific procedure, can be disseminated in Y, yet the masses are already in possession of a considerable body of realistic convictions, unpremeditatedly arrived at during centuries of actual living. In the long run, people will act upon these unconsciously accepted axioms. There is a body of tradition-preserved experience which forms an accumulation of materials comparable to the accumulation of phenomena which the physical sciences have gathered, studied, analyzed, and assessed. Where the physical sciences have dealt with rocks, plants, and animal forms, given in nature, the social sciences can look to the study of ideas and practices, that is, of folkways and mores, given in society.

It is possible, for example, to assemble a collection of proverbs of all peoples—which are pellets of folk-wisdom that have survived the handling and assessment of generations—and subject them to the stock processes of scientific method: classification, comparison, and so on. The outcome should be the identification of a residue of universally accepted rules for homely living. It is remarkable how similar proverbs are, all over the world. Whether or not their precepts have been systematically lived up to is no matter; nor is it of consequence that, prior to an examination of the special circumstances under which they are uttered or of the situations to which they refer, they may contradict one another. It is well known that the same force may produce opposite effects, as when gravitation causes the stone to fall and the balloon to rise. It is as realistic to admonish: "Haste makes waste" as to enjoin: "Let not the grass grow under your feet." At times, a single precept may seem paradoxical: "Make haste slowly." The value of such a collection, classification, and comparison would lie in the residue remaining after all proper cancellations, reservations, and other precautionary measures had been taken into account.

In a study of these mass-phenomena, the mores, which are indigenous in Y, one might start with a deduction from the vast induction known as the adjustment theory, or the theory of evolution: that the residue arrived at, having withstood incessant selection, must consist of items of lasting expediency, endowed with survival-value to any and every human society. But a warning should at once be sounded that it is always perilous to start with a deduction unless one is fully aware of what he is about. The deduction cited is from a well-established induction—that of evolutionary adjustment; nevertheless, even so, it is to be employed solely as a point of departure or a preliminary orientation. It must be critically tested, at every step; that is to say, the user of it must be able to demonstrate, in all cases, wherein the expediency or survival of a specific custom inheres, and he must be ready to drop the deduction at once if he finds it unsupported by a thorough, severe, protracted, and repeated test upon the facts of experience.

If this does not occur, the use of a deduction quickly reduces to absurdity. The evolution theory has been reduced to an alleged absurdity, in that it has been asserted to be an example of circular reasoning by logicians who imagine that Darwin was operating with mere words and concepts, as they themselves inveterately do. Rationalizing thus, they have proclaimed that the evolutionist first says that the fittest survive, and then wheels about and states that the fittest are demonstrated to be fittest because they survive—which reduces to: "The fittest are the fittest," or to: "Those who survive, survive." This empty objection might hold, if evolution were a mere exercise in logic or dialectics; it falls immediately with the demonstration, on the basis of bodies of observed and verified facts, of what constitutes fitness, and why: the Why, as well as the What of fitness.

Verbal juggling of this order has worried not a few. It should not. Is the woodpecker proved fit merely because he is alive? Is that the whole story? Not at all. He is so proved by the observable adequacy of his structure for the pursuit of his struggle for existence: the adequacy of his beak, feet, tail feathers, and so on. The Why of adjustment was the truly enlightening contribution of evolution; the What had been long known, but was so confusing and inexplicable that divine agency had to be called in to account for it. For men, unwilling out of vanity to admit ignorance, yet always hankering after some Why, have always summoned in the Who to substitute for it. They have invoked agency to substitute for cause. "Think of the What," says Goethe, "but think more of the How"—only the How is more readily envisaged as the Who.

It is sound science to infer the utility and survival-value of items in the traditional code of folkways and mores from their universality and persistence; but not unless close study of them reveals Why they are expedient under the conditions of social life amidst which they exist. Any residues that are found to occur in all places and times in the life of successfully persisting societies can be taken as possessing a high and even permanent expediency—as permanent as society is permanent. This attribute of permanency would be confirmed by the demonstration that declining societies are found to be losing these residual mores. If correlations between the presence of the residues and the soundness of society could not be established on the basis of detail studies of actual situations, the mere deduction that persistence goes with fitness would be merely an empty major premise deflated by the test on facts.

What science can do is to demonstrate, not allege, fitness or unfitness by reference to recorded experience. This is a rational performance. Science can detect the Why of expediency, in the social range as well as in the organic. Such detection is always after the act, because experience is always past, or it is not experience. Science can show the inherent rationality in what has been produced without the prior application of reason, spontaneously and automatically: in the instincts of animals as well as in their physical equipment; in the unpremeditated traditional practices of men as well as in the obviously unplanned phenomena of nature. Science can discover how and why nature does this and that—not how and why the cosmos is thus and so, but, more humbly, how and why such details as the camel's structure confer fitness in a desert environment. Science does not expect to solve the Riddle of the Universe, but generates a safer, lesser enlightenment which turns out, within the range of the physical sciences, at any rate, to be useful in living. Science demonstrates, without being in the least able to alter conditions given once and for all in nature, how to adjust to those conditions—for instance, how to profit by the changeless habit of certain chemical compounds to explode under heat or percussion.

Let us now return to the traditional precepts of experience, as embedded in the mores learned, accepted, and practised without any conscious appraisal of their expediency but only with the unpremeditated assessment of trial and error. Suppose that science has made a conscious, rational examination of the record, and is able to demonstrate the survival-value of specific mores and institutions at the time and under the conditions of their general acceptance; and also the dwindling of that value during the period of their decline, if that has taken place—for example, in the case of slavery, the why and how of its rise out of variations toward it, its practically universal acceptance and popularity for centuries, and its eventual decline and elimination. Science is then enabled to put sound sense behind the whole evolution of that practice and of the ideas that have attended its several phases.

Suppose that social science, in studying the evolution of mores and institutions, has found certain of them to have been permanencies in all viable societies, and has even discovered that their decline is correlative with that of the society rejecting or neglecting them. These are, of course, the residues alluded to above. Suppose that social scientists, becoming seemly in their humility, drop the idea of creating a new order of the ages by striving to instill grand visions into Y, and confine themselves to making the most of the residues indigenous in Y. Would they not be doing something quite similar to what the physical scientist does, in his investigation of what is given, as data, in nature? Would they not be able, in some measure, to forecast, as he does, not by divination or revelation, but upon the basis of "anticipated recurrence"? Would not the social scientist actually have penetrated a little way into Y?

In Y reside certain basic convictions, accepted as a matter of course, which science knows, from a survey of human experience, to be sound. It knows also why they are sound. The reasons why they are adjudged to be sound are often very simple and obvious, once attention is focussed upon them. But the simplicity and obviousness of anything are no guarantee of its spontaneous acceptance or even of its recognition. Attention has to be called to the familiar, or it is taken for granted. The elaboration of the obvious, of the commonplace fact or relation which is unheeded precisely because it is familiar, is a major task of any teacher, even when dealing with the X-group. Familiarity may not breed contempt, but it is a fecund progenitor of shortsighted indifference. For the familiar lacks the interest of the new and bizarre. But there is nothing more startling and interest-enthralling than the revelation that the familiar is strange. Every thoughtful person has periodically waked up to the marvel of the familiar, to the profound import of what has been lightly taken for granted. There need never be any apology for the scientific elaboration of the obvious.

If the masses could be held in unswerving loyalty to the residues or permanencies in their codes, much could be accomplished that might properly be accredited to the entrance of social science into Y. False leaders, intent upon their own dreams or interests, are always cluttering over, with their trashy castings, the sound traditions indigenous in Y, the saving common sense that has been pounded into men's codes of conduct by the experience of millennia. The sense is there. Its soundness can be demonstrated throughout the evolutionary course of society. Perhaps it can be cleared, and then kept at least relatively clear, of the smothering rubbish that buries it. Perhaps the recurring eclipses of residual common sense can be shortened. Perhaps it can be brought about that fewer of the people can be fooled for so long a time. If this is merely a pious hope, it is at any rate a modest one.

It is not as if social science had to import sound elemental convictions into Y. They are there. There are proper seeds in the soil. What they need is encouragement through the resolute weeding out of the tares, so that they can be at least recognized; then, patient cultivation. Religion once undertook to do this, and to some extent succeeded; but, withholding from it no due credit, it was one-sided, dogmatic, antipathetic to science. And it is gradually losing what grip it had. If social science is worthy of the name, it will be as dispassionate and realistic as a good husbandman.

No specific program is here presented, but only the conditions which any program conceived in terms of the theory suggested must encounter. It is possible, however, to illustrate the kind of procedure such a program would have to envisage. The residues, or permanencies, as yet left unspecified, form a sort of master code, learned through experience, mainly sad experience, which has been the only genuine teacher of mankind, and formulated in homely precepts passed down by tradition. A very large majority of Y hold to it, in their "heart of hearts," though they may stray from it, and though what is in their "heart of hearts" may be laid bare only by a painful contact with realities. For such contact dissipates the clutter of wishful emotionalism by which the elemental wisdom distilled out of racial experience is recurrently eclipsed. The fact that criminal and other antisocial elements do not subscribe to this basic social code but take advantage of its prevalence throughout society—take advantage of prevalent honesty, as "confidence men," to cheat; of prevalent unarmed peaceableness, to murder—is but added evidence of the deep-seatedness and common acceptance of the code.

Facing the issue in stark and naked form (and one of the ways of stripping the items is to ask: "What would happen to society if everyone did the opposite of the code—for instance, if everyone habitually lied?"), the great majority of Y would subscribe to the following sample items of our basic code: Industry, thrift, honesty, keeping faith, orderliness, stability, certainty, knowledge, experience, self-reliance, are good; sloth, extravagance, dishonesty, faithlessness, disorder, instability, uncertainty, ignorance, inexperience, parasitism, are bad.

One might strive for exhaustiveness in such a list of opposites, but it is not necessary at this juncture. Then there are the proverbial admonitions, many of which underscore the social indispensability of the "good" items and the disastrous results to be expected from the "bad" ones. These warnings appear in lighter guise in venerable fables, such as those of Aesop: they hammer away at irresponsibility, light-mindedness, debt, mendacity, confident ignorance, self-conceit, vanity, and many another socially undesirable quality. They applaud individual initiative, steadfastness, sense of duty, good faith; they exalt traditional exponents of honesty, incorruptibility, loyalty: a Socrates, a Cato, a Christ, in history, a Lincoln in recent times. The rugged virtues of a Grover Cleveland carry him through a period of virtual ostracism into the status, before he dies, of First Citizen of the Republic.

The stock virtues are applauded, even when portrayed in anything but subtle guise, in melodrama. Applause breaks out when Pasteur exhibits his lofty character on the screen. No matter whether the people live up to their sentiments or not, the sentiments are there, down deep, and they boil up periodically to the surface.

Upon this code of residual social virtues rest all the institutions of society. What is the indispensable function of government? To keep the peace. No government can last that does not suppress violence within its jurisdiction. Popular wisdom includes the truth that anarchy is disastrous. To avoid demoralization through internal collision of interests, there is law, which marks out rights to life, liberty, property.

Lawlessness is bad. There is marriage, which debars sexual lawlessness and establishes legitimacy as a reliable basis for inheritance, thus interlacing with property. There is the family, the very cell of any society. It is safeguarded on all sides by a respect which, rooted in millennia of social experience, repels all attacks upon it by antisocial theorists. In general, there is in Y an essential conservatism—a predisposition to preserve what tradition avers to have been conducive to social well-being—and a deep and sound, if inarticulate, conviction that proposed novelties must bear the burden of proof.

There is something, down in Y, to count upon: an unreasoning, automatically developed set of ideas that can have reason, simple and understandable reason, put behind them by a science that has expressed that reason out of accumulations of verified facts, about which, or about the processes of truth-distillation from which, the average man cannot know.

There are, of course, items of conviction in Y behind which science can put no reason at all, because there is none. Some of these are of long standing, but most of them are neither so deep-seated nor inveterate as the scientifically sound items in the code. There was once, for instance, a considerable set of convictions as to the efficacy of magic, and they still exist, especially in politics. It is the business of applied science to explode such phantasies as it can. Then there is the positive line of attack: the shoring up, by good and simple reason, of what I have called the social virtues—the making explicit of the sound sense that is implicit in most of the unconsciously accepted convictions as to what is proper living, the introduction of a conscious and rational element into that acceptance and retention.

The social scientist can renounce, once and for all, the possibility of actually introducing science from, so to speak, above, at the same time relieving himself of the discouragement of sure failure in so doing. It is probably impossible to demonstrate to Y, for instance, that clean sweeps and new dispensations are pure phantasms that have never anywhere or at any time taken on substance. It would be hopeless to attempt the popularization of any social theory approaching in its demand for comprehensive grasp the evolution theory. That kind of thing can penetrate only slightly, even into X.

There is no use assuming the presence of seeds in the Y soil which are not there: immortal yearnings after various thin abstractions, for example. What the social scientist can do is to confine himself to the appraisal and discrimination of what is already patent in Y, with the hope of promoting rational selection upon what is there. Then he is working upon what may be a real crevice in the barrier, instead of hurling himself headlong at it, or mournfully yowling before it, as before some wailing wall, or importantly tooting tin whistles and waiting, assuming the while an easy posture, for the defenses of Jericho to fall. He may not be able to make a breach, for all his patient pecking; but what less formidable alternative is in sight?

IV

SCIENCE AND "SUPERSTITION."

A RATHER PLAUSIBLE paradox is presented by the assertion: "Without superstition there would have been no science." It pleasures all those optimists who like to think of good distilling out of evil, like honey dripping out of the lion's carcass. A companion-piece would be: "Out of illusion cometh truth." Aphorisms of this sort are encouraging, and men like to be cheered up. And they are not mere empty sayings that appeal sheerly to credulity, for there is evidence out of experience to back them up, at least in part. But they should not be gulped down whole, like an article of faith. Remembering that most generalizations must, by their very comprehensiveness, do some violence to the truth, the discreet student of things social will look pretty critically into such blanket-assertions.

Consider the example in point. It might be stated in a kind of tabular form: No science without laws; no laws without sequences; no sequences without comparison; no comparison without instances; no instances without observation; no observation without interest; no interest without superstition (superstitious fear). This chain of items fits the case of astronomy. If you start with the major premise that the stars govern human destiny, you are keen to know what the stars are doing. Your interest is roused. If people nowadays were convinced that the stars governed, say, the outcome of industrial enterprises or of operations on the stock market, colleges would not so generally lack popular courses in astronomy. That study would, indeed, form a staple item in extension enterprises and in the elementary schools. It does not, because few people are interested. Intellectual curiosity, divorced from practical interest, moves comparatively few to acquaint themselves with even the rudiments of astronomy. The situation was very different in ancient Chaldaea and wherever else the horoscope flourished.

It is quite evident also that medicine and several other of the arts and sciences go back to a root in magic—in which everyone unshakenly believed and therefore had a vital interest. Chemistry must always regard alchemy as a kind of ancestor; had it not been for the ardent interest in the philosopher's stone, which is now regarded as a pure superstition, certainly there would not have been so long a line of experiments—that is to say, of almost systematically acquired observations and experience—by so many interested men.

There is no doubt whatever that much science comes straight out of superstition. That is a valuable and an enlightening generalization. But that all science thus originated is a proposition known as a "universal," and any universal can be upset by even one contradictory instance. Universals are always risky. They always need some whittling. In their unwhittled form, they are more useful for forensic purposes than for either the discovery or the exposition of truth.

As a matter of the record, while science always began with interest, that interest was sometimes not even tinged with superstition. Much knowledge came out of experience with wood, bone, and other familiar materials. Tools like the lever and devices like the inclined plane were developed without much or any superstition attending the process. Then, out of experience with them—observation, trial and error, etc. —came ways of shaping and using them that were effective and, at length, laws of mechanics or of elementary physics and chemistry. It was learned that friction produced fire, that anything very sticky glued birds' feet to a branch, that an outrigger to a canoe gave it stability, that puffing into a pipe would propel a dart, that one kind of wood was better than another for making a bow, and so on indefinitely. All this was the result of the accumulation and comparison of observed facts, plus common sense in putting two and two together.

It is true that superstition crept into the most practical aspects of living: the archer's new bowstring parted, and he blamed his gods or imputed some unwitting sin to himself. But this was exceptional because unexpected and unaccountable. In the ordinary course of events a new string would not break; there was seen in the rupture something extraordinary and inexplicable that roused superstition. Otherwise, in the ordinary course of things, there was nothing to think or worry about or to refer to supernatural agency.

I do not like to leave the term "superstition" hanging on a hook, unnoticed. I think almost everyone understands what is meant by it in the phrase about science coming out of superstition, but it will do no harm to look into that meaning a little. What the phrase signifies is that science, which we hold by our acts, if not our words, to be true and accurate, develops out of what we now believe to be untrue and inexact. It is not that, when we think of it, we blame people of the past for being what we call "superstitious," any more than we should call a child "superstitious" for believing in fairies. But we should rightly use the term in the case of an adult who believes what the child does. One is not really superstitious unless he "knows better," or ought to. A superstition is really a belief discarded by "us," the enlightened, which persists in the minds of the unenlightened. It is a survivalistic belief, something indefensible that lasts on, as the etymology of the word indicates. It is to be deplored, perhaps, but not censured, except in the case of those who could, and ought to, know better.

The kind of superstition that science grows out of is the uncensurable variety. Since the word almost always carries a shade of depreciation, very likely it should be discarded as applied to the pre-scientific period. In no case is it justifiable to brand primitive religion, magic, medicine, and the rest of those ways of primitives that represent adjustment to the supernatural with the contemptuous phrase, "nothing but superstition." In their places, we could have done no better. But if we take the word in the colorless sense of "discarded beliefs," then of course superstition has been the matrix of accepted beliefs; for beliefs, like organisms, grow out of preceding beliefs, not out of a vacuum.

There is something else besides religion and magic to which modern views go back: something intermediate in the series between the primitive way of thinking and the way of the modern world. Comte placed it between the religious and the positive states or stages. It is the metaphysical. In the colorless sense of "superstition," metaphysics is to the scientist superstitious, that is, it is a survivalistic belief. That science grew out of the metaphysical phase of human thinking is known to the informed; all sciences have had to free themselves of metaphysics, much as from a cocoon, before they could take on their distinguishing features and traits. The fact that certain scientists choose to become metaphysicians by renouncing observation and study in favor of speculation, or of some kind of harmonization or "reconciliation of science and religion," affects the case in no way. Pontificating promiscuously on the basis of a demonstrated position in science is a foible of vanity merely, though in effect it amounts to treachery, or at least to extending comfort to the enemy.

As Comte clearly enough explains and illustrates, the metaphysical Absolutes and Entities are merely the frail shadows of the once lusty gods. Speculation was a stage through which mankind, to their detriment, had to go. But there is no longer any warrant for the belief that metaphysics will get anywhere—not, at least, in the direction toward which science has been long heading. To retreat back upon speculation and deduction from grand major premises is an exhibition of superstition. It is as if a grown man were to refuse to put away childish things.

Someone once defended philosophy on the ground that it was like poetry—and not to be taken seriously. No one can have any quarrel with the poet nor with the philosopher as a poet. But when either of them pretends to know, in the sense of possessing verified and indefinitely verifiable experience, that is another matter. There is profit in keeping different things apart. Then you do not get them mixed at a pinch. Poets and philosophers have bright ideas that may be either right or wrong—you can never tell until they are submitted to verification on experience. To believe otherwise is superstition—the same kind of belief that the savage had in his medicine-man.

All my life, since I was twenty, I have prized Goethe as the wisest man who has ever delivered himself freely out of a wide experience with life. He has had wisdom for me in every decade of my life—in the latter ones a wisdom I was not mature enough to grasp in the earlier decades. His conclusions have been verified in my life-experience. He has passed over the road before me, noting what he saw, felt, and thought; and I find, so far as my experience has gone, that his observations were profound and correct to a unique degree. Many a thoughtful man will disagree with me. I cannot prove my conviction, as I might, were I a competent scientist, prove that Goethe was right or wrong as regards his biological conclusions or his theory of color. Where Goethe was a poet, I can even thrill at his sweep of imagination and his verse, as I can profit by what his personal experience with life led him to conclude about it; and, in addition, because he is revealed in his work as a wise commentator on life, I can prize him more highly than as great or greater artists, such as Aeschylus or Shakespeare.

Scientist as he was in some of his avocations—enough of a scientist to be named, in *The Origin of Species,* as a forerunner of the evolution-theory—as a poet he seems to me unique in the cool objectiveness of his observation of himself and of the world about him. That makes him, in a sense, the most useful of them all to some possible science of the future which can use his penetrating insight. Nevertheless, his observations and conclusions will then be and remain subject to the assessment of common experience, not accepted forthwith as infallible on the ground that "the poet knows." To believe anything else is to resurrect the old superstition by which Authority was conceived to be Proof.

The trouble with philosophy is that it claims to be the science of sciences when it is no science at all. If it gave itself out to be a species of poetry, there could be no complaint. Many queer things have been styled poetry, and still are. The pretentiousness of philosophy rests upon yet another superstition—that it can find and reveal truth—to which, along back, everyone assented as he accepted the witchcraft-mania now generally termed a plain superstition—indeed, a snare and a delusion. It is to be noted here that "everbody believes it" is no proof at all that "it" is true, despite the fact that you can generally make a strong specious appeal by such an unqualified assertion. All that wide belief in anything proves is that the mores are favorable to that belief. It is another way of reiterating that the belief in question "is universal because it is universal."

I have gone to some length in the contention that science has been as much hampered, at a later stage of its evolution, by metaphysical superstition as it was earlier by magical and religious handicaps. All of these chrysalis-envelopments were natural and normal enough in their day. No one could have thought differently. They were therefore not censurable in their setting. But they are now, for intelligent discrimination can "know better." They afford, however, a legitimate extension of the assertion that "science grows out of superstition," a particular extension, indeed, that is commonly overlooked by those who accept the generalization.

This generalization is therefore, as commonly received, both too wide and too narrow—too wide in that it is stretched to cover sources of science that are not superstition in any sense of the word, and too narrow because it is not extended over the superstition, which all real science has discarded, that truth can be derived from intuition, speculation, formal logic, dialectics, or anything else except the accumulation, comparison, and arrangement in series of verified and re-verified facts of experience, and the eventual derivation, out of these operations, of scientific laws. Science has, indeed, been largely developed out of superstition, but shreds of the cocoon should not be sticking still, untidily and draggingly, to the emerging creature.

V

THE ADJUSTMENT IDEA.

To LIFT "adjustment" out of current usage, to set it up as the central feature of a science of society, is the very antithesis of a strain after academic impressiveness. It is, rather, to take footing directly upon the obvious. The verb "to adjust" is so common that the conception of adjustment must be widely diffused in men's minds; and no wonder, for adjusting is precisely what men have been about, as a necessity for survival, since they arrived upon this earth. Mechanical things are always being adjusted to one another. Partners in wedlock must make mutual adjustments. Maladjustment and re-adjustment are much to the front when economic or political situations are under examination. Even religion is reported to be in process of readjustment to altered conditions. Where a term is thus in evidence, the idea it stands for is familiar to everyone.

But all such current terms are used loosely. They cover not a point but a field. They spread, like a charge of shot or a stream from a hose; they are not rifle-bullets. It is when you try to focus them down, to mean something more specific, that you encounter resistance. Focussing is what must be done, however, with any term culled by science out of common usage, or there will be no science at all but merely a random incoherence.

The adjustment idea, in the hands of science, is shaped up, or focussed, into a conformation presenting the following outlines: (1) living organisms are set down in the midst of life-conditions neither understandable nor controllable by them; (2) they persist or disappear according as they get along, or do not get along, within their life-conditions; (3) the whole process is one of automatic adjustment. This is organic evolution. In the hands of a science of society, the conformation is essentially the same: (1) a group of human beings—a human society—is set down in the midst of life-conditions, at first neither understood nor controllable, and even in the present but poorly understood and only to a slight degree controllable; (2) the society persists or prospers according as it gets along, or does not get along, with its life-conditions; (3) the whole process is predominantly one of automatic adjustment. This is societal evolution.

The moment you begin to sharpen the adjustment idea in such manner, especially in its application to mankind, you encounter a resistance that the current, undefined term does not meet. The tightening up of the looser conception causes it to bind upon preconception. The idea of adjustment takes on repellent aspects.

While men do not dislike the idea when they view it from the angle they usually occupy, they hate it when seen from certain other slants. It all depends upon what is to be adjusted, and to what. The thought of adjusting the world to the self seems noble and utterly worthy of human dignity; for there is a feeling that the adjusting element is somehow inferior to the element to which adjustment is made, just as it is the socially lower-placed person who must conciliate his superior. Self-adjustment seems somehow demeaning, an evidence of unfreedom, an absence of self-determination; for the lofty self is thereby shifted from the center of the stage and presented as somehow secondary to circumstance. There begins to be some rumbling about determinism, predestination, and fatalism. Free will, an illusory treasure that men hug to their bosoms, seems to be imperilled. This sense of assault upon human dignity is heightened when the adjective "automatic" is prefixed to "adjustment." It is bad enough if man is presented as the consenting adjuster of himself to conditions rather than as the masterful molder of conditions to the imperious self; but to state or even to imply that he is coerced by the nature of things into that subordinate function without even being conceded a chance to protest is regarded as a kind of cynical treachery to Man, the Master.

The popular, because flattering, conception of adjustment, namely, that of squaring permanencies, including "human nature," to man's thought-phantasies, is precisely that one of mankind's many delusions which has entrained our worst disasters. You might as well dream of fitting climate to organisms—better, perhaps, feet to shoes, for that can be done, as the Chinese have demonstrated, if you are willing to suffer enough for the sake of vanity. This kind of thing is not what is meant here by adjustment; this writing contemplates the adjustment of the passing to the permanent, of the changeable to the changeless, of the incidental to the inevitable—in particular, of man's associated existence in human society to abiding life-conditions of society.

No conception could be simpler than that of adjustment, however complicated its processes may be found to be. We live by it, unconscious of that fact though we may remain by use and wont, every day and hour. Deliberate neglect of it entails suffering and death. But many there are who hate the idea of automatic adjustment, as a derogation from dignity, just as many still revolt at the truth of the animal descent of their noble selves, and so, wishfully thinking, refuse to accept it. All that automatic adjustment means, however, is that life is carried on, not independently, imperiously, or self-determinedly, but as conditioned by the sort of environment in which it finds itself. This truth is so much a matter of course in practical living that dissent is evidence of crazy impracticality. Men keep away from fathomless quagmires; they do not argue about them or develop ideologies about masterfully striding through them. They neither resent nor ignore, in a vanity-induced trance, the presence and properties of poisonous fungi in the woods, of crocodiles in the rivers, of lightning in the clouds; on the contrary, they simply and without a sense of humiliation refrain from eating "toadstools," diving into unexplored pools, taking refuge under trees in a thunderstorm. While so doing, they do not cry out about limitation on their freedom, nor do they "take unto themselves the tools of thought," and, shaping what they will, turn the amanita into manna, the saurian into tadpole, the electric discharge into gentle dew. No, they plume themselves on the fact that they know their limitations and so can act accordingly and continue to live on. It would be very pleasant and lordly to set some contrivance into perpetual motion, only the nature of things forbids; and so men good-humoredly bow to the Nature of Things: "All right, Nature, all right! Just as you say." No one feels his dignity injured by the necessity of adjustment.

Up to some such point, adjustment is commonsensible; not especially praiseworthy but only discreet; awakening neither resentment against determinism (or foreordination or predestination) nor even an enervating fatalism. To admit irrevocable life-conditions is not deemed at all demeaning; to know them so as to be able to adapt deftly to them is, indeed, occasion for self-congratulation, pride, and a sort of arrogant pity for those who, knowing less, adjust more clumsily.

But now, when we get outside the range of direct relation with tangible things like rocks and food, plainly perceptible things like heat and cold, changeless ways of things like gravitation and capillary attraction, we discover a type of human attitude wholly different and contrasted; for the conditioning of life in society by the intangible and impersonal, by social law, is bewailed and resented, predestination is abhorred, and anything that seems undeniably to question free will plunges men into the despond of fatalism. They refuse to believe on compelling evidence because they have the will to believe what is more appealing to their sense of personal merit. Admitting, up to this point, the need of tuition, they now put their money on the dubious steed, Intuition, a mare that has been proved to be spavined from colt-hood, or upon the stallion, Will-o'-the-Wish, which may, in one heat, pause halfway down the stretch for a doze of free meditation, then, in the next, break pace and leap, bulging of eye, into the grandstand.

Men like to believe that good intentions entail corresponding conse-quences, for in that case there is no need to take account of conditions; whereas, if there is no such inevitable sequence between purposes and consequences, and the eye must always be on the latter, then the only sensible course is to know conditions and adjust to them. Also, men readily fall for magic because it pretends to defy or to change life-conditions, so that adjustment is rendered superfluous. To know con-ditions demands long and hard labor, and to adjust to them calls for anxious attention and self-abnegation. Neither is easy. Any kind of plausible short cut is welcome, for it seems to be liberation from an onerous discipline.

It is no true liberation. Dodging is never that. It is at best a tempo-rary escape, to be made up for in suffering later on.

The adjustment idea in its relation to society's life is that all societal arrangements—the mores and the institutions that develop out of them —are products of a process, mainly automatic and impersonal, which tries out variations against the typically immutable life-conditions of society: the physical and social environments, the aleatory element, bisexuality. If they fit, they last; if they do not fit, or cease to fit, they do not last.

It is a misapprehension to infer from this statement that "whatever is, is right." All it says is that all social arrangements are subject to the adjustmental or evolutionary process. Most of them show a triple cycle: first an initial stage, when they are mere variations, as yet un-tested; then an adjustment stage, after they have survived recurrent selection; and at length a maladjustment phase, when selection is going against them. It is in the middle stage only that they are con-ceived to be "right." Slavery is a good example. Much misapprehen-sion as regards the adjustment theory arises out of confusing the vari-ation with the adjustment, as will be seen in the next essay.

The misapprehension that attaches to the term "automatic," namely, that the adjustment idea is "fatalistic," leads to the conclusion that there is no use trying to do anything, to *laissez-faire* in the vulgar sense. But that a process is automatic does not mean that nothing can be done about it. The rushing together of two gases is automatic. No command, no regrets, no yearning can halt them, once in proximity, just as no one can stop the electric discharge between a cloud and the earth. However, provided the ways of gases are known, they either need not be brought together, or they may be located where they can unite under conditions favorable to human purposes. Man may even "harness"—though that is a grandiloquent word savoring of imaginary mastership—the lightning. Actually, in so doing, he is not a master at all but an adjuster: one who knows how to move things—water, sulphuric acid, copper, zinc—into or out of proximity. What enables him to realize desired results is not his imperious intentions but his humble knowledge: his hard-won familiarity with facts, qualities, relations, affinities—matters which he cannot alter any more than he can choose to breathe water instead of air, and get away with it.

There are social projects aplenty that even a modicum of knowledge of actual conditions despairs of accomplishing, into which ignorance adrip with noble intentions and conscious of no inexorable conditions plunges blithely, confidently, and disastrously. Some years ago there was a movement labelled: "The World for Christ in This Generation." It is uncertain whether Catholics and Jews were construed to be inside or outside the crusade. The "generation" is, according to the most liberal estimate, about up; it expired, indeed, several years since. Anyway, there are still some Buddhists, Shintoists, Moslems, and other pagans outside the fold. Some of the leaders of that movement are no less vocal than of yore, although they are now shouting up something else; but a good many of its once panting followers are laughing indulgently at their youthful gullibility. Their mirth is the grain of profit out of the whole transaction, so far as society is concerned. They know now that it is mighty hard, no matter how copious the funds, to convert even one Mohammedan; and that the savage often backslides the moment the brass wire and tin cups give out. A faith that could plug Mt. Everest upside down into the Nero Deep might have availed. Nothing less.

The adjustment idea, while it is definitely allergic to emotional follies, is far from being merely negative, discouraging, iconoclastic, enervatingly fatalistic, as respects all programs envisaging social betterment. It is, on the contrary, a positive and reliable basis for a genuine science of society: a body of theory, with sound, unemotional, practical applications. It suggests a definite program, a blue-print of a durable structure. That that program is a long-run affair, demanding toil, endurance, patience, tenacity, and renunciation of prompt acclaim, though not conducing to its general popularity, yet appeals to the discreet as characteristic of scientific soundness. It is a program conformable with the experience of anyone who knows the history of the accredited sciences. It is a program of protracted, laborious, and solitary investigation—solitary because solitude confers an immunity from the aimless chatter that balks that concentration by the individual to which we owe most of our scientific discoveries.

This program is one of study, not of mooning or moaning: a study of society's actual life-conditions, not a peering into a fog of speculative phantasies, non-existent except in an emotionally feverish brain; a study of society, not of something else, such as the individual and his psychology. If we emerge with no more than a realization that there is no end to the study, and that whatever we may be able to do in the light of it cannot be done in a day, or by passing resolutions, we have won knowledge hidden from the many and even from some who have been hastily rated as among the elect. Further, if we discover only what cannot be done with society, we shall have done much better than to sojourn at the Nowhere-destination where the sociologists, we are told, now repose.

I wish to return for a moment to a foregoing allusion to the salutary effects, when it comes to discovery, of protracted and profound solitude. We have Goethe's word for it: "A talent develops in solitude." The contemporary tendency seems to deny that aphorism, conceiving of joint investigation as a short and sure road to truth. Credulous people appear to be convinced that, by operating in propinquity, a group of mediocrities may rise to levels unattainable by any one of its constituents—that, by huddling and swarming, scholars may generate, like bees, a heat enabling them to exude wax as they could not individually.

This is an attractive superstition. Any informed man knows well enough that every discoverer stands upon the shoulders of a long line of predecessors. But if he tries to hold hands with contemporaries he is likely to be impeded merely. Instead of generating some quality that raises the communal level above its source, coöperators are likely to get in each other's way and all sink to the level of the weakest. Especially, under the influence of "arrangers of things," who have an affinity for coöperative enterprises, do the capable fritter away time, strength, and the opportunity for quiet, private thought, in program-making, committee-hashings, and other wholly unproductive, irritating, and damnable gesticulation. The great discoveries have been made, like all variations, by individuals in isolation and solitude. This fact, despite all modifying considerations, should never be let slip by anyone who hopes to discover truth anywhere, and least of all by him who sets out to find it within the societal range and by the inductive method. Coördination is quite another thing than coöperation. You coördinate results, where you coöperate in planning. The former encourages individual initiative, the latter blunts it. And individual initiative in producing variations is the first step in the adjustment process, without which the operation is halted before it starts.

The adjustment idea is merely the evolution idea: adaptation to life-conditions, or environment. To its life-conditions, society adjusts by way of mores and institutions developed out of the mores. The only way to view this process at all is over long stretches and by the inspection of the genetic series of institutions and their trends, that is, by charting the experience of socialized mankind in adjustment to life-conditions that are ever, despite their essential permanency, changing in detail.

The thing called human society exhibits its distinguishing characteristics in what it actually does, so that the study of it involves, not speculation as to what is in the heads of its constituents, but inspection of its institutional adjustments in their rising, mature, and declining phases. The adjustment idea is, therefore, to one who can distinguish between knowledge and the pseudo-knowledge that passes for it, the key to the scientific study, not only of organisms, but also of all phenomena in the societal range.

One caveat remains: one must not let the adjustment idea run away with him. Any theory may be betrayed in the house of its friends. The adjustment theory is not one of unchecked change and random relativity, any more than of the authoritarian rigidity that it so comfortingly, for many of us, dissolved. To anyone who has been reared under the rod of Authority—of the Scriptures, of the Absolutes, of some species of Ipse Dixit—the intellectual relief derivable from the adjustment-theory is so solacing that he is likely, in gratitude, to erect that theory into a dogma. Against this consummation guard must be strictly kept. The form of the dogma is that all is relative, for all is in flux. Any variation whatsoever may therefore become overnight an adjustment to ever-changing conditions. There are no fixed points or bearings at all. This amounts to sheer credulity. It might well issue in the "enervating fatalism" elsewhere alluded to, though whether or not it would do so is a matter of no scientific moment.

The common attitude of one who has let the adjustment-theory run away with him finds expression in a reiteration of: "You never can tell." He is open-minded to some preposterous Plan fathered by the wish, because, he avers, "it may work under the changed conditions that may be arriving" or "that have already arrived." There is talk of a "New Level."[1] One remarks to a young man who is all enthusiasm for the adjustment-idea: "There are mores that are not subject to change, in essentials, at all." He stares at you, wide-eyed. "Then you are going back on your own theory, aren't you?" is what that shocked gaze says, even if it is not accompanied by "What ails you, anyway?" Or he may inquire: "For example?" You reply promptly: "For example, the taboo against in-group homicide, the Commandment: Thou shalt not kill." He objects: "But there may arrive conditions when that taboo goes no longer"—and then the foregoing patter about pointless change and "relativity," ending with a reiterated, "You are going back on your theory."

Well, that is just the idea, if it means that I am going back *over* the theory—over and over. I too have traversed that stretch where I believed exactly as the young man does, where the theory was to me a kind of credo. I had perceived, as a kind of unshackling revelation, that the mores could "make anything right and prevent condemnation of anything." I had realized that the Bible was entirely complaisant to polygamy and slavery, full of survivals of human sacrifice and even of cannibalism, and I had received with astonishment, preceding entire intellectual assent, Sumner's often-stated conclusion that "any institution is justifiable in the setting of its time"—his way of stating that mores and institutions are evolutionary though, identifying evolution with progress, he denied that they were.

Now the hitch in all this relativity-business lies in "the setting of its time." It is assumed forthwith that that setting is indefinitely protean. It is not. All settings of all times are alike in essentials, so that all adjustments to all settings have followed certain basic patterns. That is why all is not everlastingly in flux of change and why certain imagined changes in life-conditions—in the "settings"—are phantasms that melt away amidst pain and disillusionment when people

1. See essay on "The 'New Level,' " below.

try to act on them. They ought to be revealed as illusory by scientific forecast, and most of them would be, were it not for the wishful thinking that betrays the adjustment theory into perversion as dogma—a perversion as gross as that of Darwinism into a theory of militaristic ferocity.

Is it necessary to develop the idea, beyond the bare statement of it, that society's life-conditions are essentially, in kind, what they always have been? Is the physical environment changed, or have we merely, more or less cleverly, adapted our ways to it? Is the social environment of fellow-men altered, otherwise than numerically, or is man what he always has been? Despite all tall talk about renovating human nature, do we not recognize the same old traits in ourselves that are set down in the Old Testament or Homer? Is the aleatory element obsolete, or is it with us still? And how about bisexuality? These are, to anybody even meanly acquainted with the course of society's evolution, no more than rhetorical questions.

And are the characteristic responses to these perdurable conditions, as worked out by trial and error in the formation of the folkways, mores, and institutions, no longer recognizable in this age, even under our alleged *Novus Ordo Seclorum?* Have we not the Industrial Organization, Property, the Regulative Organization, Religion, and Marriage? Are there not still behind then Hunger, Love, Vanity, and Fear of the Inexplicable?

Absolutes are to be rejected, once and for all, as metaphysical figments; but not so the Permanencies—only, when that word is used of mores and institutions, it means "permanent in the sense that society is permanent"—"as permanent as society." That is permanent enough for any student of society. Whether the taboo against homicide goes booming down the aisles of time after human society is no more, in a kind of deathlessness, is not within the range of scientific investigation. It is a kind of joke-question, of the same grotesque and unearthly character as the issue about infant damnation. All that any person of sense can mean by "permanency," as regards society-originated and society-maintained mores and institutions, is "permanency as of society."

In that sensible sense, the taboo on in-group violence is permanent, a fixed point, one of those landmarks from which bearings can be taken in faring forth. To those who have such bearings, a variation is not incontinently identifiable with a settled adjustment.[2] Fixed

2. See essay on "The Variation and the Adjustment," below.

points are not so rare: Commandments that are not, all ten, out of date and negligible. I have specified some of them in a little book called *Brass Tacks,* designed to correct the impression that all is relativity, which students have, with some justification, read into *Societal Evolution.*

This relativity is not to be overdone. The series from folkway to comprehensive institution is one of increasing stability. If relativity is made into a dogma, it becomes as pernicious to straight thinking as any other pronouncement of Authority. For it is then mobilized, in perversion of whatever scientific character it may be thought to have, behind the indefinite credulity of wishfulness and emotionalism. And when that pair of sinister birds of omen fly in by the window, from the left, science and common sense, omen-conscious, decamp hastily through the door.

VI

THE VARIATION AND THE ADJUSTMENT.

THEORETICALLY, a variation becomes an adjustment when it has been repeatedly, and over a long time, subjected successfully to selection. But in practice it is often as difficult to say when a variation has become an adjustment as it is to fix the time when adolescence passes into maturity. To determine what "a long time" is, is like answering the question: "How long is a long stick?" It all depends.

Some there were who wanted forthwith to call the sit-down strike an adjustment, though it was, at best, but newly submitted to selection. It was plainly a variation, though those who are wont to mistake prophecy for evidence, thus being able, to their own satisfaction, to predict survival under selection, saw it already in the mores. Others regard the protective tariff as still a variation, though it has been a policy for some time and has survived severe attacks. Still others regard totalitarianism—Communism, Naziism, or Fascism—as an adjustment, though in no one of its present forms is it over twenty-five years old. Instances could be multiplied, both ways, of hailing a variation as an adjustment or calling an adjustment a mere variation, and several more will appear incidentally as we go on. It is evident that one must take account of types, rather than of isolated instances, as he has to do in classifying the human races, or in distinguishing childhood from youth, youth from maturity, maturity from old age.

When a case is closed, it is easier to assess its phases. Take the stock case of slavery. It plainly passed through a long period of trial and failure, then became the unquestioned institution of centuries, and finally succumbed to the competition of a new variation, free labor. It was, as a variation, tried out again and again but, for a very good reason, did not take hold until a developed agriculture had grown up. Then it fitted into the situation, as being a way to get work done, and also as consistent with the rest of the mores. When it was superseded by a more efficient way of getting work done and had fallen out of its consistency with the other mores—developed humanitarianism, for example—it was done for. No one can fix exact dates for its passage from variation to adjustment, then to maladjustment, but that it went through those typical phases can be doubted by no one who is informed.

But most cases are not closed; and it is a discouraging tendency of mankind, especially under misery, to reopen antique and settled cases, resurrecting old and discarded maladjustments as new variations, then to slog through the old disillusionments until the ancient and inevitable penalty for refusing to learn from experience has to be suffered yet again. Says someone who is impatient with the jury system: "Let us have an arbitrator!" Yes, that is the way things began, and if we go back to it, we shall have the same task of gradually and with misery working through the whole series again, to emerge in the end with about what we have now—a defective instrumentality, defective like all other human devices. It is easy and popular to condemn an institution because it is not one hundred per cent perfect, and then to present as a new and utopian project some long-discarded phase of that institution from which our predecessors freed themselves with pain and even bloodshed.

One of the truths about evolution that should, along with its deliberate pace, be taken to heart, is that it never produces perfection. The phrase "survival of the fittest" has misled many; it should be put in the comparative degree, and negatively as well: "the non-survival of the unfitter." It is said that any competent optician would be ashamed to produce an instrument as faulty as the human eye, with its blind spot, age-stiffening, and the rest of its imperfections. What makes the salient impression of perfection, and excuses the rhapsodies, about the eye is that it is alive; but life is nothing unheard of, after all. The discreet student of human society will start out by expecting imperfections in all human instrumentalities, especially the social ones, and be pleasantly edified that they are as good as they are.

There is no rule to be laid down by which one can accurately distinguish in every specific case between a variation and an adjustment. That might as well be given up first as last. But that renunciation does not mean that there is no yardstick at all. There are higher and lower degrees of probability in the science of society, even though it lacks the certainty of an often-repeated laboratory experiment which always comes out, under the same conditions, the same way. Nevertheless, whatever yardstick there may be in the social sciences, it must, as in the laboratory sciences, be constructed out of experience, not caught up out of snatchings at rainbow ends. When we have gathered and winnowed more facts of experience, our yardstick will become more accurate, that is, it will register higher degrees of probability. It is not very rigid as yet; it can be stretched, squeezed shorter, or bent this way and that by the disingenuous and the hysterical; but it is not altogether, even now, of a banana-like spinelessness.

The distinction between variation and adjustment is confused by a misapprehension about evolution. To one making his first acquaintance with the adjustment-theory, it appears to be, as I have elsewhere[1] stated, a doctrine of endless and incessant change, with no element of stability in it. That is largely because it challenges all the philosophical dogmas about the Absolute, the Eternal, the Perfect, and other phantasms that have plagued the world for millennia. It is therefore, to the believers in such Ultimates, a theory of confusion worse confounded. I have no intention of arguing the case of organic evolution but shall confine myself to the societal range. Is there nothing permanent about the mores? Are there no mores or institutions that are lasting, in the sense that without them no society can long endure?

Society could persist, of course, without certain fashions, for example, the wearing of earrings. Fashion is a synonym for capricious change. A "permanent fashion" would be a contradiction in terms. There is, upon the folkways, a top layer of frothy ideas and practices whose flimsy, ephemeral presence or absence is of no consequence. But then come the real mores which, by definition, are the folkways when they include a judgment that they are important or even indispensable for society's welfare. They may not be; but if they are thought to be, that sets them in a category apart from mere fashion. Public conviction backs them up. At this point, one is tempted to stop and reflect upon what kind of a thing public conviction is; but that topic is to be put off a while, with, however, this preliminary understanding: that nothing whatever is proved true by the fact that multitudes believe it.

Taking the mores as they have developed in history, we find a residue of practices, backed by public assent or even fanatical zeal, that has existed in every known society of mankind and the perversion of which has been correlative with social decline. These selected mores might be called morals. And some of the most highly approved of them develop into rigid precedent and eventually into law. The stock method of prescribing what is deemed beneficial is by proscribing the opposite: the right to life is guaranteed by the taboo against killing.

1. Essay on "The Adjustment Idea," above.

The entrance of religion, in the guise of spiritual sanction of the taboo —"Thus saith the Lord: Thou shalt not!"—immensely strengthens every mos which it enjoins by forbidding its rivals.

Then, finally, arrives the settled institution, which is a group of mores surrounding a prime interest, such as the sex relation, when that lumpy accretion of ideas and practices has been carved by the taboo into a shape recognizable enough to call for a label, such as "marriage." Property comes out of a set of ways for attaching a thing to a person; government out of a gradually winnowed group of tentatives for keeping the in-group peace; religion out of a complicated body of practices supposed to constitute adjustment to the surrounding world of ghosts and spirits.

This series, from folkway to institution, is one of ascending significance and permanence, so that where passing modes are of small consequence, settled institutions are vital to society's life and are so recognized by the public conviction of all peoples, even of those who could not for their lives cite any rational grounds for their belief. With the passage of time, and with the selective process having, by sparing it, approved some institution—say, private property—over and over again, the element of tradition enters to cause people to forget, if they ever knew, that any other system was possible. An institution thus becomes like the eternal hills; variation goes on always, ever chipping away at its superficial features; but no one, except he be touched with some monstrous madness, like Otus and Ephialtes, harbors even fleetingly the idea of alteration in any essential of the settled order.

No evolutionist has any fault to find with tradition, any more than with heredity in the organic world, to which tradition in the social range closely corresponds. Brakes are just as necessary as motors, the discipline of tradition quite as indispensable as the liberty of variation. Nor will anyone who understands the adjustment theory be able to deny the existence of survival-value in a practice, such as the adherence to tradition, which all sound human societies have always exhibited. That is to say, the lastingness of any institution or code of morals or of laws is broadly indicative of its utility to society. The fact that things are old is proof that they have withstood repeated selection on the basis of experience with them. The presumption is always in favor of any longstanding institution, especially if it is also universal in all societies. The burden of proof always rests upon the innovator, the more heavily in proportion to the subversiveness of his proposed variation. An illustration of longevity is the family; another is religion. Indeed, the permanence and universality of any institution is commonly referred to some "instinct" of mankind, or to "human nature," or to "natural necessity," which is a naïve effort to yoke the observed permanence and universality of the institution in a cause-and-effect relation with some assumed Absolute.

The upshot of the foregoing is the contention with which we started: No proposed or initiated alteration or replacement of an institution or of a code, either of morals or laws, can be legitimately termed an "adjustment" until it has been subjected to repeated selection. All consciously devised variations are efforts to remedy maladjustments or to secure better adjustment; but that is their only relation to adjustment, for they are actually nothing but variations. The fact that their proponents mean well, even harbor lofty purposes and can see in their mind's eye and eloquently prophesy the smoothness of perfect adjustment to be attained by their pet programs, is totally irrelevant to the matter of actual adjustment. For an actual adjustment is not a thing of the mind's eye or of the "creative imagination"; it is a thing of the body's eye; it is a thing of the stomach, which has no eye and cannot feed upon futures or upon dreams and visions, not even those of human brotherhood.

No variation can be justified by anything else than by demonstrated success, and after the act. There are too many $x's$ in any social equation to allow of confidence in any "solution" that works out on paper both smoothly and too "logically." Logic can never get around unexpected refractory facts and unforeseen factors—and the social woods are full of such pests—except by evasions, excuses, and alibis that break down in the long run.

"True enough!" gladly agree the "experimenters" of the present, longing, as they do, to be regarded as scientists—aspiring so yearningly that they drape themselves in what rags of scientific terminology they can snatch up. "Quite true! That is what we want to do—try things out! Any old thing! That's the way to get adjustment, with attendant felicity! Lo! Most of our experimental variations are already adjustments! Is not public opinion behind them? Have we not a mandate?"

Does a variation become an adjustment when public opinion, as recorded, say, in election returns, is behind it? This brings us around to public conviction, a topic left suspended a few pages back. But before embarking upon that topic, let us see where we now stand.

The adjustment-process in the societal range is not merely change, random rather than otherwise, with no fixed points at all. Fixity increases as we move up the line from the folkway to the institution. Certain structures that form and hold the shape of the institutions are, to all practical intents, permanent—"to all practical intents" meaning that no society could long endure in their absence. This is the verdict of history, which is that of experience. Such provisions are the taboos: Thou shalt not kill (an in-group member); Thou shalt not steal (from an in-group member); Thou shalt not commit adultery (with an in-group comrade's wife). Any society that permits internal strife signs its death warrant, for it cannot survive in competition with rival societies that have established inner peace and order. The assurance of the right to life and the right to property within the group is, to all practical intents, a permanency. Only the wildest fanatic or criminal wants to abrogate either of these rights. Public conviction is unremittingly behind them and has never, either in theory or in practice over an extended period, tolerated departure from them.

If all is change, how is it that such relatively fixed points have been established and maintained? What is this public conviction which, though it may divagate, always returns to the traditional code?

Allow a little more illustration before coming to that question. Let us take samples out of the mores that have become morals, recognized social virtues. They are interfered with more than are the blocklike institutions, but any society that loses its bearings as regards them is always a candidate for chastisement. They too—some more than others —appear to be relatively stable.

Take honesty, once more, including fidelity to the given word and also truthtelling. Fancy a world in which the same proportion that are now honest, faithful to engagements, and truthful should be dishonest, should break promises and oaths, and should habitually lie—what kind of a society should we have? Imagination falters before the speculation. Only a madman could advocate such a change. Even the rascals dare not profess dissent with the public conviction backing these traditional social virtues, just as no nation was found ready to accept "war guilt" and glory in it, but each sought to shift the obloquy to some other.

Men on a very primitive stage of civilization had already found out that they needed to depend upon the social virtues under discussion; they took recourse to solemn oaths, which were conditional self-cursings in event of untruthfulness. "May my brains be poured out on the ground as I pour out this water, if I do not do as I say!" The gods were invoked to carry out the curse, which was often spoken before the altar and, of course, in the presence of witnesses. Nowadays we try to secure the same solemnity by the use of the Holy Book.

The presumption of honesty is strong enough so that business methods are based upon it. Goods are sent by mail-order houses immediately on receipt of the buyer's check, without antecedent investigation of his bank account; and the practice pays, despite occasional losses. Indeed, the chance of the swindler, or "confidence-man," resides precisely in the presumption of general honesty; and the very attempts to evade or suppress the truth while appearing truthful, or to "get away with" perjury, witness to the strength of the traditional code.

There is, then, a relative fixity of points in the adjustment process. All is not disorientation and random change. There are yardsticks of a sort. It is also a kind of truism that the degree of fixity varies in most or all cases with the proportion of the traditional element present in the case. Without heredity, organic forms would constitute an unclassifiable chaos of variation; without tradition, social forms would never attain configuration at all. (On the other hand, to complete the whole picture, if all were heredity or tradition, without variation, there could be only a monotonous and arid rigidity—in fact, socially speaking, a *rigor mortis* of society.)

Public conviction is strongly and tenaciously behind certain relatively fixed norms, as illustrated. That is what fixes them. This conviction is stable, barring occasional flightiness, just as a man's health can be described as sound, despite ailments now and then. But the term "public opinion" is applied also to certain mass-movements of the emotions which have always turned out to be ephemeral and capricious, although joyously hailed by the proponents of some "new truth" as a genuine, rational, and lasting apprehension of that new truth.

Is public opinion solidly and lastingly against dishonesty? It is. Is it against war? Yes. Is it against thrift and in favor of extravagance? It is not. Is it in favor of liberty of conscience? Theoretically, yes. Is it for law and order and the suppression of crime? It is.

Can anyone say that public conviction has been more than temporarily and impulsively behind prohibition, or against the Supreme Court, or in favor of the sit-down strike, or against the death penalty, or for relaxation of sexual morality, or in favor of the division of wealth, or against the money-dole, or in favor of exalting the State over the individual, or envious of the rich, or for an increase of women's rights, or against classical art and music and in favor of jazz and the new art?

You can reply to the queries in the paragraph before the last with some confidence. You cannot do so in the case of the queries in the immediately preceding paragraph. That is because the former relate to adjustments and the latter to variations. It is true that one who knows history can infer, concerning certain of these variations, that they stand no chance of becoming adjustments because they run counter to trends established by long previous selection and now constituting fixed points or highways of tradition; he might, for instance, infer that any variation that challenges, as it works out, the tradition about the value of thrift, or of law and order, can have no future as an adjustment. I shall return to this matter of assessing variations prior to trying them out. Such forecasting is of the very nature of science. Its realization within the social range can be at least prayed for.

Public conviction, as distinguished from opinion, is the power behind all the mores, morals, laws, and institutions, for they all become dead letter once it is shifted for very long from their support. But it is not often, perhaps never, genuinely rational. It belongs within the range of those automatic forces that work through the emotions rather than the intellect; and the emotions may easily fail to show any relevancy to the actual matter in hand, especially if that matter involves the destiny of a large society as a whole. The reason for this is that only men of the keenest intellect and much experience can think in terms of society: nationally instead of parochially; from the point of view of the general interest rather than of the local or individual interest. Most members of the "public," who form the composite opinion of the public, cannot but derive their bearings from the only features of the landscape that are within their horizon, namely, their own individual interests, as they see them, and those of the more or less local groups —family, kindred, sect, lodge, union—to which they are attached. Between these interest-groups there is often a complete lack of mutual understanding exacerbated by an intolerance that prevents them from making common cause save in the most crass emergency. What coöperation they show is, in general, "antagonistic coöperation": they grudgingly consent to suppress antagonisms in the interest of the superior gains which experience has revealed as the outcome of coöperation.

Public conviction, however, is further alignable with the powerful, impersonal forces operative in nature, in that it has regularly, over long periods, manifested a rationality-after-the-act—a post-rationality—where there was no ante-rationality at all—unless one chooses to stretch "rationality" to cover correct deduction from a major premise since revealed to be incorrect. Eventually, public conviction rallies behind the expedient adjustment, as has been indicated in the case of the major institutions of society (religion, the family, and the rest) and of the residual social virtues, or moral codes. This is not because these institutions and codes were rationally planned beforehand, but because out of endless variations, at all times and with all peoples, these particular ones have withstood repeated winnowing without being eliminated in favor of their competitors. Then they have come to "stand to reason" and to show the type of post-rationality exhibited by the camel's foot or the ptarmigan's seasonal change of color. Rationality-after-the-act is always a demonstration of the presence of impersonal, automatically operating forces.

So, indeed, is scientific ante-rationality, for that involves a knowledge of and an adjustment to these forces as inevitabilities. For unvarying forces can be learned about, as in the range of the laboratory sciences—which makes the charge of fatalism against a scientific system recognizing inexorable social law an example of shallow thoughtlessness.

Public conviction, then, is an automatically formed composite that comes to support, very strongly and stubbornly, certain institutions and mores of longstanding and of an efficiency demonstrated by repeated experience. This conviction is commonly expressed and held fast, among simple peoples, in the form of proverbs—traditional precepts that have circulated for ages and among most peoples, exhibiting through time and over space an astonishing similarity of essential content, though expressed in a variety of version and metaphor corresponding to different environments and modes of life.

I have taken not a little pains and some risk of repetitiousness in striving to illustrate what might be called "long-run public conviction." It is evidently something to build upon and never to ignore. It supports tested adjustments, not ephemeral variations or those as yet untested by long experience. Such are the convictions that men grow up into and accept as features of existence that are to be taken for granted. Not much, if any, thought is devoted to them, any more than to the atmospheric pressure on every square inch of skin. They are relatively few for a large society or nation, for the number of mores held in common by groups of men always varies inversely with the size of the group, so that a national code must include fewer items than that of a family or even of a geographical section.

But what of "short-run public conviction": for example, the sudden popularity of some fad, fancy, or fashion? No one would dare to risk much upon its chance of becoming a settled adjustment. Awhile ago, most women went in earnestly for enormous hats; now, they seem to despise low-heeled shoes. Some new song, or name, or piece of slang, or idea "sweeps the country," presently to be recalled only by oldsters of the "Mauve Decade." Nobody is misled into predicting adjustive longevity for such variations. There is here no confusion of a variation with an adjustment.

The point need not be labored that between these two extremes—variations that nobody of sense expects to last, and adjustments in which nobody of sense expects to see much change except in immaterial detail—there is a wide spread of variations that have a kind of graduated chance of attaining support from the long-run type of public conviction. Is there any sound way of forecasting this degree of chance in specific cases?

Recalling that scientific forecasting, that is, prediction of recurrence anticipated on the basis of experience, is what we are interested in here (not at all in any species of divination by some inspired medicine-man or in any inference from imaginary or predicted experience), we should naturally seek to align any specific case of variation with our relatively fixed points. So doing, one must conclude that the chances are always against any proposed abolition or any utterly transformative alteration of major institutions or of the age-old codes of social virtue. "Clean sweeps" and "new dispensations" are immediately and prima facie suspect. History forbids us to expect anything such, particularly if the "new order of the ages" is to come about forthwith. Nobody who knows anything about history or society's evolution can harbor the idea for a second.

All utopian schemes are to be ruled out at once, for they are nothing but the progeny of wishful thinking, of which every accredited science has had to rid itself by a species of delousing.

A number of variations presented attractively to the public can be found, on critical analysis, to be inconsonant with the relatively "fixed points." That is enough to support a strong and short inference that they cannot last to become adjustments. Opposition to them should naturally center upon the reiteration of that inconsonance, thus playing for the long-run public conviction which must always replace impulsive lurchings and temporary phantasy-chasing. For, sooner or later, and later only by way of suffering, does the long-run conviction come again to its own.

If history (experience) teaches anything—and it is the only instructor that teaches anything at all—it is that societal change of more than details takes place with what is to the earnestly yearning soul a truly damnable deliberation. Historians, playing up the dramatic, have rather specialized in the portrayal of the apparently sudden, paroxysmal, and astonishing; they have exalted the dashing Great Man who "did something" spectacular rather than the impersonal forces that were steadily and silently at work. They have exalted personal agency over impersonal cause. Nevertheless, even these emphases upon the striking, which reveal the historian as an artist only and history as no science, are no more than the exaggeration of the incidental—a case, once more, of presenting the ripple as a billow, the variation as an adjustment. What are revolution and counter-revolution, reformation and counter-reformation, but the ups and downs of a massive evolution—waves which, though they must look imposing enough to the swimmer and can be so presented on the pictured page, yet actually flatten out in the long perspective so as to leave no lofty peaks and profound chasms at all?

The illusion of suddenness is generally due to a lack of realization of what has been happening, perhaps unobtrusively, for a long time; the developing situation is abruptly realized, not abruptly arisen. When it is so realized and the emotions stirred, there may be violence at the peak of change which, by clearing out a lot of already antedated institutional rubbish, seems to have made a "clean sweep." No great and permanent change, or selection, has occurred in history without long preparation in the unhurried march of events, during which detail after detail of some system has come under test and has revealed itself as a maladjustment; and then the system has gone on with new parts in place of the old. The system is the same old jackknife, with new blades, handle, and other replacements. It is the same old ship which, having headed for some time due north, now veers a point or two to port or starboard, Left or Right.

It is very easy for the mind light in experience to believe that slavery in this country ended with the stabbing of a period after the name "Lincoln" at the foot of the Emancipation Proclamation. It is so difficult to realize that there are no sharp and fast clefts in evolution, but only blurred zones of gradual transition comparable to those of the spectrum. So many of us believe, even when we deny it or admit it shamefacedly, that when a law is once passed, a change, even a radical change, has been effected. That is because the human mind is so prone to wishful thinking. And yet the homely proverbs of mankind are full of recorded experience that is scornful of daydreaming and of the effectiveness of wishing.

"If wishes were horses we'd have a ride;
If wishes were fishes, we'd have some fried."

And wishfulness is always a matter for derision when it has to do with verifiable action. There is the fool who ardently wishes he had planted corn instead of potatoes, and even prays agonizingly for some miracle to effect a substitution, or some magic whereby his neighbor's corn can be lured over into his own field. Does he get any sympathy save for the crackpot state of his mentality? The fact is, however, that wishful thinking, while derided within the range where verification is at home, remains the characteristic and inevitable mode within the social range, where there is, as yet, no more than the beginning of verification on the basis of recorded experience. Within that range, magic flourishes; and if you cannot charm your neighbor's corn over onto your field, you can get your hand into his pocket and take away what he gets for his foresight in raising what you wish you had raised.

When there are no laws and no verification, there is really nothing to do but wishfully think. That process must have had survival-value (like the cocoon, presently to be abandoned) or it would not have been universal for so long a time. It has in it the seed of an interest that leads to variations, out of the fate of which experience can be garnered. Then this experience can, in the fullness of time, come to be handled in a more and more systematic and effective manner, that is, by the trained and organized common sense of scientific method. Thereafter there is no more need of a random wishfulness—indeed, there has then been evoked the mortal enemy of that antedated mode.

The task and privilege of the scientist are to replace, as he can, wishful, emotional thinking as regards societal variations, by assessing them rationally in advance. Thus can be forecast, in not a few cases, their probable chances of ever attaining to the stature of adjustments. He can "place" them in their relation to the "relatively fixed points" and conclude as to their consonance with what has been shown by experience to be relatively permanent. At the very least, he can show that what is hailed as new is no more than a forgotten and resurrected discard. Naturally the resurrectionists will assert that conditions have so changed, or that they themselves have so changed them, or will change them, that "it will not be so this time," or that "we will control it (say, inflation) this time"; but then it will be the scientist's opportunity to investigate the alleged change in conditions or the alleged competence of "us" to control what our forebears were unable to control. It goes without saying that one must harbor only the most modest hopes and practise the most ruthless of self-criticism in endeavoring thus to forecast upon the basis of anticipated recurrence.

A view that will invite disagreement and probably scornful epithets is now to be stated: that science is bound to be conservative. The adjective is used in its true sense, not in the distorted connotation of the day, according to which it means "reactionary," "hidebound," "hard-shelled," and similar uncomplimentary things. Science, it is to be recalled,[2] deals solely with experience; and experience is not such until it is past and even "old." Science rests therefore on history. It rests upon what has been preserved, or conserved. It is cautious rather than daring. It is least of all reckless or intent on shocking people. It is judicious rather than itching to "do something," right away. It believes in *laissez-faire,* a phrase meaning exactly what a "Do not touch!" sign upon delicate and swiftly running machinery means—it does not refer at all to the competent engineer but to the gawking and cane-poking crowd. Science is always counselling against becoming panic-stricken by an alleged emergency, recognizing the proclamation of such as a political dodge and advising: "Wait and see." It is precisely in an emergency that one should not tear off his shirt and fling it to the winds. Science never denies that in a true emergency (which ceases to be such if it becomes chronic) men must act on what they know, even if that is very little—for, unlike the impulsive, self-nominated savior of society, the scientist is quite aware of his own limitations.

All this is true conservatism, caution, and discretion. Like patience, labor, discipline, and duty, it is not enthusing, as are immediacy, ease, liberty, and rights. The scientist has to be shown, not prodded, or nudged, or "pepped up," or evangelized, or stampeded, or hypnotized. He will always view the proposed variation with what Huxley called a *"tätige Skepsis"* (operative skepticism, skepticism looking toward expedient action)—not with an eye cold and forbidding to all change but ever insisting that the burden of proof rests upon the innovator,

2. Essay on "Common Sense," above.

not upon him who holds to that which has been long tested and accepted in tradition (another at present opprobrious term). He will deliberate, in the case before us, in conferring the title of "adjustment." This is what is meant by saying that science is bound to be conservative. The scientist is as far as east from west removed from the prolific spawner of one litter of bright ideas after another, who bustles about, indifferent to checking up on his last happy thought because its successor has already crowded it off the stage.

There is one thing we can be sure of, for the case is always closed, namely, of what men have *done*. What they think or have thought is another matter. The same thing may be done by many for as many reasons as there are doers. The same person may do the same thing a dozen times for at least six different reasons. But what has been actually done is a set of facts capable of objective examination in relation to the co-existing setting of circumstance. The habit of dealing with what men have actually done is yet another characteristic that enters into science's essential conservatism.

VII

THE "NEW LEVEL."

EVERYONE is overfamiliar nowadays with the word "new": new music, new art, new religion, new order of the ages *(Novus Ordo Seclorum)*, New Deal. Reiteration of that adjective goes with an equally banal and buzzing chatter about the squalid and contemptible character of the "old": old masters, old economics, and so on. I am thinking about nothing of this tiresome sort. My title is in no sense ironic. I have in mind a difficulty that confronts the serious and disinterested student who has accepted with full conviction the view that the only way to get a science of society is to be scientific about it.

This serious student, being influenced somewhat—it could not be otherwise except in the case of a recluse—by the aforesaid heat and chatter, has come to wonder whether we have not attained a new plane or level of society's life-conditions, adjustment to which demands something else than the principles and rules derived from recorded experience or, at any rate, some radical modifications of them. As I understand those who think they perceive this new level, they do not see any qualitative differences between society's life-conditions along back and now, but observe contrasts, rather, of such quantitative significance as to seem almost qualitative. I do not know how far back they want to go to establish the base line of the old level as a take-off for the rise of the new. Sometimes it seems pretty far—say to the Industrial Revolution, when, for example, women began to attain freedom, with the result that relations of the sexes are thought to be upon a new level. Again, it is the recent invention of efficient means for contraception which has introduced a novel element into the domestic, demographic, and moral situation. But perhaps the question of how far back it is to the "old" is irrelevant.

In general, it is some mechanical invention or series of inventions, like "the machine," which is thought to have so altered the life-conditions of society that they can be said to have attained a new plane or level, upon which old ways of adjustment are antedated. Nobody wants to allege that life-conditions remain unaltered by such inventions: the compass, gunpowder, the steam engine, the gas engine, the airplane, and so on. Of course they are altered. The question is as to the degree of readaptation to their altered form demanded in order to adjust society's life to them. Must we make a clean sweep of our former adjustments, reversing current methods, or may we still rely upon our accumulations of recorded experience? Must we radically uproot—eradicate—or may we conservatively preserve?

No one doubts, I say, that the life-conditions may be altered. But that does not mean the introduction of some unheard-of element, such as the satisfaction of hunger by sawdust, the procreation of Homunculus in a bottle, or the introduction of a third sex. Everything that is developed is genetically connected with what has gone before. In that sense, there is absolutely nothing that is new. There are no miraculous creations, with uncrossable chasms of abyss between them and what went before, but only zones of more or less gradual transition from old to new. This fact, obvious enough to any informed person, needs recalling from time to time. I think it needs attention in the present connection.

There is another qualification in the offing. Sometimes the less discreet exponents of the New Level seek to establish their contention about its presence or imminence by reference to alterations, not in life-conditions but in the popular mind—that is, to shifts of public opinion. No one doubts that public opinion changes, and often as a sequel to some mechanical invention which amounts to appreciable modification of life-conditions. This is a common phenomenon of the mores, and may seem to occur suddenly if the results of a long course of development are unexpectedly visualized, as when a long wave suddenly breaks. But always the deliberate rise of the wave can be perceived if one rises above the surface to a perspective, historic survey. Something does not come out of nothing. So that, while no one can deny that public sentiment changes, he must always realize that its pronounced alteration is at best a secondary phenomenon, secondary or ancillary to changes in life-conditions.

There is a fallacious short cut here. Some of those who see a new level, by reason of alteration in what people think, proclaim that "human nature" is not what it was. Because people are conceived to be more sympathetic, more neighborly, and otherwise improved in disposition, morals, and manners, the old system is no longer geared to a now altered human nature. It is asserted that we are better than our fathers, so that what was good (virtuous) enough for them is not good enough for us. They languished along in contented dullness, we learn, under the régime of "tooth and claw," as well as under that of slow transportation and planeless skies. They thought well of the narrow maxims of some Poor Richard. It is readily seen that this contention that what people think constitutes evidence of a new level raises issues far less objective and demonstrable than any that are related more or less directly to actual changes is material life-conditions, such as the introduction of the automobile.

No careful scientist is going to be much influenced by what people think—consider what they thought about comets—unless he can be sure that their opinions are a reflection of experience with actual life-conditions. They are too prone to form opinions that mirror things as they wish they were rather than as they are. They are readily seduced into thinking in utopian terms. Furthermore, the careful student will not be led into accepting as public opinion the vociferations of some glibly articulate group which claims to speak for all, especially for the inarticulate masses. He will constantly check his conclusions by asking himself whether he is not rationalizing upon the basis of the mores of the social stratum to which he belongs. For it is an error natural to us all to judge others by ourselves.

The New Levellers seem to have no scruples about explaining even very great changes in the social order of the past by reference to general laws and to the same old factors that produce hitching along or edging along rather than saltation. They seem to regard the course of society's evolution as homogeneous and continuous, with nothing catastrophic about it. After a long time, society has seemed to rest on a new level. That is all. Instance the transition from the mother-family to the father-family, the passage of landholding from communal to private tenure. Without any planning or even any awareness of what was happening, much less why, close inbreeding, cannibalism, and many another practice now so offensive to our mores that they seem to be prohibited by "instinct," have been eventually eliminated. One seems to be looking back on them from some higher place.

There have always been plenty of these unnoticed variations or innovations, and also of unrecognized accumulations of variations in the same sense, the aggregate of which has been, in historical retrospect, revolutionary. But the generations that have lived through the long process had no sense of a mighty wave of change but only of the local ripples upon the long swell. The unconscious changes came about so slowly and gradually that there was plenty of time for sliding, also slowly and gradually, into adjustment to them, as there is not now time for adaptation to a rapid succession of even lesser changes—which therefore break upon us as something of a shock. People no longer ascend so gradually to new levels that they find their traditional adjustment-technique and kit satisfactory enough, with small alterations here and there. They may feel under the necessity of injecting into their adjustment-operations altogether new and previously unheard-of implements and processes, if they can be invented, to meet what looks like unparalleled change in life-conditions. Nevertheless, a review of past experience of mankind establishes a sort of presumption that the course of society's evolution is a kind of road that presents no chasms demanding unheard-of leaps or some kind of revelation in the line of discovery. It puts the burden of proof squarely upon those who allege that the attainment of new levels calls for a disruption of and a discontinuity in the process of adjustment.

The New Leveller seems to have his eye chiefly upon the prevalence of wide unrest around the world and especially upon two types of social organization—communism and fascism—which have dramatically risen over the horizon line in response to that discomfort of maladjustment. There are not lacking those who hail the one or the other as the grand New Adjustment to the New Level.

In reality, neither type is either new or an adjustment. Lodging power in a single hand is nothing novel in the world. It has been the regular practice in a pinch, and pinches have been recurrent. It is as old as the primitive war chief. Naturally the features of a modern dictatorship do not reproduce with exactitude those of any preceding type, but the family likeness is unmistakable. In general, fascism is not very popular in this country, and few, openly, at least, propose its adoption as an adjustment, so we may more profitably center attention on the other "Ism."

Communal organization is not new. It is older than autocracy. It is, as elsewhere shown, a natural adjustment in the sense of being the only obvious arrangement under certain circumstances, especially primitive ones. Sharing is an expedient that groups of Europeans, facing a raw frontier environment, naturally fall back upon. It is a system out of which society has had to work itself before it got very far in civilization. It has always lamed and discouraged individual initiative, the matrix of variation.

Modern communists, as distinguished from the actual primitive, and matter-of-course sharers, or communalists, are such by a priori conviction. Lacking support in history for their preconceptions, they rationalize out a "primitive communism" which, like the Golden Age, never existed at all. But not even utopian communism is new, for men have always been dreaming of things as not being what they are and, in particular, constructing in imagination unchecked by reference to actuality a world in which men would lovingly share their abundance so that all would be rich and happy. Then they have enthusiastically rushed into some variation that seemed to them new, although it led up the same old type of blind alley out of which they had once and again retreated in a discomfiture they have forgotten.

Along comes, once more, the happy thought of holding and doing things in common, and men fall for it as of yore. The Russian "adjustment" is hailed by emotional people as a kind of New Dispensation. The circumstances of its initiation are ignored or excused and pæans are sung to the inspired sages of Moscow, who have found something new in the world and put it into operation. Maybe they too thought they had done just that. Disillusioned pilgrims to the Russian Promised Land found, however, no New Jerusalem. What they found was oligocracy passed into autocracy. Readjustment after readjustment has taken place in the direction of the rejected "old" system, each "chiselling" resulting, as unearthly excrescences were chipped off, in a progressively less unmistakable likeness to the traditional organization of civilized society. Despite all the theoretical flourishes, the Soviet system is merely yet another instance of the lodging of power in the hands of the few, or of one, who is strong enough to seize and hold it.

If the New Levellers see in collectivism the one new and promising instrumentality of adjustment, they are thrown back at once—even if they could demonstrate it to be new, which is impossible—upon solely theoretical arguments for its adoption. Genuine experiments are lacking. Among other things, they must needs persuade skeptics by dialectic that an assemblage of mediocrities (The State) can rise above its source; that men will develop energy and initiative for other ends than the profit of themselves and their immediate relatives and associates, and not be discouraged by having to share the earnings of their efforts with the lazy and incompetent; and so on and so on. Enthusiasts naturally are not daunted by that prospect, but propose, simply and beautifully, to change "human nature." In brief, communism as a theory of general societal organization calculated to meet the exigencies of a New Level is exactly as hopeful or hopeless as it ever was, for all efforts hitherto to establish it as a working system have failed. It has always turned into one of the inveterate old forms, when it has come to encounter, face to face, the inveterate old life-conditions of society.

Sharing as a practice, however, here and there and in detail, goes on all the time. Some things (libraries) are owned publicly that used to belong only to individuals or small groups, and other things (churches) which used to belong to communities have become the property of individuals or corporations. They exemplify the natural and practical process of detail adjustment. There is no "-ism" about them. It is folly to talk about the extension of state regulation, say, over the mails, as "socialism." The State runs the post, not because it does it well and profitably, but because, despite its recurring deficits where a private company with state monopoly would make money and give better service, the sum of all pertinent considerations favors state operation. The arrangement was not dictated by socialistic theory at all, any more than that which makes the schools public. You cannot clap the same theory over conditions, or even nations, which are diverse. Fascism, said Mussolini once, is a home product, not designed for exportation. The German type is not the Italian.

The basic error of some of the most scientifically minded of the New Levellers lies, it seems to me, in their confusion of a variation with an adjustment—both ways. They take a variation to be an adjustment, or they view an adjustment as a mere variation presented for selection, with no verdict of experience behind it.

All the allegedly novel phenomena of the New Level are still clearly in the variation stage. Undoubtedly the steam-driven machine was an invention different enough from those that went before to demand, when it ceased to be a variation, long ago now, adjustment to it and its sequels. For a century and a half, or more, we have been producing social variations, and even inventions, in attempted adjustment to its presence in the world; and it cannot be said that we have even yet attained that adjustment. Anyone who realizes this will be very shy about swallowing any pretentious and wholesale program of immediate adjustment to some New Level.

There is in reality no new plane, or level, at all. There are more people on earth. That is a fact. Perhaps we should decimate them, on the ground that if we do not Nature will. She seems to be at it now, and not alone through wholesale slaughter. The declining birthrate, declining despite the "demographic policy" of Mussolini or the fulminations of Holy Church, seems to indicate something of the sort.

But our resulting problems of adjustment are not strange and new; they are the age-old ones, somewhat intensified. There is no catastrophic break here, any more than in Nature. Lyell's principle holds, even in the societal range. Birth, death, age, and sex remain.

That last sentence is no mere sententious falling back on Authority conferred by revelation upon an uncritically receptive soul. Basic things do remain. Everyone knows from experience here on earth that men are going on eating, procreating, catering to their vanity, fearing the inexplicable and unpredictable. They will never attain the satisfaction of their wants because there will never be enough satisfactions; for each want, being satisfied, engenders a dozen other wants. There will always be struggle and competition for what there is, and the rewards of that contest will be unequal because the contestants will never be equal. Equality of opportunity, in however low or high a degree it is realized, will always operate to let quality, mediocrity, or inferiority reveal themselves in their successes, their ploddings, or their failures. Always there will be presented a choice, no matter how glitteringly bedight, between something bad and something else not so bad.

These are life-conditions—the ills of life, if you will—that have always existed, and there is no reason at all to expect that they will cease to be. Just because experience has irrefutably demonstrated that this is a life of frustration, with defeat (if death be defeat) in the end, have mortal men pushed all compensation into, and dreamed of the absence of ills only in, some Beyond or Utopia.

It is a pity that enthusiasm for adjustment in detail is so hard to rouse while mankind seems credulously ready to take fire at any proposal of a clean sweep or a new dispensation. And yet all the variations that have ever survived to become durable adjustments have been relatively small, slowly effected, and comprehended under no swelling Plan or sweeping Philosophy. There seems to be a fatal predilection in mankind for impatient reversal of direction rather than for shifting a few points of the compass. "Away with thrift and the other traditional social virtues altogether! Down with Capitalism, and Religion, and Monogamy! Hurrah for Rights and to Hell with Duties! Enjoy!—there is nothing in Self-Denial!" It seems that there is, in mankind's outfit, no eye for anything between white and black, between the altogether good and the unrelievedly bad. And yet the whole teaching of experience exemplifies the shading of things into one another and demonstrates the total fallacy of absoluteness.

The teaching of experience, which finds its refined expression in the conclusions of science, that implement par excellence for dealing with experience, is all against this new-level idea, with the accompanying technique of reversing tested procedure or sweeping it away with the intention of replacing it by some *tour de force* which shall remake the world to the heart's desire. It is against even the hope of devising brand-new methods for coping with the ills, even when recognized as ineradicable, of a permanently unsatisfactory and unreconstructible world. The only prospect that science can hold out is that if men learn the lessons of experience, heed what they come to know, and avoid wishful thinking as they would poison, they may make sound detail-adjustments which, in their aggregates, will render life less painful. By avoidance of illusion, disillusionment—one of life's prime woes— may be cut off at its root.

If we reject these phantasies about new levels and wholesale adjustment to fanciful novelties projected suddenly into the congeries of society's life-conditions—adjustment by way of clean sweeps and new dispensations—we are left with the chance to recognize or even foresee detail-maladjustments and offer variations calculated to obviate them. To this end we must remain alert. We must take the inventor's attitude. Invention has been called "planned variation"—a designation which calls before the mind a picture of exactitude and conscious premeditation that is too perfect to be true. The inventor is less a creator than an acute receiver of suggestion.

There is always an element of luck—the unforeseeable, the unexpected—about even a mechanical invention. No inventor can possibly plot all the secondary results of his successes. All the inventor of the engine could think of was how to get steam to make wheels go round. He had no more vision of his responsibility for the Industrial Revolution than Germans had, on entering the War of 1914-18, of the fact that they were helping to win the vote for British women. This unexpected concatenation of intentions and consequences is obvious enough but is often lost to sight.

Nevertheless, he can see a little way ahead if he has his bearings out of the experience of his predecessors, and is alert, receptive, and prepared; if he is in his laboratory, with his apparatus at hand—not dozing over a fishing-rod. He is then ready for the lightning of "inspiration" to strike, for his receiving-rod is up, with its points sharpened. That is what I mean by saying that he is less a creator than a receiver, and why the term "planned variation" is not precisely what invention is. Perhaps we need not worry over precision of terminology. Anyone knows that the inventor is deliberately trying things, while the mere finder may have no interest or purpose at all, or one wholly irrelevant to his find. He may be merely strolling along through life.

If one wants to help the adjustment-process along by suggesting hopeful variations that are at the same time possible, he had better keep the inventor's attitude before him. Among other things, the inventor always aims to begin, as Edison often said of himself, "where the other fellow left off." He takes account of foregoing experience. In particular he notes preceding failures. The name "inventor" does not belong to the perpetual-motion crank who keeps on trying something that all experience, including the summation of experience in scientific law, has declared impossible. His motto is never *"Credo quia incredibile."*

Allied, and not so remotely, to these new-level views is the contention that the culture of peoples with a recorded history itself represents so elevated a plane, or new level, that no study of its antecedents can help much in its interpretation—much less in that of the contemporary. Specifically, a book like *The Science of Society* is criticized as stopping short of the only really significant stretch of human history, which is to imply that for a few thousands of years (at the very outside) out of the low estimate of two hundred thousand years of man's earthly existence, the pace of cultural progress has been so accelerated that the ninety-five (or more) per cent of society's course prior to the historic period has little bearing upon the recent five per cent (or less). It would seem that the level of "civilization" is conceived to be qualitatively different—different in kind, not in degree only—from what went before. Naturally this distinction is sharpened when the last century or so, as regards its relation to the prehistoric, ethnographic period, is under consideration.

In looking into this matter, one might start with a reservation as to the meaning of "civilization" or "culture" that has been registered by anthropologists and others. They object to the use of "civilization" as meaning "high civilization." Similarly with "culture." Civilization is civilization, and culture culture, no matter on what level of advancement or retrogression. Civilization, or culture, has had a continuous course, consisting of a long line of forms derived out of preceding forms in a connected, genetic series. There is no place in this series where a sharp line of distinction, much less a catastrophic interruption, is to be found. If there are new levels, they have been reached by ramps or by stairs with low treads, not by sheer leaps. This fact by itself disposes of the level as something suddenly attained, and as involving life-conditions so novel as to render traditional adjustments irrelevant.

As elsewhere noted,[1] the science of society, in its demonstration of the aforesaid genetic institutional series, has been practically halted on the threshold of the historic period. But there is no validity whatever in the conception of "civilization" as a kind of floating Laputa disconnected with the long prehistoric period. The connections are all there and we can, so to speak, see both ends of them. There is a relatively short section of them, in the historic period, that is so complex and tangled that it will take a great deal of labor and skill to plot it out. That is all there is to it.

It is very easy and very natural to assume any contemporary problem an unprecedented one on a new level. Then one does not need to embark upon the arduous and irritating task of disentangling, but can masterfully draw his sword and cut the Gordian knot at one a priori stroke—that is, by some such pontification as that "it stands to reason" that the glorious culture-bloom of Western civilization cannot be accounted for in any respect by the study of "naked niggers" who smell bad and may even be cannibalistic. However, each level has its characteristic odor that people on other levels find offensive, and "dog eat dog" is still, according to the most radically emancipated of the present, the loathsome law of life pending the advent of the New Jerusalem.

It is freely admitted that the New Jerusalem, when it comes, will constitute an undebatable New Level, with utterly novel life-conditions that will enable adjusting mankind to junk all its experience and start afresh under the direction of a Sanhedrin of Seraphs. But science has no data on the New Jerusalem.

The Millerites, roosting on fences in their ascension-robes, were "logically" justified in having scrapped all their previously held and earthly ideas about, say, property and the family, for they were not going to live here on earth any longer, but on a New Jerusalem Level where, of course, property (being "robbery") and marrying and giving in marriage (being monogamous and therefore monopolistic) would no longer exist. In that more abundant life, harps were going to replace hoes and there would be no more maintenance-mores to crib and confine the efflorescence of immortal yearnings. But, sad to say, until the heavens are rolled up like a scroll, we non-recipients of revelation, like the Millerites when they had climbed down, have to get along pain-

1. Essay on "Evidence," below.

fully, as of yore, on the same old level of air, water, seismic shakings, insects, germs, empty stomachs and other biological urges, human nature, bisexuality, and the rest of the inexorably permanent life-conditions in the midst of which God or Nature has seen fit, without consulting us, to set us down.

VIII

PLANS AND PLANNING.

THERE IS a kind of planning that is nothing less than godlike. Consider the "Plan of Creation." Consider "Design" in the universe, as it has been identified by the sleuthing mentalities of philosophers. Consider God's Plans—many, divergent, sometimes mutually cancelling—as revealed to His friends and confidants, to His advisers. Of a truth, when one sets out to plan on the grand scale, he is in lofty company. To be ranged in such ranks evokes a sweet and seductive sensation. It should make the heart to swell with pride of workmanship. It does. Also the head. Illusions of grandeur, as of one who, seated aloft, appoints tasks for lower beings, must amount to an exquisite experience. It is, in particular, an especially care-free, spacious, and soul-expanding function to plan the spending of other people's money.

There are two clear types of intellectual activity in the world: doing things and arranging things. The doers of things are rather rare; and they are generally off in a corner somewhere, in solitude, intent, hard at work, not saying much. Like Darwin at Down. Usually they have had slight funds and often homemade, improvised apparatus. They are on the trail of some truth, often a small one; and they do not imagine that the world is waiting agog and trembling with eagerness to hear their message. Indeed, the moment that one of them succumbs to the temptation to get out and make speeches, laying down the law upon matters about which he knows nothing because he cannot stop with what he knows, it is all up with him as a doer. Burbank instructing the country upon social issues, instead of keeping to his berries and flowers, is an example. There have been several notable tragedies and farces of this sort, most of them, luckily, coming late in the lives of their chief actors, so that, while the enacting of them has evoked light melancholy or decorous mirth, the net loss has been relatively inconsiderable. Nevertheless, it is a pity when a doer turns aside to become an arranger.

The ordinary arranger of things is a bird of another feather, in that he lacks the doer-phase altogether. He has the cuckoo-wit to discover what the doers have done, but no capacity or desire to add unto it by practising a similar industry, reticence, and self-denial. What he does is to ascend to heights above all the toiling and moiling, there to exercise the elevated function of philosophizing about the doers' results, allocating them to their proper place in the cosmos, "evaluating" them, and juggling them about. Around the doers' little heaps of actual accomplishment in collecting facts and drawing modest and cautious conclusions from them, he leaps and chants, makes passes and ventriloquizes, eulogizes and vituperates, and especially "interprets" and rearranges in accord with revelations conferred upon him as a prophet, so that after he is done the original producers find it hard to recognize their own handiwork. The arrangers are the doer's self-constituted patrons, in whose houses he is often betrayed; he ought to fear them more than he does his open enemies, for they can so damnably distort his results, in the ignorant enthusiasm of their defective understanding, as to lend to his findings an aspect so ridiculous that they cannot for a long time be taken seriously.

The arrangers of things are commonly the improvers and uplifters; in a word, the planners of new dispensations. They are conscious of the sublimest motives, especially of "service"—not anonymous service—and are generally quite unaware that, no matter how noble the purposes, they can never be transmuted into even passably expedient consequences, except by knowledge. Mere emotion will not do that. They illustrate once again Goethe's saying that confident ignorance is the most terrible thing in the world. Many of them are honest enough, but most of them are too lazy to get down to work or too impatient of the small returns of actual labor. Their vanity demands instant acclaim and notoriety. Also they dislike the solitude of laborious days. They want to be rushing about among men, chattering. They assume a busy manner, as of great minds intent upon the transaction of large matters. They are all generals and colonels; among them are no noncommissioned officers or privates. They love to charge through the illumined area, pausing to pose and posture when they pass the focus of the spotlight. History is full of personalities that have succeeded for a time in this sort of exhibitionism and have only very slowly, by the verdict of history, been demoted from their pseudo-status as great men in favor of the actual doers, who are at length hauled out of the wings toward center-stage.

Because planners have been of this arranger-type, the plans of mice and men have so often gone as the poet says. One arranger, seizing upon a few happy thoughts, sketches out a "reconstruction of religion";

another, taking off from human yearnings and undoubted human ills, proposes a scrapping of age-old adjustments in property-tenure; yet another wants smartly to reconstruct marriage and the family, first loosening up everything to the primitive level. All these are proponents of "the absurd effort to make the world over."[1] When resolutions are being proposed to abrogate this and that social practice that has evolved automatically out of millennia of experience, it is hard to understand why the resolvers do not go the whole hog and propose decrees to expunge disease and death. Why spend effort on half-measures, such as abolishing poverty? Why not hew to the root of the matter and extirpate hunger by forbidding bodily wastage? Why scatter effort in making the sexes equal? Why not get down to bedrock and, by resolution in legislative halls, abolish sex? It is enough of a trouble no longer to be tolerated. Why not highly resolve to raise human beings henceforth not only on, but in, a bottle?

"Nonsense!" is the reply. "No one expects to do that sort of thing. Let's stick to common sense!"

"All right. But just where is the line to be drawn between nonsense and common sense? Why is it nonsense to talk about abolishing gravitation, so as not to be obliged, for example, to climb stairs?"

"Because that's the way things are in the world. Gravitation *is.*"

"Because of Nature's immutable laws, then? But how do you recognize such laws?"

"By a repeated experience that common sense recognizes. It is not common sense to talk about abolishing gravitation."

"But it is all right to talk about abolishing the family or religion?"

"Certainly. Men made them, and can unmake them. Heil, Menschen! There's no telling what we can do in social matters if we set our minds to it. Didn't we abolish slavery? And rum? Well, then! All we need is a planned economy, with faith in it, and the resolution to put it through."

That, of course, is the nub of the matter: "There's no telling what we can do in social matters." There is "telling" enough in physical matters. No one in command of his senses would say: "There's no telling what we can do in corking up volcanoes and changing the seasons." In connection with the above proclamation of human prowess, the following questions are in order: Did "we" make the family and religion? Did "we" abolish slavery? Is there really "no telling" as to what we can and cannot do within the social range?

1. Sumner, W. G., Essay with that title, in *Essays,* I.

But let us come at these matters in a somewhat roundabout way.

It is evident enough that there are plans and Plans. A plan for a bridge is of one type; a Five-Year Plan (noting the capitals) is another. In the former, you are within the range of established science, that is, of trained and organized common sense, and so within the field of that technical process of winning, recording, and verifying experience which is known as experiment. You are dealing with items such as strength of materials, stresses, strains, and so on, which have been measured, calculated, tried out, and recorded in manuals accepted by all without the least idea of disputing them. No dialectics are needed. You are within the range of identified regularities, or laws.

It is not the specialist alone who realizes this. Awareness of many of these laws has been diffused so widely and so long that people who do not in the least understand the principles of mechanics, physics, or chemistry cheerfully accept the laws discovered by scientists as existing life-conditions, immutable, inexorable, to be reckoned with as a matter of course and of common sense. So far as they plan their obscure careers through life, they take account of these laws as permanent landmarks and limits. They trust the expert. They would regard grumbling over physical laws as witless. Not to accept them and live in accord with them would be to betray a lack of ordinary sense. Only an idiot would pick up a live wire and smell it.

No one thinks that one man's opinion is as good as another's when it comes to what load a bridge will carry, or what will happen from mixing substances in a chemical retort, or whether or not to operate upon the human body. Is the same true in the social realm? Do we rely there upon the expert? Do we hesitate to inject our own untutored opinions? Ah, no! And why not? Because we lack confidence in the expert and do not know enough to lack it in ourselves. And why is this the case? Roughly, because there is as yet no science of society. That type of science is so new and raw, says Sumner, that any crank can fasten upon it from any angle. Our "saving common sense," in this range, has not been trained and organized into anything deserving the name of science.

The story of social planning, of the Planned Economy, is quite another tale from that of bridge planning. There is no such check-up on experience. There is no intelligently critical attitude abroad among us, for, to occupy that attitude, there must be something definite and firm to stand on, in the shape of a block of hard facts of experience, slowly gathered, patiently verified, laboriously analyzed, classified, and compared. That is precisely what, in the social realm, the race of mankind does not possess. Hence, an infinite credulity replaces in that realm the ready skepticism in ranges subject to experimental verification. Also what little is known about society's laws is but faultily disseminated, while fanciful, cheap pseudo-knowledge is broadcast by irresponsible prophets and interested agitators. Social experts are not identifiable except by their own visiting cards.

No wonder the view prevails so widely in the social range, as in philosophy but never in the habitat of the natural sciences, that one person's opinion is just as good as another's. There is no hesitancy about rejecting forthwith the conclusions of social specialists; their judgments are, indeed, commonly alluded to as "academic," meaning unworldly and unpractical. And such an attitude on the part of the public is little to be chidden, in view of the specialists' disagreements and their disproved prophecies.

A common feature in the social realm is the urgent advocacy of some novel and hastily launched idea linked with a mood of irritated impatience with practical objections. "Don't be backward-looking!" we are adjured. "We should consider this matter in the large and in principle. The details can be left to take care of themselves." They can. There is nothing on earth that is competent to take better care of itself than a practical detail. Presently the grand program is limping because of some little sharp-edged stone in its shoe, and the tragedy has been reënacted of the small refractory fact that punctures and cripples a great theory.

The novelist[2] has sometimes pitched upon the contrast between doing and arranging, planning and Planning. "The new age is being ushered in by a new type of young man, secretly envious, superficially clever, afraid of constructive responsibility, but obtaining a sense of power from energetic interference. They call it planning. . . . They come to think of nothing but administration until there is nothing left to administer."

The truth of the matter is that the data available to the social scientist is scanty in amount gathered, is carelessly assembled, is poorly organized and classified. It is never sure of dispassionate handling. And yet it needs all the care and skill of which honest and capable brains are possessed, for it is complex and entangled, shifting, slippery, and very difficult of verification. Lacking the laboratory method, the social scientist cannot reproduce social phenomena—a depression, say—over

2. Deeping, W., *Blue Water* (1939), pp. 196, 243.

and over on the small scale, so that one factor after another can be isolated in order to study its peculiar nature and the results of its impact, by itself, upon society's life. The most that the student of society can hope to attain in his results is an ever slightly higher degree of probability, or successive approximations to the truth. He can do more and better by a more rigorous application of industry and self-discipline. Certainly the social sciences have attained no great repute nor inspired much confidence by the deductive, intuitional, wishful, and dialectical methods common since the time of Plato. There is some tendency in the present to renounce talking and speculating on utopian lines in favor of the effort to collect facts, verify them, and perform induction, after the manner of the approved sciences, upon them; but it will be some time yet before the shouters evacuate the field to the workers.

There are, in utter truth, no men living who are competent to construct for society a Planned Economy on the grand scale, as large-scale engineering enterprises can be planned. Faith in social planning is justifiable precisely in proportion to its modesty.

"But that doesn't get us forward very far," is the impatient retort; "We know that already." Do we, though? There is a startling difference between knowing things and realizing them. We accept offhand the assertion that there is a weight of atmosphere on the body; but we do not realize it until, perhaps, we acquire a cold in the head that makes us really aware of pressure on the eardrums, or until we learn the principle of the siphon or barometer.

Even that which we call obvious, though familiar in a superficial sense, may not be realized. Proverbs are essentially formulations of the obvious; then they become so conventionalized that they are tossed off as a kind of counter in speech, as one pulls a dollar bill from his pocket and pays it out without the slightest realization of what is printed upon it—whether it is a bank note, a silver certificate, or, in general, why it is more valuable than any other dirty piece of paper. One of the services of the study of many social facts is the awakening of an actual and definite realization that human institutions have taken uncounted ages to become what they are. No one who has acquired a realizing sense of that truth will ever be nose-led into believing that society or its institutions can be reorganized overnight. If this one simple item of the obvious could be injected into the mental outfit of mankind, hopes for the future would be indefinitely heightened.

Instead, we find vague and high-sounding programs for the improvement of "human nature," although there is no warrant for the belief that human nature can be readily altered, even in small details and where the truth seems self-evident. If one realizes the resistance put up by human nature in trivial instances, what will he think of projects for remodelling that nature as a whole, or of plans that involve an antecedent transformation upon wholesale lines, such as we encounter Mondays in reports of Sunday's sermons? We are told that nothing much can be done till human nature ceases to be egoistic, casts out fear, and so on; exhorters might as well declaim that the human body will remain imperfect until it ceases to perspire or can get along without a liver. But there are plenty of good souls who, though they ought to know better, have swallowed fluffy soapsuds of that sort, in blown-bubble form, and then plaintively wondered why they have felt so qualmish inside, or so depressed in spirit.

There is no other hope for us than to train and organize our common sense into science, the while we keep our merely emotional nature under stern control.

All planning calls for the prerequisite of forecasting, or prophecy. There are several kinds of future-searching: from omens, from casting lots, from the stars, from inspection of the palm of the hand or of chickens' insides, from direct revelation—all of these being rejected out of hand by science—and then there is what has been called "scientific prophecy." It has been laid down, indeed, that the test of any science is its ability to predict. Evidently forecasting of this latter order is different in kind from the variety first mentioned, which might be called divination. Let us concentrate for a moment upon scientific forecasting.

Upon what does it rest? Divine suggestion? No; there is nothing especially divine about it. All it has to set foot upon is the simple principle of "anticipated recurrence," which means that things will continue to go as, in experience, they have gone. No miracles will intervene. If you put two molecules of hydrogen together with one of oxygen, you can confidently expect to get water and nothing else; even though you pray fervently, you will not get sulphuric acid, or beer, or a tadpole. How do you know it? Because, in thousands of tries, that is the way it has come out, with no exceptions at all. It is a mighty safe bet that it will come out the same way the ten-millionth time, or the trillionth. Anyway, the bet is safe enough so that we, regarding ourselves as wagering on a sure thing, confidently live by it. It has never fooled us, or anybody else. It may not be absolutely, philosophically, dead sure, but it's good enough for us, as we show by intrusting our lives and livelihoods to it.

While we are on this matter of scientific forecasting, a warning is in place that it remains highly hazardous within the societal range. There are not enough established recurrences to anticipate. One is convinced that adjustment is sure to take place, without, however, having any confidence that he himself or anybody else can forecast the exact development which will constitute adjustment. It is as if, though sure that the evolutionary process in the organic realm will go on while there are organisms, he should refuse even to guess what the organic forms of a million years hence will look like—only, in the matter of the exact identity of societal adjustments, he would hate to commit himself even a dozen years ahead. He may recall, as horrible examples of shaky seerdom, the dismal list of social experts who were reassuring the world, just prior to August, 1914, as to the impossibility of another great war.

Nevertheless, though discretion is the better part of intellectual, as of other types of valor, there are such things as general tendencies in society's evolution; and they are not likely to execute a rightabout and retrace their course, any more than the earth is likely to reverse itself and begin to rotate from east to west, or than mankind can be expected to give up the struggle to live and, lying prone in platoons, let hunger and cold have their way with them. There is some little diversion and a good deal of profit in reflecting upon these tendencies.

Scientific prophecy resting, as it does, upon anticipated recurrence, the basis of anticipation is experience. It is common sense to learn from experience—the commonest sense that we poor humans can have. One who rebels at learning from that schoolmistress is a fool, because he lacks the commonest garden variety of common sense. Unless he is a defective, he presently gets that sturdy perennial drilled into him. Indeed, there has been no human learning at all, except through experience—one's own or others'—and not so often others', as all parents know. The simple and splendid thing that science has done is to collect and compare experience, reproduce it in experiment for closer study, get rules, called laws, out of it, to go by in future cases—in short to organize and train common sense to handle experience successfully and expeditiously in living our lives here on earth.

In so doing, science finds out laws. It does not create them, nor can it alter them by a jot. It maps out the permanent conditions of living, so that men may the more readily and painlessly adjust to them. It says: "This substance is dynamite. Its nature is such that if you hit it with a hammer, unless experience is false, it will explode and blow everything near it into fragments, the striker included." Science having thus spoken, it is now up to the individual to decide what he wants to do. Science cannot make dynamite not dynamite; it can simply tell men what it is and will do under percussion on the basis of what it always has done. Men then have the evidence of unvaried experience to go by, if they want to. If the now instructed wight wants to die, he can; if he wants to live, he can do that too, so far as the dynamite is concerned. He knows how to adjust his conduct to the end that he chooses, because he has been informed as to the experience of mankind in the matter. He is now in a position to plan for the future as to this particular matter of hitting or not hitting. A feeble-minded person may befog himself with metaphysics to the extent of regarding both the stick of explosive and the hammer as no more than brain-eddies; but philosophy usually evaporates before actual situations. If not, and the meditator on mystery hits out, it is a case of the removal of the unfit.

Evidently, the more perfectly and exhaustively experience has been subjected to scientific investigation, the more expediently can men act in adjusting themselves in living.

In the absence of science, the prime instrument in human adjustment, what is there, or has there been, for men to do? Nothing but groping and fumbling—about what they have been doing all along, and up to date, in their social life: applying what untrained and unorganized common sense they had to practical situations, and "thobbing" for the rest. All the "planning" of the social order that men have done throughout history, and most of what they are still mouthing about, rests squarely upon thobbery, that is, wishful thinking, with no basis in experience, least of all in science, and therefore with a conspicuous absence of common sense. "It must be so—for how unpleasant if it were not."

If ever, in the social realm, experience can be gathered, preserved, and analyzed as it has been within the physical range, then wishful thinking and the seeing of visions will give place to that other type of prophecy which is based upon anticipated recurrence.

Take as a contemporary example anyone of the government's water-power projects, to point the contrast between forecasting in the physical and forecasting in the social range. Nobody doubts at all that what is proposed in a physical way—the digging, the reforestation, and all the rest—can be done. Bigger things than these have been accomplished in constructing an interoceanic canal. But will the social results come to pass as planned? Sharp difference of opinion prevails as to that. Take the case of inflation of the currency. It would seem that there has been misery enough recorded in human history as the consequence of inflation; but do men learn from experience in this matter, as they learn to keep their hands off live wires? Oh, no! The present case is "different" from those of the past. The live wire is not going to behave, in this case, at all like former live wires; it is going to spark and spit gently, for our eternal good. Are the inflationists cautious in proposing their measure, admitting that it has always proved to be perilous and advocating a step-by-step process allowing of easy and safe recession if prospects begin to look dubious? No. Cheap money and soft is set forth as a cure for an indefinite number of social ills. Its prophets file a blanket claim for it. You cannot have too much of a good thing. To be critical of it is to them almost sacrilegious. It is a kind of revelation, and its advocates become as impatient of doubters as the orthodox religionists of the heretic. The dispassionate attitude of the laboratory is not in evidence; it is replaced by heat and partisanship. Fancy partisanship and slogans in laboratory experimentation! When heat and emotion enter the game, science gets out.

The scientist is avid of criticism, for he wants to get the truth. Are social theorists and planners that way? Was Bryan? On the contrary, the peerless leaders claim everything, concede nothing, and conceal or minimize all objections. Where is your protectionist who, in addition to being disinterested, conscientiously warns the people that they, not the importer, pay the duties he advocates, and to the protected industry? Where is the ardent free trader who states candidly that the self-sufficient country, capable of producing everything it needs within its own territory, is better off for war? Where is the opponent of birth control who concedes it anything; or the advocate of abolishing all censorship who admits that crime is, in this country, presented by the newspapers in such a setting of the heroic as to create strong suggestion to the feeble-minded; or the opponent of capital punishment who will acknowledge that execution is a deterrent, at least to the executed? All is a partisanship that is not after the truth, but is intent solely upon establishing, by a parody on reason, a position pre-selected under emotion and interest. Hence it is full of extravagant claims, suppressions of evidence, alibis for failures or interpretations of manifest failures as "after all" successes, charges against opponents of unfair tactics and against supposed friends of selling out. The result is not a cool deliberation or honest experiment but a calling of chosen names and a vending of malicious gossip.

Examination of planned social orders reveals at once that all such grand-scale enterprises are rooted in emotion and that the mental process connected with their origination is wishful thinking. The more sweeping the plan, the less can this tendency be checked by such experience as men possess in recorded and verified form, and the wider the stamping-ground over which unbridled aspiration and "ideology" can rare about and kick up their heels.

One of the characteristics of acting on emotion is an uncritical indifference to cost. What matter if prohibition enforcement is expensive? That is merely incidental to the nobility of the ends envisaged in prophetic ecstasy. Cost is one of those details which has proved itself capable of taking care of itself. What if the veterans' budget is high, a number of times higher than that of countries with many more widows, orphans, cripples, and other war casualties? Consider our elevated exhibition of generosity—with other people's money. Not to count the cost in a private enterprise is an evidence of irresponsibility; yet in the social realm cost counting is represented as a kind of petty and ignoble affair. The eye is always, and always emotionally, upon the grand and noble aspects of the case—or on getting into the steal.

Furthermore, as intimated, if there is a lurking tendency to count the cost, it is lulled to rest by the conviction that, anyhow, somebody else is going to pay. And it will be good for him to pay, too. That makes for easy generosity and loose-reined extravagance, together with moral self-approval. In general, it is the State, or Society, that will foot the bills. It is Uncle Sam. But what is the State, or Society? Some supernal Entity that blesses at no cost to citizens? Where does Uncle Sam get what fills his pockets? Out of "thin air"? Does he somehow earn it outright? Or does he simply print it? If he collects it, can he do so merely by "soaking the rich"? Does he derive it merely from the relatively few who pay an income tax?

No. None of these have enough. If Uncle Sam could not levy on the pennies of the poor, he would soon have to put up his shutters. The State is all of us. All of us pay for the public works, and the battleships with their brief span of life between launching and scrapping, and also the grandiose gestures that our representatives endorse. One of the chief sources of our foolish action lies in the fact that, chiefly because of indirect and so unrealized taxation, we are not "tax conscious." If everyone who has even a little income had to pay a direct tax upon it, no matter how small, this tax unconsciousness would be rectified toward the development of a sense of sober responsibility in ourselves and of an insistence upon the same in our representatives. For the counting of costs to ourselves is another thing from counting them to others. It is a sharp corrective to enthusiasm for some sublime scheme to realize that our endorsement is to be followed by payday. We are even now learning the pinch of payday for years of extravagance and picturesque posturing; and the thought of how noble we looked along back is proving to be not so much of a solace.

Grand Plan always costs. Creation cost the Deity Himself enough effort so that he rested on the Seventh Day—and that despite the fact that He knew what He was about and got, except in the case of disappointing Man, what He aimed to get. Human planning in the social realm not only costs but generally winds up with something quite different from what it has set out to get. The more spacious the Plan, the more likely is the result to be one unforeseen; for when the social process has been once started, factor after factor enters into it so unpredictably that its entrance is characterized, helplessly, as an Act of God or of Providence. Every time that expression is used, it marks a failure in forecasting; and it stands also for an alibi, so that the Planner can forge on, at once, without diminution of self-confidence, toward his next vision. For the genuine Planner is always an idealist and rejoices in it, holding realists to be carping, backward-looking conservatives. The Planner never stops, either, to clean up the mess he has made; it is the realist who cleans up, and his scavenging, besides affording sanitary service to his generation, often pays pretty well. Instance Napoleon, with his fog-dispelling whiff of grapeshot.

The reef upon which the big Plans come to grief is, of course and primarily, ignorance—non-realization, above all, of the intimate interconnection of all the constituent elements in the social order. The Planners, in their enthusiasm, always oversimplify and underestimate. They do not know that tampering with private property means tampering with the family—that the effect of yanking violently at one of society's institutions may readily turn out to be a dislocation not at all expected or desired in what has been assumed to be a remote part of the societal structure. The structure of society is too intricate and delicately balanced to allow of the hammer-and-tongs method of readjustment. The watchmaker cannot ply his trade with a maul and wedges.

But the Planner of a New Social Order has no time or patience for study of that upon which he is to operate. He has a conviction that something must be done, right away. Also the people he is to bless are in a hurry. All the great social plans start with impatience of discomfort, springing thus from emotion. That is normal enough, for emotion, as the etymology of the word suggests, is the basis of movement. But then they go on being emotional; in the absence of positive knowledge about society, they are incapable of entering a rational stage. It is reasonable to hold all Social Planning, as that term is now understood and preached by the heralds of a new economics, a new social order, and so on, as realistically futile and hazardous. Neither the beneficiaries of the new revelation about the obsolescence of the law of supply and demand, together with the rest of the "old" economics, nor anyone else, knows enough to forecast on the grand scale for a large society over a wide field and for a long time ahead. The very proclamation of the capacity to do that is a confession of ignorance and incompetence.

The realist discards at sight, therefore, all revolutionary programs whatsoever that promise much and soon. It seems to him that, despite the youthfulness and greenness of what science of society we have, it does at least inform us that the social processes are very slow in their working and cannot be hurried much without throwing society into disorder—that, in a word, they are like those of nature in being impersonal and automatic; that, therefore, the best that man can do is first to discover them by serious and patient study and then adjust to them as he has done, with lasting profit to himself, to the inevitable processes of nature. The more he knows about what can, and especially what cannot, be done with society, the safer he is in his forecasting—provided always that his plannings are very modest. The failure of even the most modest social planning means cost and loss. The cost of failure in the case of a gigantic Plan is incalculable.

Anyone who proclaims that dictatorship will solve society's problems, because it is an ideal system, or that communism follows the "law of God," is talking ignorantly and wildly, no matter whether he means an autocracy or "the dictatorship of the proletariat." The facts about a personal dictatorship that interest the realist are such as the following: Always at a pinch, especially in war, it has been found expedient in society's experience to lodge power and responsibility (both together, or neither) in one hand. "No war was ever won by a debating-society." The realist is not averse to dictation as such; he favors it when needed. We have for some time been in a pinch not so much lighter than that of war. Therefore he is not frightened and repelled at the idea of clothing a president of character once again with such powers as Lincoln and Wilson wielded—together always with the corresponding responsibility. It seems to him that, as a carpenter takes out of his chest a chisel when he has work that calls for a chisel, so society picks a dictator out of her box of tricks when the situation calls for him. Society does not especially "plan" to do that; she fumbles in the toolbox until presently, so to speak, she finds that tool in her hand.

There is all the difference imaginable between dictatorship as an expedient and "dictatorism" as a doctrine. The realist has no more faith in political doctrines than in religious dogmas. He would just as soon subscribe to the doctrine of infant damnation as to that of imperialism or protectionism. When you take on a doctrine, you abdicate your critical judgment, which means that, prejudging, you resign your right to apply your common sense to situations as they arise. And the review of rising situations commonsensibly, without commitment to some pre-selected doctrine, or authority, or other entanglement, is the distinguishing mark of the intellectually free man.

Allow some further illustration, to throw into relief what a realist thinks about plans and planning; what we can hope to do and what we cannot. The plan of anarchism proclaims no-government as the ideal. A moron would reject it, because even he can understand that no society can exist long without control and discipline. Socialism would have the state do everything. The realist rejects that too, for the state cannot, to judge by human experience, rise to that function. The fact that an individual gets into the government, though he must then, it is true, assume to know all things, does not endow him with omniscience and rectitude. Communism holds that we should all share. The realist sees clearly enough that that means only that those who can get must share. He repudiates all these "-isms." However, he agrees that some peoples have been governed too much for their good and others too little, and that there are a lot of hoggish wights who might, for everyone's good, do some sharing. He says that relaxation and tightening of governmental control and enforced sharing are merely practical expedients, to be employed or not according to circumstances.

To him "capitalism" means nothing, except that he is sick of the very sound of the word, as bawled by doctrinaires. If anyone tells him that economic distribution has lagged behind production, he agrees at once, and wants to be told by some expert what to do about it. But when someone asserts that under socialistic doctrine the economic system will become altogether lovely, he smiles sadly and wraps his toga about him, preparatory to departure thence. When, perhaps, he is told that his own books support economic determinism à la Marx, he is about as interested as if he were informed that they advocate nudism, and no more. If he is enlightened as to the fact that the public school, which he thinks good, is socialistic, or that reserving a space in the center of a city as a public park is communistic, and that those who advocate these two measures must be socialists or communists, he feels about as misnamed as did one writer when a person who signed himself merely "A Christian" called him an atheist because he happened not to swallow Catholic doctrine, hook, line, and sinker.

Is there any sense in all this doctrinal labelling? The realist knows as well as the doctrinaire that certain things have to be done by central authority. He is aware, and may even admit, that they are likely to be done expensively, often inefficiently, sometimes corruptly; yet, with all the drawbacks, he is for letting the state do them. He is thereby far from being a socialist, committed by doctrine to having the state do a lot of other things—rearing children in barracks, for instance—for which it has never betrayed the slightest atom of competency. On the other hand, because one believes in the existing property-system as the best available in a faulty world—being quite willing, however, to modify it in directions where it is demonstrably a misfit—he is not thereby proved to be a dogmatic capitalist.

The reason for all this yearning to label one's self and everybody else is partisan belligerency. The big principles professed by Planners of a new world-order are nothing but fighting slogans—battle cries of discontented men. The cry of "Equality!" is raised by him who wants to be lifted up as high as others are, or to pull others down to his own level. It is the Have-Nots who want a sharing-system. All the high-sounding "principles" are nobler after-thoughts supplied by poets and philosophers. Who can think and plan in terms of society? No one; and only a very, very few can remotely approximate to that power, commonly assumed to be an attribute of "the people." Men can visualize personal and local interests with some approach to accuracy, and that is all; if they think they can plan for society at large, they fool themselves, for they can no more than generalize on their own experience. Even careful and conscientious parents may go all wrong in their planning for the next generation. In some few and obvious respects self-centered generalizations will be correct, since there are items common to all human experience and interest; but beyond these, which are sure, in any case, to take care of themselves without any campaigning, all is diversity.

There is no safe attitude, except a cautious skepticism, toward any swelling social program. There is no justification for credence in the possibility of abolishing or radically remodelling any long-lived social structure. Changing a name should not be confused with altering a thing—in essentials, Sovietism is still Tzarism. If history teaches anything, it is that statesmanship consists in noting and removing small maladjustments before they have a chance to grow very bad. This strikes Planners as small business.

The trouble with Plans, Planning, and Planners is that they aim too high upon an inadequate equipment. And there is some little equipment available. It is despondently complained that the only thing we can learn from history (experience) is that we can learn nothing from history. "Does history repeat itself?" is the rhetorical question. "Well, then!" Of course history does not repeat itself—not exactly. Neither does the weather; and yet we have learned to predict weather well enough to do business on our forecasting and not be disillusioned too often. Anyway, we do the best we can on the equipment we have and do not pay attention to any "—isms" in the matter.

History does not exactly repeat itself any more than does personal experience. But it is yet possible to disengage from history, by analysis (which is not so good as experiment, yet not altogether to be despised), certain broad and general conclusions, such as that any society that has discouraged individual initiative and ambition has suffered for it. That kind of truth may not be much, but it is something; and, such as it is, it is sure. It is a fact that society needs inequality, and even that the equality of opportunity that reformers call for is, at bottom, a chance for inequalities to reveal themselves. "Careers open to talent" means the unleasing of superior human beings from handicaps that prevent them from winning out over others. Thus "quality prevents equality."

Unassailable facts on this order can be derived from the study of the past experience of the race; but they are about all we can get in the present state of knowledge. They enable us to be critical, if not constructive; to find fault with pretentious plans, if not to realize them. But clearheaded criticism, while not so godlike as Planning, is at least something; and, a greater truth, the capacity of intelligent criticism must as surely precede sound constructive planning as childhood and youth must precede maturity. You must know exactly what is the matter with a faulty construction before you are capable of setting up a faultless one. The successes of men have been more like the caulking of the leaks in a strong and tested old boat than the complete scrapping of the whole in the hope of building a new and perfect craft, from the keel up. All plans of the latter type are fantastic and unscientific, and argue ignorance and incompetence in the planners. In some far day when, by hard work and study, we know more about society and its laws, far-reaching planning may become less visionary; but that will not be until we have real social experts comparable to the chemists and engineers of the present, with a body of tested truth and technique behind them, and a convinced clientèle of understanding laymen to back them up.

It is hopeful that criticism is gradually becoming more acute and rational. Norman Thomas's specific criticisms of definite maladjustments, for instance, are in the main as conclusive and realistic as his general doctrine is inconclusive and visionary. If someone comes to the realist coolly and says: "This high tariff is absurd; this veterans' bonus is ruinous; this hanging-on of the war debts is disastrous; this monkeying with the currency is perilous; let's jump on them!"—then the realist will reply: "Lead on, old man! I'm convinced. I'm with you." That is the kind of realistic plan that he can understand. Social planning will be safer when it begins with: "What shall we undo?"

But when someone else approaches him, frothing at the mouth and with bedewed or bloodshot eyes, and begins to bawl about making the world over, quoting about how faith can move mountains, etc., one moves cautiously off until he can dodge around some corner. If a seer offers to show me how he can move East Rock, along with its monument, down to Lighthouse Point, I am perhaps willing to spend a bus token to gawk at the sights; but I will not invest even those eight-and-one-third cents on some pipe-dream about realizing human felicity in this generation by sweeping political action. Everybody hankers after that felicity ardently enough; but that desire, unless restrained by common sense, leads to a lot of wishful thinking, idealism, and other soft cerebration. What social science the realist knows has convinced him for life that the only trustworthy way to adjust, in our day and age, is to try to remedy, in an objective manner and one by one, any obvious and definite maladjustments in the system we have received as the tested heritage of the ages.

IX

SOCIETY AND THE INDIVIDUAL.

No ONE who strives to present a scientific theory of the nature and evolution of human society can hope to escape the charge that he has ignored the individual. It is the aggrieved individual, naturally enough, who arraigns him, for society is not in the way of lodging protests. The individual, not society, is articulate about his condition: his satisfactions and his discontents; his hopes and his fears; his loves and his hatreds; his significance, as conceded or ignored. His vanity causes him to be deeply concerned about that significance. He likes to be in the foreground for the mere sake of being there, not to mention the practical advantages—first helpings—attached to that strategic position. But even the serious student who can rise above his personal interest into a region of detachment and perspective is puzzled by the recurring question: What is the relation of individual and society, anyhow?

The predisposition to look with disfavor upon any relegation of the individual to the background is natural enough, even to the thoughtful. To set him back seems even morally questionable, for, intimidated before the inexorability of social as of natural law, he may sink into a state of mind represented by the phrase: "What's the use?" Such peril, incurred by enlightenment, is without substance, as I have elsewhere[1] shown. In any case, science cannot suppress the truth because someone fears the consequences of its discovery and dissemination.

The question, generally conceived of as highly "academic," as to the relation of society and individual takes on a severely practical guise in times like the present, when Communists, National Socialists, and Fascists are proclaiming that the individual exists only for the State, while Anarchists of all hues are shrilling against even the slightest limitation, in act or utterance, on personal liberty. When an issue has thus broken out of the theoretical range into the arena of practice, an intensified effort toward its clarification has become a kind of instant necessity. But no light upon so basic a relation can be shed offhand, either by emotion, intuition, or logical exercises. First must

1. Appendix to *Societal Evolution*, revised ed.

be established something in the way of general bearings, by the identification of objective fundamentals. Then there may develop some soundness of policy as to particulars.

Stable bearings—landmarks that are not going to shift overnight, even though some exponent of Faith bids them be removed and cast into the sea—go far back and down deep into the nature and evolution of human society. To get the society-individual relation into some perspective, let us recall certain basic features of societal evolution.

A human society is a group of individuals living in a coöperative effort to win subsistence and to perpetuate the species. The *coöperation,* ensuing upon *specialization* consequent upon differences in sex, age, mental equipment, and so on, constitutes *organization.*

Expression by individuals of their differences constitutes *variation,* the first stage in any process of adjustment, or evolution. Then comes *selection,* resulting from inevitable conflict or competition, whereby numerous variations are eliminated, leaving the more apt to survive as "the fitter." Surviving variations are handed on, vertically down the generations or latitudinally between contemporaries, by *tradition*—which corresponds in function to heredity in the organic range. When the group habitudes and traditions, the *folkways,* have attained a relative stabilitiy and authority, they are *mores.*

Selection under conflict and transmission by tradition are processes automatic and impersonal in character. There is not much of the rationally planful in them. After the individual has produced a variation, it thrives or not according to the degree of survival-value it possesses for the society as a whole. Will the society survive longer with it or without it?—that is the crucial question as regards any newly launched variation. The individual drops his variation, so to speak, into the evolutionary current; then his part is done, for the stream does with the novelty what it will. The variation is carried on until it becomes a folkway, an item in the mores, or even a constituent part of a long-lived institution; or it is whirled away against some unyielding obstacle and shattered once for all; or it encounters some destiny between the two extremes. But what happens to it is determined by the set of the current, to alter which the individual is impotent.

The masses are the current:

It is not the individual who brings about changes in the social fabric. It is not fanatics, not reformers, not inspired leaders. It is the labored working of the mass, and the working of the mass brings forth and casts up fanatics, reformers, leaders, when it has gestated them and prepared the way for their birth. The individual is futile; his aims and plans are futile save as they are the outcome of the trend of the mass.

But the individual is not at all "futile" as the necessary agency of variation; he is indispensable. This rather colorful writer[2] is thinking of the individual's function in selection, to which his adjective "futile" applies.

Let us look into this society-individual relation from the standpoint of society's interest in what militates for society's survival. It is evidently to the individual's interest that society shall persist, society being his own milieu of existence; but we may begin with the impersonal interest of the group. What does the individual mean to society and how is he utilized?

The prime utility of the individual to society is that he is its one sole agency of variation. We must always go back to that fact. This function of his must always be safeguarded in society's interest. To discharge it, he must not be cramped and confined; he must have *liberty*. He must be able to give play to whatever initiative he has; otherwise the best that society can hope for is stagnation. But no sluggish society is safe, if there is any competition at all, against elimination; and, as group-competition never ceases except under conditions of the extremest isolation, societies must always be readjusting by way of outreaching variations. There is a perennial need of individual liberty of initiation, then, if never-ending adjustment is to be accomplished. In society's interest, the individual must have a measure of unrestriction, or freedom.

This is but one side of the coin, however. The individual must coöperate as well as initiate. He must therefore submit to restraint. Individuals are close enough together in social life to have to keep out of each other's way. Coöperation is characteristically "antagonistic"; since no two human beings have interests that are identical all along the line, a number of cross-purposes have to be subordinated to larger interests held in common. It is seldom that this subordination can be accomplished rationally; it is endured with more or less resentment or resignation, rather, as one of those ills of life that are felt rather than understood and are not to be removed or evaded. Wherefore, men have to be subjected to *discipline* as well as accorded freedom, if society is to go on. Members of society must be, at one and the same time, both bond and free.

2. Kelland, C. B., *Youth Challenges* (1920), p. 297.

Evolution by restriction, it should be recalled, was nothing new in the world even before the advent of human society. Restriction is only a kind of cautionary provision against elimination by selection. Organic life is by no means "free," any more than the "noble savage" was free. Society's institutions have been shaped by the restrictions of the taboo which, by carving off excrescent variations, leave something shapely enough to be recognized and named. "Property" and "marriage" are illustrations. They are institutions.

Discipline, indispensable for society, is expedient for the individual as well; only he is not likely to realize it until such time as it ceases, with resultant relaxation and disorder. He knows he wants security; but he seldom sees that security is conferred by discipline and paid for by a sacrifice of liberty. No eloquence is required to persuade him that freedom is to his interest; and he can see that discipline is good for others—at any rate, the imposition of constraint and regulation upon the rest is plainly to his own interest, for that leaves him freer, and he can readily rationalize this situation as "good" for them. But no matter what he thinks; the fact is that individual self-realization has always called for both liberty and discipline, so that the same pair that are to society's interest are to the individual's also.

If there is a more comprehensive, more clarifying, and truer perspective of the relation between individual and society than one attained by viewing them under this Liberty-Discipline aspect, it has not occurred to me during many years of concern with the matter. For some time, when a young man has come to me with the old, vexed question: "What are the relations of the individual and society, anyway?" I have suggested that he try out the Liberty-Discipline blend and see whether it would not precipitate his mental muddle a little. It has regularly done so, by assisting the mind to visualize the issue and to focus down upon something definite and substantial enough so that, as one youth commented, "we can get our teeth into it."

Any such device for attaining a clearer perspective must have the defect of oversimplification, the drawback inherent in rising above the trees to get a glimpse of the woods. But there is nothing to prevent descent into the woods thereafter, to test out the bird's-eye view or the relief map one has made during his ascension, to determine whether it may not help him in threading his way through the jungle.

The expression "Liberty-Discipline *blend*" has been used. The two elements do not occur apart from one another, unless in a kind of mental-laboratory analysis such as produced the "economic man." Any other type of isolation than intellectual analysis is, alas! impossible in the social sciences. The liberty which the individual gets in society is never untinctured with restriction, nor is the discipline he is under ever complete, definitive, hermetic. Freedom and discipline are relative, not absolute terms; mixed, not pure. This item of truth can be tested, out of his experience, by anybody capable of the most elementary observation. Nevertheless, like the other examples of the obvious, it is worth elaborating upon.

Evidently, neither society nor individual could profit by the pure article, liberty or discipline, but only by the blend of the two. The chemical elements of the atmosphere furnish a parallel. Silently and automatically, society gets the blend in proper proportions, or society degenerates. The individual twists and squirms, and is mightily vocal about it, calling, as is the way of mankind, for a superlative: perfect liberty, pure liberty, when he really means a comparative: some more liberty, a larger proportion of freedom in the blend. He exaggerates to attain a more telling effect. But when he gets more than a little more of liberty, as in the days of the French Revolution, he begins to hanker after the security that he has forfeited and is ready to deify Discipline in the person of a little, rotund man—L'Homme—on a white horse. Most individuals do not know what they want, except that it is something other than what they have; but even a moron can perceive that there can be too much of even a good thing. The unpremeditated thrashings-about of ever-discontented individuals issue in the automatic proportioning of the blend to society's interest.

Anarchism is the ideal extreme of freedom; despotism an exaggeration of discipline into regimentation—for all but one. Human history can be envisaged as a series of oscillations inside an arc of which these two are unreachable extremes. Periods where individual liberty is so untrammelled as to become license are succeeded by swings toward discipline so strict that it is charged with the banishment of all liberty and the substitution of enslavement. A period of disorder and insecurity under unrestraint is followed by a tightening of control; one of intense restriction by a revolution whose battle cry is "Liberty! Give me Liberty or give me Death!" The sequel may be a loosening up into chaos and anarchy. Masses of men, following what they think to be their personal and local interests, lurch now one way and now the other.

No durable blend of discipline and liberty, despite the tendency toward it, is ever reached. If it were to be attained at any moment, it would be lost the next, amidst ever-changing life-conditions—ever-changing in detail only, that is to say, but sufficiently altered to upset the blend. These tightenings and relaxations, ever succeeding one another, generally occur on the small scale and are not widely felt; occasionally, however, on the grand scale, the convulsions attendant involving a good part of the world. This rhythmic or undulatory movement has caught the eye of a number of observers, though they may not name the waves "liberty" and "discipline," but, as did Pareto, "residues" of combination and of persistence. Pareto's residues seem to me to amount to variation and tradition, or even to liberty and discipline, viewed from a somewhat different slant.

Let us now focus attention rather more sharply on the individual. Manifestly, the interest of society and that of the individual must be, at bottom, the same: to attain a blend of liberty and discipline expedient for society. For the individual interest can be realized only in a sound society. There only does he enjoy a reasonable security. But that fact is not at all clear to the individual, for, with very few exceptions, he cannot think in terms of society's interest if he would. He sees society only vaguely, at best. He is interested to execute his own set of variations, and he readily wanders off into disharmonies with the master theme, society's massive destiny. Then his dissonances seem to him to argue defects in the theme. He only is in step. The world is out of joint. To all of us, our own little affairs crowd our horizon. This results in an age-long antagonism in men's minds between society's interest and the individual's, where society's interest is identified with discipline as the individual's is with liberty.

At the root of this antagonism lies the fact that the individual likes to do what he likes to do, and not to do what he hates to do. He wants to do the easy thing, following the line of least resistance. That, to his mind, is liberty. Discipline, on the contrary, lays a curb upon impulse, requiring the individual both to do what he hates to do and to refrain from doing what he wants to do. He must do the hard thing, overcoming resistance. Freedom is the status of the chip on the tide of impulse, discipline that of the swimmer against its current. The free following of impulse is passive, like falling, while discipline means strain against inertia or positive resistance, as in pulling against weights. Passivity develops no fiber; the overcoming of resistance does. But fiber-development, to be interesting, has to be pretty well disguised.

"The achievement of liberty, even though the existing servitude is merely fanciful, is one of the strongest motives by which man can be inspired." The appeal of liberty is direct, immediate, vivid, exciting. Its cult easily evokes phantasms, such as the "free and noble savage." As I have elsewhere[3] taken some pains to align the natural attraction of "Starry-eyed Liberty" with the natural repulsiveness of "Fishy-eyed Discipline," I shall not repeat myself here, though tempted, but shall dwell rather upon the unpopular and neglected member of the pair.

I shall always recall my startled realization of the truth of Sumner's remark that discipline is quite as essential as liberty. The idea had never struck home to me. It fails to strike home to any young man before he has been deliberately, abruptly, and bluntly confronted with it. It is a truth that has often evoked resentment, for youth is partisan to liberty by reason of exhortations from the cradle up; but it is nevertheless a truth provocative of such re-adjustment of ideas and such development of a critical sense as amount to a genuine "learning to think."

In society, the most evident and galling limitation upon the freedom of a member is at the hands of his fellows, so much so that it is common to charge up cramping restrictions, where they cannot be identified as the doings of some particular individual or small group, against "Society," or "The System." An examination of the relation of the individual to society amounts, then, to a study of freedom and discipline inside a society. This relation presents itself mainly in terms of the discipline exerted over the member by the community. Society, except in pale theory, is seldom assigned credit for the freedom it confers—exemption from unremitting concern, for instance, as to the bare struggle for existence, with its hazard of death by starvation or violence—because its services are taken for granted. The very "right to life" which it assures its members is commonly accredited without ado to Nature or God.

Naturally, then, when it comes to squaring up with society for these services, paying disciplinary dues of self-denial and self-restraint, the bill is discharged grudgingly, as if it were a gratuitous, tyrannical imposition. You have merely to thank Nature or God, where you have to pay Society; and even when you pay divine tithes, you dare not grumble over them as you do over taxes. Centuries will still be needed to disabuse mankind of the idea that Society is some kind of superhuman Entity that could bless us all if It would, instead of choosing to remain seated heavily upon men's shoulders, bearing down, like a heathen god or a feudal lord, in the weight of an arbitrarily set

3. *Brass Tacks,* last chapter.

tribute. Doubtless the taxgatherer, even in scriptural times, used to try to explain that his levies were to pay for the *pax Romana*, the Roman roads, and so on; but he, the publican, was unpopular enough to be traditionally hitched up with the sinner. Taxes lie, as an unmistakably objective item, upon the disciplinary side of the society-individual ledger, being, in theory at least, payments for forms of liberty guaranteed by the society. But their weight is felt while their lift is not appreciated.

The element of sense in the resistance to all forms of discipline imposed by society, is, aside from the incapacity of most individuals to realize society's legitimate and vital interests, that the discipline appears as if imposed, not by some Entity whose ways are past finding out, but by fellow-members of society, whose ways are not at all inscrutable. There is a suspicion that, the state being "all of us under the direction of some of us," the "some" are collecting from the others considerably more than is necessary for the routine cost of recognizable governmental services and diverting large remainders to themselves. "What do I get out of my renderings unto Caesar?" was the sentiment of the Jew, as he dug out his much caressed shekels and bade them an eternal farewell. Many men of today can sympathize with that agonized bereavement, despite the knowledge they can acquire, sometimes by merely looking at the back of the tax bill, that certain percentages of the amounts they pay are actually allocated to and spent upon projects which they can understand and approve.

But the great majority of mankind can hardly penetrate beyond the fact that some of their hard-won substance, for which they feel pressing individual need, has been taken away from them under duress. Who has taken it? Society. Then Society has "robbed" them, or at least has forced a loan upon them and is in their debt. If, then, Society refuses to repay, down with Society! This attitude is reinforced by the remembrance of sundry unfulfilled promises, given by those who represent society, to reimburse all forced contributions by an assured and continuing "prosperity." No wonder that simple-minded men acquire the idea they have of society and their relation to it. It is to them a kind of unholy alliance between a supernatural Power and a set of predacious officials. What do they know about the cost, or even the value, of law and order, until they have seen what happens in their absence?—in which case they fall at the feet of him who can restore them. They thus assume the services of society as matter-of-course, failing to prize the liberties it confers while grumbling at the forms of payment that it must exact.

And this situation is further muddled by another persisting misapprehension as to the nature of society. Society is "all of us"; but it is wholly misleading to attribute to the composite of us the attributes of the individual. To talk of the "social mind," or to speak of a society or state as loving, hating, oppressing, or taking vengeance, is only a figure of speech. The trouble is that collective terms, like The People, The Society, The State—terms indispensable to language—lend themselves readily to personification. One arrives at a very much safer conception of society and its doings if he realizes this peril of personifying or personalizing. The individuals who compose society are the only ones to enjoy, suffer, love, hate, resent, and seek revenge. Society, the aggregate, merely moves on in a massive way toward the necessary goal of all living things down to the lowest: self-preservation, including self-perpetuation. It realizes this destiny, as do all living things, by adjustment to its life-conditions—adjustment secured by its institutions. In a very true sense, it cares no more for the individual and his fate than does the organism for what happens to some particular, dispensable, constituent cell. Society uses individuals, and whether it uses them up, or not, is to it of no concern.

The relation between society and the individual is, then, highly impersonal. Society does not brood over the destiny of its members, like a hen, nor does the individual worry much over the interests of society. Very few human beings apprehend them at all. What happens is that society goes its way and the individual, however much of a free agent he believes himself to be, must go along, or drop off and be left behind—and it is not healthy to straggle along alone. If he goes along cheerfully, or at any rate submissively, he gets considerable sweet with his bitter—not a little freedom along with his discipline. If he chooses to defy all conventions, he gets very little freedom and a double helping of discipline. Liberty is a kind of reward of merit for good behavior under a discipline imposed, largely automatically, by society preoccupied in its own self-realization.

Both the liberty and the discipline of the individual are accorded, then, in the interest of society; but discipline is more instantly indispensable for society's very preservation. A society can get on for a time with a minimum of freedom; but if it is not to collapse at once, its use of the individual to its ends means that he must behave in certain ways prescribed in the mores, for if he had absolute freedom to follow impulse, society would crumble forthwith into chaos. Absence of freedom might be considered the lesser of the two evils, for by constraining all to the same rigid pattern of behavior, society, by renouncing variation, would lose merely its adjustability—a loss not immediately, even though eventually, fatal.

Here is, in broadest outline, the relation of society and individual: how much liberty is the latter to have; and how much discipline? And never to be forgotten is the truth that the balance between liberty and discipline, even if attained for the nonce, has always, and soon, been tipped one way or the other; and the mores and the theories have shifted accordingly.

Most people love freedom and hate discipline in a general sort of way, without importing much specific content into either term. Freedom is a fine word to cover fine things; discipline is a kind of epithet for the disagreeable, a stick to beat up any squalling alley-cat idea or practice of a restrictive nature. Parallel to these two terms are "liberalism" and "conservatism," which, one readily perceives, correspond closely with our two main "red threads." The "antagonism between the living and the dead" is an aspect of the clash between liberty and discipline, or liberalism and conservatism. I propose to center for a time upon another pair closely enough related to our original complements to be their children: Right and Duty. What men talk about most is not abstract liberty and limitation but rights and duties—above all, rights, for duties, as disciplinary by nature, share the unpopularity of discipline, while rights are always nobly enfranchising.

The aspect under which the issue between liberty and discipline, right and duty, presents itself to the as yet undisciplined individual is this: Liberty for me; discipline for others, so that they will not infringe upon my liberty. This would be Caesarism: all slaves but one. Many a child is taught it in the home. Such a sentiment is natural to egoistic humanity, and has to be disciplined out. Considerable enlightenment from experience is called for before the individual can feel, not merely say: Liberty for me insofar as it does not trench upon equal liberty for others; or: Liberty for me, combined with enough discipline for me to keep me from infringing; or: Rights for me consonant with the rights of others; or: Rights for me, together with duties for me representing acknowledgment of the rights of the rest.

Rights and duties are thus correlated with liberty and discipline; they are the aspect under which liberty and discipline reveal themselves.

A right is, at bottom, a guarantee of non-disturbance, non-interference by others, that is, of liberty; and the duty resting upon all other people, that corresponds to every right, is that of refraining from interference, that is, the obligation of self-discipline. The rights and duties distributed by society, first in the mores, then in law, define the measure of liberty accorded to, and of restraint imposed upon, the individual by society.

What the individual, caught up into the automatic process of society's evolution, happens to think about all this, is of small consequence. Indeed, few think about it at all; for, when society has effected a distribution of liberty and discipline that is apt to its own persistence and welfare, the individual, living in the mores of his time, regularly sees it altogether right and just. It is when a distribution of such long standing as to be immune from criticism is becoming a maladjustment for society at large that numbers of individuals, feeling vague discomfort and acquiring a grievance, begin to grumble and to try to evade it by random squirmings. Thus do they automatically, under pressure of discontent, evolve variations from the traditional. Illustrative are the multiform tentatives among savages away from the sharing-system or communalism in property-tenure; or, at the present day, under a showier dress of argument, away from the modern system of private property, vaguely but resoundingly labelled "capitalism."

The essential point of the matter, all along, is that the distribution of the rights and duties, the liberty and the restraint, of the individual is solidly based upon society's interests, not upon those which the individual thinks must be dominant because they are his own—least of all upon those which he has persuaded himself are natural, absolute, immutable, inalienable, and so on. In short, the individual is aboard Society as he is aboard "the good ship, Earth," and in the one case, as in the other, his well-being as a member of the crew, or even as a passive passenger, hangs upon his ability to adjust himself to his life-conditions. His "freedom" is a choice between standing out against the Inevitable or, having learned what he can of its ways and laws, adapting himself, by way of self-discipline, accordingly. This is by no means a counsel of despair or of fatalism. To follow it is the only sensible way to live.

Having attached to liberty the corollary of rights and to discipline that of duties, I wish to return to the contrast in sentiment evoked by each, as it works out into systems. It is easy enough to heat up enthusiasm for Liberty. Propaganda for it never goes against the grain. History is full of sentiment about it. From Marathon down, saviors of and martyrs to Liberty have been exalted into Valhalla. "Freedom shrieked when Kosciusko fell." But it is not so simple a matter to raise up and inspire votaries to the somewhat sourfaced, severe, austere, formidable goddess of Discipline. That demands an ungrateful rubbing the wrong way of the fur. You can feel at once the inner, compelling, logical reasonableness of doing what you want to do. The human mind is an agency primarily busied in finding good reasons, before and after the act, for doing or having done what the emotions suggest, whereas it may be only long after the event that you perceive, or rationalize out, the blessing of restriction, frustration, or chastisement. "Whom He loveth He chasteneth" has been a rueful explanation of last resort. Men are forced to Discipline's altars by the fear of pain and loss—hence the value of fear—rather than by the prospect of unlimited self-realization; and even then their paeans are thin and unconvincing, not loud and joyous, and their offerings something less than copious and ungrudging. After a while, there evolves an "inner compulsion" to duty, which comes out of the mores by traditional, painful experience, and is always an uncomfortable thing: namely, conscience.

To acclaim freedom is less necessary than usual, in the present age, for we, in this country at least, have been for some time at the high point of one of those oscillations away from discipline—poised already for, perhaps already on, the return swing. And so concern is here primarily with the doings of the sour goddess to whose altars mankind are now being dragged, kicking and struggling, by the scruff of the neck.

Extremes of the liberty-discipline alternatives are now afloat. At one end of the scale is the zero of discipline, anarchism, where theoretically all is liberty and unconstrained personal self-direction; at the other hundred per cent end are the systems of socialism, communism, fascism, naziism, where the state, theoretically again, initiates and does everything and disciplines all but a few favorites. Anarchism can never be put into practice because it would promptly destroy the society that should permit it. Statism would make for stagnancy by withdrawing inducements to individual initiative and thus nullifying variation; in actuality, it exhibits a small coterie of by no means superior persons, centering in a Committee and focussing in some *primus-inter-pares* leader. This minority does as it likes, or as the Leader—Führer, Duce, or Vozhd—likes, he reaping much liberty, commanding all the rights, and imposing an interfering, rigid, often savage discipline upon all the rest. Socialism and communism run out readily, by way of an oligarchy, into a dictatorship, with which fascism and national socialism frankly started.

If anarchism be figured as a revolt against excessive discipline, then communism and socialism might be regarded as a reaction against an excessive liberty, under democracy, that is displayed in a competition resulting in inequality—a lack of disciplinary control permitting an "unrighteous" exploitation of one class by another. There is sought, in theory—and communism and socialism are mere theory, never yet verified—a levelling-down, not up, toward equality under sharing, or division, of the wealth.

Between these two extremes lies the long-tested system of liberty-under-law, or civil liberty, distinguished from the anarchistic type, as its name indicates, by the admixture of discipline—civil discipline to meet specific cases, not total discipline as a doctrine. The individualist, whose eye is upon the services to society discharged by individual initiative, though he might, if he had to choose, prefer anarchism to its opposite, is heart and soul dedicated to civil liberty. He strives to maintain liberty and law, rights and duties, in some reasonable, realistic relation to one another.

If anarchism be dismissed as sporadic and as generally disavowed, the issue of the day lies between the kind of looser discipline to which we have been used in a democracy and the severer type under approaches to, or in the culmination of, dictatorship. The tendency toward the latter indicates that a general automatic readjustment of societal organization, involving stricter discipline, is impending or is here. We seem to be heading toward less liberty under more law, less freedom under more discipline, than we have been used to. The relation of the individual to society seems likely to alter in the direction of more duties for him corresponding to more rights for it. His interests and prerogatives seem destined to take a back seat as compared with those of the State.

The appearance of these various "movements" does not mean, as we are adjured to believe, that "the people" have begun to "think," except wishfully—and they do not have to begin that sort of thinking, for they have always done it. What they have done is not to think, but merely to feel and then to rationalize. The people's only perception of society's interest lies in their personal sensations of discomfort and discontent. When things are going pretty well, they want to let them alone. It is the discomfort, plus the envy and hatred of the Haves, that promotes credulity while it dulls critical common sense in those who harken to the glib promises and fiery diatribes of social doctors. The latter are fully aware that "thought" can be stimulated by emotional appeals to envy and covetousness between "classes." The text of all the exhorters to revolution is "Liberty and Rights"; they remain discreetly mum on "Discipline and Duty" until such time, perchance, as they are settled in the seats of the mighty Committee.

Nevertheless, discipline is always in the offing. Tradition, along with its suppression of variation, has been present from the beginning. Limitation on freedom in variation, be it recalled, is a stock phenomenon of the organic world. In nature, most of the variations perish from a restriction that undoes them. If any are to survive, there must be a great many of them, to allow of adequate selection. Variations are tolerated only when they are in line with the course set by previous selection; selection has long been making the horse, for instance, into a single-fingered and single-toed being, and variation back toward multiple digits is, we are told, excluded.

The case is similar with variations in the mores. Though very numerous, most of them perish because they are off the course set by previous selection, now established in tradition. This amounts to a limitation of the freedom of the individual variation-producers, who are thus under discipline of an automatic order. In the matter of foods, for instance, all seems now to be variation; nevertheless, certain types of nutriment, such as human flesh, or even that of dogs and pigs, are traditionally tabooed. This is a disciplinary limitation upon liberty, established long ago by a selection quite irrelevant to the food-values of the forbidden nutriment. Perfect liberty in sex relations would leave the individual to sit as his own judge; but society insists that he shall behave in this matter according to its traditional norms. Perfect freedom in property-relations would allow theft as a regular and respectable means of acquiring possessions; there is, indeed, theft enough, but it is against the traditional code, which prescribes ways for winning property by proscribing other ways. The professional thief (re-distributor of wealth) finds his land of liberty only under a government where law and order have broken down.

The disciplinary agency, par excellence, throughout society's evolution has been the taboo, a traditional "thou shalt not" backed up not only by the secular powers but also by the vastly more effective sanction of fear of supernatural beings, from ghosts to gods. For, in the main, discipline arrives in the wake of fear, of a dread that runs all the way from uneasiness at the thought of others' disapproval to panic fright at the prospect of eternal and infernal tortures. In brief, discipline works through fear of punishment for infringement of the societal code, a fear which becomes conscience in the individual who has been adequately disciplined. Since, also, the most tangible and definite items of the code of any society appear as legal enactments, discipline stands forth most recognizably in connection with law, secular or ecclesiastical. The "unwritten law" of the mores too has its penalties, which are more direct and sure than those of the written code in that they are imposed without process, spontaneously, and at once. There are no arguings, no expert witnesses, no retaining fees, no lawyers' strainings after prestige, to muddle or pervert the verdicts of the unwritten law. An upstart with bad manners bores into some circle to which he does not belong, and a verdict is ready at once. It is conclusive, unanimous, arrived at without need of even comparing notes. The upstart is disciplined.

This treatment strikes its object as "unjust." He begins to talk about rights in a "free country." He protests: "I'm just as good as they are" and begins to howl for equality and "social justice." That is what an Eskimo might feel if he were snubbed for sticking his fingers in the stew at a foreign mission's love feast. There is, of a truth, nothing inherently wicked about "gargling" soup, any more than in the odor of a skunk; both of them merely convey sensations to the sensitized which demand distance and detachment. It is possible to suffer just as sorely from listening to a tittering person as from having the soles of the feet tickled; both are damnable sensations. There is no question of "justice" involved. Distinctions and restrictions merely and simply are as they are, and that is all there is to it. Nobody devised them to plague someone else or to reduce him to a gibbering wreck. Manners were not evolved with the purpose, but with the consequence, of squelching the unmannerly; they merely came to be, and then the unwary straggler encountered them and was bounced off. Fish did not devise water with the idea of maintaining an unjust exclusiveness as against beings with lungs; water is the medium of the fish to which they have become adjusted; if alien beings are not adapted to it, that is their own lookout and their personal hard luck if they stumble in. The codfish aristocrat merely turns upon them a fishy eye, with the opposite of "Come hither" in it.

It is absolutely vital to an understanding of societal evolution to realize with full comprehension that the restrictions on liberty, as developed automatically in the mores, never have been, and are not, aimed at individuals with the idea of imposing malignantly upon them. Society never "has it in" for an individual or class. She is not cruel, but big, and, to our eyes, gauged as they are to smaller bodies, clumsy. She merely goes her way, with as little intent of injuring specific individuals as has a man who, striding across a field upon his own affairs, sets an unconscious heel upon some small insect in the grass. He would probably have avoided it if he had seen it. Only in fairy tales may the insect rise to protest that it has a "right" not to be trodden under foot and to exact compensation for the loss of a limb or the destruction of an abode. The whole process of societal discipline is impersonal to the last degree, so that to insist upon personalizing Society is a sure way to befog what little insight we have won into the nature of things in the societal realm. It is very dangerous to talk about "Society"—even in the terms of analogy innocent of "reasoning," as has just been done—and call it "she," unless one knows precisely what he is about, namely, using a shorthand expression for "the aggregate action and product of many societal laws."

To enforce this contention concerning the automatic development of disciplinary provisions in society's life, let us reconstruct a situation which, while it probably never existed precisely as presented, is yet typical and revealing. Society X, let us say, allows blood-vengeance, permitting the individual or small kin-group to settle private wrongs as he or it can. As a result, internal feuds are going on in X, more or less intermittently. Society Y—no matter just why or how—has arrived at a stage where it has a chief jealous of his authority, who insists that he himself shall arbitrate all cases of bloodshed. Even at the cost of "injustice," he stops wrangling and keeps the peace. Presently X and Y fall into competition and conflict. Other things being even approximately equal, Y, with its closer-knit organization under better discipline, wins. Here is plainly a selection of the fitter system. X may be extirpated, in which case its lax organization goes with it; or may be reduced to subjection or absorbed by adoption, with the result that the disciplinary measures of Y are extended over the defeated, and private vengeance-taking is tabooed for subject as it has been for master. There is nothing personal about it.

Before the collision, X and Y each thought its mores the best possible. Each has now participated in a practical test. The Y's are not surprised but confirmed in their opinion; the X's may be disillusioned or not, shaken or unshaken in conviction—that makes no difference, for they have to submit. And, in a generation or two they will have come to share the conviction imposed in practice upon them, and in accord with which they have since been living. The young do not think back and compare; it is not men's "thought" but the automatic collision of unreflectingly accepted, operating codes of mores, that has brought about the transformation in attitude.

Of course, agency rather than cause, the personal rather than the impersonal, is accredited with accomplishment. It happens that society's constituted authorities are individuals and that they "do" things— execute the private vengeance-taker, for example. They do this on the grounds that he has trespassed upon the prerogatives of authority or, more simply, has defied the will of the chief. Then if the chief personally knocks him on the head with a royal club, it looks like a relation between individuals. It is not. It looks so simply because it is easier for any observer to apprehend the case in terms of agency rather than of cause—indeed, impossible except for a disciplined mind to apprehend it otherwise. Similarly, the chief is said to own all the land when he is merely trustee for the group; if he should undertake to do something arbitrary in defiance of the mores, such as to execute the sinner with a gun instead of the official mace, or to sell a piece of land to an alien, he would speedily hear from the elders or the people as a whole. What imposes the discipline is the utterly impersonal code of precedents held by the society. One cannot say that it makes no difference who the transgressor is, that none ever get off more easily than others; nevertheless, the longstanding precedents could not have been aimed at any individual. Exceptions occur in application. They are corollary adjustments. The rule remains.

The impersonal nature of societal discipline comes out even more clearly when it is enforced simply by adversity of untraceable provenance. We are under discipline of that type in the present. "Dire economic pressure is the great reformer." The normal human tendency, under that pressure, is to blame some one or more individuals—to seek agency, not cause—especially since political capital may be made in the process. The handiest modern goat in a democracy is the Administration, especially when it cannot conceal or brazen out a trace of hangdog shamefacedness over the contrast between its attractive promises and forecasts, while it was seeking for votes, and the actuality. To resume the list of ills referred nowadays to agency, there are the War and its leaders; Wall Street and its spokesmen; Prohibition and its noble experimenters. Critics speedily get down to proper names, in the case of both culprits and saviors: Hoover, Coolidge, Harding, Wilson, Mellon, Morgan, Foch, Clemenceau, Lloyd George, the Kaiser, Lenin, Mussolini, Hitler.

There exists in the present, however, strangely enough, a growing body of opinion which holds that a world-depression is too vast to be charged to any individual or small group—not even to "the old," in their casehardened refusal to learn from the young and forward-looking. This conviction that blame can be attached to no one leads to some little search for causes rather than agents, which is encouraging; but a grotesque line of culprits is passed in review: "fear psychology," for instance, because it sounds wise, though it means nothing beyond what everyone knows, namely, that people are afraid when there is something to be afraid of, as well as "when no man pursueth"; that when they are scared about losing everything, they hang onto "hoarding" a few gold pieces in a sock. They are in a perfectly normal "state of mind" under the circumstances, and the way to change that state is to change the circumstances, not to call it "psychology" and then preach about the ignobility of hoarding and the patriotism of spending.

(That word "psychology" is cruelly overworked nowadays; it keeps long hours. Galvanized into an unnatural vivacity, it prances pompously ahead of a pretorian cohort of tired paraders—platitudes, proverbs, and wisesaws—but with such feverish twirlings of its drum major's baton as to hypnotize the unwary onlooker into seeing a heavenly host in shining mail.)

Some lifelong students of society, scouting all the learned patter about the cycles and conjunctions of economic planets, have stated bluntly that the causes of the world-depression are yet to be identified. There is, however, one a posteriori way of doing that: if we note what kind of foolishness discipline is sweating out of us during a period of adversity, perhaps we can guess better as to those causes and even identify and isolate poisonous elements and focuses of infection in the body politic.

For the moment, interest attaches only to noting how very far from planned and personal is the discipline imposed by a sheer Adversity whose source is wholly in dispute. The situation is one produced by automatically aroused and automatically operating factors which, though their identity may not be clearly or at all revealed, leave nothing to be desired as regards the disciplinary actuality of their results. During a period of economic maladjustment, as when a war is on, there is occurring an exhibition of selection whereby the means and methods of a while ago are about to be, to a large degree, replaced; and there is a great deal to be said for a *laissez-faire* policy and for resignation as regards the outcome. A certain mortality in human enterprise is bound to ensue; and, while that is hard on the individuals who have put their money on the wrong horse, it is not so unfavorable to society. The fact that a plunger "meant well," i.e., meant to win, when he bet on the wrong horse—or crop—does not justify making up a purse for him at the taxpayer's expense, so that he can speed forthwith to some bookmaker and guess again.

No one who lives in a society can evade its impersonally imposed discipline; he cannot become a member even tolerable to the rest unless he develops some sense of duty and responsibility. He must know what rights are, not only from insisting upon his own real or fancied ones, but from submitting to the limitations and practising the duties that correspond to the rights of his fellows. Society may be figured as delimiting, in the mores, the spheres of rights of its members—determining where and how they flatten out against one another, like soap-bubbles in a basin—as a necessary condition to the formation and preservation of a peace-group. Each member has his rights and is charged, if he wants to keep them, with defense of them against encroachment; but no more strictly than with the duty of respecting and even defending the rights of others. Those who cannot fit into society, even to the extent of recognizing others' rights to life and property, are thrust out—out of life altogether, or into seclusion; minor antisocial offenders are disciplined in one way or another, the modern object being to reform rather than to deter or punish; but if they refuse to reform, even the soft-heads lose patience with them after a while.

Society is the medium within which the human individual lives, moves, and has his being. It is for him what water is for the fish, except that the societal medium is not a fixed combination, like H_2O, but can be, to some extent, rationally and purposefully modified by its living indwellers, if they have learned to win by adjusting to the changeless. For, in addition to his function as variation agent in the mores, the individual has in their selection and transmission a part which he can make somewhat better than a passive one. He can indirectly apply something of rational selection to some of the mores. This function has been covered elsewhere.[4] In general, he struggles to win and to maintain what he considers to be his rights, with his own interests and those of his immediate family and interest-group as his motive force—not the interest of the enclosing society, much less that of world-society, which he can but seldom even visualize. That has to be taken care of by the automatic process, as regards which he is privileged to learn all he can, as he has learned about the processes of Nature, and to act, with what dexterity he has, accordingly.

The individual pursues self-realization within a sphere of freedom bounded by the limits of discipline set automatically by society in its own interest; and he succeeds in proportion as he recognizes those limits and conforms to them, while using all the liberty of individual initiative available to him. There are always, in any society, unexplored avenues for that initiative, or variation, to strike into; nevertheless, liberty must never cease to be under regulation if it is to be worth anything to society; and if its manifestation turns out not to be expedient for society, it is presently metamorphosed into a curse for the individual. That which is ill for society cannot long remain good for the individual, while many a form of discipline that seems to the individual bad and irksome, being expedient for society, turns out eventually to be a blessing to the individual also.

4. Keller, *Societal Evolution,* chaps. iv ff.

X

NUMBERS.

THERE WAS a time when France was the only civilized nation to show little or no natural increase of population. French statesmen were much concerned about it, while the enemies of France, secretly rejoicing, seized the occasion to moralize: "Aha! their moral looseness has caught up with them!" Allusion was heard to the decadence of the Latin Quarter, to absinthe, and so on. Manifestly, such a light people, atheistical and unethical, were marked for domination by a stronger, more upright race. Evidently they had no spirit or endurance left for fighting. Verdun eventually offered a rebuttal of the last conclusion.

The numbers question, including the morality matter, began to present a broader aspect as lowered birth rates came to be reported for Great Britain, Germany, the United States, Italy, and even Spain. Up to recent years, we found ourselves used to them, and the sense of foreboding that was stirred by the earlier statistics seemed to have been succeeded by an attitude of incurious indifference. Those who reckoned up the figures did not howl mournfully nor draw moral lessons; editors tucked them into some convenient corner as if they were matters of no more than routine reporting. Evidently something had happened to the cult of numbers, quantity, and size. The population shrine seemed to have lost devotees and penitents. Apart from the heated adjuration of the dictators in totalitarian countries, that is about the situation at present.

In dealing with long perspectives, not much attention is being here accorded to these noisy harangues. In the main, they have encountered a stolid indifference on the part of the peoples adjured to increase and multiply; and it is what the masses do, or do not do, that makes history. The Duce has rewarded and penalized to small effect; and the Führer, as is plainly evident in *Mein Kampf,* is not much interested in the increase of racial stocks outside the "Aryan," and specifically the German. In neither case can it be maintained that the populations concerned have been made fecundity-minded. Even if they had been, under special conditions, and for the time, it would be but a variation of uncertain future. While it is natural enough, during a tense period, to assume that radical alterations are being introduced into the long course of society's evolution, it is to be recalled that many an alleged billow has flattened out into a ripple in the long perspective. Pareto, realizing that judgments formed during a war period have been notoriously shaky, refused to carry his famous treatise beyond 1912. In brief, there seems to me to be no reason to hedge as to the contentions arrived at in this essay because of totalitarian propaganda of recent years. If, ten or twenty years hence, it is seen to have been reflected in vital statistics between now and then, proper corrections can be made.

Everyone of sense agrees that there are too many people in India and other areas productive of "the white man's burden." Even in this country have we been warned that there are too many, at any rate for the jobs, and there are those who add: "Too many anyhow." But how many are "too many"? How many are just enough? What has determined opinions about proper numbers, the optimum, the happy mean between over- and under-population?

If the primitive peoples could have visualized a population policy, it would doubtless have been, "The more of us the better," meaning by "us" the clan or tribe to which the speaker belonged. As for alien groups, the fewer the better, because the safer for "us." All that the savage had by way of an opinion was what tradition and personal experience taught him; naturally he could envisage no population policy, formulated to serve group-interest by minds capable of thinking in terms of society. His sole motive was self-maintenance, involving for himself and his small circle of family and kindred protection from hunger, the elements, and the enemy. As he prayed for health and wealth, so he besought numerous offspring who should support him, both in the weakness of age and also, by their sacrifices to his manes, in the life to come. Economic considerations, with a strong dash of the religious, called imperatively for numbers.

Then, too, in the matter of the fighting that had to be done: though even the lowest savages have their convictions as to the value of leadership and tactics, they believe in numbers. Military strategy, even yet, aims at concentrating a preponderance of numbers at some crucial point. Even undrilled, poorly armed mobs, casually armed, have overwhelmed professional soldiery by brute weight, as locusts have prevailed against all human resistance. War has always demanded numbers, even if only for cannon fodder or to level up fosses with their bodies. This demand is so characteristic of militarism that the alarm at a falling birth rate has been typically the fear of being overwhelmed by a faster-breeding hereditary enemy, as France dreaded Germany; so characteristic of warlikeness, that when Il Duce enjoined upon Italy a higher birth rate, the inference, right or wrong, that leaped to men's minds, despite his disavowals and his evidence as to the reclamation of waste land, was that he was itching for a fight. This is the groove along which men's thoughts have been shuttling, time out of mind, and it will take them a good while to get out of it.

Economic, religious, and militaristic motives for rapid breeding are very old and deep of root. Man has apparently agreed with nature, which may be figured, someone has said, as preoccupied with the effort to cover the earth with the thickest possible layer of protoplasm. Numbers under nature tend to increase up to the limit of the supporting power of the land, that is, up to the limit of the food-supply derivable from the environment. But man, by the development of the various arts of hunting, herding, and tillage, has managed to extend that limit so as to allow numbers beyond those possible under nature. So to speak, he has gone nature one better. He has not deliberately aimed to do that; what he has done has been accomplished mainly, for untold ages, under pressure, defensively and for self-insurance rather than as the result of any positive policy. In developing the productive arts, he has been trying to make sure of maintenance for himself and his, rather than to provide for the growth of population. It is because he has managed to win more than he and his actually needed that societal surplusage came into existence, so that the group-limit to increase could be moved outward.

Nor was it very long, as evolution goes, before nature's terse law of population was further amended by men, as respects themselves, through the development of a standard of living, which appears most rudimentarily in an unwillingness to live more meanly and precariously than has been usual and traditional, to fall below the status quo. Sturdy and lucky effort to maintain that status may, however, overshoot the mark, so that a higher level may become for a time, and recurrently, the status quo. The standard of living has thus, more or less accidentally, risen. Then men begin to visualize an ever higher standard and to struggle toward it; the element of idealization enters, invention is encouraged by hope as well as forced by necessity, and the standard of living becomes dynamic where it once was static. Men struggle no longer solely for bare self-maintenance but for comfort and luxury, that is, self-gratification. What their fathers had is no longer good enough for them.

This they have done, in the main, by increasing production through improvement of the arts, not by controlling consumption. The eye of the world is upon production and its furtherance; no one pays much attention to the consumer except as he is a production-supporting purchaser. No protective tariffs are enacted in his behalf. At best he is shielded against being poisoned or cheated with outright flagrancy. He is adjured to work and sacrifice in order to raise the prices he will have to pay.

It has not been the productive arts, but the standard of living, that has had within it the germ of an influence making against the quantity-ideal of population. As it visualizes quality of existence rather than number of those existing, its rise means that what product there is, at any time, shall be distributed in larger portions. It is unlikely, however, that production can ever provide a larger share, or even any share at all, for every member of an incontinently breeding race; it certainly has never done so in the past. The abolition of poverty remains a dream. What has happened is that the powerful and organized few, who have known exactly what they wanted, have raised and maintained a luxurious standard for themselves, by a monopoly that has excluded the weak and unorganized many, who have not known what they wanted. This might be called predatory standard-raising. No moral judgment need be passed upon it; that was the way life was lived in those days, and nobody bewailed the loss of rights of which he had never heard or dreamed.

Despite predatoriness, for decent people the elevation of the standard of living has meant, not climbing up on the shoulders of the oppressed, not taking handouts, but self-limitation and personal renunciation; it has called for negative rather than positive action, for frugality, thrift, self-denial, and a choice between quantity and quality—specifically, between the number of offspring in the family and the quality of life assurable to offspring by parents. Parents have found that they could not eat their apple and still have it. In short, a rise in the standard of living makes directly against numbers. The less civilized the state, the class, or the family, the higher, in general, its rate of breeding; compare India with England, professional classes with hand workers, shiftless families with ambitious ones.

Deliberate limitation of numbers, so-called "prudential control," is deemed to be a modern phenomenon; nevertheless it has its roots far back in the evolution of the standard of living. Even the veriest savages exhibit occasional instances of subordinating their numbers to their standard of living, such as it is; among peoples constantly on the move, if a succeeding child is born before its predecessor can walk, the strain on the mother of carrying the extra infant in addition to her regular burdens dictates infanticide as the only recourse. If it were not, the savages would keep all their children.

When primitive peoples, as is usual with them, favor numbers or refrain from reducing them, there is in their minds no dogma about the sacredness of human life, the holiness of the vital spark somehow conferred by a Creator Who resents the assumption of any right to quench it. The life of an enemy has no sanctity at all, nor is anyone deterred from suicide, upon what seems to us like slight provocation, by any considerations of divine resentfulness. The savage's religious scruples against limiting offspring are not, in a word, demographic.

Primitive religious ideas favoring unchecked multiplication have eventually been subjected to alteration without losing their essential stamp. Somewhat as production has been speeded up to meet the development of commercial competition, and as the military arm has been more intensively organized when groups have enlarged and come into more serious conflict, so out of the simple trunk-ideas regarding post mortem maintenance of the departed by their survivors have sprouted certain dogmas that have made it a sin not to increase and multiply, though no longer solely in the posthumous interests of the parents. The children, too, were held to have their interest in non-limitation of procreation on the part of their progenitors: married pairs, it came to be taught, had no right to withhold "the gift of life." For this gift, benevolently bestowed, their children owed them a debt they could never repay. The progenitors were assumed, apparently, to be conscientiously discharging a duty, not to be pleasuring themselves, by conferring that gift. Every act of prudential restraint was, then, a sin; some soul was always "knocking at the portals of life" who, if not admitted, could not sin, repent, attain salvation, and be received, at length, into eternal bliss. Thus to cheat a soul out of life eternal was worse than murder.

It is manifest that the age-long motives for increase and multiplication, among which the foregoing are outstanding, have in varying degrees and along with the advance of civilization, lost their traditional drive. There is considerable doubt, for one thing, about the gift of life being so priceless a boon. If decline of the birth rate has accompanied the rise of culture, so that the higher the degree of culture of a nation, class, or family, the more evidently is it practising prudential restraint, then what has been happening to the motives, economic, religious, and militaristic, which during the past millennia drove mankind to multiply and, in some Oriental lands, still whip them toward manifest overpopulation?

There was a time, in this country, when no one thought of restricting numbers. The family broods of the forebears bear witness to the fact: they seem to us incredibly, even discreditably, large; the fecundity of our grandparents even embarrasses us. And yet that natural increase, copious despite a high infant death rate, was inadequate to meet felt needs, for voluntary immigrants were welcomed almost without discrimination, and members of the white as well as the black race were kidnapped and brought here to work as redemptioners and slaves. Even after the age of the machine had come along, there were heavy, hand-labor tasks enough here in reducing a raw environment to call for even greater numbers of the unskilled. Public works and railroads developed an insatiable demand for navvies. To have restricted the increase of population, natural or by immigration, would have been to stunt the economic growth of the country. Hands were wanted, and it did not signify what kind of heads were attached to them, or what was in the heads, at least so long as the skin was not yellow. The "melting pot" would resolve all differences in the imported mores into a single, American type. Men flowed to our empty lands like air under pressure into a vacuum, their shift making toward an equilibrium between the density of population in the Old World and the sparsity of the New.

This mania for numbers is now becoming difficult to visualize. It is not alone concern as to the efficiency of the melting pot that has led to the virtual reversal of our immigration policy; it is far more the decline of the demand for unskilled labor, which goes back, it is asserted, to the application of labor-displacing machinery. Where the machine turned out to be an expedient adjustment, unskilled labor was at a discount, and vice versa. Cotton picking had to be done by hand for a long time after the sowing, cultivating, and reaping of grain had been turned over to the machine, because it took so long in the case of cotton to perfect the machine-adjustment, the efficient, nonwasteful cotton picker. Because, too, the gin preceded the picker by many years, the unskilled laborer was relegated altogether to the field.

The opening of the new countries confirmed and protected the old quantitative theory of population; nevertheless, new country or old, the machine, we are assured, is bound to lessen the demand for mere "hands"; that, while it does make new tasks, its net effect is to weaken the call for brute numbers. Whether or not this is true, it is generally believed. And it is not altogether reassuring to be told that the displaced hands will happily be shifted to nobler and higher tasks. When the New World was younger, the superseded cottage weavers could migrate and take up a new life, or a new lease on life; but that is no longer possible, and never will be again, so far as can be foreseen, unless a new planet can be opened up for colonization. All change is difficult, especially for the mature; when youth is past, it is already too late for most men to make a sweeping readjustment to other, even if nobler, tasks, granted that such loftier services are in actual, not theoretical, demand—in such demand as to be paid for. The hod carrier may be able to turn himself into a concert artist, but if too many of the horny-handed do that, they will not all make a living. This theoretical shift to nobler work is a sublime thought. Would it could be realized!

Not much more reassurance resides in the contention that, even if the older must accept, as the consequence of their maladaptability, extrusion from the industrial organization, yet the younger generation will smoothly adjust itself. To rise from ancestral levels is not easy, no matter how free the country. The next generation may not be capable of readjustment at all; and even though it is, it may lack the prerequisite preparation and opportunities. For chance has always played, and will ever discharge, a crucial rôle in the life of mankind.

The pertinency of such considerations to contemporary social policy is evidenced by "labor troubles" of various description, centering about unemployment, and chargeable, according to bitter critics, to the displacement wrought by the machine. The readjustment proposed most fanatically has been the "socialization" of the machine, as against "capitalism," which is identified with its private ownership. The rock-bottom fact to be considered is that the machine is here, and to stay. Advance is not going to stop because it hurts someone. A mahatma may have a vision of multitudes squatting nude over primitive spindles; but Gandhi's days of silence, rather than his economics, is that about him most worthy of emulation. The machine cannot be run away from. For one thing, there is nowhere to run.

The upshot of the whole matter is that there are too many competitors for the jobs available; and that men naturally turn first to the expedient of increasing or dividing up the work or, if they can get at it readily, the wealth, instead of imposing any limitations upon themselves. The next obvious expedient is to choke off competitors. In the days of the craft gilds, concern lest there be too much competition led to the limitation of numbers of apprentices. Trades-unions have seen the same sort of light. Limitation was tough on the excluded, but it was practical; and when it comes to a pinch, realism generally pulls through. Enlightened self-interest may not be so noble as idealistic altruism; it is not so sonorous; but it spurs to action and efficiency where big talk breeds only more big talk.

There is always an interval of alternative-exploration before people get down to self-limitation; for it is much more agreeable to feel that we need not deny ourselves but have only to exert the positive power that is in us in order to meet the increasing demands of a rising stand-ard of living. We are easily taken in by visions such as that of an Economy of Abundance, or by the fallacy that The Rich can pay all the taxes, or that Society owes us the kind of living we want, which is sometimes truculently demanded as a right by persons engaged solely in conferring upon society the boon of living, digesting, and procre-ating within its confines. If a grievance can be presented as discomfort for no fault of our own, but a legitimate claim for damages, we can be very righteous about it. Laziness, envy, and greed can thereby be sublimated into a noble thirst for Social Justice. There are many ways of wriggling away from the offensive need of practising the sturdy independence, involving self-direction and personal responsibility, those qualities which all so loudly profess to admire as national char-acteristics.

Nevertheless, throughout history, and despite all wrigglings, men have been forced, by the impersonal and automatically acting forces that propel societies whither they must go, toward renunciation of heaven-scaling demands and eventual restriction of numbers. They may do so groupwise, deliberately and of policy, when the pinch is near and local enough to be visualized; but the more general and un-accountable the discomfort, the more unconscious and unpremeditated the response.

In cases local enough to be readily visualized, actual restriction of numbers by prudential control has long been practised. For "the people" may exhibit a hard common sense and realism that those with less experience of straitened life-conditions lack. They realize that half a loaf is better than no bread; probably the idealist is dimly aware of that, though he does not know from direct experience what "no bread" means; but they know also, out of experience in estimating "how many times ten goes into roundsteak," that for each to get a decent helping there must not be too many at the table. They know in practice, not by theory, that the domestic fraction, $\dfrac{income}{numbers}$, can be increased, when augmentation of the numerator is improbable, by keeping down the denominator. This is practical folk-wisdom, which is down there in the bottom of people's minds, however overlain by viscous emotionalism. At a pinch, it crops out and through into a kind of dim visibility and is met by a certain concurrent, non-doctrinal response.

With the steady increase of population, and so of competition, life-conditions have been tightening up on the average man during the last generation while, at the same time, he has been losing any sense of duty to religion or state whereby he should not practise limitation in his own family. So, viewing with concern the cost of children and the threat of numbers to the family standard of living, he has been reducing his own denominator. The declining birth rate is not due wholly to such restraint; there are also celibacy and postponement of marriage to take into account; but when all other possible factors have been reckoned in, there can be no doubt in any unprejudiced mind that the decline in fecundity is due, even in the Catholic countries, not to any organic degeneration but to methods of prevention, individually adopted.

There is one noteworthy fact about prudential control of the birth rate: it does not incur the charge of selfishness lodged against the craft organizations that limited their membership to maintain their monopoly. Selfishness implies that someone is wronged; Crusoe could not have been selfish or otherwise immoral. No competitor is harmed by prudential restraint; no one's living is taken away from him; no one's economic chances are lessened, as they are even by restricting immigration. Potential competitors for the jobs of the future are simply not summoned into existence. If harm is done at all, it is done elsewhere than in the economic range.

There are factors in limitation other than the economic ones, as will presently appear; but anybody can readily see that they are being progressively ignored, and that as they wear off and the underlying economic aspects are left exposed in relief, limitation comes to appeal ever more strongly to ever-increasing numbers of realists as the most expedient adjustment to life-conditions in a rapidly filling modern world. The ultimate choice presented to mankind is between numbers and a maintained or elevated standard of living; and as soon as people come to know enough, they inevitably gravitate toward the latter. The Indians who, under the miseries of Spanish rule, renounced cohabitation altogether lest their offspring sink to their status, are no more than the extreme case; they saw a zero-standard in prospect and met it by their one hundred per cent limitation. Postponement of marriages with a higher standard in view is different from what the Indians did only in degree. So is control of procreation within the marriage institution.

The non-economic aspects of limitation are, broadly, the religious and the political (militaristic). The relation of religion, especially in the West, to all matters involving sex has been a singular compound of obscurantism and meddling. At times, celibates who have professed to hold aloof from sex in fastidious holiness have laid claim to a knowledge and authority about it quite exceeding their admissible credentials; they have exhibited also an unflagging interest in the matter, thus confirming the often-noted affinity between the religious and the erotic. In general, it has been the pious who have been the prudish and often the prurient, scenting the obscene where the rest of us, not being so hot on the spoor, detect nothing of the sort.

If sex is conceived to be somehow unclean and shameful, and any consideration of sex matters improper—so that pious parents cannot bear the thought even of informing their children as to the phenomena attending puberty—then, of course, the topic of prudential control is under taboo. It certainly was so when those of us who are no more than elderly were young; even the discussion of limitation was out of order, and Malthus—a clergyman at that!—was anathema. Topics involving procreation, despite Biblical preoccupation with begettings, ran all the way from "not nice" to "damnable"; but that does not mean that they were not interesting, even to those who proscribed them— who could not have been so piously horrified had they been less susceptible. It is a sordid story of hypocrisy, deliberate or unwitting.

Religion has been consistently unfriendly to limitation of numbers, not only in ancestor-worshipping countries but everywhere else. Multiplication (and subtraction) was God's prerogative upon which He did not brook infringement. If, then, the Occident reveals, through statistics from one after another of the most civilized states, beginning with "atheistic France" but winding up with the domain of the *Reyes Católicos,* a declining birth rate, what conclusions are to be drawn concerning the present and future control of religion over procreative conduct? If whole peoples are not practising restraint, then has something untoward been happening to their reproductive powers? That is highly problematic, as indicated by the large families of emigrants from all these countries to frontier settlements. Consider the French in Algiers or Canada.

Some of the clergy deprecate limitation through contraceptive means as compared with "old-fashioned continence." What this phrase means and how, except by way of some modern legend of a Golden Age, the adjective "old-fashioned" was acquired, it is impossible to imagine. The expression cannot mean celibacy nor yet such pious renunciation as that of the medieval spouses who became saints by virtue of their diurnal resistance to self-invited temptation. People do not sleep with swords between them any more. The fact is that Nature has never allowed herself to be flouted in the grand manner and on the large scale—not even in the petty manner and on the small scale. Old-fashioned continence is like old-fashioned honesty, a concept fathered by wishful and wistful thinking.

In any case, the fact of limitation witnessed by the vital statistics is clear enough evidence that people are no longer either so fearful of hell or hopeful of heaven as they used to be. And religious authorities must have let up considerably upon the score of literalness. Religion may thunder away against prudential control, urging that all such matters are the business of "The Man Up There"; but the plain tendency is toward self-help in maintaining and raising domestic standards of living by producing fewer mouths to feed and fewer bodies to be clothed withal. In this particular, religion has lost, or has relaxed, its grip upon private conduct. Plainly speaking, more and more people are arriving at the conclusion that religion has been meddling here with things that are not its business. Behold yet another of those rear-guard actions between theology and scientific enlightenment where there can be but one issue; indeed, certain of the clergy, and by no means the least of them, are even now ready to surrender, in this matter of limitation of numbers, if only they may march out with the honors of war.

If practical economic considerations, no longer concealed by dogmas, impel men of this age to adhere by their actions, if not their words, to the limitation-adjustment, how about the hoary militaristic urge toward numbers? Has it too lost its drive or merely its allies?

"No," answers some psychologist, "it has not lost its motivation: for there is an innate instinct of pugnacity which, at best, may retire temporarily into abeyance." Temporarily "inhibited," one supposes. If there is anything that a serious student of human society comes to loathe, it is this easy chatter about "instincts"—the "instinct of workmanship," for instance. Beyond the "instinct of self-preservation" and the "sex instinct," that is, except for the natural drives toward self-preservation and species-preservation, the human germ-plasm seems singularly free of determinants of social traits. Traits of that order are in the mores and, as acquired characteristics, are learned, not inherited. As for the alleged innate pugnacity, it cannot be demonstrated in fact; it cannot be shown by cases that mankind is "by nature" either warlike or unwarlike. What man is always engrossed in is self-preservation, self-maintenance; and he takes the shortest cut he finds to that goal. If robbery and killing form the line of least resistance toward making a living, he has recourse to violence; and the prospect of being robbed, killed, or kidnapped has always roused him to a frenzy of resistance. It is not violence as such that he has loved. He knows the value of peace and of being let alone. The formation and extension of the peace-group have been characteristic of mankind everywhere and in all times.

In brief, the vast majority of men have always wanted peace. Society itself must be a peace-group or cease to be a society, and the most elementary and characteristic function of government has always been the keeping of peace inside its jurisdiction. All through the ages, the peace-group has been expanding to take in ever greater numbers, and the inevitable collisions of societies have been mitigated by various limitations on war. If a world-referendum could at any time have been taken as regards armed conflict, there would have been an overwhelming majority against it—as an alternative, say, to peaceful trade; the automatic adjustments of mankind along this line reveal an unmistakable trend or drift toward peace. Certainly the sentiment of peoples nowadays is against war. No nation lays proud claim to the paternity of a conflict, but all hasten to repudiate responsibility—the phrase "war guilt," indeed, implies plainly that war is regarded as a crime or even a sin.

The primitive peoples did what they could to prevent war; we are doing what we can. They were afraid to disarm, and so are we. They always wanted numbers for the sake of safety; so did we, up apparently to recent decades. Latterly we seem to have become willing to reconsider the matter. Why is this? Is the "instinct" of pugnacity, along with fecundity, dwindling? Or is the fear of aggression lessening, unconsciously, so that we can look without misgivings upon a declining birth rate? Is militarism weakening?

A wise man once argued sharply against the proposed Hague Tribunal as follows: "If people are mad enough they will fight; if they are not, the ordinary means of diplomacy will do." With all due submission to the logic of this answer to the question as stated, the issue as to actual war goes back a little deeper. "If people are mad enough they will fight," certainly; but cannot their anger be headed off while still short of "enough"?

There is a general principle here involved. It may not attain the scope of *tout entendre est tout pardonner;* but it runs in the same direction. Why does the pacificator in an industrial quarrel try to get the disputants together as soon as possible? So they will not get "mad enough" to want to fight. Why is it said that a few days' delay might have obviated the World War? Because facts and aspects might have been presented by the economic and financial authorities, had they been accorded the chance, that would have cooled the "madness" below the "enough" point. Up to a certain degree of rage, discretion can still intervene. When a tennis player is angry enough to make a display of temper but is not too angry to ignore all consequences, he hurls his new racket, indeed, but selects his spot.

The upshot of the whole matter is to get potential belligerents together; for the result is almost invariably a better understanding. Bismarck arranged it that there could be no time to rectify the misunderstanding he created by distorting the historic telegram. He wanted war. The humble people concerned did not, and it is doubtful whether their representatives, if they had had the chance to speak, would have allowed it—at any rate, Bismarck acted as if he thought they would not. The human fact is that two antagonists who can see each other's point of view generally find something in it. Hostility and suspicion thrive best at a distance; many a man has found his supposed enemy a pretty sound fellow, when they have once got together, and his own hostility largely a misapprehension nursed up by distance, silence, and misconstruction. Even aborted conferences are not always in vain.

All through society's evolution man's actions have witnessed to an unconscious perception of this human trait. Truces, go-betweens, parleys, and embassies are very ancient devices whereby understandings and reconciliations might come about. It never has mattered much that some one or more of these expedients have failed. It does not matter so much that our own post-war conferences have accomplished little that is tangible, or that the League of Nations has run aground. It does not matter so much, in the long run, that such organizations have no formal powers. I recall a remark made by an expert on railroads that a certain commission was stronger without power, for it was thus less under suspicion of intent. It had only one power, namely, publicity; but that turned out to be formidable, for publicity is no mean weapon when it comes to influencing public conviction. When Mr. Wilson contended for "open covenants, openly arrived at," that was the weapon he was reaching for. Even the gibes poked at the post-war conferences have been effective in securing further publicity among the many to whom the flout, sneer, or joke are the prime call to attention.

That we are at war once more is no disproof of the foregoing. The whole matter will have to be taken up again, presently. And there has been a brutal openness during the preliminaries to the present conflict, even in the announcement of intended aggression. The common man faces the issues of the day rather more squarely, though he does not reason them out. They are presented in terms that impinge more directly upon his experience in life.

Men would not be men, nor women women, if they did not yield to the excitement and glamor of a war once started and blown hot by propaganda. Uniforms speak, and not to women alone, of godlikeness —but less than of old, unless I am deep in error. The experiences of the last decades have contributed powerfully to the unpopularity of militarism in many countries. The type of novel based on the former World War has distinctly portrayed disillusionment, centering upon the mud, cold, stench, vermin, and general debasement of bodies, minds, natural beauties, property, and spiritual values, rather than descanting, Pindar-fashion, upon the glory, the elation, and the laurels of victory. And the destruction of city and countryside by assault from the air is bringing home to peoples as wholes what the front-line fighters alone used to see. There are plenty of extremists who hold that there is no gain for anybody from a war, who want peace at any price. It is the pinch that persuades. No one had any doubt, after the act, that Cassandra's gifts were authentic. Insofar as a spawning-policy as respects numbers is a corollary of militarism, it seems to me that it rests upon a base that is steadily weakening, that is being sapped at source, despite the scheming and brawling dictators, who are incidental ripples on the evolutionary stream. Not even a dictator seems able to evoke babies by either fiat, bribery, or penalty.

Even though hordes of modern barbarians are now ravishing the world, I do not find it necessary to retract what has been said about the decline in popularity of militarism. I have made no forecast of a warless world, at any time. Assuredly the conquered and enslaved peoples have no love for militarism. It is stated on good authority that no such hatred of military oppressors has ever before existed as that which the reduced peoples harbor against the Germans. Many thousands of even the oppressor-nations hate war as bitterly as do the more conspicuous victims. All of them will hate it still more before the present convulsion is over. This latest exhibition of what has become a German habit is, in reality, unfinished business of 1918, with all the former detestation of violence much exacerbated.

We started with the fact that birth rates are decreasing in the most civilized countries. We have seen that, throughout history, the popular sentiment has been in favor of rapid increase, and that economic interests, religion, and militarism have been behind that sentiment. None of the three any longer support it unreservedly; the labor-saving machine is believed to have reduced the call for hands, religious dogmas unfavorable to limitation have lost much of their authority, and militarism has come under deep suspicion. The result has been that, under changed economic life-conditions, families have taken the direct route, once forbidden by an authority now questioned, toward maintaining and elevating their standard of living by reduction of the denominator of participants in its proportion to the numerator of supplies.

People have not analyzed the changed situation; they have shown apprehension of its presence only by living into it through adjustment to the thousand small details of it which they have encountered in the daily round. Why should they not take the direct route toward quality of existence when the lions, religious and militaristic, in the path had lost their teeth? Even the savage knows that the more numerous the sharers the smaller the share. Then why lessen the share, especially since no disservice is being done to the prospective extra claimants by not summoning them into existence? The idea about cherubs knocking forlornly and wistfully at the gates of life is no longer convincing; its pathos is like that of Cinderella, as compared with the tragedy of the unwanted child whose advent is awaited in despair.

One more factor in the declining birth rate remains—a most significant one, once the idea of limitation has become tolerable: the technique of contraception. Despite all efforts to ban or hinder the dissemination of knowledge and of effective methods of preventing births, the ignorance hitherto prevalent is sure to be dispelled. Then the birth rate is likely to take a drop of startling proportions. Maybe this means that civilization is to seal its own doom by letting the world become a prey to counter-selection through being overrun by recklessly breeding races. Perhaps a knowledge of the technique of contraception will favor sexual immorality. Possibly some transcendental spiritual values may be sacrificed—although a celibate clergy evidently feels small personal responsibility for summoning souls to earth. Many of us apprehend no such dire results, though we can by no means prove that we are not unduly tranquil.

In any case, however, the standard of family living can be raised by prudential limitation. Insofar as there is a conscious motive behind the decline of the birth rate, here is where it has lurked. No one advocates contraception for the sake of promoting sexual immorality, or counter-selection, or any other of the results its opponents honestly fear or disingenuously pretend to dread. Of course, any student of social programs realizes full well that consequences have no necessary relation with intent; but we cannot resign ourselves to timid or fatalistic inactivity because of fear lest, despite all our care, caution, and calculation, we may come out wrong. All that we can do is use our best knowledge and go ahead. The solution of the purpose-consequence relation is by the interpolation of knowledge between them, for that is the only stiffening bar that can hold results rigidly in line with intent. If we have studied a situation hard, thoroughly, and candidly, we must not hesitate to trust the truth as it appears to us. Any other course is fortuitous and irrational. It seems to some of us that the advocates of birth control have examined the situation from all sides much more thoroughly and with much less prejudice than have its opponents; and so we are willing to go along with them until they are demonstrated in the fact to be wrong, or until they become mere advocates acting hotly under revelation.

The plain fact is that there are too many people in the world—or, at least, in the parts of the world favored by mankind as dwelling places; and that, no matter how much we improve the arts in those regions, for people who cannot or will not do that for themselves, population there will speedily rise to a new level, so that conditions will be improved only momentarily, in the manner in which opium improves them. What good does it do to teach Orientals to raise two bushels of millet where they are now producing one? They merely raise two children, or more, where there has been one. Then famine and disease return upon the new level. There is no end to this sort of thing, so long as breeding is uncontrolled. If men want to evade those natural and capital penalties of overpopulation which Malthus long ago pointed out, and cannot steadily, and of themselves, and without limit, increase the productivity of the arts, then they must let up on breeding.

Sooner or later the "swarming, spawning multitudes" have got to quit either their spawning or living; and the sooner they control themselves voluntarily, the later will they face the Malthusian checks. They will at any rate stop spawning when they have died off. It is a false humanitarianism to take away from prudent people that which allows them to live on a more comfortable standard, in order to enable ever more of the thoughtless and shiftless to drag out a sluggish minimal existence. Why should they be summoned into life, anyhow? Their presence on earth is no boon to anyone, least of all to themselves. Some day the race has got to give over fantastic sentimentality and take account of plain facts.

It is not to be hoped that rationality will arrive very soon; that the race will rationally adopt limitation (or even so sane a practice as cremation) on its merits. It is the automatic forces that have lowered birth rates by so adjusting society to its altering life-conditions that it now pursues a road over the opening to which once hung warnings stating: "No Thoroughfare," signed by Moses and others in the name of the Lord. No one could have foreseen this, for the automatic forces were not working directly upon numbers but were producing the machine, altering religious creeds, making people sick of war, opening the way toward contraception. As the situation has been altered, limitation has begun to appear to more and more people as a natural, unobjectionable, crucial, and inevitable mode of adjustment.

XI

WHAT IS HAPPENING TO RELIGION?

To ONE who has been piously reared, whether or not he has held to the narrow faith, it is something of a shock to find young people knowing next to nothing about the Bible. Tom Sawyer, called upon to name the first two Disciples, was able, at any rate, to mention two authentic scriptural characters. They were merely the wrong ones; but the Sabbath-school background was there. If the boy of today is asked to name any one Biblical person, he can perhaps recall "holy Moses" or connect "jonah" with Jonah. A parallel benightedness envelops the Greek and Roman classics, in particular their mythology. One may wonder what Milton can mean to a reader who, to follow *Paradise Lost* otherwise than afar off, must look up nearly every allusion in some concordance. Who was this wight who fell all day and lit upon Lemnos? The fact is that authors like Milton are moving rapidly into the same status as Dante, whose masterpiece is unintelligible without a deal of learned apparatus attached. The Bible is in the same predicament; if anyone finds himself about to allude before college undergraduates to "Armageddon," or the "Cave of Adullam," or the "Witch of Endor," or anything out of Revelation, he had better shift over to the *New Yorker* for his allusion; otherwise his target is likely to remain indifferently blank and, if he undertakes to explain his scriptural allusion, he will get just about the sort of response that is evoked by a learned footnote.

The reason for this situation as regards the classics is plain enough. Once the ability to speak Latin, as the *lingua franca* of culture, and a dexterity in embroidering conversation with classical tags and allusions, were marks of superiority in the world. They conferred prestige. They impressed the common herd, to whom, in addition, the *Aeneid* and other classical works were fetishes, instrumentalities of divination, repositories of mystical wisdom. Even yet the classics are, to some, exempt from the sort of criticism encountered by profane literature; the attitude toward them is worshipful, not discriminating. The suggestion that the long lists of exceptions in Greek and Latin grammars may be, in part, a roster of original errors and defects arouses a kind of rage. It is possible to hear persons with a keen sense of humor as regards everything else, laugh heartily over the feeble jests to be found here and there in the classics—sallies which, had they been uttered by a contemporary in some modern tongue, would have elicited a species of pity. But that laughter is not precisely "counterfeited glee"; it is a kind of tribute, akin to merriment over the clumsy witticisms of some dull monarch. Amidst the tiresome stretches of unbending gravity, even a mean little oasis of let-down is magnified into unreal proportions.

The classics were once about all there was to know. For some time now there has been a variety of other things to study. The glamor of prestige and the fetish-quality have faded out of the classics, leaving them, with the removal of their walls of high protection, to stand pretty much on their actual merits. The merit of Homer and the Greek tragedians is a solid and enduring quality, the like of which is rare at all times; they have had no trouble in facing the competition of later literatures. Nevertheless, the classics as a whole have lost their grip upon their once almost universal occidental clientèle; national literatures have appeared and the peoples have shifted their allegiance, patriotically if not discreetly, to Shakespeare, Goethe, Dante, Cervantes, Camoens. Certain of these national heroes, it is true, present versions of the classics, somewhat adapted; but eventually even Dante could not rescue Vergil from the slide into obscurity. "Tully" has flattened out to the thinnest kind of a shade.

Something similar to all this has taken place as regards the Holy Scriptures. If the study of them were any longer regarded as the key to life eternal, they would no doubt be as familiar as they ever were; as it is, the prevalent ignorance of them merely registers either an indifference to that which they were once thought to confer, or skepticism as to their competence to confer it—"it" including not only immortality but all the rest of the benefits once accredited to familiarity with the Word of Life. The reasons now assigned for study of the Bible are not on this order; reading courses which treat "the Bible as literature," or attend to its historical or cultural aspects, or take it apart to show its composite character as an accretion of contributions from many sources arbitrarily adjudged to be authentic revelation are far removed indeed from a reverential study of the Word of God, the inmixture into which of any critical attitude would have been sacrilege, even though such exercises were prefaced by prayer.

One often hears serious young men say about the Bible: "We know we ought to read it. We know it is a great historical and literary document that an educated man ought to know about. But it's so long, and a lot of it, to judge by what little we know of it, is so dull. It's boring—and then there isn't time." Fancy what the Mathers would have replied to that sort of talk! About the same sort of student comment is made upon the classics. There is no inkling of the erstwhile attitude as toward divine revelation. Even the young collegians who identify themselves, for one reason or another, with campus religion have a pretty shaky acquaintance with the Bible as compared with that which was once drummed, even birched, into some of us who are not yet senile. The backs of many members of college religious organizations shed, as those of wild geese shed rain, references to Jael, Absalom, Balaam and his Ass, Zaccheus, and other figures once presented to edified childhood in vivid chromo-form; you might fully as well allude to Atreus, Mimi, or Manu. The way to "get a rise" from juveniles nowadays is to cite something considerably newer than Alice in Wonderland or Moby Dick.

If Jonathan Edwards were to revisit his old haunts and preach his sermons on hell-fire to an audience in a college chapel, he would be in constant peril of transforming a decorous detachment into laughter —in something the same situation as the visiting clergyman who, one Sunday morning, not knowing the disastrous outcome of yesterday's baseball game, gave out as his text: "Where are the Nine?"—or the more earnest than wary Greek instructor who, at the harrowing crisis of the *Oedipus Tyrannus,* intoned tragically; "And then they bore in two biers."

There can be no question but that the attitude of the Western World, even though Russia is excluded as partly Oriental, has altered considerably as regards what used to be called "religion." This is recognized in the charges of godlessness that have issued from high ecclesiastical sources, as well as by the frantic effort to prove by statistics that churches are "really" gaining in attendance, membership, and influence; likewise by the compromises and the new "interpretations" of traditional dogmas that have been appearing at short intervals since Genesis was shown, somewhat belatedly and too incontinently for accuracy, to have anticipated geology.

There were many who firmly believed, at the time of the Reformation, that "true religion" was going to the dogs; there are some nowadays who are convinced that religion, in whatever sense, is on its last legs; nevertheless, when the shocked conservative laments that it is all up with religion, or private property, or the monogamic family, it generally means no more than that he foresees correctly the end of that phase of one of these institutions which has been traditional to him. Anyone who has any sense knows that private property will always go on, in some form; that there will always be government while there is human society; and that society's adjustment to its life-condition of human bisexuality will always involve a combination of parents and children. To those who despair, this question is always pertinent: "Is it religion (or property, or the family) that is about to pass away, or is it only what you personally regard as religion?" Is it the entire, long-lived, long-unquestioned institution that is to be no more; or is there merely a sloughing-off of certain dispensable details which, because the observer is so short-sighted and short-lived, look to him, since they are all he can see, like the whole thing?

Did the Reformation end religion? "Oh, no!" replies the Catholic, "the true religion—ours—remains." "Not at all!" is the Protestant answer; "religion—true religion—reformed religion—took on a new lease of life with us." It was nothing, then, but a re-formation; there was no destruction. And nowadays Catholic, Protestant, and Jew admit, with varying degrees of reservation, that they are all religious together. A marvel! There are even Christians who concede that Buddhists are religious, though Buddhism is "a system which knows no God in the Western sense; which denies a soul to man; which counts the belief in immortality a blunder, and the hope of it a sin; which refuses any efficacy to prayer and sacrifice; and which bids men look to nothing but their own efforts for salvation."[1] There are even those who make so bold as to declare that all men "naturally" have religion. Even Dante cannot see how, in fairness, the people of India who lived before Christ should be damned because they were born too early to know and confess him. That Dante's question, under stern rebuke, was hastily retracted as an inadvertent criticism of the Almighty does not expunge the relevancy of that query. The small boy who once propounded the query: "If God can do everything, can he make a stone so heavy that he can't lift it?" received, sixty years ago, substantially the same illuminating reply that Dante got: "Do you presume to criticize the Almighty?"—except that the boy was tersely and crudely bidden to "Shut up! Never let me hear you ask another wicked question like that, or else . . ."

1. Huxley, T. H., "Evolution and Ethics," *Popular Science Monthly*, XLIV, 35.

You can even "prove by logic," if you are so minded, that religion has always been and will be. When you have a spacious major premise, out of revelation, you have something. Socrates "must have been" religious because he was so noble. An eminent clergyman once declared that Goethe "was too great not to have known God." To be religious is great; Herr X was great; ergo, Herr X was religious.

We are sliding down the usual chute into the bog of definitions. Evidently, first of all, the term "religion" is not adamantine. It is protean, rather. It puts up no inexpugnable resistance to re-shaping; indeed, there are times when it seems more like a chunk of wet modelling-clay which can be squeezed together and pinched out into various forms. This is when it has been powdered up somewhat during a period of selection ensuing upon its hardening into a maladjustment; when, for its survival, variation is indicated. In the case of the clay, whatever its form, it remains the same substance. Can the analogy be applied to the case of religion, by one who realizes that analogy, however suggestive, proves nothing? In all its forms, is religion one and the same thing? Are all changes in its contours merely superficial adjustments? Or has something recently happened to its essence, as never in the past, whereby the sentiments now expressed concerning its final passing within a generation or two are different in kind from similar forecasts of its dissolution uttered in former crises, and since then interpreted as no more than the defeatist misgivings of those against whom some theological battle was going?

Religion, in its evolution, is an adjustment to the spirit-environment —directly to that spirit-world, less immediately and more realistically, as will be seen, to something else that is verifiably actual. Superficially, as an adjustment to something quite intangible in comparison with the environment of things and men, it is to an increasing number of persons wholly illusory. But religion is more than a response to that which has no actuality; it is fundamentally an adjustment to the aleatory element. Elsewhere treated with some fullness,[2] this element may be briefly characterized as that of the inexplicable and impredictable in life, the sum of that which we commonly and without analysis call "chance" or "luck." The spiritual environment, with its ghosts, daimons, and divinities, is a kind of personalization of the inexplicable, together with an attribution of agency to that mental construction. These two features in life's landscape, chance and the

2. *The Science of Society*, II, chap. i.

spirit-environment, the former as actual as the rocks and weather, the latter a personalization of the former, offer a point of departure for the study of the evolution of religion and for the assessment of contemporary religious trends.

Let us take up the spirit-environment, and what has happened to it, first. It was destined to be the sole available instrumentality or recourse for rendering the aleatory element, as it entered primitive experience, capable of being grasped and dealt with; nevertheless, it has its own beginning apart from that element, in the illusions of the dream, with the thence inferred supernatural agencies. What has happened or is happening now to the spirit-environment as a conception? And does it still continue to discharge its age-long function of visualizing, by personalizing, the chance-element, so actual in life?

For long ages the ghosts of the dead were regarded as the agents that controlled human destiny; then came the super-ghost, the daimon or deity, an evolved conception that plainly enough revealed its ghost-parentage by remaining anthropomorphic—modelled throughout upon the likeness of man—the god made in man's image. Some advancing peoples worked through to several ranking deities among many or, in some rare cases, to a single God; even He, however, was a personal being, with human attributes—a "jealous god," for example. Only very gradually, and in late ages, was the conception of the spiritual somewhat detached and elevated; and even then God became a kindly and generous super-person instead of a touchy, bad-tempered, arbitrary head-man of the tribe or nation, a benevolent Father of all mankind instead of a dispenser of narrow favoritism in behalf of some chosen people.

The inevitable outcome of this expansion from the particular to the general was that the anthropomorphic spirits were eventually rarefied out into metaphysical entities: First Causes and Absolutes. But, whatever the denizens of the spiritual realm are to those who can no longer accept the view that they are anthropomorphic persons, or that the Great Spirit is one Person (or Three in One) who likes flattery, gets angry at human sins, and so on, always They, or He, or It is recognizable as the genetic aftertype of the earlier anthropomorphic conception—recognizable by the same kind of evidence that establishes the descent of the vertebrate animal from the amoeba. In the one case as in the other the derivation is not immediately obvious; first, the transitional forms in the series have to be arduously sought, discovered, and set in place. The God of Christ was far along the scale from the

God of Jacob, and the Supreme Entity, or the First Cause, or the "Power not ourselves that makes for righteousness" reveals a considerable stretch of evolution covered even during the last couple of millennia.

As readily apprehended, the conception of the spirit-world has been losing all of its former sharpness of outline; even that of the spiritualists makes a vague, uncertain, and grotesque picture. The old spirit-environment has long been in process of replacement by other conceptions where, indeed, it has not been simply dropped, with no visible substitute, as illusory and gratuitous. This is due in no small part to a change of attitude toward the aleatory element, as will presently appear. It can be confidently contended that if religion is to rely for its validity upon belief in the spirit-environment of aforetime, then religion is moribund if not already defunct.

There is another aspect of religion, having to do largely with the spirit-environment, namely, theology. It is unnecessary to rehearse the decline of creeds and dogmas once held to be essential elements in religion; that survey was accomplished, not once and for all but well enough for several generations, by Andrew D. White, who introduced the world to the undefeated victor in "the warfare of science with theology in Christendom." No one holding forth outside a divinity school—and few inside, to judge by the eagerly advertised changes in the no longer ghostly curricula—can even get an audience any longer for a discourse on theology. The best that some of the most hotly disputed doctrines—*homoousion* versus *homoiousion,* infant damnation—can now elicit is a scornful laugh or a flash of irritated incredulity. Their ordinary effect is stark boredom. No intelligent person can any longer be scared into being holy by the menace of hell, nor yet be bribed into sanctity by the prospect of heaven. No one yearns, indeed, for the banal joys of Paradise that used to be dangled before half-culture. The traditional panorama of the next world is slipping rapidly out of focus for this age and its mores, and naturally enough, for it corresponds to other times and other manners. In short, if religion is pallid and freakish theology, it is even stiffer in *rigor mortis* than if it holds to the old ghost-theory; for there are not a few who still believe in specters, while those who can stick theology and doctrinal dialectics are, or soon will be, inhabitants of institutions frankly designed for segregation from the world.

Reference to those who are still credulous enforces an apparent digression that is really nothing such but a kind of *caveat* needful whenever any assertion is made about changes in the mores. The *caveat* shall be brief. It is always the part of discretion to keep reminding one's self that the mores are in the "masses," that the masses are overwhelmingly numerous, and that they are not to be moved by theoretical considerations. I shall not elaborate upon this warning, which may be regarded as a self-admonition that any writer on social matters recurrently needs. Its bearing upon the present topic of trends in religion is this: that much of what has here been said, and of what is to come, is superficial in the sense that it deals with ideas current only in the upper strata of culture and unrepresented among the masses. Hence the movements we may think we discern among ourselves must not straightway be taken to pervade the whole body of our own society, much less that of the human race as a whole. Plenty of human beings are unshakenly credulous of what we regard as imbecile ideas, long discarded. It is not at all certain, either, that what we of the emancipated think today the world will be accepting tomorrow. What counts is not what we imagine the masses to be *thinking,* whether or not we are reading our own conclusions into their mental outfit, but what they *do;* for what they do is what they are stressed toward by the automatic forces that govern society's evolution; and the stress exerted impinges upon the emotions of the masses, not upon their intellects. This is what saves the situation in the end, for it eliminates the errors to which the mind seems to take as naturally as the duck to water. Though an effort is being made in this essay to indicate as we go along what changes in religion are matters of thought and what are matters of action, this admonition against reading the "emancipation" of the few into the tradition-bound many can never be a genuine digression or irrelevancy.

It is no exaggeration to assert that religion was once almost wholly faith in various conceptions now credited by the naïve alone. But those who held the faith could not merely sit there and hold it. There was something to *do* about it; there were the "works" as well as the faith, and just because of the faith. Faith and works have been perennial fellows in a stock formula, if not in any other way. There has been, indeed, a long-standing disagreement about how the reality of a man's religion should be judged: by what he professes or by what he does. The primitives assumed the faith as axiomatic and not to be bothered about; they were realists who dealt with acts, not states of mind; who, in passing upon results, did not feel the necessity of reckoning in the intentions or purposes. Our forebears, however, became involved in the *prepense* and we still pride ourselves, often justifiably, often fatuously, upon judging by the state of mind behind the act. The center of interest, however, between the two, always somewhat shifting, has been moved toward the behavior-side of this issue—in religion, away from the credo, which was once so crucial that if a sinner could mumble it just before he died, to the right person, a lifetime of scandalous "works" could not weigh him down to hell against its heavenward pull. Nowadays, on the contrary, it seems that anyone who behaves himself pretty well, who is honest, truthful, generous—who, in a word, approximates the gentleman-as-he-should-be, is called a "good Christian," or a "Christian gentleman," no matter what he believes or cannot accept. He may not even go to church, though if he occasionally does, much is made of it, as in the case of certain of our Presidents, to show that he is really religious, religious "after all." Even God is sometimes regarded as a "gentleman" Who will, after all, act in a reasonable manner and not as, in the Scriptures, He says He will. If these are not variations away from traditional religion, it is difficult to classify them; they raise, in fact, the very question of religion's identity. Is it faith alone or works alone, or must it include both?

I wish to illustrate this situation by a somewhat detailed example. In a little, old *Life of Lincoln,*[3] published not long after his death, there is an assessment of both the faith and the works of the Emancipator. With plenty of good will and an eagerness to twist the facts to their limit of torsion, not much of a case is made for the first: Old Abe, Honest Abe, simply was not a "professing Christian"—and "Oh, the pity of it!" On the other score, he was a pretty good sort, in fact, a remarkably Christlike soul; and the impression conveyed is that that ought to count for something in the reckoning. Confront this nervous apologia with what an eminent American divine[4] asserted, in February, 1933: "It is part of the surprise and grandeur of the life of Lincoln, with his early fatalism and his growing cosmic piety, [that] he should be accounted one of the most Christ-like men of his age." This liberal clergyman regards it as "impertinent" to "ask the old question, so much debated; 'Was Lincoln a Christian?' The answer depends on what we mean by being a Christian. If by Christian we mean one who holds certain dogmas about Christ—the manner of his

3. By W. C. Gray: "For the Young Man and the Sabbath School." (Cincinnati, 1869.)
4. Newton, J. F., reported in the New York *Times,* February 14, 1933.

advent, the nature of his person, the works he wrought—then Lincoln was not a Christian; he did not reject the creed of the church; he ignored it." This is about where Sandburg, in his prolonged researches on Lincoln, came out.

The implication of this seems to be that Lincoln was "essentially" a Christian. If so, then the dogmas do not count: the Virgin Birth, the Divinity of Christ, the Miracles, the Resurrection. Quite a contrast to the feeble defense put up by that Sunday-school biography! But let us return to that apologia for a moment, realizing that it does not by any means sweep faith aside as immaterial but merely puts in a kind of shamefaced plea for extenuation on the grounds of good works accomplished by the accused. There was, however, in all honesty, one item among Lincoln's "works" that was pretty awful, too flagrant to suppress or even to whitewash: he was in a theater on the fateful evening—and it was Good Friday, at that. There seems to have been in the mind of the apologist little doubt that God was sorely enough irritated by such looseness of conduct to let Booth do his worst, and also that somehow the assassination expiated for the victim his bad slip in behavior. That argument is as laughable today as it was seriously taken by the good people who wanted "Father Abraham" in their blessed fold on Judgment Day and could not believe that God would send him shambling off with the goats, even though he had met his end in a playhouse. Excuses were made for him, at the time and later: it was the woman-serpent combination—Mrs. Lincoln's frivolity—for he would not have gone had he not been badgered into it by her. This was not so but was the usual "good reason" and good enough. Their very eagerness to excuse is clear evidence as to the enormity of the offense in the eyes of pious admirers who, aware that they had no case for attributing the status of Christian to their hero on the score of faith, hated to see a flaw in the inferior, though acceptable, evidence from works.

Everyone has encountered the expression used in reference to some agnostic: "He's as good a Christian as anybody." It has been employed even in the case of a militant infidel like Colonel Ingersoll who, being a great orator, remained in high quadrennial favor with the most pious of Republicans, sinking only betweentimes into the ranks of unredeemed. What is the significance of this? Nothing else than that the non-believer has behaved himself decently, morally, even generously, unselfishly, and in a "Christlike" manner. Here is another instance of metaphor. Lincoln, once again, was, it was admitted, not technically religious, but his behavior was such that he "ought" to have been, or "must" have been, or "really was" a Christian. His works were so praiseworthy upon Christian criteria that an underlying faith, even though not expressed or professed, "must have been" there to account for them. At any rate, he was religious, for he referred to his "Maker" and otherwise expressed himself in religious terminology. If he found no credo broad enough to secure his allegiance, what of it? Look at what he was and did!

If such criteria were admissible, then "religious," we recall, would mean nothing more than "good" or "admirable." But that is a misleading and improper perversion of a term that has its own special, fixed, and traditional significance. If "religious" is to be extended to take in unreligious or irreligious persons who behave themselves, then it becomes at best merely another synonym where none is needed, and a term that has meant something definite is lost to the language. That has happened often enough. It is one of the ways in which language evolves. But the thoughtful person should clearly realize that terms suffer such change only when that for which they stand is changing— in this case, that religion is becoming for the reflective something very different from what it has always been before. What is happening to religion? is our main topic. Bluntly, to certain of its popular champions it is becoming so different from what it has traditionally been that the well-behaved atheist, agnostic, or heretic can now be juggled into the fold.

This Lincoln case was being thus threshed over not so long ago. Nowadays, a clergyman, especially of the go-getter type, is not likely to lay much stress on faith; nor is he squeamish about the old trio of devilishness: dancing, cards, and the theater. In urging you to join his church, he may reveal an indefinitely expanding latitude. "But," you object, "I do not believe the articles of your creed." Your conscientious scruple is waved aside: "Oh, that needn't deter you. Believe what you like. You're interested in furthering public morality, aren't you? Well, then! [Aside: "What's biting you, anyhow?"] You ought to belong to the organization which has been, all along, the grand agency for that sort of thing. Creeds don't amount to so much: it's what you do and how you live. Come along in!"

With all respect for the doers of things—the quiet ones, without "pep"—and a complete distaste for the noisy and showy arrangers of things, I nevertheless submit that this emphasis upon conduct or ethics as contrasted with faith is not religion in the sense understood for centuries; that to call a man religious simply because he is moral is a perversion of both terms. I know well enough that if a sunflower could be called an orchid by enough people for a good while, it would come to be known as an orchid to everyone; but that is no reason for withholding objection to an unannounced re-naming that has no utility at all—unless it be an *alias* designed for causing confusion of identity in the mind of everyone except the re-namer. Uncalled-for re-naming is on the order of changing the figures on a bank note while it is in circulation, or of withdrawing a coin for an interval of clipping or sweating, thereafter to slip it back into the trustful hands of the unobservant unwary. It is at best an unsportsmanlike trick with its source in a not disinterested intellectual dishonesty.

Old-fashioned pious people complain that the clergy no longer preach religion but chatter about everything else under the sun: politics, literature, sex—in a word, comprehensive of all their divagations, "sociology." Where is the theology of aforetime? That was religion. You could get your teeth into that. Indeed, it had teeth of its own.

The opinions of the clergy on business and politics are inevitably crude and amateurish when they seek to be more than hortatory and utopian. Each week, throughout the land, there are Sunday whinings over the general situation, plus hasty improvisings of wild courses that people "must" pursue—of programs that even a Stalin would despair of enforcing upon an intimidated population. During the former World War the clergy were stingingly arraigned, under the charge: "Peter sat by the Fire Warming Himself," [5] for a lack of both insight and courage. The fact is that the clergyman, having descended from the pulpit into the arena, has become criticizable under observation at close quarters like anybody else; and his outfit and conditioning for the arena do not inspire any of the awe that once invested his priestly detachment within the realm of theological mysteries.

Why did Mr. Jones, a sexagenarian, formerly go, Sunday after Sunday, to listen hours on end during those Lord's Days, and also several times during the week, to discourses by some youth of tender years—possibly by even Bill Smith's boy? Why did he crave advice from young Reverend Mr. Smith, whose trousers he had himself dusted for juvenile misdemeanors, concerning his own elderly private life or social conduct? Had he not been involved in these questions of living long before the youthful oracle was born? Then why go and listen?

5. Odell, J. H., *Atlantic Monthly*, Vol. 121, no. 2, February, 1918, pp. 145–154.

Because young Smith had something in him now that could be acquired by, and only by, protracted study of the inspired writings. He had, as a consequence of that immersion and attendant revelation, a priestly, fetish element in him; his utterances on life were not at all the raw opinions of immaturity but eternal truth revealed to him by immersion in the Word of God and in the interpretations of life set forth over long ages by the inspired wisdom of fetish-men: church fathers and saints. The young preacher may have had small experience in life—nobody was deceived as to that—but when he began: "Thus saith the Lord"; or "According to Saint Paul"; or "Saith Saint Thomas Aquinas," you were getting stuff straight from Authority Itself. Bill Smith's son had been behind the scenes among the mysteries; he was no longer Bill, Jr., but, even to his sire, a being transformed in something the manner of the initiate into the primitive secret fraternity, born again, with a new name and a personality become portentous. If he ever stole apples and got birched for it, that was in a former incarnation, a pupa stage irrelevant to his present full-blown splendor; for now he had become a Minister of the Deity.

The case is even more striking when one asks himself how a sensible, hardheaded man, with a lifetime of experience behind him, could ever have endured with patience, could even have listend with deference and reverence, to the ravings of a crude, unlettered, welkin-punishing "evangelist." But the explanation is the same: the performer was inspired; the crazier he was and the more bacchanalian, the more evident was his "possession" by spiritual power. It is all very primitive, and also very human and exciting and entertaining. If the medicine-man turned out later to have been a charlatan or even a scoundrel, that did not discredit his successor at all, for the cure for disillusioned credulity is more credulity.

But how is it now? Let us set aside the case of bacchic inspiration and return to Bill Smith's boy, who never charges up and down the aisles, or pants, or sweats out his decorous collars. Nevertheless, he has lost his fetish-quality—perhaps, in part, just because he remains cool and sane. Common enough is the priestling who has had a "course" in social sentimentality in some forward-looking divinity school; or in college, years back, enough elementary economics to lend him glibness of terminology. This youth now encounters and straightway senses an affinity with certain exponents of a "new" economics, to whom Adam Smith and Mill are merely though pardonably antediluvian, and spacious "planning" à la Moscow a revelation; then he

expounds the new philosophy with uncritical fervor to elder men who
have been infected with green enthusiasm and eventually immunized
while he was still in knee-pants. What mature man can endure to
listen to criticisms and exhortations on social conduct from upstart
youths with a quite inadequate outfit of knowledge? Are these amateur generalizations and platitudes the forms under which God now
reveals Himself? If so, most of us who are older would vastly prefer
the thunderings from Sinai.

The trouble is that men of experience can check up upon the
modern revelation as they could not aforetime, or dared not, upon
Revelation—where if it was written that the number of the Beast
was 666, that was that. The clergy have surrendered Authority in
deserting theology and mysticism for ethics and the practical. Of the
latter pair they cannot make a religion. As to them, authority is not
conferred by inspiration nor can it evade criticism. To speak of making
"a new religion" out of eugenics or social service is merely to employ
a truth-betraying figure of speech.

Any discussion about religion keeps circling about the vital question
as to what religion is: the definition of religion. A definition is a
description commonly accepted. The dictionary is the definition hand-
book. How does it derive its definitions? Manifestly by recording
usage. It recognizes, of course, not only common usage but also variations that are beginning to look hopeful and meanings that are fading
out; however, it does not fail to indicate by its notation the new and the
obsolescent. Now, anybody who should look only to the novelties under
a dictionary entry could not be said to have acquired a genuine definition. If a foreigner knew "racket" only in the sense of "tennis bat,"
his understanding of the term would be nothing to boast about. Similarly with "religion." If anyone wants to write understandably about
it, he cannot pitch upon an appealing definition that some eccentric,
or he himself, has evolved out of his inner man, and make his readers
accept and stick by it. They won't do it, especially since he himself will
inadvertently depart time and again from his plotted straight and
narrow lane. The only way to discuss religion profitably is to quit
trying to set up special definitions and start with what it has meant
and still means to most people. Then you can get somewhere.

A religion has always been "something to believe plus something to
do," faith plus works, but always unmistakably oriented from the
supernatural, not the natural. You start always with the grand major
premise of the spirit-world and proceed by deduction; there can be

no "scientific religion," working along inductive lines. To speak of the "religion of the scientist" or the "religion of the agnostic" is, again, highly and dangerously metaphorical, for it is like speaking of white blackness—dangerously metaphorical, I say, for it is a menace to truthfulness to call white black unless everyone likely to be affected knows that you are only fooling or romancing, or unless you deliberately warn your hearers that you are proposing a new terminology involving the scrapping of the old. Otherwise you are using "weasel-words," that suck out all vitality and honesty from the issue they fasten upon.

If this word "religion" is to be used at its face-value, with no slippery understandings implied that it is to mean something else, its "something to believe" must relate to the supernatural and its "something to do" must be a set of actions directed toward reconciliation or ingratiation with the supernatural. It will not do to say: "We will say so-and-so. Our audience will think we mean this; the press will think we mean that; we ourselves will know that we mean this other." No good can come of such shiftings and shufflings, however copious—not if we want to understand things as they are, here and now. Of course, shuffling is, in the long run, the inveterate method by which the waning of pet ideas and of loved maladjustments is interpreted to be their persistence. Something new and inconsistent with the old is given the name of the old and then, as among savages, the name is conceived to be the thing. "You see we were right. We said the Bible was infallible. Well, you see now that geology is merely a rehash of Genesis, don't you? Of course, we now know that our nineteenth-century theological brethren who were anti-evolutionists merely failed to see that evolution is, after all, a part of religion; that it is God's way. They had too little faith, not too much. They did not perceive that it is less godlike merely to create things than to create a ground-process like evolution, which itself creates things. It is clearly nobler to create that which creates than merely to create a plain creature."

One has some respect for uncompromising tenacity, no matter how forlorn the hope; also for a plain and unadorned confession of error; but for the face-saving squirmings to bolster human vanity, to show that "we were right after all" (though they are exactly what the emotionless process of societal evolution most commonly uses to bridge transitions from one set of mores to another), there can be nothing better than an indulgent contempt; "Yes, it's a loathsome sight. Men will never get over the itch to be thought infallible. Too bad. But that's the way the thing's done."

It is here maintained that no definition of religion, as religion has been and is still to the masses of mankind, as evidenced also in their current usage of the term, is valid if it leaves out the conception of a spirit-environment. This conception involves, necessarily, conceptions of the soul, the future life or immortality, and a number of others which have been used, over and over, as criteria of religion. A religion without the supernatural is no religion. The "religion of morality" is accurately and understandably describable as "morality"; the "religion of science," as "science." There being no supernatural in either, there is religion in neither. All that "religion" means in these phrases is that men are pretty earnest about their morality or science, somewhat as they used to be about a faith that included the fear of God. Religion characteristically "puts the fear of God" into people; it is doubtful whether anything else can put anything similar into them. That question will turn up later on; for the present, it may help toward a distinction between the religion of reality and that of metaphor to realize that no figure of speech—no trope, metaphor, simile, or even *hysteron proteron* ever put the fear of God into anybody.

Thus far in our survey of what is happening to religion we have found that the idea of a spirit-environment, which is an essential to religion, has recently been rather rapidly fading out from the consciousness and conscience of at least the more emancipated. Ghosts are gone; vampires are no more; familiar spirits have shrivelled up into little imps portrayed, playfully, as attendant upon prestidigitators; angels and devils with their wings of swan or bat; heaven and hell with their crowns, harps, seas of glass, and jasper portals, or their fire, brimstone, quaking bogs, burning marls, sheets of ice, their doors upon whose hinges "grate harsh thunders," and their "shrieks and shapes and sights unholy"—all these are of antiquarian interest only. Dante and Milton have lost their erstwhile drive; modern youth experiences no more than a passing wonder that men could have taken "all that dope" seriously. For the educated and, indeed, for the rest, in cultured countries, there is little left of that spirit-environment once conceived to be as real as mountains, plains, plants, or animals. If that environment, plus the theology attendant, were all there were, or had been, in religion, there could be but little doubt about its eventual disappearance. Essential to religion as the spirit-environment is, however, it is not all. To the lover of paradox, it might be called an essential incidental—essential to religion as such, incidental as a mere instrumentality of independent origin, present and capable of affording a visualization of an abstraction—the aleatory element—too volatile (though an absolutely basic and in no sense illusory life-condition of human society) to be seized upon directly by unsophisticated minds.

I have been speaking of a fading-out of the idea of the spirit-environment rather than of an abrupt rejection. Occasional individuals may be able to execute a direct about-face, but that is not the way of societies; nor, indeed, do many individuals change their former views as they change their clothes. The process is much more gradual, being far more likely the reputed replacement of body cells every seven years. It is more by way of rationalization and interpretation than consciously. The old wears out and drops away. The parts of the old jackknife are replaced but the owner may insist that it is the same old knife, until, some day, it dawns on him that the original tool is all gone.

There are a number of intermediate stages between an original belief and its virtual rejection, even in the case of the highly educated, who have always been the most subtle justifiers, apologists, and interpreters, because their wits have been sharpened in the direction of argument, logic, and dialectics. They have been the most expert squirmers. Some of them, like the pious scientists, have exhibited a kind of hybrid mentality, part-time agnosticism along with a covering orthodoxy; an ability to hang up their religion, along with their hats, in the vestibule of the laboratory. Pasteur seems to have been somewhat of that type, even though he was goaded to protest against the invasion of his laboratory by noisy heresy-hunters. Then there are those who think for themselves in part and in part let others do it for them; or think for themselves weekdays and merely absorb, with entire docility and credulity, on Sundays.

The dominant agency productive of the fading-out of the spirit-world into pallor is, of course, science, with its essential feature, free investigation. I shall have much to say about that agency later on, but I want to introduce it now, together with an anticipatory warning that its devastatingly transforming effects are attained indirectly and its influence exerted wordlessly via its observed performances rather than by any direct frontal attack. For it is this influence of science that occasions the various rationalizations, apologies, and reinterpretations just mentioned, for which there would be no call except for the advance of positive, verified knowledge. It is not immediately significant that scientists tend themselves to become agnostic;[6] but the long-time

6. See J. H. Leuba's two surveys, nearly twenty years apart, of the "Religious Beliefs of American Scientists."

import of that tendency is very momentous, for thus is gradually generated an atmosphere unfavorable to the raw and florid coloring of primitive religion.

I have centrally in mind the question of what is happening to religion, not in the experience of the intellectually most alert, but in that of the "People." Evidently, they cannot any longer be rallied to old-time beliefs, though they have never deliberately rejected them. The "times" (meaning "mores") have changed and the traditional creeds have lost their force. They are no longer even interesting. Presented anew, they seem strange and even trivial or ridiculous. Church authorities have realized this and have quietly dropped a number of them. Ritual has been modified so as not to insist upon what is offensive to modern taste, e.g., the parts in the burial service about "worms," in the wedding service about "burning" and even "obeying." The populace will no longer stand for the old crudities.

One single illustration, to portray the inevitability, and the pain, of change; also the sure diffusion of doubt from the afflicted individual to those about him. Then will appear a partial list of discarded religious ideas and practices.

Fifty years ago, as a certain protesting clergyman[7] puts it: "God was God. He was Jehovah, King of Kings, Lord of Lords. What else mattered?" This was a "simple, sincere religious faith exhibited by my parents and our neighbors." He goes on: "My own utter confusion is distressing as I try on the occasion of ordination to . . . give any conception of God." "We see with each new age a new definition of God. . . . This redefinition process is certainly in full swing today." If one is in doubt about this, let him read the evidence in Henshaw Ward's *Builders of Delusion*.

This reluctant protestant is a sort of rueful agent of change; for he is sure to pass on something of his confusion, and eventually of his rationalizations, to those who merely receive what is told them. Only the priest with a prescribed, unquestioned doctrine and dogma behind him can do otherwise; and even the dogma is not utterly changeless and unadaptable to changing conditions. If God Himself is rationalized and adjusted, minor religious items are not immune. The formerly stable and vivid spirit-environment is becoming a set of unsteady, confused, complicated, tenuous, colorless, metaphysical symbols and rationalizations.

Rationalization has been widely applied to the following religious

7. Marsh, T. H., "A Preface to an Ordination Paper," *The Christian Century,* August 2, 1933, pp. 978–980.

conceptions and acts: the fear of death;[8] the soul, in both the living and the disembodied; mortuary practices and the funeral; mourning; the nature of the future life; sacrifices to the dead; fasting; the Messiah; dualism; deities; fetishism (relics; holy places; the altar; the holy day [holiday]; the Word; the Book; the image; the holy man; the People [*vox populi vox Dei*]; inspiration; "possession"; etc.); the evil eye; omens; prophecy; the taboo (on work; on foods; sex taboo; marriage taboo); holy discomfort; self-discipline; mortification of the flesh; sin (remission, confession); baptism; amulets; cursing (anathema); worship (ritual; sacrament; renunciation; continence; vows); redemption; salvation; covenant; faith-cure; miracles; social position of clergy (no longer an inspired, fetish group); conservatism resistant of all change as such.

Retention of the old in literal form is rare. It is most marked, perhaps, in the following: projectivism (conception of the next world and life in terms of earthly existence); funerary practices; opposition to cremation; property (money)-sacrifices; hero-worship (saints, Messiah); polytheism; fetishism (see above); the evil eye; lucky and unlucky; the taboo (see above); baptism; ritual; sacrament; fasting; prayer; magic; faith-cure (Christian Science); conservatism as to selected details; the conviction that religion makes morals.

Certain of the items in this tentative list will come in for more extended attention below, where the effects of religion upon conduct are to be considered. In any case, and despite divergence of opinion as to the several items just cited, the net impression as to the fading out of the idea of the spirit-environment among the religious is confirmed.

So much for the spirit-environment. We now turn to the aleatory element.[9] In actuality, direct adjustment to the spirit-environment has been indirect adjustment to that element. Thus is the life-condition of luck or chance—the inexplicable and unpredictable by other than spiritual agency—thrown into the foreground. Has anything been happening to that element whereby religion, as mankind's expedient in adjustment to it, has been superseded or is likely to be; has been vitally altered or is it likely to be? Is the aleatory element now seen, as and for itself, so that visualization through an instrumentality is no

8. See the following essay.

9. Familiarity with this term (as developed in Sumner and Keller, *The Science of Society,* II, chap. i; Keller, *Man's Rough Road,* chap. xi) is assumed, but should not be merely assumed for himself by the reader, if he cares to know just what, from this point on, the writer is talking about. Space to re-state is here unavailable.

longer needed? Is the chance-element bigger or smaller than it used to be, more vital or less, more or less readily dealt with?

It is not debatable that much of the previously inexplicable and unpredictable has become accountable and subject to forecast. Success along this line has been a consequence of recording, verifying, and comparing experience. The acme of that procedure is science, which has explained many previously incomprehensible things and has been able to predict by announcing anticipated recurrence. In so doing, it has been subtracting not a little, during its as yet brief career, from the range of the aleatory element. It has thus narrowed the scope and importance of chance, the unanticipated, by establishing a method of anticipation. Is the aleatory element, then, on the wane, like the spirit-environment, so that men need no longer feel that they must anxiously provide against it by getting the supernatural on their side? Does the decline of the aleatory element thus account for the fading out of the spirit environment, the form under which it has been visualized? Is that element of chance, to which religion has been an adjustment, passing away or so changing form that religion is no longer needed?

It is not. Nobody who has thought about it believes that the aleatory element will ever cease to be a major life-condition of mankind. Keeping, for the moment, to its more homely manifestations, can we say that there is less "luck" now than formerly? Abraham could not have had bad luck in the stock market, nor could Job have lost his job in a depression due to extravagance, overproduction, and wild foreign investment, following on a world conflict. It is certain that much of the race's cultural advance has been accompanied by the assumption of new risks, so that civilized people can be said to live more and more dangerously. Each nation has its own hazards; and then each participates in the fortune of every other. Not only is every citizen in a state under hazard because his fate is bound up with that of his fellows; he is concerned also with what is happening to people in China whom he will never see. Mankind has, in becoming civilized, surrendered ever more hostages to fortune. He is ever more vulnerable to mischance.

What did a Western European of the early Christian era care about what was going on in China? There was then no "white man's burden." Nowadays the West is distinctly vulnerable in the East, because the advance in transportation, commerce, and so on, has made their good luck our good luck, their mischance ours. Instance the case of the Philippines: in 1898, as a humorist said at the time, many Americans did not know whether they were islands or a kind of nut; and now that we possess them we are thereby vulnerable, along with the several millions of "brown brothers" of those islands.

The immense complication of modern life introduces many a hazard that was unheard of a little while ago. Wherever people live in large numbers in proximity, untoward things are sure to happen, running all the way from an epidemic of disease, due to a polluted water-supply or imperfect sewerage, to petty collisions that may assume huge and destructive proportions. A natural phenomenon like an earthquake may scare the savage to death, or suggest a special kind of architecture to peoples somewhat higher in civilization; in great modern cities, its destructiveness becomes many times as serious, for it fractures gas-pipes and water-mains and presently there is a conflagration and wide-spread exposure to hunger, the elements, infections, and violence.

There has been a loss of self-sufficiency all along the line, as civilization has developed. Individuals and groups—yes, whole nations—have specialized; and they have been able to do so only because they could depend upon the coöperation of others. But this dependence means that we have put our fate in good part into the hands of others; then if something happens to those others, it happens to us, and if they turn uncoöperative or hostile, as the Germans in 1914 and recently, they may take advantage of our lack of self-sufficiency to harm us. Protective tariffs are measures rooted ultimately in fear of just that situation.

From this point of view, certainly, it looks as if there had been no diminution of the aleatory element, but that, on the contrary, its scope had been much widened. The protective device of insurance, magnificent as it is, does not lessen risk, but merely distributes loss so that it can be more easily borne. The very exuberance of insurance, covering as it does risks all the way from having twins to losing theater tickets, witnesses to a lively sense of hazard in modern civilization. The savage would have liked to insure himself against twins, but he could have dispensed with plate-glass insurance or protection against the mischances involved in a presidential campaign. We have many more chances than he to get hurt, just as a man in a room full of close-packed, rapidly speeding machinery runs more risk than a Gandhi spinning in the solitude of the lockup. Third rails, live wires, headlong autos driven by irresponsibles, grade crossings—what were the hazards of the much-enduring Odysseus, in number and peril, compared to these?

The inexplicable and unforeseeable will always be present, so long as men are men. Science, it is true, has explained many things once hopelessly mysterious; but—be it noted and never forgotten—with every one of its advances it has opened new vistas of the aleatory. When it had discovered the operation of the chromosomes, the sphere of the inexplicable and awe-inspiring suddenly expanded before its very eye. The capacity for wonder acquired by whoever is even moderately acquainted with the disclosures of science is completely beyond that of the most rhapsodical of psalmists. Unless the scientist with insight is very patient and courageous, he is likely to throw up his hands and mutter: "What's the use?" Every time he makes a hole in the sand bank, it caves in and only the prospect of more toil remains; and the poets and prophets who "know" dance about the scene of his discomfiture and chant: "Didn't we say so? *Now,* perhaps, you'll give it all up! Science has to change its theories all the time. Does Homer have to be altered, or does his work stand? Well then!"

Theoretically, since the range of the aleatory element is infinite, at least so far as we are concerned, it can be neither increased nor diminished. As a practical consideration, however, this and that can be found out and lived by, to the diminution of certain pains and losses. Pasteur opened vistas of the inexplicable while he was finding out about germs; but he did find out about the germs just the same, and that exploit was not in vain.

The fact is that, under civilization, the aleatory element has been both increased and decreased. But the decrease has been more widely apprehended and applauded. Civilization has reduced certain real and tangible risks that were constantly taken, perforce, by earlier peoples, and has cancelled also a number of imagined hazards explicable in their day only by reference to the supernatural. The first class needs to be no more than indicated: consider the relief won for those who have sense enough to receive it, from smallpox, yellow fever, diphtheria, malaria, rabies, and the rest of those diseases which were once regarded, along with frogs, fleas, and minor plagues, as the scourges of the Almighty. Job needed a tonic more than philosophic discourse, together with a prompt lancing under antiseptic conditions of the ripest of his discomforts.

In a general way, civilization has exempted men from the immediate hazards of the actual struggle for existence: hunger, cold, and violence; for within a peace-group, whether family, clan, tribe, or state—indeed, within the human race itself, except in time of war—it is thought to be a reflection upon civilization if relief is not rushed to those who have been struck hard in the battle of life. It is a "shame" to us, we are indignantly reminded, if the Oriental victims of inundations, disease, famines, and unrestrained breeding are not instantaneously fed, clothed, housed, and cured of their maladies—the last not including, however, their spawning proclivities. It is our "duty" to renounce raising our own standard of living in order to keep them alive, in greater numbers, on theirs—which they have no idea of raising. We lower their risk by loading it upon ourselves.

But the question of multiplicity and brute quantity of risk, as between the past and now, between uncivilization and civilization, especially between the prescientific age and the present, is of minor importance as compared with the metamorphosis in ideas concerning the nature of chance which science has brought about. It is not so much that real risks have been distributed or lessened or increased as that imaginary ones have been shown up for what they are, and that the old religious explanations of the real ones have been superseded, or, at any rate, corrected and refined—whether replaced by something non-religious or rarefied into something more "truly" and "nobly" religious, depends upon the meaning assigned to "religious."

It may be that the "masses" still hold to the old views; that they are daimonists, accepting the accountability of supernatural agency for everything except the most obvious, everyday exhibitions of mundane agency and effect or, much less frequently, of impersonal cause and effect. Certainly no one who fails to realize the essentially primitive nature of contemporary "reasoning" is competent to advise upon social policies. Nevertheless, there has been an automatic process steadily going on, as the result of which there has percolated into the minds, even of the masses, a certain tendency toward realism in action, no matter how unearthly and fantastic the beliefs which the actors profess. A striking case is that of the Christian Scientist who, in a pinch, sends for the doctor; the fact that, after the pinch is over, the doctor is again derided and libelled has no bearing upon what was actually done.

The contention is briefly this: no matter what people say, they live and act as if they had an utter trust in the reliability of science. All do not get their lawn mowers and automobiles blessed or even christened; they expect them to work without the laying on of hands other than those of the mechanic. If the engine stops because a wire has worked loose, that is not regarded as a case of the intervention of the devil—unless, of course, some unusual catastrophe results from it—but either a result of carelessness or nobody's fault, inasmuch as "such things are always happening." Contrast this with our Homeric hero whose bowstring, a new one, snaps just as he is about to get a great result: "O, Zeus!" he roars in uncontrollable rage over his disappointment, "no one of the gods is more malicious than thou!" Doubtless if the shot had not been important, he would have muttered merely "*O popoi!*" and peevishly or patiently put on a new string.

That is what men have always done, to some degree—they have resigned themselves to the fact that an apparently faultless bowstring, or steel axle, or bridge support, or strut to an airplane's wing, may yet have a flaw in it, and have not bothered to lay the imperfection at the door of the supernatural. They have unconsciously practised the "law of parsimony," not calling in the supernatural when the natural explanation would do. Only when the ill-luck element has been excessive, was it felt needful to look further, outside the range of common sense. Now what has happened in recent decades is that common sense has been subjected to such schooling, drill, and organization that it has needed a new name for its disciplined phase, which is "science." Once the supernatural had to be invoked at once to explain, say, the original water-barometer; the inventor thereof was rebuked by a flight of stones for collusion with Satan. Otherwise than by infernal aid, how could a little wooden figure in a glass pipe know enough to pop up when the weather was to be fair and retire before a rain! Or how could water run up hill, through a siphon, without there being "big medicine," i.e., "big mystery," about it?

Of course, everything is, at bottom, "big mystery." The scientist is the one who knows that best. The ordinary run of humanity knows it not at all; a primrose is to them a primrose; it is no marvel that grass grows, or that tides flow and ebb, or that a child is born, or that the sun rises. That is the way things go, "as everybody knows." When they do not go that way, then comes the "big medicine": the comet, the rain of blood, the two-headed calf, the twin-birth, the albino, the genius who is near to madness.

What has happened is that more and more of the givings of science concerning the erstwhile inexplicable have become "what everybody knows," and that much of what was once "big medicine" is taken not to be mysterious at all but matter-of-fact, like the sunrise. The thus explicable does not belong any longer to the aleatory element, for it is viewed as explicable, even though those who see it as such could not explain it to save their lives. Few of us, indeed, intelligent as we think we are, could save our lives by explaining what the doctor is after when he inserts his fingers, "with eyes on the end of them," into an incision and feels around; all we know is that he gets results. And that is what the rank and file of mankind are coming to feel, unintelligently perhaps, but ever more consciously and unshakenly, about science. The Italian peasant knows nothing about the life-cycles of the parasites on his trees, nor yet of the chemicals with which Il Duce's experts make him spray them. He used to climb up barefoot to a mountain-shrine to pray his pests off; now he has no occasion to do that any more. What will he come to think about the matter? Presently, he will be saying that "everybody knows" you should spray your trees, as the Duce ordered. Here is another unmistakable bull's-eye for science by way of the Duce, though the peasant, never having heard the word "science," doubtless lays it all to the Duce, as once to the local saint.

The scientific way of dealing with the heretofore aleatory is thus supplanting the daimonistic, even within the much limited horizons of very simple people, who, when they have constantly to do with the products of chemistry, for instance, and learn some of the chemical vocabulary, cannot remain untouched by what is behind both the results and the terminology. Not all the drivers of motorcars understand what went on in the laboratories before the gas engine, the storage battery, and the rest of the assembled devices become available, or even what goes on under the car floor; but they all talk glibly of magnetos, carburetors, and short-circuiting, and most of them know enough about the working of the gears and valves to identify the seat of trouble and perhaps to patch things up temporarily. In any case, even the Filipino chauffeur knows that there is nothing spiritual about his machine, as he may have thought when he first saw it—as the Africans used to think about the gunlock, with its little oil-fed, clicking spirit. Repeated experience with the products of science, in short, diffuses an impression that spiritual agencies need not be consulted incontinently to explain everything which is, at first sight, inexplicable. In any case, that consultation is postponed until there is a conviction that the old, slug-shotted, spiritual guns are needed.

All this means that science is now dealing with a good part of the aleatory element, as it affects practical living, where religion once dealt with nearly all of it—indeed, science has cancelled it out or abolished it insofar as it has been reduced to predictability. While, to the scientist, science has at the same time opened prospects of the inexplicable never even sighted before, to the great majority of people its exploits have meant the removal of the everyday happenings of life from the range of chance into that of regularity. In times when life is jogging smoothly, serenely, even sleepily along on an even tenor, most people are "materialistic," practical-minded, callous to "spiritual values," followers of common sense based on experience; it is only at a time of inexplicable catastrophe that they flee back to their old gods and religion "revives." Fright makes them religious again, as it made them so in the first place. *Primus in orbe deos fecit timor.* The salient aspect of this whole matter is that, having become, when not in a panic-fright, less easy to scare out of their reliance upon science to deal with what they cannot understand, they are seeking refuge less and less frequently beside their altars. They do that when science seems to have fallen down. The gods are receding to an ever greater distance, more difficult and less necessary to span.

Even the "common man" in a civilized state does not rush to the churches when an epidemic appears; he summons the health officer, or joins in cursing his inefficiency. This calamity need not have been. If one accident follows close upon another in a certain industry, he does not pray about it but damns the managers for not installing safety devices, and tries to get them convicted of culpable carelessness. If a surgeon has case after case of wound infection, the conclusion is not that he is hoodooed but that he has operated with "dirty hands." What used to be called the "death-corner" in a Civil War hospital would now be called the unsterilized corner. And the offending doctor can no longer employ the shaman's alibi of some enemy's counter-magic to disguise with a spiritual camouflage his own now patent deficiencies.

Perhaps this reiteration of illustration from the range of the verifiable is uncalled for; it is designed to throw into relief and contrast the situation within the realm of the as yet imperfectly verifiable. If all the social doctors could be checked up by an examination of their hands, instruments, brains, information, and results, it would be a safer and a happier world to live in, and one might justly be censured for harping so unremittingly upon the one string of verifiability. In the present, at a time when experts in social science, the real and even the self-nominated, admit that they do not understand what is the matter with the economic system, or what to do about it, there seems to be nothing left, in default of science, but to retreat to original daimonistic principles and prayer-wheels; and already whirling petitions are ascending. Already, too, the parsons are smelling out national and international sins and zealots are condemning airplanes and an abandonment, during the summer, of "God's time," as furnishing a choleric Deity with occasion to vent His pent-up wrath. The medicine-man and his familiar thrive much better in legislative chambers than in the laboratory, for the dry, cold, calm, sterilized atmosphere of the latter is discouraging to the incantation that thrives in a muggy area of intellectual low pressure.

Nevertheless, and despite all the waste lands of chance not yet cleared of their tangled brambles by the blade of science, there is yet to be recorded any conflict between science and theology or any other of her challengers, where she has not eventually won. Further, the truth that victory has become a habit with her has not been concealed even from the lowly, while, with the informed, confidence in her has become virtually boundless. The belief is held by some that what science cannot explain is not otherwise explicable at all—indeed, that, given time and opportunity to investigate, she can explain anything and everything in the universe. If that were so, then there would eventually be no more aleatory element at all and so no more call for religion.

Consider the logic of this contention. One mystery after another has yielded to scientific siege; one miracle after another has been shown to be, where not an empty fancy, no departure from law and order but an exemplification of them. Portents and wonders, of old assigned immediately to the inmixture of the supernatural—the comet, the earthquake, the rain of blood, the thunderbolt, the plague, the genera and species of plants and animals, the species and varieties of *Homo* —all have been shown to be the normal products of natural processes. Must these victories stop anywhere short of the confines of all things? Is it not the foregone conclusion from the trend of experience that science can be looked to eventually to explain the universe? And if that is so, what becomes of the element of the inexplicable? Then, if religion is an adjustment representative of that element, what is to become, ultimately, of an adjustment to what does not exist, except that it too must cease to exist?

This is a logical inference. It is not drawn formally or consciously by many; yet an increasing number are unconsciously accepting the practical view that if science has explained so very much of the previously inexplicable, where all other agencies have fallen short, and is going right along imperturbably with the process, then science is the best bet for any man. They do not think very much about the density of mystery that underlies all things, so that life floats upon it as "the earth rests upon the waters"; they do not realize those new mysteries that open out from the frontier of every science; they merely sense the way things have been going and, as practical-minded realists, fall in with the trend. Religion as it used to be, with all its daimonism, its theologies, and its metaphysical dialectics—and with all its primitive emotionalism, eroticism, and hysteria—leaves him who is even slightly inoculated with the scientific spirit of this age at best cold and indifferent, at worst contemptuous or even intolerantly, militantly hostile. It is clear enough to him that religion, as that term has been known, is passing—and good riddance!

That may be so; but the passing of an institution as long-lived as the religion known to past millennia has never been a sudden decease or, indeed, a cessation, or annihilation, at all. It has been a transition into another phase. It has passed only as the chrysalis passes. Property in land used once to be communal; it is now largely private. Marriage was once prevailingly plural; it is now largely singular. The family was once matrilineal among many peoples; it is now almost universally patrilineal or bilineal. But never have property, marriage, or the family ceased to be. Religion was once identified with the ghost-cult; then with daimonology; then, among a number of the advanced peoples, with the worship of a few gods or even of a single Supreme Being. Each form was *the* religion of its day; but all were merely adjustments and readjustments to the same persisting life-condition, the aleatory element, under its varying phases.

This life-condition, to which religion is an adjustment, has been, we repeat, one that has persisted throughout man's time on earth. Science, in explaining part of its mysteries, has encountered another Hydra, for, one of its heads having been struck off, the stump has sprouted manyfold. No matter what logic may infer as to the eventual passing of the aleatory element, in actuality it is destined never to disappear. Its end is in the same place where parallel lines meet or where a variable reaches the limit which, as human things go, it can never touch. Logic has, so far as practical living goes, nothing to do with the matter. One of the warning signs for the student of human society is: "Beware of Logic!"

There are always the Unknown and the Inexplicable. Whether either is knowable or not is, perhaps, solely a matter of unverifiable opinion. Spencer divided phenomena into: (1) the Known; (2) the Unknown but Knowable; (3) the Unknown and Unknowable. Since it is manifestly a waste of time to bother with the third category, the sensible course is to concentrate effort where it has, or at least seems to have, some chance to count, namely, upon the As-Yet-Unknown Knowable. There is plenty of that available to keep men busy; and if it turns out that what has been thought Unknowable is really Knowable, then we can take that also into our list of agenda. To the scientifically-minded, the Unknowable covers phenomena to the investigation of which scientific methods are probably forever inapplicable, because there can be no verifiable evidence; and other methods are rejected as having yielded nothing better than religious and metaphysical fantasies. It is not alone the scientifically-minded, but also the practical-minded (who, often unconsciously, are shifting their allegiance to science) who are ignoring the religion of the past in taking whatever attitude they assume toward the inexplicable mysteries upon which every path of knowledge debouches.

Some scientists, it is true, manage to keep their science and their religion of the orthodox type in separate sound-proof compartments. They can pass out of one of these chambers, closing the door upon its contents and atmosphere, to enter, sterile of all infection, into the other. There is for them no intellectual carry-over from one to the other; no sense of inconsistency perturbs their serenity; they are like the youths who go from a Latin class to one in English, aware of nothing in the one that is relevant to anything in the other. There are also certain scientists who profess an ability comfortably and comfortingly to reconcile science and orthodoxy. They are the favorites and the noble examples to which the church, when it is on the defensive, triumphantly points. There is a certain disposition that derives the keenest and most spacious self-satisfaction in "confiscating science to the uses of theology."

It is not of these types of mankind that I am thinking when I speak of the new attitude that has arrived in the wake of science, toward the inexplicable, the aleatory element. I am thinking, rather, of that attitude which Huxley named agnostic. Agnosticism is the position of him who lays no claim to knowledge of that which is beyond the reach of scientific methods of verification. When the thus verifiable evidence gives out, he makes no further judgments but says merely: "I do not know." He cannot declare: "I know there is a future life"; or, "I know God's purpose." To him the dogmas of theology carry no authenticity whatever, no matter on whose authority they are issued. He is sure enough that the universe is a realm of law and order; that is a fact of concurrent observation; but he draws no shaky logical inferences as to Law "necessarily" implying a Law-Giver, or Order a supernal Police Commissioner. Because what he calls his intelligence perceives laws and orderliness in the universe, he does not leap to the conclusion that there must be a creative Mind at the bottom, or behind, or at the top of it all. He has no depth bombs for attacking such profundities; about them he knows nothing and says so; in fact, since he generally cherishes no hope of ever knowing, he contents himself with pecking humbly away at the discovery of the Unknown Knowable as the best thing, though perhaps not the "noblest," that he can see to do.

This is the attitude toward which a number of leaders in the intellectual life of the race have now for some time been tending; and they have a considerable and constantly increasing following. Their band may not include the most brilliant mental exhibitionists but it numbers its growing thousands of cool realists who at any rate regard what used to be called religion with augmenting indifference and in their practice reflect what Comte called, in contradistinction to religion and metaphysics, "positivism." In a very true sense this whole following, however little they reflect upon general principles and world-theories, are representative of the shift in attitude exemplified by scientific leaders.

There are those who hold that attitude to be "really," or "after all," a religious one. The expression, "religion of the scientist," is often encountered, and not in quotation marks. Are these terms, which to some of us sound very strange, descriptive or metaphorical? Is the agnostic attitude a "religious" one? If so, is it a new phase of an age-long attitude—a novel posture—or is it a new thing altogether, different from what went before in kind, not alone in degree, so that when it has been called "religious" there has been a shift of meaning in that term such that it can no longer be properly applied to the old, traditional, age-long attitude?

There is one absolutely crucial factor which religion has always had —indeed, which religion has always been—and that is *faith*. Let no one be misled by religious apologists who proclaim that religious faith and scientific conviction are one and the same article. Science goes as far as there is evidence susceptible of scientific handling. Intimations, intuitions, revelations, and all the rest of that sort of thing can never be so handled; they are matters of faith. Faith is highly emotional and subjective; you feel it or you do not; reason has nothing to do with it except to "justify" it after the act. It is a grand major premise, first accepted, then vindicated; a thesis to be proved. Limitless deductions are drawn from it as an infallible major premise or axiom. It is set up by some Authority, generally supernatural, which only the sacrilegious would wish to subject to criticism. It is a parody on candor to say: "Religion is just like science. You form a hypothesis and then test it in living. Believe, and then see how happy you are. *It works!*"

Most religious exhorters, prominent among them Bryan, never attained to the distinction between an hypothesis and a pure guess; Bryan thought that Darwin guessed. And who can tell a scientist how to "believe," as an act of mere will, when every cell in his brain cries out that belief in the absence of evidence is neither common sense nor scientific honesty? A scientist cannot believe simply because he wants to. He knows the deadly danger to truth that lurks in wishful thinking. He recognizes no "will to believe." The nub of the whole matter is that scientific confidence rests upon dispassionate induction from experience, while religious faith is a compound of emotional and supernatural elements not subject to test. To confuse the two is evidence only of the kind of mind the confuser has, of the sort of content it tolerates without ejection. Religious faith and scientific conviction are as far from one another as the East is from the West.

The attitude of the agnostic, rejecting "faith" as it does, is not religious unless one shifts the current connotation of that term. And I insist that it is as intellectually dishonest to juggle a connotation as to manipulate a pea under a shell, without warning the audience that a trick is being pulled off. A shell-game is a shell-game, no matter how noble the motives of the performer, no matter whether the peas are pearls of price and the shell a hemisphere of jasper.

This is not a mere dispute about terminology. Here is involved another instance of effort—effort very likely unconscious of its own aim —to "confiscate science to the uses of theology." It is very easy to deceive one's self in a matter concerning which he feels deeply; it is not hard to believe that self-deception has been the explanation of the above-mentioned confusion of religious faith and scientific conviction. This is a wholly venial affair, as compared with the performance of certain scientists of the present who, venturing far beyond their equipment, employ their prestige in some branch of science to cater to their itch for the spurious glory of having "reconciled" religion and science. One of them is described by a sharp-tongued critic as having "leaped sobbing into the baptismal tank." Their conduct tempts the observer to the wrath reserved for traitors to a worthy cause; but such beggarly strutters can do no lasting harm, even if their lust for notoriety and adulation from both sides somewhat prolongs a rear-guard action.

Science, because it has removed from the range of the inexplicable so many items that have engaged the attention of religion and evoked daimonistic "explanation," stands as the solvent of much religious structure: the creed, the dogma, the ritual of worship, and so on. Religion has regularly recognized science as its most formidable enemy and has sought to belittle and persecute it as such. It is for that reason that one who seeks to discover what has been happening to religion should not hesitate to incur the charge of prolixity or even an otherwise damnable iteration in enlarging upon the contrast between the principles and attitudes of the two. The divergence of science from daimonism is wide enough to seem almost a face-about, a wholly novel and previously unheard-of attitude toward the problems of living. It is not that at all. It is no more than a systematic development and extension of a realism that has been present from the outset.[10] It is a mere alteration of emphasis rather than a startling novelty. But that alteration and the training and organization of common sense consequent upon it have been so solvent of the older emphasis upon the "higher cause" that the contrast between the two emphases cannot be made too clear.

The agnostic scientist, having no religious faith, in the common acceptance of that term, has no creed and no theology. He can never, in honesty, profess any codified credo. He cannot even aver that he "believes in God," or "loves God," unless he allows himself to do so with reservations that amount to a rejection of that formula as understood by those who stated it originally and also by those who accept it for what it says. He cannot talk glibly about the supernatural as contrasted with the natural because he recognizes no such distinctions as those rising out of daimonism.

Miracle and magic being all one to him, he discredits the one along with the other. He sees no sense in prayer or praise or any other religious exercises, in their original sense. He recognizes no "Lord's Day," reads the Bible only as literature or as a repository of lofty ethical sentiment. He knows what a crime is but cannot recognize a sin, for that is a trespass against the injunction of a god, and he cannot be sure that gods, if there are any, have enjoined or tabooed anything, even

10. Essay on "Common Sense," above.

the Tree in the Garden. And so on. Wherein, then, lies the scientist's "religion"?

There is another aspect to this "religion of the scientist." The lives of the great agnostics—of Huxley, for instance—have been those of serious men. The insight to which they have attained through long acquaintance with and arduous study of Nature is not calculated to consort with the flippancy that was often the stock in trade of the "skeptic" of aforetime. The astronomer is in a much more favorable position to perceive how "the firmament showeth forth His handi-work" than is the chanter of emotional ravings over the evening-red or the twitterings of God's little feathered creatures. No man can study the stars even superficially without a sensation of awe; and if he gazes through the microscope into the nucleus of the egg, instead of through the telescope into space, he experiences that same thrill which, says Goethe, is man's best part. (*Das Schaudern ist der Menschheit bester Theil.*) Fabre, whom Darwin called "the incomparable observer," reports events and processes in insect life that simply stagger and stun the imagination.

The more one comes to know about what has gone on and is going on in the organic and inorganic world—and, indeed, in human society —the smaller do he himself and his knowledge seem in comparison with the illimitable unknown. The sensation he feels as he comes to realize the overwhelming complexity of what at first looks simple and is passed over with the blind indifference of familiarity—a blade of grass, for example—may not be reverence—certainly not, if "rever-ence" has its original meaning of "fear." If "love" means attachment as to a person, it is not love. It is certainly, however, wonder and awe; but these are impersonal. It is a feeling of helplessness leading to solemn resignation, rather than either fear, love, or any other more intimate and personal emotion having as its sequel the hope to please, propitiate, persuade to one's own advantage, alter in this or that sense.

This resignation to the necessity of self-adjustment to the eternal may be of the same species as submission to the will of God; but one should not let himself be misled by superficial similarity. The attitude, which is an essential of essentials, is not the same in the one case as in the other. What the scientific eye sees is a vast set of complicated life-conditions, inexorable, inspired by neither love nor hatred, desiring neither to reward nor to punish, knowing neither good nor bad accord-ing to men's ethical systems, intent upon nothing in the way of design, and not making for "righteousness" or "justice" in man's wavering sense of the terms. To these conditions, life, if it is to continue, is seen to be in constant need of adjustment. If it is "right" for life to go on, which is perhaps reasonably to be assumed from the instinct of self-preservation, then the adjustment-process can be figured, if one so desires, as "right" and even "righteous" in its expediency—though our moral preconceptions and judgments in the case are wholly irrelevant.

Of one thing the scientist, even of that type which is not playing to the galleries by questioning the "very foundations" of science—of physics, let us say—is serenely sure, namely, that he need not fear the entrance of whim and caprice into the cosmic process which he perceives. There is no use to pray for daily showers in the Sahara or that milk may substitute successfully for sulphuric acid in a wet cell. A spreading realization of that fact explains why we are now told that prayer is an attitude of soul toward the inevitable, though that piece of wisdom may be dressed out in more vague and pompous phraseology. Prayer used to be a petition to set aside the laws of Nature in the interest of somebody's pet, petty desires. It is now presented as resignation or as complaisant encouragement to the Omnipotent to go right ahead. "It's all right with us—in fact, just what we want most. Thus let it be! Amen!"

The scientist, I say, expects from Nature, on the basis of experience, not of yearning, a dependable regularity, so that if he has once found what her ways are, he can rely upon her not to change them, on a whim, overnight. Anticipated recurrence can be trusted to recur. The universe is regular, not helter-skelter. That is something; and something to count on. Here is scientific confidence in contradistinction, again, to that religious faith that holds natural law readily contravenable, even to the extent of sliding Mount Washington down into Connecticut if you only believe hard enough that you can do it—if you repeat often and ardently enough some formula on the order of "All good, good all, good good, good God, good gracious, livers, lights, bones!" or the Connecticut Yankee's: "Constantinopolitanischerdu-delsackspfeiffenmachersgesellschaft!"

Though not instinct with fear or love, the scientist's attitude is, at any rate, highly respectful, and results in an unquestioning obedience —not, again, an unreasoning obedience as to a person beloved, but a cheerful acquiescence in the Scheme of Things because of the demonstrated inexpediency of any other course. Miss Fuller once announced that she was reconciled with the Universe. Someone repeated the sentiment to Carlyle. "She'd better be!" growled the dyspeptic sage. As the scientist sees it, the universe is the constant and mankind the variable, whereas most religions, anthropocentric in practice if not in theory, have tried to make the cosmos over to suit the human heart's desire, by importuning its Ruler to ease up on them or to come down hard on their enemies. I do not know which attitude is more religious, but certainly one of them is more dignified than the other, as well as more promising of result.

Then what is the scientist's idea of what has been called "The Supreme Being"? He sees in the universe irresistible, inexorable, implacable Force operating along constant lines of Law and Order. He knows that his conceptions of regularity and orderliness come from observation of the Way Things Go, of the process to which he is now applying them. He sees that the logical upshot of the matter amounts to: "Things go as things go," and he does not feel so puffed up over the discovery that he cannot perceive the humor of it. He observes, however, that if he adjusts himself to this perhaps logically absurd principle, he gets along, and that if he ignores it, he suffers. That is at least something, and not a case of *e nihilo nihil*. It is on the order of "Two and two make four," a banality, but useful in crossing this vale of tears with fewer scarifications than if one were to charge in a noble frenzy through all the briar-patches. The scientist sees mankind within the range of Power operating in accord with Law. He marvels deeply. He respects utterly. He conducts himself with a resigned discretion, hoping to learn the Law, not change it, and to obey it to his temporal benefit.

Having no evidence of the kind he demands, he can infer no spirit-world, no immortality. He does not know ritual sin or penitence for it. He is free of the terror of transgression and of eternal punishment by an "angry God" which once tortured generations of men; so he is not afraid of death.[11] Therefore he takes no stock in theology, with its confessions, cleansings, remissions, ransom and redemption, damnation or salvation. Furthermore, he has no cult. He does not try to beg himself off from the consequences of his errors or to please, reconcile, or bribe the Power behind the Law. He knows it is of no use; that this Power is not tricked by "praise," not rejoiced at the smell of burnt offerings, which is no more than a little matter of chemistry amidst much bigger odors of combustion—say, from volcanoes. Shall an emotionless Force that manifests itself in cosmic processes be edified by its

11. See the following essay.

own manifestations? Shall it plume itself upon the good opinion of its creatures? Shall it faint over human protests?

In Kipling's "Children of the Zodiac," Leo belongs to the House of the Crab. In the end, he feels the grip of his Master on his throat.

Why have you come for me *now?*" [he asks.] "You were born under my care. How can I help coming for you?" said the Crab, wearily. Every human being whom the Crab killed had asked that same question. "But I was just beginning to know what my songs were doing," said Leo. "Perhaps that is why," said the Crab, and the grip tightened. . . . Leo was standing close to the restless, insatiable mouth. "I forgot," said he, simply. . . . "But I am a God too, and I am not afraid!" "What is that to me?" said the Crab.

The sharpness of the contrast between the religious and the scientific attitudes raises the question as to whether they are related at all. Should they be classified together under any rubric whatsoever? Have they any common stock from which both are derived? Have religion and science any common factors or any likenesses that persist out of their relation to the aleatory element, to which both are adjustments?

One of the main roots of science reaches down into religion and magic, for, within certain ranges of phenomena, religious and magical beliefs have enforced observation—say, of the stars—without which as a basis there could have been no science. Religion has been one way of adjusting to the ever-present aleatory element, science another; but the ways have widely diverged. The method of religion has been to deal with that element of the inexplicable by way of an interpolated spirit-environment; that of science to close with it directly, on the basis of actual experience or experiment, or not at all—not at all, when and where genuine evidence is not to be found. There is a vast difference here.

It should be realized that these two contrasting methods, the spiritual as against the objective or empirical, grew up side by side from the outset. Recourse to the spirits as agents has always taken place in direct proportion to the element of mystery or chance sensed in rising situations. In many everyday objects and relations, the primitive man saw no mystery to speak of or to get worried about—not nearly so much as an educated layman of today, to say nothing of a scientist, perceives. The savage faces with indifference, as matters of course because familiar, phenomena before which science stands with corrugated brow: the cycle, for instance, of impregnation, gestation, birth, and growth to maturity; or the development of property-tenure, marriage, and social organization in general. And where the mysterious is not forced upon him by circumstances engendering fear, man has been objective and empirical from the outset. Out of trial and failure he has learned, for instance, to use the lever, the roller, the inclined plane, without thinking much or at all about the spirits. Common wounds he has come to deal with directly and adequately where in the case of disease he has rushed to incantation because there was nothing to go by. Where he could accumulate objective experience he acted upon it directly, without any spiritual interpolation, by common sense.

The whole history of science has been a progressive enlargement of the empire of common sense. Science has progressively taken over, against the opposition of religion, area after area where spiritual agency was once regarded as unquestioned. At no time could the religious and scientific explanations of the hitherto unknown exist side by side without collision, for they were basically at odds, despite the shock-absorbing "interpretations" thrust between them. The result has always been the eventual retreat of the spiritual into regions where science, unable to find a footing in factual evidence, could not penetrate. The retreat has always led into some "mystery" or other, that is, into rarefied regions of the aleatory and inexplicable, and finally into the vasty reaches of the Unknowable.

To establish any relationship between two methods that are by their very nature mutually exclusive is difficult indeed. The two seem to have conflicted from the outset, the vital point of difference having been that common sense went straight to experience in this world for factual verification while the other rested upon the unverifiable major premise of a spirit-world—a world of difference. The fact that religion and magic were forced into workable harmony with actuality, or that men accidentally discovered, as in the case of massage and curative drugs, what turned out in practice, and after the act, to be a real adjustment, has no bearing at all upon the irreconcilability of the two methods. Nor does the fact that their purposes were similar argue them related; the thief and the honest citizen are both seeking a living.

In sum, the evident fact is that science and religion have always been two mutually uncongenial methods of dealing with a constant life-condition, the aleatory element; and that the fact that they are adjustments to the same eternal life-condition is about all the relationship, could it properly be so termed, which they show. Any "reconcilement" of the two will scarcely be accomplished by the artificial establishment of blood brotherhood between them.

A practical question of weighty import arises with the assumed replacement of a declining theology or religion by science, or by anything else which no longer recognizes the spirit-environment in its impact upon the life of mankind in society. How, indeed, can religion possibly decline when its survival-value to society, through these disciplinary and solacing functions, has been so outstanding? Are discipline and morale-inspiring peace of mind no longer needed? Have men ceased to be obstreperous and resentful of limitation set, by nature or by society, upon their individual liberty, or to need solace in a world no longer difficult to live in? If these two services of religion were to be withdrawn, what would happen to society? Are these functions which constituted the reason for religion's persistence capable of being discharged by science?

To the evolutionist it is unthinkable that adjustments so demonstrably indispensable to society through past millennia shall ever suffer selective elimination. So that when he sees before his eyes the loosening of the grip of religion on conduct, he looks about to find out what other instrument of morale and discipline may be developing to take its place. When he notes that an increasing number of human beings can no longer, by "casting their burdens on the Lord," attain serenity of mind, but must fume and rebel and curse and restlessly squirm under them, he sees that the less there is of comfort and content the greater will be the need of discipline. And where is that to come from?

Let us consider these matters in order, beginning with morale. The reason why religion has conferred peace of mind is because to its votaries it has amounted to insurance against calamity, or even assurance of the absence or non-existence of calamity, in this world and in the life to come. It has been like a glorified extension of old age and accident insurance. The next life has, indeed, come in for the bulk of attention; for when the proposition that happiness attends goodness failed to verify on earth, faith and courage were galvanized by the promise that it would all verify blissfully where it really mattered, namely, in eternity. The effect was to minimize the present existence into a mere stage between birth and death—a kind of qualifying or trial heat—and to look for the final and certain victory, the sure maturing of one's policy, in the next life. This certainty has enabled the faithful to endure a great deal cheerfully—indeed, to bear physical tortures gladly and eagerly; for, although this life, in and for itself, did not matter, nevertheless if one fought the good fight and kept the faith for a few fleeting years here, his title was clear to mansions in the skies. Such a conviction was no "opiate" at all; it was rather a pick-up, an excitant, a tonic.

There can be no question whatever as to the effect of faith both upon state of mind and upon conduct. The two are of course closely connected, but let us keep to the former, for the moment. Not only did the Jesuit missionaries to the Six Nations suffer atrocious tortures, such as having a red-hot axe-head bound between arm and body, but, having been carried to France and patched up, they came right back for more. Why not? They were winning a sure salvation. The more pain, the more certainty. Mortification of the flesh has been accomplished by generations of the pious with a kind of holy exultation, in the anticipation of eternal reward. Merit was eagerly stored up in Heaven, as a thrifty person might strain to deposit sum after sum, large and small, in a bank. Renunciation and self-discipline became the prosperity-policy of many human beings, if not for this life, then surely for the life to come. Such faith is not a phenomenon purely of the past; almost any mature person can recall cases out of his own observation. A widow, subsisting precariously upon her needlework, with no provision whatever for herself and her dependents, exhibits an unmoved and enviable serenity which amounts to an undeniable asset in her struggle, not only because it is favorable to her health and spirits, but also because it creates admiration, respect, liking, and a wish to assist.

No one can doubt that the faith of the Moslems or of Cromwell's Ironsides was energizing; if morale is, as Napoleon said, as three to one in comparison with any other item in military equipment, then its efficiency for the battle of life cannot be doubted. Every doctor of any acumen counts heavily upon his ability to inspire confidence and hope. But no other factor has begun to compete with religious faith in that respect. Often it has carried men sublimely to the very threshold of death, and beyond.

There is evidence enough, however, that this function of religion is on the decline, and not among the more sophisticated alone. The poor, for instance, used to comfort themselves with the promise of compensation to come. They were, if also meek, to inherit the earth; before them, at any rate, lay a comfortable refuge in Abraham's bosom, whereas Dives had at best no more than a camel's chance of squeezing through the needle's eye. In view of a rich compensation beyond the grave, many could cheerfully renounce prosperity in this shallow vestibule to eternal felicity—indeed, not a few deliberately refused to be prosperous in this life, thriftily driving a sharp bargain by vowing themselves to poverty here, in order to gain the richer compensation there. The rich were not to be envied. Let them wallow in their transient softness! Their lot was about as enviable as that of one who had sold himself to the Devil.

But now there came along, to many, a waxing doubt concerning the existence of heaven and hell, and of the future life, and especially concerning the compensation-feature of the latter. What, then, was the course suggested? Evidently an evening-up in this life. Hence the rising enthusiasm for a sharing and levelling system, here and now. It is significant that communists are seldom religious and not infrequently contemptuous of and hostile to religion as an "opiate" for the "people," the "proletariat," meaning the less fortunate. And it is not communism alone that furnishes evidence that faith in compensation in the hereafter—to which the reward of happiness accorded to goodness was adjourned as a result of disillusionment, despite scriptural assertions, as to its inevitability in this life—has waned almost away.

It cannot be maintained that science affords the peace of mind, contentment, and hope provided by faith. The agnostic who refuses to believe anything outside the range of natural law and so unverifiable by the methods of science cannot very well feel the emotion that underlies religion-engendered morale. What he accepts is the product of cold intellect, not of hot faith, and his mood is one not of uplift but of acquiescence and resignation, often melancholy, seldom joyful, to the inevitable and changeless. What hope he has is sober, not intoxicating, not inspiring in the sense that the prospect of eternal felicity was. He knows what he has to expect, namely, that if he can correctly gauge his conduct to the ways of life, he need not fear so much as to the outcome. No jealous deity is going to alter the set-up while he is in process of adjustment to it. Caprice is forever out of the picture. But to the miserable this is cold comfort.

Nevertheless, though confidence in dependable regularity may be only a mild reassurance, it is a steady one. One can be maturely calm, if not youthfully joyous. It also verifies, not in the problematical future life, but here and now—which is also something. One does not need to swallow the alibi—counter-magic, interference by Satan, original sin, and the rest—which has so often constituted the excuse for faith's frustrations. He cannot be put off by the stock religious reply to criticism: "Wouldst thou question the Will of God?" (Answer: "Oh, no!

Far from it! Please excuse me! I'll never do it again!") He can paddle his own canoe, confident that if he studies the course and strokes aright, he stands a chance of getting somewhere. He can be sure that in proportion to the knowledge he can acquire, he can fit his consequences to his purposes. He knows what he knows, and that he does not know everything; hence he accommodates his purposes and desires to his prospects of realizing them. He is clear upon the truth that things are neither thus-and-so, nor can be made thus-and-so, by yearning or praying that they should be according to the heart's desire. He does not expect any results from wishful or wistful thinking. He feels about his destiny: " 'T is little, but mine own."

He does not ignore the aleatory element. He knows he cannot control it. But he makes allowance for it until such time as what can be made explicable can be made explicable. His dish of herbs seems to him actual and sustaining as compared with the flesh of the stalled ox, to be enjoyed in some place and time undefined and problematical. This aleatory element, moreover, does not unduly frighten him; there is no grisly ghost-fear about it. It is there, like a precipice, and it is dangerous, also like a precipice. But it does not shift about, as a precipice does not, at the will of capricious, anthropomorphic beings. He knows it is there, and can often locate it closely; then he can keep away, as one avoids the proximity of chasms when it is dark. Or, to look at it from the positive side, he knows that there is a reservoir of power in the Unknown from which, with faithful study, one modicum after another can be drawn into use for promoting the welfare of mankind. The inexhaustibility of this reservoir is impressive. The very sight of the works of the Lord, runs the lofty "Prologue in Heaven," lends strength to the very angels of God, "even though they cannot fathom them," or "just because they cannot."

> *"Und alle deine hohen Werke*
> *Sind herrlich wie am erstem Tag."*

Such an attitude promotes a mood of quiet resignation. I wish to enlarge upon that topic a little. The lesson of all religion, too, when you get down to it, is resignation, and to something more profound than the will of the gods; for your gods cannot control the aleatory element. They are at best only another name for it. The Greeks put it, under the title of Fate, above the gods. Because the priesthood has promised so much more than they could perform, they have become, throughout history, the chief exponents of face-saving, and have taught the art, in its several branches of interpretation, misrepresentation, and plain falsehood, to the rest of us, who have been eager pupils. "Mr. Tyndall does not know what prayer is," was the sacerdotal squawk when that scientist proposed his simple statistical test of the kind of prayer that was being offered by the million at the instance of the clergy. Now we hear that prayer is an "attitude of soul"; and what is that attitude? It is resignation to getting no answer to the petition you are handing in; it is a bolstering of mind, or soul, against disappointment. That is well enough, and quite sound, only it is wholly defeatist as regards any efficacy of the prayer advocated by the priesthood, which asks for something definite and positive.

Because faith can move mountains, you ask for the impossible. "Ask, and ye shall receive." You do not get what you ask for. Why not? Because either you do not have faith enough, or because it is not the Deity's will. So then you merely perpetrate the absurdity of begging Him (or events) to have His (or their) own way, as He (or they) will have, in any case. If this is not fatalistic, what is? And yet fatalism has been charged up against those who would try to discover what immutable social law is, and conform to it without any palaver.

Resignation, as preached by religion, is negative and fatalistic. It has been enervating, too. That is why religion has been called the "opiate of the people." Relying on the promises of the clergy who, unable to deliver in this sublunary sphere, have shoved their engagements forward into the life beyond, the people have endured lethargically or patiently, awaiting compensation beyond the grave. They have resigned themselves to earthly misery because they were told such stories as that of Dives and Lazarus. Now if, say the Communistic Anti-God societies, you remove this opiate from their reach, then they will be alertly up and doing, and there will be an evening-up here and now. Otherwise Lazarus will merely endure under a false hope created by the priesthood under the thumb of the capitalistic Dives-plutocrat. There is not a little logic in that contention, however little historic sense and however much wily hypocrisy in the self-seeking junta that is its proponent—a gang which recognizes in it a rallying cry capable of evoking discontent and then energizing the aggrieved.

What could be more futile than to pray against the war now let loose upon the world? Throughout history men and women have feared and hated war. Agonized appeals to their deities have ascended in every age: "Spare us this calamity!" When the supplications have failed, the priesthood, like the Indian medicine-man, has been ready with face-saving devices. Knowing the mind of the gods, they have dug up some patent or obscure taboo whose unintentional violation explains the deafness of the deities to prayer and reveals war, simply and beautifully, as a punishment for sin. It then becomes something to repent about and to endure. That is to say, there is nothing to do but, with beaten breasts, to practise resignation to the inevitable. Only, the inevitable masquerades as the divine and inscrutable will instead of revealing itself as what it really is: the working of changeless law. After the war is over, with all its waste, misery, and cruelty, then is it seen in retrospect to have been due to causes quite mundane, and not to an arbitrary divine peevishness at all. But by that time the people have forgotten that they have been praying against war in vain, and are ready to be cajoled again.

Any right-minded man deplores much more heartily the disingenuous junta, who know exactly what they want and are about, than the generally self-deceived clergy. The priesthood, in these days, seems not so much hypocritical and timid as dumb. Self-seeking rascality and conscious charlatanry have not characterized even the primitive shaman. Black sheep have not dominated in the clerical flock, no matter how ovinely they have bleated, and still bleat.

Furthermore, religion, by emphasizing resignation, has taught rather unwittingly, a crucial lesson in living. Resignation is what every individual must come to, as he nears the end of the road; and it is what every race must practise as a condition of its very persistence. But the religious lesson is scarcely the same type of resignation that science teaches. Science interpolates a wide and widening zone of positive action in the light of recorded and verified experience between the incidence or anticipation of ill and a flight to the altar. It makes possible, so to speak, a deferment of resignation until it grows to be man-size —no longer childish and helpless. It teaches that God helps those who help themselves, an idea conspicuously absent from all systems of paternalism, whether the pater is God the Father or the State. It does not countenance running to either incontinently, with sobs and tears and petitions, until the stock of knowledge has run dry. It advocates that quaintly named Law or Parsimony, whereby, stingily reckoning up what outfit you have, you do not rush to fire off your "higher causes" when the lower will do the business, any more than you unlimber a field-gun when there are some sparrows to be eliminated.

If religion is going to stick by such expedients as seasons of prayer for the averting of threatening social calamities, it cannot hope for much of a future. This is perhaps sensed by members of the clergy who have turned, however feebly, from theology to what they think economics and sociology to be. Their offerings may constitute a sorry exhibition of emotional amateurishness, with tatters of clericalism still flutteringly attached; but that is perhaps the unlovely status of an emergent variation in the direction of better adjustment.

Evolution is the most reassuring theory in the world—not "optimistic," for optimism and pessimism are alike impertinent in science, and not at all personally comforting to the short-lived individual—for while it promises no present "progress," the process has always worked out into adjustment. Seeing no way out of the world's present maladjustments, we can nevertheless be certain that painful misfits will be eventually swept away. That may take place only when we are no longer here, although we are the ones who suffer the pains of the elimination-period; but an evolutionist must have his eyes upon the species, or society, through the ages rather than upon the individual, through his few years, and not be always counting his own petty, personal joys and sorrows. He must take toward the de-personalized aleatory element an enlarged and impersonal attitude that is not so unlike the unworldliness prescribed by certain religious systems. Then his own earthly fate, or even that of the generation he knows, does not matter so much—not because it is going to be compensated for, but because the self is too insignificant a thing to feature in the center of, or even visibly upon, the immense evolutionary canvas.

All this is very far from being a religion in the current sense, but it does contain elements making for a resigned peace of mind and a hopeful activity that is the antithesis of an enervating fatalism. It is religion and philosophy, not science, that are fatalistic. For one thing, science always has its practical applications; there is always something to do besides mooningly sitting down and wringing the hands. If one does not insist upon breaking his head over the relation of God to the universe, or agonizing over other religious and metaphysical issues which can never be either proved or disproved by any type of verification known in actual living (besides being of no practical significance, even if solved), he can get a good deal of mental and spiritual serenity out of his intellectual life. A group of people who have the scientific point of view have morale enough, though it is not of the type inspired by mahdis with their portrayals of the houris of Paradise.

For those who have "lost their religion" and yet cannot take the impersonal attitude here indicated, there is usually some utopian Cause available to enlist a fanatical interest and enthusiasm. Communism is one of the most prominent of these. Though Russian Communists in theory reject all religion, in practice they have their mummified hero to gaze upon; to many he is doubtless the kind of substitute fetish they can understand and accept in place of the "Little Father" of Tzarist days. The works of Marx and Lenin form now a kind of fetishistic Scripture, the object of an uncritical, quasi-religious Faith.

Withal, however, for that element of reassurance which religion gave to its devotees, insofar as it is lacking to modern life, there seems, for the present, to be no adequate substitute in sight. There is an element of truth in the assertion that the woes of our day are due to a weakening of faith, though the prediction that they will disappear with its revival along the good old lines needs heavy discount. People must again learn, we are told, to submit patiently to the will of God; then we can once more have "the Thirteenth, the Greatest of All Centuries," or the other samples of the fancied "Good Old Times." Of course all our woes are not due to loss of faith, nor, if they were, would it be of any practical consequence; for that faith cannot be restored, not even as old-fashioned furniture can be, by any art, or even "planning," known to man. Despite all the whittlings, scrapings, and veneerings to which it has been subjected, the old faith is hopelessly out of joint with the rest of the mores. It is simply increasingly incompetent to discharge its traditional morale-generating function. For the time, society lacks the services it once performed.

As regards, finally, the disciplinary function of religion, the case is not dissimilar. The terror of ghost-fear and of the fear of God is no longer what it was. As late as forty or fifty years ago, children of tender years were threatened with the wrath of the Deity for petty acts of mischief; and many a child was frightened into a state of mental and spiritual invalidism or abnormality by the violences of "evangelist" leaders of religious bacchanals. Farther back, even grown men could be scared to death as the result of having unwittingly overstepped some petty religious taboo. It is recalled with a kind of incredulity that to such a transgression the woes of the whole human race were once solemnly, devoutly, and nonsensically attributed. "In Adam's fall we sinned all."

This kind of dread was a tremendous influence upon conduct, completely eclipsing the fear of constituted human authority. No governmental organization could ever exercise over men the unintermittent, sleepless surveillance of the "All-seeing Eye." And in its day, because it could reduce turbulent, unruly human beings to coöperation within a peace-group, it possessed the highest survival-value for society. Within a comparatively short time, however, it has lost much of its terror, and the priest, its agent, has no longer his fetish-quality whereby he once represented God on earth and was intrusted with the distribution or cancellation of penalties resulting from the wrath or appeasement of the Almighty. Religion was once so powerful a sanction of morals that it was supposed to have created them, and is even now, we have seen, confused with morality. If it prescribed any line of conduct—kindliness or ferocity in men, chastity or prostitution for women—the one who so conducted himself or herself was regarded as moral or even holy. Only it was not realized that religion took whatever it sanctioned out of preëxisting, secularly approved mores. Thus it was held that religion makes marriage, which is about as true as that marriage makes religion, or that marriages are made in heaven.

A slang expression often conveys a shrewdly if unconsciously observed truth. What is meant nowadays by the expression to "put the fear of God" into somebody? Several years ago a bad boy drew a revolver upon a lady-teacher—at an unpropitious time, for it happened that the young woman's affianced, a sturdy, energetic, and deeply enamored youth, was just opening the door of the schoolroom. He manhandled the juvenile desperado in faultless style and, it was stated, "put the fear of God into him," as evidenced by his subsequent polite treatment of the pretty schoolmarm. Evidently the expression "fear of God" has become metaphorical, as slang expressions so often are, and means simply a lively fear of definite consequences of a wholly mundane order.

These are the only consequences that are much or widely feared nowadays. To some, an excommunication is doubtless a fearful thing; but since Luther and others risked it and, to judge by Protestant views as to their present status in the Beyond as well as by their earthly repute, came out whole, the threat of expulsion into outer darkness is much less formidable than aforetime. Cursing was once a doughty weapon; nowadays nobody "cares a curse" for it. Once, taking the name of the Lord in vain was a perilous exploit; nowadays, a genteel female may utter her "mein Gott!" her "mon Dieu," or her "damn" and be thought rather fetching. Literature designed for the cultured sprinkles a "Jesus!" (even a "Jumping Jesus!") or a "Christ!" upon every other page, paragraph, or line, together with a strong peppering of pruriency and obscenity that would once have been regarded as not only in bad taste and immoral but sacrilegious.

There is no question that this age and generation, as elsewhere demonstrated, is undisciplined. Unlicked cubs snap and snarl in many a family lair. Prophets of "freedom" hold all restraint up to scorn, chanting that self-control is ignoble and that the presence of desire warrants its instant satisfaction, at peril of physical and mental disaster under "inhibitions." That word "inhibition," or "repression," has been given a sinister meaning; then it has been taken to account causally for all forms not only of misdemeanor but also of a decency and reticence which themselves are thus brought, as "psychologically" abnormal, under suspicion. The result is unscrupulousness of conduct, especially in the matter of consideration for others, and an individualism that erodes away that respect for the rights of one's fellows which guarantees the integrity of the society as a coöperative peace-group. All is talk about rights and little or nothing is heard of duty. The slogan is "Enjoy!"—a kingly word! Extravagance has replaced thrift, for the latter requires forethought and self-denial. Nearly every woe of the present can be referred, directly or indirectly, to an irresponsible juvenility of attitude on the part of an undisciplined generation, under spoiled brats as leaders.

A certain unconscious realization of this state of things is shown by the rise and popularity of masterful rulers like Mussolini, Stalin, Hitler, Kemal Pasha. After a period of running wild, men generally react toward law and order under discipline. Along comes the Man on the Horse, with his theories about "a whiff of grapeshot" and other forms of realism, and an orgy-wearied nation hands power over to him, with a sigh of relief, and then half-deifies him because he re-presses them into orderliness. Limitation has always been as essential to society, and to individual happiness, too, as freedom. Men may get property, not by stealing, but within the lawful ways of acquiring it; that is to the advantage of all concerned except, for the moment, to the thief. Men must satisfy their "libido," not in emulation of the blue-bottle but along lines laid down in the sex code of civilization. And if they cannot restrain themselves, the automatic process of societal evolution will raise up an agency to do it for them. For discipline is the very life-principle of society.

We must not be deceived into taking the temporary aberrations of a decade or so to represent either an age-long trend or yet a definitive departure from a secular tendency. This present is a period of selection, of which 1914–18 were only the first phase. After the rapids are past, the stream returns from its plungings in all directions and up and down, to resume its interrupted course. Under any conditions and despite the status of religion, the present would be a chaotic and undisciplined time. Nevertheless, the criticisms of religion for not having prevented or stopped war and for its shortcomings in the post-war period, as well as the tearful exhortations to return to the faith and the confident prophecies that after we have done penance enough such a return will take place, all witness to the fact that something untoward is thought to have happened to religion.

For the present, and probably for the future, the discipline which religion used to impose is on the decline. The drill to which it has subjected mankind will have to be accomplished, if at all, by some substitute agency. Even if dictatorships have risen in these days to compensate for the enfeeblement of discipline, yet no form of governmental control is of the same quality as the religious; though adherence to a new political régime may have its emotional aspects, it does not lay hold upon the individual so intimately as did the religious fear that issued in conscience—the dread of that sleepless Eye scrutinizing at every instant of life, day and night, the very secrets of the heart.

"But," someone objects, "you have made no account of social approval or disapproval as disciplinary factors." No; because they are always present, in all types of society and in practically equal degree. The real question before us is as to the religious sanction of the code according to which social approval or disapproval is distributed, not as to the power of the mores themselves. Since religion has always sanctioned any and all forms of the mores, our question resolves itself into the probable specific effect of the removal of the religious sanction, while general social approval or disapproval remains always a kind of constant. Similarly one might regard temperature as a constant, to which no attention need be paid, while carrying on an experiment in isolation of some other factor in environment. This would by no means signify that temperature was unimportant.

There is no adequate substitute in sight for the discipline that religion gave, except for the most enlightened and mature of mind. There are many persons in every civilized nation who have no need of religion to restrain them within the bounds of rectitude set by the mores. They obey whatever decalogue there is, not because it was "given," amidst awful thunderings from some Sinai, but because it is expedient for society and all its decent members that there shall be no murdering, stealing, or other infringement of rights to life, property, and the rest of the human desirables. They have a conception of "right" conduct, that is, behavior proper to a member of society, to which they strive to approximate. At the same time that they are standing up for their individual rights within the code, they are mindful of those of others and of the society as a whole. They have self-respect to guide them both ways. There is no emotion to speak of in this attitude, any more than in that of the expert husbandman who knows what he must do to get a good crop and faithfully does it, or in that of a wise parent who, over and above his natural affections, puts his mind and life-experience into the service of his children. Both father and farmer make their errors and deplore them with various degrees of bitterness; but neither ever regrets having thrown into the task all there was in him.

Nor does the good citizen regret having lived as he has thought a member of society ought to live, even though he has attained no public acclaim for it and has seen others profit by his very conscientiousness as well as by their own lack of scruple. Not being vain, he can forego applause from others; being proud, he must have the approval of his own judgment—upon his motives if not upon his actual performance. There are a good many people in the world now who do not have to be scared into propriety of conduct. The number is probably increasing. There is gradually filtering into the mores the conviction that we all sink or swim together—and not only "we," as meaning the members of our own families or local communities or nations, but "we" as including the concourse of families, local groups, and even of nations. Few of us will ever become genuine "world-citizens," but we are nearer to that status than our ancestors were.

Some have suggested that we do not need discipline as we once did; that discipline is for the culturally as well as the temporally immature; that we "have learned our lesson." That is a highly optimistic contention, especially for an American to make; for among us discipline has been conspicuously frivolous as well as feeble, beginning with slackness in the family and winding up with an incredible inefficiency in the state. Education in particular is moving nowhere in particular by fits and starts, like a ship with a deposed captain, run by a soviet of paranoiac mates, vociferous pursers, chefs, and bath stewardesses, passenger representatives highly self-confident upon a negligible outfit, a squad of psychoanalysts, and a sprinkling of fundamentalist clergymen voyaging as missionaries. They have raised the skull and crossbones of "Unrestricted Liberty" and are evidently seeking to realize the conditions in the jungle when Hathi, the Elephant, went away for a while, deputing rule to the Gray Ape. "Brother, thy tail hangs down behind."

This is, it is to be hoped, a passing stage at which our successors will incredulously marvel. I repeat that the present era is chaotic, oscillating, transitional, a period of selection typical only of periods of selection, a stretch of troubled and muddy waters in which not a few quaint fishermen are eagerly angling with grotesque bait and hooking up the kind of gaping, goggle-eyed, hairy monstrosities one sees under the microscope.

Behind all the constructions of religion has always lurked the chief of all disciplinarians, Adversity. The old idea was that the gods sent it, whereas it was the original aleatory element and the deities were merely the form under which it was visualized and approached with a view to some sort of evasion or reconciliation. The world is at present being disciplined by Adversity in person. Its god-mask is pretty much torn and unconcealing. "Ah, me!" Zeus ponders, "how now do mortals find fault with the gods! For they say their woes are from us, whereas it is they themselves who, by reason of their own acts of blind infatuation, suffer calamities beyond measure." It seems that, after many centuries, the insight of Olympus is percolating into human minds. Naturally, as the idea dawns upon us that the fault is in us, the immediate tendency is to "pass the buck." But even the appearance of that device for creating an alibi is hopeful. The buck is found, sooner or later, in the possession of parties who have not been alert enough to hand it on. Then, however painfully, its meanderings can be retraced, as they could not when the eventual source was mystical. Science has been the efficient buck-tracer.

If the conviction gains power that adversity is due to maladjustments that can be avoided or rectified by knowledge, a disciplinary factor that has real power enters the field. It is no longer irrational terror in prospect of divine punishment for the breaking of some arbitrary taboo; it is more like a reward for success based upon self-conditioning for a contest, the conditioning being the discipline. Naturally the prevalence of this substitute for the older type of attitude is yet a long way off; but it has been quietly extending its range for a considerable time. In fact, it was present in certain ranges where daily and practical verification was enforced upon men, from the very outset.

Its spread to the field of social relationships has been rendered all but impossible by reason of the lack of verifiable knowledge about society and societal processes and of the presence of metaphysical speculation of various stripe. A genuine science of society, if that can be developed, would open a broad way for this sort of discipline.

For the present, it seems scarcely debatable that religion has been and is losing the two items of survival-value which have been before us: its power to confer peace of mind and its disciplinary function. I do not see that they can ever be restored—perhaps never even replaced. Efficient substitutes seem not to be present except, perhaps, in immature and unrecognized form, inaccessible as yet except to the relatively few. The many are still in good part under the old system of solace and of discipline. Perhaps when, and if, they outgrow it, the substitutes now satisfactory enough to the few will have evolved to meet the need of the many. What will happen in the meantime can be forecast only by a prophet or the son of a prophet. Meanwhile what can't be cured must be endured.

But one thing is sure: these two services of religion have been indispensable to society. The time will never come when morale and discipline cease to constitute survival-value to associated mankind. It is safe to say that they will continue to be discharged by some agency or other—one eventually rising responsive to the need—or society will break up. The latter alternative is scarcely to be harbored. If civilization were thus to lapse into savagery, doubtless religion would resume its old function with the vigor of aforetime, and the course of evolution would be virtually repeated, until, at length, some future millennium would front the situation we face today.

The aleatory element—the inexplicable—is always with us in practice if not in theory. There will always be a vast Unknown, whether or not it is Knowable. The Inexplicable must be adjusted to in some manner. Chance can never be ignored. But the spirit-environment and religion are falling out of confidence as factors through which adjustment can be, directly or indirectly, effectuated. How, then, is the aleatory element to be met?

That which has made the great turn in the evolutionary trend, if it is a turn, is science. It probably carries its own replacements for the factors long serviceable to society but now weakening. These substitutes have been indicated, perhaps, in the attitude covered by the metaphor, "the religion of the scientist." The agnostics—Huxley, the inventor of the term, for example—have not been lacking in either morale or self-discipline. Agnostics have been, in the main, good citizens, respected and honored in their generation and after, for character as well as for their professional exploits. They have not fallen into an "enervating fatalism." And they have died without fear and with serene dignity. A society composed of such a membership would be a community worth living in.

XII

THE FEAR OF DEATH.

Years ago, Metchnikoff[1] came out with the idea of "natural death." His contention was that certain organic beings seemed to approach their demise rather gratefully, much as a weary man his bed. They had arrived at a stage of decline where the next natural and apparently welcome step was their passing. Of animals it has been said: "How patiently they die!" There was attached to his presentation the solacing suggestion that something like the same contented resignation might eventually be attained by man. Then his fear of death would be no more. This relief would come by way of scientific knowledge, not of religion or metaphysics, which "are content with passive fatalism and silent resignation."

Here is at least an approach to one of those easy analogies to which men have been wont to accord evidential value. Though far superior to most analogical attempts to align the superorganic with the organic, it yet has an unmistakable kinship with them. There is no objection to comparing man as an organism with other organisms. That practice has demonstrated its usefulness. But when it comes to setting side by side the organic and the societal, any likenesses between them are bound to be misleading, for factors enter into the evolution and nature of society which render its phenomena at best only to a small degree comparable with the organic. Analogy has never proved anything since the world began, and insofar as Metchnikoff is analogical he is under suspicion. His subtitle is against him: "Studies in Optimistic Philosophy."

The fear of death that man harbors was put into him not by nature but by religion, a purely societal development; to be more exact, it was put into certain human groups by a certain kind of religion.

The fear of death is not "plain fear," such as impels the animal to flee physical peril or the man to dread burning at the stake. It is not a form or corollary of the instinct of self-preservation, but a terror before a creation of the imagination. It is, in a word, ghost-fear: fear of the supernatural. "For in that sleep of death what dreams may come." To

1. *The Nature of Man* (1903).

get to the bottom of it, it is fear of what may come after death, not death itself. It was left to mankind, who have often acted as if they found life not miserable enough as it is, to invest a natural event with a set of phantasmal horrors. The obverse of that idea has been another phantasm: the sacredness of human life.

This fear of death is one of the gifts of religion; nevertheless, it seems not to have been conferred by most religions, least of all the primitive. There is plenty of evidence that primitive peoples have not feared death at all, nor yet esteemed human life as sacred. They have sought death when tired of life, or irritated by some petty disappointment, or for revenge on others—for many a reason that strikes us as highly frivolous. Oriental ideas and practice touching death differ markedly from our own.

A popular novelist[2] makes a Japanese Prince remark that "we do not dress Death in black clothes or fly from his outstretched hand. We fear him no more than we do the night. It is a thing that comes—a thing that must be."

Primitives do not fear death but the dead. They are not concerned much about their own fate after death but rather with what the ghosts of the dead, or the spirits that evolve out of them, may do to them in this life. Here is a type of anxiety quite different from that as to what may happen "when we have shuffled off this mortal coil." Evidently the distinction hinges upon diverse conceptions about the next life. If it is viewed as a mere continuation of earthly life, under perhaps more fortunate circumstances for all in some happy hunting-ground, and if it is so unshakenly thus conceived that action on belief is a matter of course, there can be no horror about it.

A real fear is imported by the theory of damnation through all eternity, with attendant notions about endless roasting over undying fires or about similar grisly tortures in retribution for sin.

There is some little adumbration of the heaven-hell phantasm in a number of religions; but the "hell of it" is generally pretty mild and the imposition of dire penalties much restricted. Primitive ingenuity in torture seems to have expended itself on the living subject, where some "higher" religions have taken their sadism out on the dead. Where there is any idea of future reward and punishment, it is the "good" who are thought to have a future life of a more desirable order than the "bad." In a number of cases, those who have been a public menace simply have no future life at all, being forthwith annihilated

2. Oppenheim, E. P., *The Illustrious Prince*, p. 75.

in the matter of soul by some special disposition of their dead bodies. Moreover, the conceptions of good and bad, as held by many peoples, cannot be brought into line with our own except through tortuous rationalization. "Virtue" was once simply "manliness," and is usually synonymous with "courage," the acme of manly virtues. A young fellow is a good chap if he withstands the ordeal of initiation with fortitude; a woman is what she ought to be if she is a capable worker and fecund. A king is bad if he is stingy, whereas a bloody tyrant may be altogether royalty as it should be. Goodness and badness, in short, are such by the local code and have nothing to do with faith but only with works.

It has been seen while considering religion that the entrance of this faith-element leads to great confusion and to strenuous efforts to reconcile it with the works-element. It is the same confusion that begins to plague men when they try to assess guilt by reckoning in purposes and intents instead of sticking to plain consequences. The primitives are not subject to that particular kind of muddlement.

The Western world alone, together with converts to its religious dogmas, has been pretty thoroughly infected by the heaven-hell idea, which has invested death with terrors elsewhere no more than adumbrated in rare variations whereby certain sinners, such as Prometheus, Ixion, and Tantalus, not at all sinful in our sight, have been condemned to eternal torture, in a kind of special hell, for *lèse-divinité*. But in the doctrine enforced upon the West by Christianity this variation was nursed up into the status of an adjustment (or of a long-persisting maladjustment) that has determined the thought of generations, to remain stubbornly in the mental outfit even of those who have rejected the dogma.

It has seemed to me sometimes that the less religious a member of a Christian nation is, the less he fears death—indeed, the less he dwells on his own dissolution at all. He has not been exposed to the traditional line of threats levelled at the sinner, the inveterate *memento mori* of the priesthood. He can look even upon the *Dies Irae* with composure and with admiration for its stateliness without being frightened, as Gretchen was, in *Faust,* by the prospect of Judgment Day: *"Quid sum miser tunc dicturus? Cum vix justus sit securus."* The agnostic simply does not know about such matters. Neither do the pious. Only he is honest enough to say so. Huxley's epitaph,[3] composed by his wife, about covers the case:

3. Huxley, L., *Life and Letters of T. H. Huxley,* II, 426.

"Be not afraid, ye waiting hearts that weep;
For still He giveth His belovèd sleep,
And if an endless sleep He wills, so best."

As to the matter of retribution and post-mortem punishment, the aforesaid fadeaway has been in evidence for some time, naturally by way of interpretation and face-saving. The dogma involved does not really mean what it says, and theologues are indulgently sorry for their predecessors who thought it did. Six twenty-four-hour days for Creation? Of course not! We know better. Didn't Caesar's "day for deliberation" lengthen into weeks? Does the day that every dog has mean some August fourth? And how about things that happened in "Luther's day"? Is not a day with the Lord a thousand years and vice versa?

Many a dogma is dead or moribund; but it has died hard. Its protean quality endows it with more lives than any cat. Assailants, thinking they have some dogma cornered, relax vigilance a little; and when they attend again, they find it in some other corner, full of vigor and vim.

Furthermore, long-lived dogmas leave behind them, in their evacuation of position, residues that cause recurrent infection. People get into the habit of acting on some doctrine and go on so acting long after they have rationally rejected it. Those who acquired a fear of death out of what they have discarded go on fearing death by a certain inertia or momentum. The habit of dread lasts on when no man pursues. Reasoning about that fear does not help much, for it is in what is called "second nature," namely, in the traditional code. And, of course, there is no actual disproof of a genuine doctrine, any more than there is proof. No dogma can be tested as a perpetual-motion machine can. It is always open to the orthodox to demand a disproof that cannot be furnished, any more than they themselves can produce proof. Ask them for it, and what do you get? A retort that the doctrine is "above" all such evidence as they themselves demand in disproof.

Dogmas have nine or more lives not only among the unreflective and uncritical but also among those who have painfully emancipated themselves from a thralldom imposed by early training. I knew a man once who said that death meant no more to him than going upstairs to bed at night; but he added that he hoped he would not lose his grip before he died, and make a fool of himself. What was in his mind was a fear of such mental weakening, under age or sickness, that he might return to discarded phantasms and provide an example for his edified detractors to crow over. There have been so many pious lies repeated with holy gusto about the deathbed repentances and agonized terrors of the Voltaires and other dogma challengers. The agnostic wants to be judged by what he has believed, or not believed, in the days of his strength. He hopes to rival the many "unbelievers" who have faced death with full mental clarity and free from a trace of such fear as religion has imported. "I am not in the least afraid to die," said Charles Darwin, the morning of the day which, as he knew with unimpaired senses, was to be his last.

Doctrinal propaganda has eventually succeeded in making the process of dying into something to be feared, entirely apart from the post-mortem retribution. This venture into fiction can be checked up upon. We know that the alleged penitential deathbed writhings of certain great doubters are pure fabrications disgraceful to nobody but their authors. We know also that the edifying deaths of the faithful occur mainly in pious fiction wept out by such emotionalists as Dickens and Stowe, not to mention the spawners of the Sabbath-school abomination. I am not forgetting the heroic deaths of the martyrs who passed away at the stake or on the rack amidst visions of eternal bliss; that is why I use the adverb "mainly." I am thinking of all such reports of sinful and saintly departures as contrasted with what the doctors have to say about the phenomenon of death. They assure us, on the evidence of much experience, that the end usually comes under coma, so that there are comparatively few "deathbed scenes" of any sort which are not staged by the supporting cast at the bedside rather than by the chief actor. That one piece of verified fact is rather discouraging to the religious propagandist.

For all these devices and attachments calculated to enhance doctrinal comforts and terrors have just the degree of truthfulness to be expected in propaganda. I do not need to review them. Sermons have been adrip with them and they have been prodigally warbled in gospel hymns.

It has sometimes been alleged that, whether or not the sinners are scared into godliness by the fear of hell-fire or are allured to righteousness by the hope of salvation through repentance, at any rate the saints are relieved by the prospect of eternal bliss from fear of death, so as actually to welcome it as a necessary incident prior to a glorious resurrection. Experience does not always sustain this glowing motif of religious fiction. The most orthodox seem to harbor some little reluctance to act upon their professions. Where the savage reveals no lack whatsoever of assurance, but makes his preparations for passing on with the casual demeanor of one purchasing a ticket to a neighboring town, the most fervent in the faith, who sing loudly about how every passing day brings them happily nearer their long home, seem, when the prospect of departure hence really discloses its proximity, to want to put it off. They want to go, but not yet awhile. Eternal life, not across the river but on this bank, would seem to be the eminently desirable future.

Such inconsistency is not to be censured. It is cited merely as evidence bearing upon the attitude of the pious, when it comes to the pinch, toward dissolution. They seem to be in about the same box as the rest of mankind. They too cast "a last, long, lingering look behind," not resigning" this pleasing, anxious being" without a qualm, as they certainly might be expected to do if they were as sure of what they sing about as they give the rest of us to understand. I cannot believe that a faith which has deliberately made death fearful can face about and make it desirable. Having put into death a sting that it had not before, it then asks triumphantly where the sting is; and having enlarged upon the corruption of the body, in terms now rejected by refined taste, it asks of the grave a rhetorical question: "Where is thy victory?"

The facts witness that Western religion has instilled a general and gratuitous fear of death, whether or not it has been able, with the other hand, to administer to the chosen an antidote to that repulsion. In any case, the fear-attitude has been infused into the mores, so that almost everyone has the infection, whether or not he has ever heard of the antidote.

A notable sequel, or inference, from the fear of death is the sacredness of life. I do not recall any such conviction in the minds of those who take death nonchalantly. The idea of life's sacredness is now embroidered with a heterogeneous fringe of sentiment which represents the fraying out of the old religious dogma. It is in the mores and is rationalized upon by many persons who are not religious at all as "humanitarian," as part of the "dignity of life," and so on. It has blunted the edge of selection.[4] I do not say that this is either desirable or undesirable, but merely that it is true. Other doctrines, less sharply formulated, have taken the place of the one about sacredness.

4. Keller, A. G., *Societal Evolution*, 111 ff.

Nor is the contemporary sentiment, or sentimentality, nor was the older attitude, due primarily to doctrine; to believe that it is, or was, is to endow doctrine with too much origination; for doctrines are not original but derived, and no formulations can lay hold of people unless the mores are ready for them. A doctrine summarizes, gives shape to, and sanctions—gives a show of logic and supernatural authority to— what is already present in inchoate form. "Humanitarianism" derives out of the ancient necessity of social solidarity, which, like patriotism, is called for in any society as a condition of its persistence. The sacredness of life is an extension on the right to life, which must be guaranteed by any society to its members, to widen later on, with the extension of the peace-group, into a "natural right" conceded in theory to all mankind.[5]

The basic facts about rights, including the right to life, bared of all interpretation, are these:

(1) A human society is a group of human beings coöperating in self-maintenance and self-perpetuation.

(2) The coöperation essential to living together demands internal peace and order; otherwise the society collapses in the inter-society conflict.

(3) These essentials are secured by the automatic distribution of rights —to life, property, spouse, and so on.

But the operation of impersonal cause is a conception too demanding for the untrained mind, which can comprehend agency only. Enter now the gods, guarantors of the mores, to personalize the impersonal. Then the infringement of any of these rights becomes more than a crime against the group, namely, a sin against the deities. Rights are now sanctioned by taboos—by "Thus saith the Lord: thou shalt not"— that call for no abstract thought but only for unreasoning obedience. Along with the gods, sacredness has arrived; it is sacrilege to kill or to steal. Thus life is sacred, and property, and all the rest of the untouchables. There is now present a doctrine, a generalization easy to carry in the head, which is thus relieved of reflection—one that summarizes a set of automatically developed practices, conferring on them a logic and coherence that they do not have but which, like all classification and organization, enable them to be handled.

For a long time the doctrine confines itself pretty closely to the ordering of actual relationships, such as those of kin. That is what it does in the Old Testament. The lives of the in-group comrades alone are "sacred." Eventually, however, it cuts loose from its practical moor-

5. *Ibid.*, 133 ff.; Sumner and Keller, *The Science of Society*, §§ 168 ff.

ings and begins to develop from within itself by a dialectical process. By deduction it ascends into regions of rarefaction. It develops logical necessities. Returning from such flights, and while still possessed of its original, expedient powers, its prescriptions and proscriptions throw actual human relationships into disharmony with realities, thus promoting maladjustment where it once enforced adjustment. I need instance only such religious divagations as the sanctification of poverty or celibacy, or the elaboration of doctrine into such absurdities as infant damnation, original sin, and the long line of acrimonious or even bloody disputes over purely imaginary issues.

Accept once the doctrine about heaven and hell, with attendant corollaries about damnation and salvation, and you are caught at once in a logical net and must agree, let us say, that prudential restraint is worse even than murder—for you are preventing those who are "knocking at the gates of life" from being born, sinning, repenting, being redeemed, and entering into blessedness. You are not merely taking away mortal life; you are refusing eternal life. Of course, human beings in general have never lived up to all these doctrinal refinements; I am merely citing instances to demonstrate the correlation between religious doctrine and the conception of the sacredness of life. Having arrived, in theory, at the doctrine, as peoples of a different religious development have not, we then apply it as a kind of yardstick to the assessment of war, crime, and other issues that need to be adjudged variously upon a variety of criteria of actual social expediency. For they are not simple issues capable of being settled by the application of any single formula, however practical, much less on the basis of a noble sentiment fathered by a doctrine developed under faith or even "free meditation." That life is sacred, given by God and to be taken back only by Him, is, no matter how holy a thought, nothing but an "argument" against war, or suicide, or capital punishment—not at all the kind of realistic consideration that can issue in expedient action.

All this may seem rather remote from the main topic before us: the fear of death. It is not. It is a set of short inferences from the doctrine that made death fearful. What made death terrible made life sacred. Without all the theological complex about the supernatural and its relation to mundane affairs characteristic of Occidental religion, it is likely enough that our major premises as regards death and life would be quite other than they are. And I venture to believe that we are in considerable degree maladjusted to reality because of the doctrine about life and death which we follow, even afar off. I think we are better adjusted to our life-conditions for having abandoned ancestor-worship and the other practices of an overtraditionalism while they are still handicapping the Orient; but I do not share the view that our religious doctrines and practices have been the dominant factor in our cultural successes, however much they have been refined. One might take more stock in the assertion that we owe our vaunted superiorities to our religion if he had ever observed that we had lived by that religion. There is point in the skeptic's reply to the question: "You say Christianity has failed?" "No, I didn't say that. How could I, when it has never been tried?"

Are we better off because of our fear of death? Or by reason of our conviction that life is sacred? I doubt it much. Our renunciation of the latter, on occasion, seems to indicate that it may get in our way. At a pinch, as in self-defense, or even for the promotion of pleasure or excitement, we promptly forget that life is sacred, invoking that quality chiefly on emotional grounds or as a grand gesture. We fail repeatedly to practise as we preach or are preached to. We are always interpreting our axiom away in the special case, while proclaiming it as an universal proposition. This is natural, human, and even sensible; but it means that we are always under the necessity of dodging grand principles when they do not fit realities. And we are always applauding those who have not, or do not exhibit, the fear of death, nor yet confine their earthly doings to the increase of their merit-pile or treasure in heaven.

In short, it looks as if we should have been better off if theologians had never worked out their *memento mori* at all. If these various phantasms gratuitously set up by them have in the past scared people into righteousness, they have been no more than passing extemporizations. With their inevitable loss of effectiveness, the West has the original problem of societal discipline still to meet. The priestly apparatus was worked up far aloft in a stratosphere and never got down to earth without deforming modifications. Such improvisations have worked, it is true, after a fashion. They were better than none, which is their justification—and nobody who knows what he is talking about ever blamed evolution for developing only comparatives; but they were far from being the last word or revelation of perfection that they were claimed to be.

For one, I am evolutionist enough to believe that any institution (an interest plus a structure) that has lasted as long as the Western Church, has possessed survival-value to the society that housed it. I have no doubt whatever that it was an inevitable development, under the circumstances. I do not question the sincerity of the priesthood as a class, no matter if it has included charlatans, rascals, and ruffians. Even one black sheep among twelve—a rather high proportion—did not corrupt the apostolic band. I know what the fear of hell and the hope of heaven have done for morale and discipline. But I am not at all sure that the Occidental variation adds up in these particulars to an algebraic sum of effectiveness that confers on it a clear superiority over all its competitors.

Here is a moral judgment: There is something singularly ignoble and offensive, to my taste at least, about the cultivation of a bugaboo, complete with trappings such as Dante and Milton picture at length, that has been used both by the self-righteous emotionalists and the coldhearted self-righteous not only to frighten adults into hysteria but also to change the normal thoughtlessness and innocent high spirits of childhood into anxiety and terror of damnation or into a premature and altogether damnable smugness. It looks sometimes as if, finding life not hard enough, men have invented ways of making it harder for themselves as well, though not so enthusiastically, as for others. Always the gods have delighted in seeing men unhappy. Always men have furtively concealed their happiness, lest divine envy become aware of it and take them down a peg or two. The Puritan Sabbath is a mild example of this gratuitous but holy discomfort.

I know that all this superstition is falling out of fashion, and I am glad of it. We are now invited to contemplate a loving Father and not a jealous God. Fulsome praise has long been hymned to such a Father, with much the same placating flattery and obsequiousness as to an Ivan the Terrible—this being a kind of hold-over from anthropomorphism and but another reaction to fear. I have myself heard those who proclaimed themselves redeemed, and even "sinless," praising the Deity and reassuring Him as to their adoring love, in terms that could not but disgust any self-respecting God—or man—to his marrow.

At the bottom of all this kind of thing lies the fear of death and the beyond. An inevitable development, with an undoubted survival-value to society? Certainly. But its long persistence, in survival-form, is deplorable. It is difficult, though necessary, to maintain while contemplating it a dispassion that future generations will have no difficulty in exercising.

XIII

SEX DIFFERENCES.

THIS TOPIC was treated, to the extent of the evidence available to me fifteen years ago, in *The Science of Society*. I have been somewhat astonished at the emotional heat occasioned, even in some of the young men attending my classes, by the conclusions arrived at in that book. First of all came a schoolmarm rebuke from a didactic lady-reviewer who was especially revolted by the etymology of "hysteria" and counselled me to make the acquaintance of Sumner's *Folkways*. Thereafter there began, and still continues, a recurrent gush of "argument" on the part of predisposed persons who had taken umbrage at my "unfairness" to woman. The argufiers harped on one string: "Give woman her chance, and you will see"; and I have found it quite useless to explain that prophecy is not evidence, that evidence can never be presented in the future tense, and that where evidence is lacking the attitude of science is agnostic. Any time that any of the objectors could have cited evidence in the nature of verified facts of experience, I have been ready to welcome it; but argumentative, "logical" prophecy, in damnable iteration, is about all they have had to offer, except that now and then one of them has hopefully snatched out of history something or other that has not sustained critical examination. Therefore I stick by the aforesaid conclusions. I hope I may be excused for any personal matter presented above or below, in this resumption of the topic.

I do not propose to defend those conclusions here or to challenge misrepresentation, willful or not, of them—for instance, that they include allegations of superiority or inferiority of one sex to the other— but I shall state them briefly, as a take-off for what is to follow.

(1) Sex difference of an innate, biological order is the most basic and pronounced of human differences.

(2) That difference, in its profundity and immutability, is alone capable of accounting for, as adjustments to it, the essential and durable diversity in the sex mores.

(3) Environmental conditions, natural or social, including "opportunity," have played, at best, a relatively slight modifying rôle in the evolution of the sex mores.

(4) It is not to be expected, forecasting on the principle of "anticipated recurrence" as contrasted with prophesying on the basis of wishful thinking, that any catastrophic changes impend within foreseeable time. That this or that will or will not happen can be neither proved nor disproved within the societal range; but higher or lower degrees of probability can be scientifically calculated.

It is to be understood that the above conclusions rest largely upon general principles of societal evolution derived from the study of the mores in general, not the sex mores alone. The evolution of the latter is not detachable, as a special case, from that of the rest. I do not rehearse here the general case, as set forth in *Societal Evolution* and *The Science of Society*.

The inconclusiveness of the issue as to sex differences is due to the fact that so little is as yet known about some of them, not only by the embattled partisan but also by the dispassionate truth-seeker. Sex differences may be roughly classified as (1) physical, (2) neural and mental, (3) social. There is little dispute that is not merely captious about the first and third categories. As regards the third, far from being disputed, neglected, or needing illustration, social sexwise discrimination has been incessantly complained and raged about as an obvious, hoary abuse—attributable to agency, of course (Man, the Oppressor), and not to cause. It is not the existence of such discrimination that exercises the partisan; the quarrel is over how it came to be, who is to blame, and how it can be annulled. No one of sense denies the physical sex differences either, but only those who grasp wildly at controversial straws.

No serious critic, then, alleges the equality of the sexes as respects physique or social status, the latter being correctly envisaged as a complex of rights conferred and duties imposed by society. The debatable ground lies between the first and third of the above categories: the neural and mental differences; and heated disagreement is fostered owing to the lack of a body of laboratory evidence. As regards the purely physical disparities, there is a visible, measurable, experiential contrast between the sexes, so that, for instance, a collection of skulls of unknown origin can be classified as male and female crania; but, so far as I know, not even the most skilled anatomist can pronounce upon a stray nerve-fiber or a random slice of brain-substance, that it is of male or female provenance. The only criterion of nerve or brain quality resides, not in what the nerves or brain are, but in how they

act—not in material structure but in function. This introduces at once
a chance for conflicting opinion not present where evidence is so clear
as to leave no room for anything better than a quibble.

During the years when *The Science of Society* was being put together, I made every effort I could to find out what was known about
the neural and mental sex differences by men of experience with them.
I found in books like Dr. Eugen Kahn's *Psychopathic Personalities*
that such differences were mentioned casually, as matters of course;
and I was informed that medical literature was full of such instances,
though I was warned no layman would be competent, even if he were
to take on the colossal task of digging them out, really to understand
them. An appeal to an old friend, the late Dr. Frederick Tilney, yielded
nothing much better than the usual "net impression" of the veteran
practitioner: that differences in "man and woman nature" could be
counted on as constants in dealing with neural and mental states. One
doctor, to whom I referred a spacious pronouncement about sex
identity in respect to nervous reaction, commented drily: "Any married
man knows better."

This is all that I have been able to find out about what, in the experience of medical scientists and practitioners, male and female
nerves and, to some extent, brains, are and do. When, now, we come
specifically to the case of mentality, brain-quality, intellect, we have
no evidence at all except the historical, and must perforce judge upon
the record of experience as to what the male and female minds have
to show in the way of actual accomplishment. I conceive that nobody
makes bold to deny the historic facts, but that even the partisan confines himself to deploring the conditions which, as he thinks, rendered
them what they were. That is all right enough, provided he does not
stop at the deploring stage but goes on to a serious study of those conditions. It is not altogether futile to infer what might have been, had
not conditions been what they were, for if those conditions can be
removed a more acceptable result may be hoped for in some future
conjuncture. But the possibility of such removal is a crucial issue whose
determination is never at the hand of mere enthusiasm or yearning.

The historical record is clear enough for him who runs to read. The
names on its roster are almost all masculine. Men have attained eminence in all the various divisions and subdivisions of social life: economic, political, military, religious, artistic, scientific. Exploits demanding power and originality of mind, as well as strength of body, are,
with vanishing exceptions, accredited to his sex. His has been the

variation-producing, inventive, organizing capacity. Such is the record of the past, both distant and recent; and the present reveals no essential departure from it. Judged by what mentalities of man and woman have to show in that record, there is between them no identity or parity of mental quality. In the spectacular, eminence-conferring activities of social life, man has had an age-long recognition and woman next to none.

One qualification is to be attached to this summary: that the historic record does not say much of anything about eminence within the domestic range: marriage and the family. If it did, woman's record there, if emblazoned, would doubtless be at least as significant as man's.

There can be no question of altering innate sex qualities any more than sex itself; they are, indeed, constituents of sex. But limiting conditions change, and certain minor ones can be eliminated or altered, with the result of removing handicaps to those hitherto disadvantaged, whether by sex, age, or any other disqualification.

What has caused some of woman's handicaps no longer to "count" has been the advance of civilization, which may be figured as having built, above the raw crudities of nature, a smoothed platform upon which those disadvantaged under natural conditions get a more nearly even chance with the rest. Not the "weaker sex" alone, but the old, the young, the victims of accident—the weaker in general—profit by the development of civilization. Woman's physical handicaps, real enough under nature, do not "count" for so much where there are skilled gynaecologists and obstetricians, devoted nursing, a developed governmental structure for peace-keeping, and the rest of the protective apparatus of an advanced culture which accords her a chance she did not have under ruder conditions.

One handicap, based squarely on illusion, of which woman has been relieved relatively recently, is the stigma of "uncleanness" which reputed her a peril, especially to man, during parturition and menstruation. This notion, whatever its origin, was accepted as in the order of things, by the women as by the men, as a life-condition. It gradually faded out into a general misprision of woman on more general grounds, an attitude preserved in legends of antiquity in the stories of Eve and Pandora. All this is now practically gone, with science launching the *coup de grâce*. There is no question that woman's status has been thereby relieved of a fantastic incubus. But there is also no question that such relief came about very slowly and unpremeditatedly, not by any agitation on the part of horrified smellers out of grievances.

It is very necessary to note, before leaping to the conclusion that conditions can be changed overnight by realizing some happy thought or bright idea, that all the alleviations of the weaker members of society have arrived automatically, gradually, and by indirection; by, in the main, quite unforeseen adjustments in the mores to life-conditions of society, effected through discoveries and inventions not aimed at all at female enfranchisement, such as the steam engine, the germ-theory, the processes of law.

That these alleviations are here to stay is always open to question. There is plenty of evidence to show that conditions of violence, especially those of war, enhance the social prestige of the male—in the eyes of women as well as in his own. This situation is a reflection of physical sex difference. In war, woman has not "counted" as have men. If you assume a warless world, her physical disqualifications for combat cease to count against her. Then they can be ignored. But as that assumption is a hazardous one, it is far from safe to do any ignoring in the case, prior to certainty that war, as a condition, is removable, and has been definitively removed—a consummation devoutly to be wished but not yet to be counted on. War plunges societies back into near-savagery in many respects other than the most obvious ones. Whole sections of the "platform" collapse, precipitating entire populations into the crude conditions out of which civilization has so slowly and painfully emerged. War may stand as a fair representative of mischances perilous to the very structure of civilization. There are others, such as the manias under which men chop and wrench at the supports of their platform, or merely neglect to keep them in sound repair, while they rush off on a crusade, even jauntily scoffing at the need of any of the supports, even regarding the platform as adequately borne up on thin, hot air.

You cannot be sure that what counted once may not count again. The doctors tell us that only by the most constant and watchful care do we avoid a recurrence of decimating plagues like the Black Death. Most of us have no idea of this situation, but lightly assume the pest a thing of the past. Some imbeciles want to discard all precautions and abandon such defences as vaccination. This is a perilous state of mind. It is reckless to assume the entire and permanent irrelevancy of what used to be relevant to the highest degree. It is fair enough to say that certain innate weaknesses of women—or of men, or of children, or of the aged—no longer count, *at present,* as they once did all the time. That is safe enough, for the qualification, "at present," stands for watchfulness and forethought; but the swelling universal proposition is neither safe in itself nor yet sound in the mood it engenders.

Situations still occur, oftener than sporadically, where the sentiment, "Women and children first" fits the case, involving an unconscious recognition of the abiding fact of difference, superseding all wishful thoughts about equality. Legislation in favor of women, however unpalatable to the fanatical partisans of sex equality, appeals to the common sense of the common people, not to their "humanitarianism" or "brotherliness" alone. The basic physical sex differences are too self-evident to be ignored in practice, even though, between the pinches, they may be argued away. The most obvious of them continue to "count" all the time and others may have to be taken into account at any time. Concealed for a space by a camouflage of grotesque word-paintings on flimsy fabrics, they are, and remain, down there underneath.

Whenever such expressions as "Man the Oppressor" or "Man-made World" are encountered, another case has turned up of the benighted tendency to seek explanation in agency rather than cause. No one who has any clarity of conception as to what society is, and how it has become, can harbor for a second the idea that its millennial and massive evolution has been determined by the petty spite or even mere self-centeredness of one half of the race intent upon overreaching and reducing the other half. No society could have long persisted whose women were systematically brutalized, cowed, and unhappy; and the first item on society's list of agenda is survival.

To talk about one sex making the world, meaning the social order, is evidence only as to what sort of a mind the speaker has. Even infants and idiots are in on that enterprise. Each sex "gangs up" on the other to some extent, but the ensuing skirmishes do not always return the same victors nor do they all turn on physical force. Woman has always had her powers, as any unprepossessed reader of ethnography and history knows. Individuals and groups try to get what they want, and make a good deal of noise about it; but what they get, in the long run—and the evolutionary course is nothing if not long—is what makes for the persistence of society. If society does not get on by reason of their squabblings, they get nothing, or worse.

A tribe drifts into a war, and immediately those capable of fighting get all the favors; and if hostilities last on, they keep on getting them.

Though the warriors always want attention, they do not get it for that hankering but because they alone can cope with the instant situation. The women are among the first to sense that fact and their relation to it. They coddle and flatter Man the Protector, and do not feel oppressed at all.

Credulity concerning the possibility or ease of rectifying sex discrimination increases as you move away from crude, physical actualities toward the range of the social codes; for many people assume the mores in general to be readily alterable by the taking of thought, where they would not hope by that process to add a cubit unto their stature or to apportion childbirth pangs more equitably between the sexes.

I am tempted toward yet another re-statement as to the nature and mode of evolution of the mores. That would amount to an abridgment of several books. I shall go so far as to indicate certain bearings of general principles to the case in hand.

The mores are automatic adjustments by society to its life-conditions; and these life-conditions, where the mores are long-lived and widespread, as are the sex mores, are always something big and solid. One of these conditions, and a major one, is bisexuality. Adjustment to it is represented by blocks of sex mores chiselled by automatic selection into shapes characteristic and permanent enough to have acquired names and to be called institutions: marriage and the family. These institutions show readily distinguishable varieties, also named, such as monogamy and the father-family. No men or group of men ever enacted any one of these; men lived on into them under the impulsion of a variety of personal and local interests whose realization was, or was thought, best served, at various times and places, by the local social code—that is, the various persistent types of institution had each its survival-value to the society of its day and place. And to each and every type of adjustment to bisexuality the rights accorded to the sexes corresponded. If the automatic societal process be called X, then all that X has ever appeared to care about has been that society, not the individual, should persist. Whether male or female was thereby to have what men call justice was a question that never rose at all, not even in the mind of male A, when the women jeered him because he had prudently run away from a bigger man, or in that of female B while she was being beaten unmercifully for having borne twins.

The mores as they have existed and exist are that which any scientific student of society must begin. Then he can try to discover to what they are adjustments. And there is just one thing that he can be unshakenly sure about, namely, that they are not adjustments to the puny whims of short-lived mortals but to something in the nature of the eternal hills.

The mores do not rise out of nothing nor do they persist without justification more authentic than man's endorsement of them. Sooner or later they are found to have constituted, in their prime—and the big blocks of them are always in their prime—adjustments critical to the survival of the society practising them. It is always the part of caution to inquire to what actuality an institution is an adjustment before starting, under the spell of emotion, to eradicate it. Uprooting it may be like lifting the Midgard Snake or pulling up the oak Iggdrasil. The question always is as to the roots of the thing deemed desirable to eradicate. If they are shrivelled up, well and good; if not, men will pull their hearts out in vain. Further than that: though the roots may not be as sound as they once were, if they interlace with those of a neighboring institutional tree, the pulling does not promise so well, for, while you may gouge out the original growth, you stand the chance of destroying something else which you cannot afford to disturb. You tug at private property, let us say, as a base monopoly. It is of the Iggdrasil family. Even supposing it defunct at the root, it is yet intricately bound, through ages of a common monopolistic intergrowth, to the monogamic family. People who still esteem that type of family had better not set out to uproot private property, even if they are rash enough to believe it rotten clear down to the ground, and below. A few unsightly branches do not prove a tree either dead or moribund. To fell the tree because of them is something like beheading as a cure for toothache. The tree merely needs pruning.

To attribute anything like petty spite to an automatic process is manifestly imbecile. The moment one catches sight of the mode of origin and evolution of the mores, at that moment personalization of the impersonal begins to look foolish, and along with it the idea that woman has been deliberately put upon.

Inequality of rights, often cried out against as "injustice," is undoubtedly, and often, supported in the mores. Society does not accord full rights to children or idiots. Is this an exhibition of spite or prejudice? "No," bursts forth the partisan, "but it is an insult to align women with the mentally immature or with defectives." This is an example of close reasoning. However, the implication as to insult is in the eye of the objector; there is no ground for scenting insult in a citation of facts so obvious as to be instantly accepted. There is nothing similarly derogatory about age, at any rate; but if a female under the age of consent is assaulted, it is a more serious matter than if she were older. Is this a discrimination in favor of youth, or a mere recognition of the nature of youth? A minor has not a few disabilities aside from ineligibility to vote, yet many a boy or girl of fifteen could vote more intelligently than many a man or woman of fifty. That all sane men who have reached their majority have been accorded the right to suffrage is no proof that they are all equal in their superiority to all minors. Is there malice prepense in all this, or are these merely such classifications as are necessary in social practice, even if they result in border-line cases of "injustice"?

Inequality of rights is, moreover, not seldom in favor of woman, as of minors. A man and a woman conjointly murder someone and are convicted. The man is condemned to death, the woman to imprisonment. If a female criminal proves to be pregnant, public opinion does not tolerate her execution; it favors mitigation of her punishment. A while ago the secretary of a woman's rights association protested against woman's exemption from the death penalty; she did not favor capital punishment for anybody, but if men were going to be executed, women must be their "equals" and insist upon the right to be hanged. Women have been the beneficiaries of legislation designed to protect them during pregnancy; it was once hailed as eminently expedient as well as humane; later, though, it was criticized as offensive to woman's dignity because indicative of her "inferiority." These protests are evidence enough that rights are not always distributed in man's favor; but consider also the husband, who pays alimony where the wife does not, is responsible for her debts as she is not for his. In short, in marriage and after its dissolution by divorce, rights are hers to which he has no claim; and, prior to marriage, if the jilted man sues for breach of promise, he only makes an ass of himself, while the girl may get much sympathy, and in a tangible form, especially if she is tearfully pretty.

Now, why all these discriminations? Do spite and sympathy turn whimsically and emotionally now toward one sex, now toward the other? Is sex prejudice really at the bottom of the discrimination, or is there here an adjustment to actual sex differences?

With sex and age, as biological bases for preferential treatment as to rights, may be aligned a number of others that are social. The fire chief has a right to disregard traffic-lights, where the ordinary citizen has not. The doctor may interrupt a procession and get through a street closed to the rest of us. Congressmen may frank their mail. Once upon a time there was a preferential item known as "benefit of clergy"; and literacy is still demanded as a qualification of suffrage. Italy has restored capital punishment for murderous assault upon the King and Premier, which means that their right to life is enhanced over that of others. Presidents must have bodyguards, whether they like it or not. Does all this mean that there is a display of arbitrary favoritism for the fire chief, the doctor, the legislator, the literate, the ruler—or, as several fearless executives have felt, a persecution and a needless intrusion upon privacy that have left them envying the ordinary citizen? Because various people—the blind, the crippled—have privileges that we have not, do we feel put upon? Does any man rebel against "women and children first" as a logically indefensible discrimination against his sex?

Of course not. Here is merely a set of practical arrangements in living that no one cries out against as "unjust" and humiliating. They are all a recognition of inequality that is inevitable as between members of society. Consider the deference of even the toughest neighborhood for the nurse or sister in her uniform.

These cases are intended to set the whole issue of discrimination in the distribution of rights, confusion of detail and all, before us. What emerges out of them is, first, that a distribution which is inevitable in the circumstances of society always entails instances of "injustice" to the individual, by reason of its being a mass-phenomenon, the only kind of an expedient of which society can avail itself. It is very irritating to one who realizes, as an axiom, that no human instrumentality is perfect, to see isolated cases of the "miscarriage of justice" so played up as to invite the inference that the whole system of the administration of justice is a failure. Such a performance presents irresponsible agitators with equivocal evidence readily swallowed by the emotional and discontented. They gladly sense yet another grievance.

The second conclusion to be drawn from the foregoing cases of alleged or real inequality is that when society does make discrimination there is behind its action not human spite or overreaching but a recognition of the same sort of diversity that Nature recognized in forbidding chickens to swim while urging ducks to take to water. The contention here is that since woman is not "framed up" as man is, any more than the child as compared with adult, she is not able to do many a thing that he can do; and that that fact, like all other realities, is automatically taken account of by society in the mores. Exactly the same contention applies to the case of man: not being "framed up" as woman is, he is not able to do many a thing that she can do—sing soprano, for example. Thus results a difference of placement or allocation of the sexes as constituents of society that is consequent upon sex differences, some of them obvious, others disputable. If men and women were exactly alike, that is, exactly equal as constituents of society or as instruments to be employed by society, then one might use the term "discrimination" in the sense of arbitrary favoritism; as it is, the word means no more than a recognition of significant differences, as when a naturalist discriminates species one from the other, or a breeder discriminates varieties, or as when, in the present exposition, it is sought to discriminate between two meanings of the term "discrimination."

The upshot of the foregoing is that woman's rights and social disabilities, being in and of the mores, have been and are impersonal, realistic adjustments to actuality and actualities, not vagaries begotten of fancy, caprice, petty prejudice, or a deliberate intent on the part of one sex to reduce, impose upon, and humiliate the other. It would seem superfluous to develop the obvious to such an extent except for the fact that it is not obvious at all except to those relatively few who have become acquainted with the nature and automatic mode of evolution of the mores and of the institutions of society that rise out of them. The rights accorded to the sexes in the mores have never been the same, nor are they now identical. Contrasts in them can be referable only to underlying sex differences to which the mores have adjusted. Unless the sex mores are different from all other mores, these differences must be not only actual and realistic but also sharply in contrast and deep-seated.

The above generalities touching the mores have an especial bearing upon the matter of woman's alleged lack of opportunity: her "chances." Admittedly she has chances now, under civilization, that she never had before. The implication or assertion is widely accepted that she had next to no chances up to recently. Prophecy is immediately advanced under the guise of argument: "Now you will see what she can do." It would be more compelling if it were accompanied by past and present instances. Women, we are told, have had much more extended chances for some time, but when one inquires for evidence of accomplishment, there are only isolated and by no means clear instances to be adduced, and one is likely to be warned that time enough has not yet elapsed, that the chances are not yet copious enough, to reveal results unmistakably due to them.

There is no quarrel about the importance of this time-element. Any serious student of societal evolution comes to have a kind of passionate respect for time. It is about the only constant he can reckon on. But he finds that the embattled enthusiast calls on time only as a kind of afterthought or alibi. Also, when he is proclaiming in the future tense, he is always talking about the appearance of results "soon" or even "now" and hailing this and that as a harbinger of a New Dispensation right at hand. Then, later on, like the prophets of the End-of-All-Things and the coming of the New Jerusalem, he has to fold up his ascension-robes and set a new date for the Second Coming. The emotionalist expects to vault over sharp boundary-lines into a Brave New World, while the student of society's course of development looks for such shadings of transition as those between the colors of the spectrum, between races, or elsewhere in nature.

But how long is "for some time"? There seems to be a general consensus that woman has not enjoyed greatly augmented chances for more than, say, a century. Some date her emancipation from the Industrial Revolution, subtracting discreetly and quite correctly a considerable period during which the influence of that change in society's life-conditions was getting under way. No serious student is disposed to quarrel with that allowance, for he knows that the Western world has not yet nearly accomplished general adjustment to that Revolution, even within the range of the industrial organization. Others date woman's enfranchisement from the establishment of higher education for women. It would seem that, whatever the period during which woman has enjoyed an undoubtedly larger chance in the world, and in view of the confident prediction of startling contrasts in her performance as sure to result promptly upon the loosening of her bonds, there should be by now a considerable body of compelling evidence available to support those who assured a past generation that all she needed to prove her "equality" with man was the chance.

The outcome of this prediction cannot but remind an observer of the prophecy which accompanied the specific agitation for woman suffrage, promising all manner of instant reforms of age-old ills. I do not say this cynically. I wanted women to vote if they wanted to. I should have been more than willing to disfranchise hordes of men, at the same time. But there are the prophecies, which I never credited at all, though I wished they might be sound.

The plain truth is that what measure of added chances woman has been accorded has not as yet had any appreciable effect in overcoming the long lead man has had over her along the various lines of historic accomplishment. One is willing enough to believe that she needs more time; that her spokesmen have proclaimed too much too soon. But that is, as yet, an academic question. Time will tell, one way or the other. Meanwhile, the record stands about as it was prior to the heralded emergence of the bettered chances. The stock in trade of the partisan remains, almost wholly, prophecy.

The common assertion that woman has had no chances to speak of, throughout the long past, to make her mark, should not be passed over without examination. Her exclusion from opportunity has been assumed, deplored, denounced. But is the allegation true? As I read history, it is not. Let us consider, for a moment, the case of the eminent man. He has often been under what looks to be a hopeless handicap. Nevertheless, a consuming interest in some direction, a career-interest, has driven him over what looked to be insurmountable obstacles—poverty, illness, and the rest—to conspicuous success. Consider the famous invalids or the highly temperamental and unhappy geniuses who might well be classed as defectives. No one can combat the truth that a goodly proportion of eminent males have started out with little or no chance but have pulled through. *"Per aspera ad astra"* is a proverbial recognition of barriers to aspiration. "The best things arrive by the hard way."

One should reflect that even a few cases of supreme accomplishment by women would count quite disproportionately to their number. How is it that the historic record shows so little in woman's column to match a long list in man's? Was it a matter of career-interest, after all? No sensible person can believe that it was because of a conspiracy to suppress woman's triumphs; indeed, such women as Hypatia and Sappho are renowned just because they are women. If a man had written only those few lines attributed to Sappho, there would have been no Byronic outburst about the isles of Greece, "where burning Sappho loved and sung." Women's historic feats have always received the disproportionate attention accorded to the exceptional. They have profited by the rarity of their performances, and the performances have been exaggerated. Their inadequacy is still condoned; when a woman has attained a prominent position and serves but poorly, she is exempted through an old-time chivalry from the savage candor of criticism which a man must expect. It is the sheerest nonsense to allege the suppression of the record of woman's attainment in the interest of man's.

As the case stands, then, many men have borne heavy handicaps—have encountered mischances, not chances—and yet have come through to distinguish accomplishment as recorded in history; whereas few or no women have hung up a similar record.

It has been asserted that all women have been under an arbitrary disqualification different in kind from those encountered by man—an absolutely insuperable one—a disqualification in the mores so drastic as to prevent any woman from even contemplating certain lines of endeavor. A stock instance is the European taboo on the stage for woman, and it is pointed out that when the taboo had been removed, women almost immediately took equal or superior rank with men as artists. There have been cases where women could have a public life only by becoming courtesans—too high a price, it is alleged. Still, there were those who paid it and attained a certain renown, exaggerated or not, in tradition. That chance was open for the woman interested enough to pay the price. Men have repeatedly sacrificed much, if not that much, to their careers.

It is fair enough to say that women were shut out of war, exploration, and other adventures in strenuosity, so that there were no female counterparts to Caesar or Columbus. It was not in the mores for them to aspire to such careers, it is true; but that was no more than a recognition of their physical unfitness, like that of the very young or aged, to stand the gaff. They had no chances along such lines any more than they had to vie with men in lifting weights, running races, or other feats of strength and agility. All this kind of opportunity was excluded in the nature of organism. The situation was taken account of in the mores. No one seems to doubt that.

Then there were what might be called derived exclusions. Since war and physical force were a large part of the function of government in the earlier days, women were naturally, not artificially, excluded from ruling, in the sense of officeholding. It was not that they did not participate in war operations in woman's traditional way, or that they did not exercise a strong influence, by way of their men, upon tribal and national policies; but no woman was likely to get her name enshrined as a national heroine by nursing the wounded, attending to the commissary, or curtain-lecturing her sachem-husband.

Here are historic facts about woman's disqualifications, and some of them can be removed; but I do not see that women were similarly disadvantaged all along the line; and, if they had the same chance as men along even a small section of the line, why have not individual women attained some specific distinction? Why did they not profit by their somewhat preferred status under the mother family? Take the industrial organization. There are some who hold that woman invented agriculture—indeed, most or all of the processes of industry. That is nonsense. The truth is that the sexes have pursued most of the arts together, barring the most strenuous ones such as mining, smithery, or heavy building operations. Had woman no chance to improve, as man has done, on the arts she did practise? Were women ever forbidden to improve or invent? The question is merely a rhetorical one. There is for the primitive time no actual record, with names, as regards either sex; but the legends, with due allowance made for their male slant, accredit invention to culture-heroes rather than culture-heroines, to demigods rather than demigoddesses.

Absence of evidence—in this case, of women's names among originators—is no sure proof, though it has its weight as it approaches totality. When we get down to the eras of records and names, I can see no reason to believe that mere lack of opportunity, or opportunity withheld, could have prevented the emergence of some few women with distinguished contributions to industrial or other invention, along some practical line traditionally in woman's hands. Midwifery, from which men were generally excluded, owes its improvements to men.

Consider another eminence-creating variety of activity: art. No matter about the primitive case; take that of historic Europe. I have never heard that women were debarred from painting or music either by edict or in the mores. If they were, still no unconventional individuals broke through. Viennese ladies knew great composers and their work, and could even hire a Beethoven to give them lessons. Music was in the air and composition a noble activity. Why did not some one woman overcome whatever handicaps the sex really had— something that, proverbially, genius is always doing? Was there any absolutely insuperable social taboo to prevent Mozart's sister from composition even remotely comparable with that buffeted genius's performance? In Italy, with many masters engaged in painting, was woman disqualified from trying her hand at it? These, too, seem to me rhetorical questions.

Not to prolong illustration in the vain effort to be exhaustive, let us consider a final topic: sex opportunity in education. In a sense, it not only resumes all those chances or lack of chances mentioned, but it covers as well, and from a revealing angle, the set of the mores that is held responsible for woman's lack of opportunity.

Recent decades have been ahum with harpings upon woman's lack of educational opportunity. Then partisans have roundly sworn that, under the swinish monopoly of Man, the Oppressor, she never had any. This is rhetoric of an inferior order. Of course, she has always had some education. All children do, even among the Hottentots. The fair question is: "What kind of an education has she had, as compared with man?"

Among simple peoples, she had the kind of training that was conceived to be preparatory to a woman's destiny in the world, as determined by the code of time and place. The boy was tested at puberty— examined on his education up to that point—as a prospective warrior and worker; the girl as a prospective worker and childbearer. Both had to show fortitude under pain and strain. What was taught was strictly practical, then, and vocational in the sense of teaching man's work to him, woman's to her. If education had remained specialized thus, sexwise, there might be some reason to allege that woman has had no chance to distinguish herself in anything but woman's traditional, monotonous tasks.

But woman's education has not been so cribbed and confined, in the Western countries, for a good while. Girls in well-to-do homes have long had schooling, access to books and to educated circles, chances to see works of art and to hear music. If educational opportunity means so much, why has it not begun to have at least a show of result?

Consider the most elementary education, hardly more than the "three R's." In modern times children have had that training rather widely, with small distinction between the sexes. Many men of distinction have had no more than the bare elements. Some women, it would seem, should have emerged into similar distinction out of the same meager educational opportunity.

Over and over again, some women have had educational chances superior to those of men who have come through with eminence. I cannot see how, if women had had it in them, some few of them could have failed to crash through, even by chance, whatever obstacles lay in their way. I am myself obliged to conclude that something more vital than circumstances—something innate—has been determinant. This seems to me to be the upshot of the whole historic situation. And I cannot, in its face, assign the slightest weight to prophecies that all will be different presently. All that kind of forecasting is of a type quite diverse from the "anticipation of recurrence," which is science's way of estimating future possibilities. It is merely a case of the wish fathering the thought.

It is objected that "any career-interest is social and cultural, not biologic, and women could do well in any career if some career-interest took them into special lines." This is prophecy, once more; it is not forecasting upon the basis of anticipated recurrence. Certainly some women have had such an interest, which has led them into careers ordinarily confined to men, and have subordinated all rival attraction to it; but without attaining, except for a vanishing few, successes comparable to man's. And why does not "some career-interest" come along, to take them "into special lines"? Why have they cleaved so closely to a single, domestic interest?

There is no evidence that woman's career-interest, or man's either, is wholly cultural, without strong biological ingredients—I might say, without a profound biological basis. The evidence seems to me to indicate that the biological structure, functions, and urges of woman, inevitably reflected in her mental attitude and outfit and in the mores, have simply eclipsed for all women but a very few the kind of career-interest that has led to the sort of eminence recognized in the historic record. And I see no evidence on which to forecast any essential change. Here is yet another case where the "emancipated" are wont, forgetting that the mores reside in the masses, to ignore the masses or rationalize as to their sentiments and ambitions.

I believe the nub of the whole matter to lie in this "career-interest." Every distinguished man about whom I have read seems to me to have had a consuming, almost irresistible, interest in the work that made him famous. Nothing else has been permitted to take precedence over that which has enthralled him: his passion, or obsession, or mania, or lunacy. In a very true sense, many such men have run head-on against the mores, to say nothing of having sacrificed what is commonly thought to make life worth living. Thus have they brought about the variations for which society depends upon the individual and for which he is rewarded by renown, though that may be long after his death.

Career-interest might seem to be both nurtured by the mores and frustrated by them, at one and the same time. But whatever happens to it is sure to be a long-run affair. One who has the most elementary knowledge of society's evolution will discard at sight the idea that any individual interest or sex interest could ever have been realized for long if it had not harmonized, in the long run, with the interest of society in its own preservation and reproduction. It is safe enough to say that the prevalent individual or sex interest of any time must have been subordinate to that societal interest, and must have been what it was because society's interest was what it was. For long ages the mores as respects sex, representing society's interest (just as the physique of sex, representing the race's interest), have prescribed and delimited the sex interest (just as Nature—to personify the process of organic evolution—has held sex functions and processes to what they have been).

From this point of view, the futility of talking about "sex equality" immediately appears. It is as foolish to debate about the "natural equality" of the sexes as to wrangle over the equality of the constituents of gunpowder in producing its explosion, or, more generally, over the superiority or inferiority of indispensables. Indispensables are superlatives; the comparative degree is out of its depth, outclassed, in their company. Gunpowder will not go off unless it contains all three of its components; in fact, without any one of them, there is no gunpowder. Women are indispensables in the Scheme of Things as it applies to the life of human society. So are men. Without both there is no human society. This means that male and female are neither superior, inferior, nor equal to one another. Society needs the services, now of men, now of women; it is better off, and so are they, for their diversity. If, for their services, women seem to have received less public regard than men, we have merely another instance of how the cosmos might have been more nearly perfect if we had been present in an advisory capacity on Creation Day. Then we should have clamored for "justice." As it is, we shall be much happier to realize that justice is a conception of our own, not existing in the Scheme of Things, one which we are privileged to realize as we can; and that it can never be attained by dint of tears or rage or sulking, but only by an acquaintance with the facts and laws of life, gained by hard labor and study, followed by as adroit an adjustment to them as we can make. The mere fact that some women are sorry they are female and want all the prerogatives of men, instead of, or in addition to, their own, signifies nothing—not even that they will be any happier if they get what they think they want (and do not get men's special disabilities and woes at the same time), and least of all that society will benefit by their attainment of it.

Woman's career-interest, I am convinced—though I do not expect to prove it to anyone who revolts at the idea—lies inflexibly in a different direction from man's; toward marriage and the family. It is undeniable that she has long been propelled in that direction by the mores and largely also by specific training. The sex codes have doubtless been superficially responsible for this. But it is incredible to me that these codes would have been what they have been, or could have exercised so compelling a stress through the ages, unless they had been responsive to "man-nature" and "woman-nature," that is to say, to innate impulse, the expression of constitutional sex differences, physical certainly, and probably also neural and mental. I believe that the stress of the race-interest, propagation, bears much more heavily on the female than on the male, and that therein lies the reason for the difference in career-interest. This, I think, is the sex heredity in the case, the constant element through time, modifiable only in the details of its expression under various environmental conditions. In consonance with general principles, the scientific method of dealing with the "sex question" would be to learn all possible about the nature of the impersonal forces in the field and in all action to take account of them as constants.

In man and woman we have a double instrumentality, a coöperation of two highly specialized elements evolved originally in nature to her special ends. This is the condition of bisexuality, to which, as inalterable, the mores had to adjust and must continue so to do. They have taken account of characteristic sex differences in physique, in nervous system and mind, in temperament, turn of mind, and interest. In so doing the sexes have been treated differently because they are different, and the "injustice" involved is a construction of our own.

This is the long-time trend. The inference is that, with modifications in adjustment to altered life-conditions of society along other lines, the sex mores will fall into consistency—for all the mores must eventually harmonize along broad dimensions—but always without surrendering their characteristic stamp. There is a man-nature and a woman-nature, different and complementary, as permanent as the "human-nature" which we are always being urged to "re-make" but never shall. Concerning this sex nature all predicates of equality or inequality are irrelevant and without sense. Misfits in relation to bisexuality will be settled, as they ever have been, automatically in the interest of the whole society whose welfare they always prejudice.

Actual illusions cannot resist this automatic process. Instance once again what has been, doubtless, the most senseless, though wholly innocent, of all the sex phantasms, the uncleanness-idea. It has vanished, but not on some afternoon at four o'clock, as the result of denunciation from some forum, or even of an hour's laboratory activity on the part of some Great Man or Woman. It gradually faded out, over long decades, as the experience of daily living, picking it up for a moment, cursorily and unexcitedly examined it, and casually, almost indifferently, assessed it as negligible. This is the way lasting changes come about in the mores. Comparatively few members of society are susceptible to direct persuasion by the most faultless logic or the most unimpeachable evidence. Agitation, it is true, can accelerate a change already on its way, or "in the air"; but unless the air, or the ground, has already been prepared by the automatic processes, the leader in the unfamiliar cause is as futile a person as a jazz-propagandist would be among the Heavenly Hosts.

The essence of the matter is that sex differences are complementary, the sexes uniting to form the man-woman unit, which is, or soon normally becomes, the cell of human society, the family.

XIV

WHAT MAKES MODERN MARRIAGE, AND WHAT OF THE MODERN FAMILY?

"REASONING" about marriage, in the absence of knowledge as to its evolution, easily leads to the conclusion that "sex makes marriage." It "stands to reason" that, since without sex there could be no marriage, therefore sex must have made it. This is another of those many matters that stand to reason but cannot stand up to fact. It is obvious enough that there could be no marriage of unisexual beings; but that bisexuality entails the institutional relation of marriage is a generalization of which the animal world reveals the imbecility. What is in the minds of those who loosely allege that sex makes marriage is that human beings have always married for the sake of securing sex satisfaction. But that is not true, either. The assertion merely reveals a rationalization on the part of its maker—some little indication of the modern persuasion that marriage is now a preferred means of securing that satisfaction. That marriage results in carnality is no evidence at all that it is contracted with that objective solely in view. The prospect of the sex relation is naturally present to the minds of the normal betrothed pair; it may dwarf all other considerations; but, again, it may be incidental. It has been, in history, no more than one member of a group of impulsions to entrance upon the social status of wedlock.

Marriage, like all other institutional adjustments, has been restrictive upon freedom. In the interest of society, it has been disciplinary over natural appetite and impulse. It has allowed of freedom in some definite direction by proscribing liberty in all others. It has kept the sexes apart rather than brought them together; it has isolated them except for a limited and specific permission to unite.

The sex impulse is naturally going to be satisfied somehow; Nature has always seen to that. She has heavily penalized all schemes for renunciation of the sentiments and acts that lead to procreation. She does not care a fig about how increase comes about. But then, there is Society in the offing, bound to care and to prescribe orderliness by proscribing a promiscuity that would lead straight to social chaos, amidst which she could not persist. I am personalizing Nature and Society as a sort of shorthand; stated impersonally, the situation is this: in the automatic process of societal evolution, the mores have always imposed discipline upon natural impulse up to a degree of repression short of raising resistance to the explosion-point. The mores are always repressive of natural impulse up to the vicinity of a danger-point beyond which, or short of which, it is perilous for society either to advance or to stop.

As the restrictions of the code have tightened, along with the strengthening organization of society, a number of alternatives to marriage, for the satisfaction of the sex appetite, have been proscribed. Freedom in sex relation has been much abridged under civilization, with the result that conscientious adherents to the code have come to feel that the only proper avenue to sex satisfaction is marriage, while the contumacious and "emancipated" rebel at the code and challenge it, by act or word, as repressive of "natural" rights and liberty. They evolve the spacious sentiment that whatever is natural is right and that everyone has a natural right, not to say a duty to himself, to be natural—a proposition that would strike Nature as sound enough but which Society could not tolerate for a split second.

In the simplest societies known, there are a number of alternatives to marriage: premarital license, concubinage and other types of plural mating, easy divorce, wife- or daughter-lending, permissive adultery, sexual hospitality in general—so many, indeed, along with the practical universality of marriage, that there is no call for prostitution in any strict sense of the term. The civilized observer of primitive life, accustomed to his own categories, confuses several of the above-mentioned examples of looseness, together with "temple-harlotry" and other ritual practices, with what he calls, quite incorrectly, "the oldest profession in the world," whereas professional sex service for hire is relatively modern.

In occidental civilization, most of the foregoing primitive alternatives have long been under formal taboo. It might be contended that the only legal alternative to marriage nowadays is prostitution—legal in the sense that measures taken in regard to it are aimed at control rather than elimination, the latter having proved hopeless; but the practice remains under condemnation by the mores. The "free love" that has been presented as so instinct with nobility, liberty, and poetry is alleged to be readily distinguishable from prostitition; but it envisages sex satisfaction outside of marriage, which it affects to ignore and despise. It is largely tall talk and attitudinizing. Most of the variations toward liberty recognize the marriage institution. There are those who align easy divorce with harlotry, but divorce pays at least lip-service to marriage; it is not informal but recognizes ritual. Similarly with the concubinage that attaches, in some countries, to the marriage of economic or social convenience; the love-consorts are not regarded as "common prostitutes" but as mates for protracted periods or even for life, with establishments of their own. In the case of royalty, there has been a return on occasion to monogyny, with the "side-wife" designated as morganatic, and regarded as at least partially within the pale of wedlock. There are other variations on the accepted adjustment to cover exceptional situations.

Occidental codes reflect the Christian tradition, which has made much of the sentiment that it is better to marry than to burn; that if one cannot sublimate his carnal impulses into something spiritual, let him marry, by all means. This rather coarse and contemptuous attitude toward marriage has recently been eliminated by improved taste from the wedding ritual. It really amounted to a religious confirmation of the general conviction that the only right way for a good person to gratify the sexual impulse is to marry—a conviction doubtless strengthened by the Western idea of romantic love; for while romance is not synonymous with passion, love could hardly be romantic if it did not include that element.

While attention has thus been focussed upon the rôle of sex passion as a dominant urge toward matrimony, nevertheless it has been the part of propriety to minimize and cloak over the physical aspect of wedlock, so that persons with any respect for convention would recoil from stating bluntly that they were marrying because they "burned." Probably if one had to pass upon a collection of alleged reasons for marriage, he would conclude that prospective sex satisfaction played but a vanishing part in making marriage.

There is no evidence as to motivation in the fact that sex passion inevitably attends marriage. It follows readily enough upon even a union contracted between persons who have never seen each other. There have been unions between orthodox pairs with little sensibility, together with much suppressed and repudiated sensuality, into which desire has straightway entered. No amount of pious protestation that sex relations were being joined solely in obedience to the injunction, *"Crescite et multiplicamini,"* ever gained credence. No such cases, genuine or not, have any bearing upon original motive; they exhibit no more than natural sequels to a proximity brought about by wedlock.

There are several side-lights upon this question as to the part played by sex passion in the making of marriage; and one of the most clarifying is that sex impulse alone has never been able to hold man and woman to one another for a lifetime. It is much too episodical, emotional, and unstable to form the basis of an enduring relation. Throughout the ages, those who have arranged marriages—generally the unemotional and realistic elders—have had the wisdom, out of experience, to realize this fact and to minimize or ignore the sentimental element in favor of the practical.

Another side-light on the topic in hand is the unequal weight of the code upon the two sexes, which, for the female, has eliminated alternatives to marriage that were at the disposal, even if under some reprobation, of the male. There has existed for ages a "dual standard" of sex morality. "Wild oats" is a different crop according as it is sown by one sex or the other. There has been good reason for this double standard as judged from the interest in it of the numerous societies— all but a very few—that have instituted and perpetuated it, not by way of discrimination against one sex but as a matter of course. Did not the woman bear the child and therefore, by irregularities plainly detectable, throw inheritance and succession, absolute certainty as to which was indispensable to orderliness, into confusion, as the male could not? His irregularities did not touch such essentials. Hers did; hence the penalties she incurred and feared, and the consequent pressure toward chastity. Literature is full of the woes of the unmarried mother, to say nothing of the dismal lot of the illegitimate child.

That the dual standard is under question in the present, if only by theorists, is something new in the world, indicative of slackening in the ancient sanctions. If the woman can bid defiance to the traditional code and not pay for it, will she not do so?

It is probably idle to conjecture on this score prior to experience, which, because knowledge is bound to be disseminated, will be afforded in time. Even if all that young women are waiting for is to be freed from the consequences of unchastity, still there would be, at the worst, a modicum of gain from contraception; for premarital license might, to some extent, offset prostitution, and with it such special evils as go with it. Also the relief to the family consequent upon control of an increase capable of swamping the standard of living at its launching is indisputable. This is the case at its worst. But tradition and religion are still to be reckoned with. Most of this talk about the outbreak of premarital license is by censors of morals who know nothing about the evolution of morality, as well as by persons who seem to believe that everyone shares their own Freud-nourished, absorbing preoccupation with sex. The sex itch exhibited in a certain lewd type of modern novel is about as close to real and wholesome life as the rashest romance. Before the unmarried leap all boundaries they must vault over conventions that are exceedingly old and very firmly established by reason of their survival-value to society. There are always some of the emancipated who are hopping back and forth over the fences set by society's discipline; but the vaulting-pole of contraception that carries some over them is not going to raze those boundaries or make the masses able and eager to jump them.

There is another change in process that is deserving of attention: in addition to the demand for premarital chastity, the postponement of marriage and the monopoly of monogamy have increased the strain upon natural proclivities. They have contributed, it is believed, considerably to the development of prostitution, as well as to the antisocial theories of those who moan and pant under a Freudian obsession. Always a philosophy or "psychology" can be found to support individuals who rebel at discipline, whether or not the discipline is an exaggerated one.

To sum up: if young people among savages who permit premarital license were asked: "Why marry?" the reply would be anything but "To satisfy sex impulse." Nowadays a similar query could scarcely elicit an honest answer that did not cite that impulse. In a union contracted solely and brutally for sex satisfaction, the wife or husband would be a legalized paramour. Probably such unions—admitted so to be—are of the rarest, for the motives are regularly mixed, and there is a great deal of rationalizing and idealizing. Still, where religion has sternly tabooed sex relations outside of marriage, so that "immorality" has long meant, in common parlance, sex immorality, these relations have become more than a crime—a sin; in such case it is inevitable that the prospect of satisfying the sex urge should figure among the motives to marriage. What the stresses other than the sex urge are, becomes of greater rather than less significance when it is realized that, while passion is always there, its incidence is likely to be determined by those other factors.

The more sex relations outside wedlock are restricted, the severer must be the stress, in contracting matrimony, exerted by the sex urge; also the higher the bars set before wedlock, the stronger the temptation to attain sex satisfaction outside. These truths are obvious enough; nevertheless, they have been ignored through whole periods of history during which men have seemed intent upon mortifying the flesh by enforcing obedience to futile counsels to unearthly perfection—to a virginity which, indeed, is not perfection at all but a reckless abnormality heavily penalized by the ineluctable, automatic forces of nature, and therefore a costly societal maladjustment.

Closest, perhaps, to the motive of sex satisfaction is the desire for offspring. Possibly there is a kind of "instinct," carried by the germ-plasm, for nature's ends, in the case. At any rate, from the standpoint of society's interest there must be children, for they render possible society's self-perpetuation. And so there has been developed in the mores a sentiment, entirely apart from any mere biological urge, not only that married pairs shall have children but, farther back, that matrimony, the prerequisite to legitimate heirs to property and social position, is the only normal human status for adults—yes, even for the unborn and the dead. When people marry because "it is the thing to do," they are following the more than subtle behests of society; then, when they are wedded and the really subtle pressure of the social environment begins to impinge, they find it "the thing to do" to have children.

People begin to look askance at the persistently single and to gossip about them or poke tart fun at the bachelor and old maid. A certain disapprobation of the same order occurs in the case of the wedded childless. This pressure to conformity with the mores becomes uncomfortable; the only relief is to dive back into the herd and mill about and propagate the way the rest do. Thus has public sentiment secured the interest of society, over and over again, at the expense of that of the individual, by penalizing under various forms of unpopularity—not only celibacy and the childless union but even the postponement, at the behest of the individual interest in a higher standard of living, of marriage or of the acquisition of a family. Society, be it noted, while it has not been indifferent to numbers of offspring of whatever quality, finds its special interest, as nature does not, in children born in wedlock, for they only can be socially "located," so as legitimately, that is, plainly and regularly, to carry on inheritance and succession, and thus keep the property and rights arrangements clear and definite—adjustments that are confused at peril to society as a peace-group. For this reason, society is the more intent upon the universality of stable wedlock, as the mores reveal.

The original idea in primitive people's heads was, and is, that children are an asset in maintenance: would help in the day's work where there are no laborers to hire; would, if girls, bring in wealth at marriage; would support and defend aged parents; and, often above all else, would continue this support for their deceased ancestors by the filial performance of sacrifices and other religious duties. To be childless, therefore, was a great peril and calamity; and to have fewer children was to incur the greater risk. Primitives pray for health, wealth, and progeny; various practices, such as the levirate, adoption, and teknonymy witness to their preoccupation with offspring. It is not that savages are not humanly fond of their childhen; but that was taken for granted, and whatever wedding-preliminaries there were either ignored or assumed it. Negotiations about marriage commonly took place between calculating elders totally devoid of sentiment.

Among the better-to-do of the present, by contrast, the child is an economic liability, not an asset. That he is not allowed to become the asset he might be, in tender years, is the complaint of not a few, in this and other countries, who resist the laws about child-labor or schooling. Upon our own frontier, the child had his tasks in the domestic economy; and it is only with the development of culture that the parents renounce claims upon him, accepting as incumbent upon them the duties of the relationship and laying claim to few or no rights. The old right of support in old age by one's children is now being passed over, as an obligation, to the State. There is probably, however, a great deal more of the primitive attitude in the masses than one who views them from afar is likely to suppose.

I pause to remark that when the self-styled and noisy emancipated proclaim, as they are always doing, that the world is utterly changed— that the family is moribund, free love about to be recognized, woman about to equal man in all respects (or vice versa), religion gone, capitalism on its last legs, democracy doomed, and so on and so on—one should always reflect that the proclaimers of a new dispensation are a minimal percentage of mankind, vociferous all out of proportion to their numbers. They acquire few converts in each generation who do not learn to know better as they become older. The mores are in the masses, not in these incontinent spawners of variations. Not with impunity does the student of society take his eye off the masses.

Despite the stress toward self-perpetuation imposed by society through the mores, it is doubtful whether very many young people marry for the sake of having children, however much they may want them as the years go on—especially if they do not come. Negotiators of alliances between families of great wealth or high social position undoubtedly plan for the carrying on of the family fortune or name, and probably the contractants to such unions know what is expected of them and conventionally approve of it; but this is something else than marrying for the sake of offspring. I do not say that right-minded lovers do not come to envisage children of their bodies; but I believe such thoughts are, as one might put it, secondary or even foreign to the more immediate concerns of lovers, and that the actual wish for children is a conjugal rather than a premarital sentiment.

After marriage, the pressure of the mores in society's interest, of which I have spoken, begins to take hold upon a pair and they observe that the thing to do is to have progeny. It is a little queer not to be like the rest. "What is the matter?" say their reproducing contemporaries, in looks and implications if not in words. Of course when and if the mores of the ages change, all this will be reversed; but, once again, it is not the few, self-consciously enlightened pent-house-dwellers who carry the mores. There is probably something down under these inveterate folkways even deeper than the automatically self-realizing interests of society—possibly some strain of an instinctive, biological order, felt by the individual, toward self-perpetuation in accord with nature's laws. There is something in the long-tested folk-wisdom of proverbs; and possibly the adage that as "a man is but half a man until he is wedded, so a marriage is but half a marriage until there are children," has its element of perceptiveness of the ultimate facts of individual and societal life. In any case, programs involving the removal of children from parental care and responsibility, to be raised crop-fashion in barracks, merely reveal a crass misunderstanding of these vital facts or a fanatical and disingenuous policy of ignoring them when they seem to stand in the way of some "ideology." Then, to support such aberrations, along comes a "psychology" of mother-love that displays a few imperfect experiments and analyses to "disprove" the existence of a biological phenomenon present in all higher organic life.

Though the desire for children seems not to be any longer of great importance in making a marriage, their presence certainly tends to stabilize wedlock. Throughout the past, the childless union was headed for dissolution; and while comparatively few divorces are now granted for childlessness—one of the dissatisfactions summed up or dissembled under "incompatibility"—it is true that the presence of children in various ways slows up the tendency to separate.

Vanity still has its part, either directly or by way of evasion of others' disapproval, in the making of marriage. I have alluded to society's method of safeguarding its interests by bringing it about that the nubile unwedded shall not only be under popular disapprobation and even ridicule but shall even be regarded as an offense to the gods. Some governments have gone so far as to tax the celibate, while rewarding the prolific. There is a constant pressure from self-respect, during youth, toward matrimony; one sees almost all the rest pairing off and feels the humiliation of "being left out in the cold." This pressure is naturally heavier among the masses than among those who have been trained to think for themselves in the face of public opinion.

The element of vanity in prestige which has, in the past, led to alliances between families of wealth and "blood," has suffered somewhat in recent times. There are always class-lines across which for various reasons, some of them very sound, unions are discouraged upon the grounds of difference in property or social position. The real disharmony is generally one of which this inequality is an outward and visible manifestation, namely, incompatibility in the mores of "higher" and "lower" social strata.

Until not so long ago, marriages were a regular means of consolidating alliances between states. There is little left of this in the present. In any case, deference is paid to romance by intimating, in the case of a royal match, that the contractants have fallen in love like any other pair; and princesses have been permitted to marry for love beneath their station where once they were regarded as pawns for eventual queening on the political chessboard. How much of this concession to romance is no more than pretense cannot be judged with any accuracy; but the presence itself of the concession, even though insincere, is significant.

The international alliances of commoners have been much in the public eye; and they may, like the unions between different races in this country, have a political effect in drawing the nations together; but if so, that result is not planful enough to render the use of the term "motive" justifiable in the connection. If an American heiress marries a European title, the popular suspicion is that the attractions are, respectively, prestige of position and economic advantage. All the unplanned and unforeseen social results belong to the automatic societal process.

I have been trying to clear away certain of the asserted motives to modern marriage that have little, or less than a little, to do with economic considerations, so as to be able to concentrate upon that motive and upon what is called "romantic love." The conclusions thus far are that there are many more marriages for sex satisfaction, pure or mixed, than there were upon earlier stages of culture, and also more prostitution; that unions are relatively seldom contracted for the sake of children, that the vanity-motive, while regularly represented to some degree, enters indirectly, in the main, and, though directly to some degree, probably to a lesser degree than aforetime; and that the political alliance is on the wane.

Now comes the question as to how far the age-old economic motive still prevails. Always without any intent or wish to make invidious distinctions, we must here distinguish between—to use the current deceptive jingle for the sake of brevity—"the classes and the masses." The classes in this connection mean the advantaged, cultured, leisured, educated, well-to-do; they are those who are or could be most emancipated from subserviency to tradition. They are relatively very few in number, a truth which, I reiterate without apology, must be repeatedly called to mind—indeed, must never be allowed to absent itself from the attention of whoever sets himself to the task of understanding the nature and evolution of society.

There is evidence upon all sides that, except among these "classes" and among those in the masses who are emerging from their inherited status, the economic motive to marriage is still very strong—in most cases, determinative. The primitive mores have not passed away. Let us look at them a moment. For long ages marriage was an economic coöperation between differently endowed and specializing sexes, distinguished from other forms of such coöperation by the added function of self-perpetuation. What the woman was looking for was a brave and efficient mate, as indicated by the nature of the initiation test or ordeal prior to male marriageability—also of the special premarital tests of the suitor, and of certain symbolic ceremonies in connection with courtship and wedding. What the man wanted was an industrially efficient and fertile wife, as indicated by the puberty tests of woman, her reputation as a worker, "trial-marriage," and, again, by certain symbolic performances prior to and in the wedding-ceremony. A man could divorce a wife for laziness or infertility, and often a woman her husband if he were an inferior protector and provider. It is probable that sterility or fecundity counts for less than it once did; and it is also realized, though not so generally as it will sometime be, that a husband may be responsible for the childlessness of a union; furthermore, that sterility, once regarded as an irremediable curse from the gods, is often readily rectifiable by surgery. In short, sterility is not the awesome calamity it once was. Very few divorces are granted, at least formally, because of it; doubtless, as in the case of adultery, it is likely to be disguised as "incompatibility" or "mental cruelty."

As for the economic virtues, it is clear enough that they are demanded in the husband in scarcely less degree than aforetime; the girl's parents do not become infatuated with a good-natured, handsome good-for-nothing, even when she does. There is in the mores a strong preventive to the acceptance of a ne'er-do-well, taking the shape of young women's gossip about the young men they know; a slacker, in peace as in war, is condemned in advance. The question as to whether a man will be a "good provider" may doubtless be lost to sight if passion is strong or romance has distorted a sense of realities, but with people who look upon life as a business, marriage, certainly the most important controllable grand crisis in life, is not to be settled upon emotion or caprice. In fact, it is possible that people who feel that they must not appear materialistic in the matter worry as much over the economic situation as those who, coolly and in the open, discuss it as a prerequisite.

A woman may not want to marry a man purely because he is a good provider—even primitive girls will not wed a hopeless freak, however wealthy—but he must generally be a prospective provider, by his own efforts or otherwise, or he will not be considered at all. And how about the woman's economic efficiency? The fact that it is relegated to the limbo of "materialism" by the youth whose mind is full of "the world well lost for love," and who knows of life little more than he has read in the poets and novelists, has no bearing upon the facts of life as lived by the masses of mankind. It is only the relatively propertied man who can dispense with the actual economic assistance of his wife, because he can hire a substitute—an "office wife." For one who cannot, the other member of the team must pull with him, if they are to get anywhere. Where the husband has to do the woman's work in addition to his own, his state is deplorable and generally desperate. Even where the wife does nothing to help him secure the wherewithal, she is the spender, and upon her wisdom, skill, and loyalty in disbursing, largely depends the stability of the domestic economy. Many a man of moderate capacity has risen in the world because his wife was a good manager, and many a potentially successful one has lagged and fallen behind because his mate has failed to hold up her end, not to mention giving him a lift with his. Wifely affection is beyond price, but it is often not enough, by itself.

Many thousands of pairs have run a business as full partners while each has attended competently to his or her special sex duties in the family. Consider the part borne by women upon the American frontier-farm, or on the small holding where today the family lives almost wholly on the land. A man with an invalid wife was and is severely handicapped, and the promptitude with which a widower married again simply reflects the truth that the man-woman economic unit is the appointed one—appointed in the nature of things, not by law, or introspection, or idealism, or meditative philosophy. The small restaurant or store is run by man and wife, not by the husband alone; and it becomes clear enough, even to the unobservant, in fact, it gets into the mores, that a man had better look to his prospective wife's economic utility if he is going to get on in the world. There may no longer be hoeing-marathons, whose winners are snapped up by cheering swains or by their shrewd fathers for them; but there is a strong and lasting tendency, especially in small communities, for the swains to size up the damsels, as the latter do the former, in the matter of their usefulness as co-workers. The ideal, if it can be so called, has always been the healthy, sturdy, competent, fecund mate. Even beauty cannot prevail against, however much it may enhance, such an endowment. The actualities of the battle of life are too imminent.

If the sexes in wedlock do not supplement each other the union is a virtual failure, no matter what the circumstances may be; and where, as with masses of mankind, self-maintenance outranks all else, the qualities demanded of either sex are prevalently those that count in the raw battle of life. Of a consequence, the conclusion is not over-venturesome that what makes modern marriage is still very largely indeed what made primitive and historic marriage.

Of course the young college fellow, who is proved to be one of the advantaged by the very fact that he is in college at all, objects excitedly to any such conclusion. "My girl and the fellows-I-go-with's girls aren't of that sort at all. They aren't gold-diggers! With them and us, it's a matter of higher values. Why, my girl would marry me if I hadn't a cent, and I don't care whether she has a nickel or not! I grant that it looks as if the savages always had an eye to the main chance. So do the French, I guess. But with us it's different and we don't like this materialism. All this calculation makes us sick. With us the whole thing's on a higher level. It's spiritual. It's idealism, and I guess it's been ideals that have made life go! Anyway, my girl's a peach, and that's all there is to it!"

Now, there is a good deal of substratum under all this volatility. The moment that maintenance is assured (though it is better realized, of late, that such assurance is relatively rare on earth), there is a chance to shift values and to idealize with impunity. Woman is not man's complement in labor alone. When a husband is quite able by himself to maintain his establishment, so far as income goes, he comes to need a different kind of aid than before. His wife must still be able to manage the domestic economy—even Queen Mary of England is reputed always to have been a careful and successful manager—and to take an equal place beside him, to whatever height he can climb. Even in politics, many a man's success or failure has been due in no small degree to his wife. In brief, when technical economic maintenance has been assured and the struggle is for a higher standard of living, sex coöperation takes place upon less material levels and consequently calls for different attributes in both man and wife. The primary qualities once demanded fall somewhat, but by no means altogether, into the discard. Then it seems, as it does to our young man, highly materialistic even to mention them, and unspeakably crude to hold that they still prevail over the earth and even underlie the idealistic structures which he envisages.

From the standpoint of society's interest, the first question about any union is: Can the pair pay their way? If they cannot, then somebody else has got to carry them. If parents and others can do so, the immediate interest of society is satisfied; if not, then society is directly burdened, as in the case of other types of unfitness—which means that those who can take care of themselves, the members of society who constitute its essential strength, are to be further handicapped, and to unproductive ends. However disguised this situation may be by glosses of humanitarianism and other noble or showy veilings, it is always there at the bottom. The assurance of liberty, in this case to marry and reproduce, without an exaction of responsibility, can never be other than antisocial in its effects. If there is any canon of societal morality or justice, it is that each individual and pair shall be expected to pull its own weight in the boat. There are enough who cannot do that to constitute always an extra strain upon those who can; but strain, however normal, should be implacably kept down. Those who can pay their way, and are sturdily expecting to do so, must in any sound economy, be burdened as little as possible by those who cannot or who are expecting to be carried. A certain amount of charitable sacrifice is imposed, as a practical necessity, upon all provident members of society; but to profess a theory of communistic sharing, or wealth-division, and try to live up to it honestly is to go back on all the experience of the race.

Thus, even under the highest culture, maintenance-considerations are basic. But if they are taken care of by accumulations of capital, then there is a chance for the development of the other values to which allusion has been made. It is possible then for the woman, and for the man as well, to be valued for qualities other than those which make directly for maintenance. As various peoples, or classes, have gathered capital and culture, the woman has come to be prized for qualities other than industry and fecundity. Easement from the bare struggle for existence always affords men the leisure to attend to self-gratification in its several forms. Woman's beauty and her sex graces of body and mind replace, as attractions, her brute strength and endurance. This has been the case, beginning perhaps with the professional sirens, priestesses, or courtesans, and extending to the wife. And then, in some parts of the world, there has entered the factor of romantic love.

The extent to which romance has entered into the relation of the sexes among the leisured classes of the Western world is truly amazing. Chivalry and Virgin-worship doubtless had their share in promoting idealization of woman. The passing of the long-standing conviction that woman is a peril freed her from misprision. Then poetry and romance in general set up their impossible images of her for youth to dream about, and their preposterous pictures of wedded bliss that have landed many an idealistic pair in disillusionment. Prudery at the same time long exacted ignorance of sex facts in the name of virtue; so that the net result was often a protracted and painful readjustment, after marriage, to unknown realities that were an open book to the primitive realist.

All this idealization, however, foolish though its exaggerations may have been and painful as the results have often showed themselves to be, discharged its usual function of promoting variations that made adjustments to changed life-conditions of society possible. The less materialistic valuation set upon women by men—and also by women on women and by women on men—is part of the elevated standard of living rendered possible by the attainment, on the part of the more successful, of relative security in self-maintenance. This attitude undoubtedly tends to enter the mores so as to be passed on in some degree to the less cultured who have not developed it for themselves; but it is very hazardous to conclude that it is deeply rooted outside the limited strata of its origin. Nourished as it is by fiction of various sorts, the idealistic conception of woman and of marriage was long kept alive and flourishing only among the readers; the popular taste is perhaps being re-formed, as never before, by the talking picture, but the most popular films are generally those which emphasize the most banal aspects of the relations of the sexes, premarital, marital, and extramarital. The virtues that are applauded most are those which appeal most directly to emotion. Indeed, the appeal of the pictures is not seldom so purely physical, despite all the appanage of pseudo-culture in which it is bedight, that standards are debased rather than uplifted by it. In any case, the socialization of attitudes developed by the more advantaged classes, if it is to be more than a superficial thing, is not to be accomplished in a day. Nor can it exist unless upon a solid economic substructure.

Still less representative of more than a narrow circle are the emancipated notions of certain exponents of "freedom," soul-affinity, and so on, whose buzzings remind one of the wantonness of fly-time. I shall not go into their case because, despite their verbosity, they are no more than a squad of utopians among the many squads which have flourished ephemerally throughout history. The great body of society carries them along and tolerates them somewhat as a rhinoceros plays host to the ticks that live, propagate, and die on his hide—and which probably hold him in condescending contempt and think they are guiding his perambulations through African solitudes.

From the above it is possible to conclude that those classes of today which are freed from the immediate necessity of self-maintenance may marry for a variety of reasons not represented, except perhaps in the germ, in the long primitive period to which the so-called era of civilization is but the briefest appendage. The advantaged youth may want to wed his lady, not because she is a good gardener, or a competent housewife, or because she has a generous dowry, but because she is pretty, or graceful, or charming (a "cutie"), or has a good education, or high ideals, or is otherwise soulfully attractive in one way or another out of a thousand possibilities, no one of which is really mundane. And the girl will, of course, try to make herself into the attractive type or, at any rate, take on its outward semblance at considerable cost of pain or paint. It is perhaps cynical to note that, possibly, when her object is attained, like the man who has sprinted for the trolley-car and got on, she will run no more. And the maiden may long to wed her man, not because he is a brave warrior dight "Plenty Scalps," or a mighty hunter, or otherwise a good provider with a steady job, or because he is worth a million, but because he has all the social graces of a gigolo, or is instinct with the joy of life, or is a "good sport," or seems to need mothering, or is a soul-affinity to some degree in some way or other.

In brief, marriage may be envisaged as desirable for self-gratification in any of its myriad forms rather than as part of the business of making a joint living and rearing a family. As is regularly the case, I repeat, where there is a relative exemption from the bare struggle for existence, there self-gratification enters, whether it shows itself in the pursuit of luxury, or of the fine arts, or of gaming and gambling in general, or in a special preoccupation with the super-essentials in the matter of love and marriage.

The regular function of self-gratification has been that of a scouting-party that explores possibilities in advance of the main force and provisionally occupies ground until the mass can come up, take it over and "consolidated" it, or reject it. The luxuries and wonders of yesterday are the necessities and the matter-of-course of today or tomorrow. When the masses eventually limber up, there will be a selection among the variations, expedient or otherwise, set up by the widely ranging, responsible or irresponsible, pioneers. But the masses have too much momentum in their long-vested traditions to execute a right-about or even a sharp turn by reason of the excited alarums of a few hysterical scouts.

To try to envisage modern marriage without touching upon the family is not so bad as to leave the Danish Prince out of *Hamlet;* but it may be as unfinished an enterprise as *Hamlet* would be without the Prince's mother, the Ghost of his father, and Ophelia. In any case, the reiterated contention that the family is doomed certainly indicates a belief that marriage is not what it used to be.

In origin, the family is the unit-society; it is the smallest aggregation to which can be applied the definition of society: a group of human beings coöperatively striving to win subsistence and perpetuate the species. It has been organized in several different ways—father-family, mother-family, joint-family, and so on—but its essential nature has always been the same. It has ever remained a peace-group and, to be that, it has had to be a disciplinary organization, defining and guaranteeing rights and duties between its members. When it is proposed to abolish the family or to relax its longstanding relations of specialization, coöperation, and discipline, the proponents are really contending for the disintegration of society. It is as if the body were to be adjudged competent to take over and discharge all the cell-functions. In brief, it is nonsense. Economic specialization between the sexes may somewhat change its form; coöperation in maintenance may somewhat alter in its terms; discipline, with allocation of rights and duties, may shift its incidence somewhat; but even in the purely economic range, there are limits to these possibilities. And when one comes to the other function of the family, namely, the propagative, the limits are still more definite and less remote.

The family, with its extension, the kin-group, has provided a line of descent which inheritance and succession have utilized much as a vine climbs a handy trellis. Suppose the trellis, after all these millennia, were to vanish—would the growths stand up of themselves? Or could some rational device be inserted in its place? A figure of speech, some-one objects. Very well, let us drop it, though it is a good and enlightening one. Suppose the blood-tie could be annihilated—what other possible relation between persons and generations could there be, capable of being employed to allocate individuals where they can be found for the various purposes of society, and especially for the certain and undisputed passage of property? Would any sane citizen trust a states-man, a commission of them, or even a philosopher of the caliber of Socrates himself to devise something to take the place of what the mores have worked out over ages of tested experience? The question is merely rhetorical; of course no sane person would have the slightest confidence that such a thing could be done.

Or suppose that children were hereafter to be reared in some en-closure other than the family—who believes that that could be done better so than in the medium of the family, with all its faults? Nobody but inflamed fanatics. One might almost as well propose to raise fish in the stratosphere. And if the comparatively few children of the "upper classes" are reared largely outside the family, in camps and private boarding schools, the expediency of that variation is not thereby demonstrated.

It is not the mere proximity of parents and children but the "atmosphere" of the family that counts. That may be an imponderable, but it is as actual as those historic imponderables with which great statesmen know they must reckon. The "home" is inimitable and of determinative influence. The fiction-writers often portray a social situation more understandingly—or, at any rate, more vividly—than the compilers of treatises. A sound novel[1] devotes much attention to the home, skillfully marshalling the various detail-items that go to make it, and winding up with the sentiment: "At this time of stress our country needs to guard the home even as it guards the coast line. Without our homes our nation has no foundation, nothing for which to fight."

It is evident enough that a virginal, soft-spoken, instructed, and cultured nurse could better the physical care and training provided by a bibulous slum-mother; but it merely conscienceless propaganda to deal in such extremes. Coming down honestly to real and average cases, while the experience of copulation and conception, parturition, and even of lactation, do not impart any knowledge, say of *caries dentum,* they put the mother into a qualitatively different class in the matter of emotional attitude toward her offspring from any that even a Pallas Athene of celibate wisdom has ever attained. It is an essential feature of this attitude that it is not an instructed one, but to some degree, like that of the animal mother, instinctive and intuitive—not needing any tuition at all but experience to bring it into being. No man ever gets more than a distant adumbration of it. And its results are piece-work that cannot be standardized in a barracks under drill. It calls for a special highly individualized interest.

Here are two good reasons why the family should not be abolished, if it could be. The kind of person who harbors the possibility is the sort that pants after anarchy, the shallow-pated, precious idealist, who leaps frantically when touched by the whip of discipline; or he is the type that pretends to believe in utopias in order to daze stupid asses into opening their jaws for the bit and patiently carrying him, despite their galled withers, whither for purposes of his own he wants to go. He even hangs out a bunch of hay-scented straws to bob tantalizingly before their elongated and flapping ears.

The way to abolish the family as we know it is to destroy its monopolistic character by free love, easy union and divorce, "socialization" of women, children, and property—in short, by returning to the mores of a low culture out of which, by pain and struggle, the more

1. Bartley, N., *A Woman's Woman* (1919).

advanced races have pried themselves. If we did that, we should merely begin all over again, thereafter and eventually, by going through all the painful stages we have traversed, to arrive at the point we now occupy. The family is not to be abolished in favor of some lunatic vision any more than friction is to be neutralized by the perpetual-motion crank. When roosters become broody and hens get to be cocky, then we may view with more assurance programs for converting the family into something contrary to what it has been.

The fact is that those who bawl for the abolition of the monogamic family use "abolition" as a kind of excited superlative for "alteration," just as the expression about the camel passing through the needle's eye means merely that it is a superlatively difficult thing to do. Some of the proposed metamorphoses of the family into unrecognizability remind one, in their naïve quality, of the way the savage disguises himself from the ghosts of the dead—"makes different"—by setting a little dab of ashes upon his brow or leaving off his nose-ring. For example, we used to be told that when women got the vote, the family would lose its identity under the new dispensation; that women would no longer submit to this and that but would get out into the open and drive all social ills into limbo. But this little daub of ornamentation has not made the men into childbearers nor provided the women with the political asset of whiskers à la "Plumed Knight"; nor has even the Lucy Stone nomenclature yet neutralized bisexuality in *Homo*.

The changes forecast for the family by responsible students of its history touch upon both its economic and propagative aspects, but they do not abrogate either of its main functions; it remains the miniature society, with self-maintenance and self-perpetuation as its basic activities. The style of family maintenance is, however, to be different, involving, as one of its results, readjustments in the rearing of offspring and even in the manner of their evocation into the world. The common statement of the case is something like this: the exterior environmental conditions of the family have changed a great deal by reason of urbanization and other societal developments, at the same time that the internal relations have been altered by the "emancipation" of woman; it follows that profound readjustments in the organization of the family are imminent if not, indeed, already present.

It needs no ghost new-risen from the grave to tell us these things. We know that the age of marriage is greater than it used to be and that the family shrinks in size along with advance in the standard of living; that a number of unions remain "companionate" for a good while, if not permanently, largely because children are so costly nowadays that the risk of having them is put off, or because people want pleasure without responsibility; that the city-flat is not a home in the old sense, for we are being "born in hospitals, fed at restaurants, married at mayor's offices, and buried from funeral parlors" as in no preceding generation; that the home may therefore become a cramped and chilly roost rather than a nest; that hasty partings and new pairings, especially when there are children, render out of the question a permanent rest, or even roost; that there is no longer a chimney-corner for the aged; and so on through a long list of more or less important alterations in the societal medium wherein the family, so long as it lasts, must exist.

There is no doubt that a number of wives have become positive breadwinners as a result of the opening of economic opportunity. Some women are intent on doing away with the traditional sex-specialization in favor of joint activity, or even of competition, in the same sort of occupation. To them the specific propagative functions of the female cannot but constitute a handicap; they cannot take time out to bear any, or at any rate many, children, and certainly not to rear them in the time-honored fashion. They are keen to retain their individual identity by subordinating the race interest to the individual interest. They are as vain of their individual names as a Plantagenet. Hence the logical "argument" advanced by minds intent upon producing a show of reason to justify their desires and ambitions, that the "state" or "society" should attend to the race interest in all respects except those where it is manifestly incompetent, namely, in the matter of conception, gestation, and parturition. It is too bad that woman's contribution to the race-interest amounts to a tax upon her that is not levied upon man, so that the situation involves, in certain respects, a preferential treatment of him; but the only ways of meeting this inevitability are: (1) to deny it and try to forget it; (2) to remain celibate; (3) to remain childless; (4) to demand recompense from society for doing it the favor of reproducing.

Let us glance, for the moment, at the proposals of the new sexual, marital, and familial dispensation. The current publications upon sex matters, especially the symposia which present looseness and "liberty" as alone worthy of emancipated spirits, might be ominous of coming degeneration if they represented the sentiments of more than a small and itching clientèle. Their authors seem to be either exhibitionists in words without the courage even to strip and stand at windows; or the avatars of the lewd-story purveyors who once squatted upon cracker-boxes in the country-stores and spat at the redhot stove; or "philosophers" who know that to startle people by patronizingly challenging their accepted code is a way to acquire reputation, together with profitable contracts for books and lectures.

The former types are probably sincere enough in revealing the animal preoccupations of their own low minds, only that now their reveries are committed to the printed page instead of being indited upon board fences and the walls of latrines; they are in need merely of soapy mouth-wash and what used to be known as the "patter of the shingle." Probably dirty-minded adolescents, no matter what their tale of years, must always be with us; the pity is that their concentration upon organs and processes that the animals and savages take unself-consciously in passing must be flaunted in the face of not unreasonably fastidious readers—people who, while recognizing the presence even of the orgasm, do not want to be nudged and leered at: "Listen to this one!" "Here's another hot one!" "Did you get that one!" It is pleasant, and seems also reasonable, to believe that this kind of thing is beginning to pall. There seems to be present in the advertisements and write-ups of this literature of detestable taste a species of anxiety and strain as of one aware that his grip is failing. The polecat will presently, without a doubt, return to his ancient haunts.

The "social philosopher" who, free of any pornographic tendency, wins his acclaim by simple proclamations such as that "the family is only a kind of conditioned reflex which is bound to go, and . . . looks forward to the time when all children, along with the family wash, will be put of the home," is a bird of another feather. He suggests that "in the future motherhood may become a well-paid profession," to be undertaken by those who can pass tests as to their fitness from a stock-breeding point of view." At this moment, he says, we do not have to decide what tests should be imposed upon sires and what proportion of the male proportion the begetters should form. He might as well speculate, were that topic equally attractive to his impressionable but sparse audience, upon what we can do with the moon when it is found to be of green cheese. It has always been a favorite diversion of certain types of mind to speculate upon the consequences of that which has not happened and cannot take place; and he who can lead such airy revels has always been sure of a kind of reputation and often of substantial dance-caller's fees.

"Philosophers" of this order are certain of a following, but it is a small one, composed almost wholly of those who will shortly outgrow their credulity or are incapable of so doing because half-baked from the outset. There is no permanent element in the human mind or in human experience which speculation of this order can titillate, as perhaps undiluted lewdness may. The appeal is merely to the restlessness, the hankering for novelty, the impatience with the deliberateness of societal adjustment-processes, and the antipathy for protracted labor in the securing of small results that are characteristic of untried youth. It will get over them under the discipline of actual living, as the colt gets over his skittishness and begins to pull soberly in harness instead of kicking and rearing and drawing down the lash upon his hide. And experience shows that most of the young are capable of learning something out of the experience, so that they cannot be nose-led for so very long by cheap solvers of ages-defying problems.

Furthermore, and of still deeper significance, this sort of philosopher does not touch the masses of mankind at all. To follow him takes a kind of sophistication which the crowd does not possess; and so it does not either accept or reject him. Embarrassing as it may be to him, it does not even know about him. It is therefore quite immune to his influence. The register in which he hums his tenuous melodies is beyond its auditory range. He is about as influential outside his little sphere as any other philosopher; and what he spins is about as ephemeral.

There is therefore no reason for anyone to be anxious because of, even though he is annoyed by, the buzzings of the various insects that dart about the body of some long-lived thing like the family. Their stridulations do not prove anything, not even that it is sick, much less moribund or already a cadaver. Pretty soon it will rise and brush them all off. And even if they puncture the somnolent animal so that it grunts a little, that is no matter. The family is not an ox, nor do the insect pests pack the lethal weapon of the tsetse. Maybe they are annoying, like the black fly; but their bite is of no lasting significance. And they are seasonal, too; so that, at any rate, one can look forward confidently to a change of pests—which is something, just as is a shifting of galling harness to a horse.

For those pairs who do not reproduce, the family is, of course, abolished. Renunciation of the family-estate has been common enough in history among those who thought they saw eternal salvation or some other desirable to outweigh it. Possibly society suffered from counter-selection thereby, though those who bid defiance to nature have never furnished proof positive of their societal fitness. But propagation and the family have gone on just the same. The case is similar with the contemporary strivers after "higher values"; they are a relatively vanishing quantity in the equation of racial life. The masses of mankind are virtually untouched by the erratic, however noble it may be in intent. They are not vocal and what noise they make is like the inarticulate rumble of a great city—a thing we get used to and do not notice as we do a shrill shriek from someone near by or the drumthumpings of a passing salvation-seeking band. But if we listen for the *vox populi,* we become aware of the same old, monotonous, eternal tune.

Certainly there have been readjustments of the family to its environment; assuredly there have been rearrangements inside of it. But there is no gain to be made by exaggerating them into first steps toward final dissolution.

The family, like the economic organization, property, government, and religion, is an adjustment to permanent life-conditions of society. It has survived millennial selection. Its theme was set when man and woman came to be, and then to coöperate in maintenance and reproduction, according to their sex qualities. If bisexuality can be replaced by unisexuality or trisexuality, revolutionary changes in family organization may be anticipated. Otherwise not. This is not a prophecy but a scientific forecast.

As regards any one of society's major institutions, a discreet choice between the small variations that are constantly arising in them can be made, provided the nature and the past of the institution are known. The reward of discretion in the matter is the relative comfort of being in harmony with the automatic movements and rhythms of society's evolution. Men are indiscreet at their peril, the peril of being out of tune, not with the infinite, but with the steady throb of forces over which they have no control whatsoever. Society's symphonies, so to speak, are not going to be thrown off their themes by our thin and scrannel pipings of peevish discontent; if we sharp and flat too often, out we go from the orchestra. And the number of catguts we rend in our effort to outsaw the rest and drown out the theme is at our own cost.

XV

YOUTH.

THE DUTCH ETHNOLOGIST, Wilken, who spent a good part of a too-short life in the East Indies, has remarked that "we must go to school to the savage." We have done so, to no small degree. Frontier populations have found it necessary to their existence, not to say comfort, to imitate the ways of the natives. They have adopted native foods, clothing, water-craft, hunting-methods, and other items of material culture. In New England they "indianized" even to the extent of scalping. But they have generally stopped with the obviously indispensable or profitable. Where the natives were honest or peaceable or pious, the white man generally took advantage of their virtues instead of adopting and emulating them. Is there anything to learn from the simple peoples about the handling of the young?

One of the common practices of primitive peoples, around the world, is to subject youths to maturity-tests before according them a place among the adults. Ordeals, often very severe and protracted, not seldom crippling or fatal, tested the salient virtues: in the male, courage, strength, endurance, ability to do man's share in the maintenance of a family; in the female, courage, industry, fecundity, ability to do woman's part in family-maintenance. Warlike peoples laid emphasis upon militant qualities, hunters upon killing game and utilizing the meat and hides, agriculturalists upon efficiency in the various tasks of tillage. Failure to qualify as an adult by sustaining these tests left the candidate among the minors until he could pass. Among other penalties of failure was a continuing ineligibility, as of a child, to marriage. Pressure toward demonstration of maturity was so constant and traditional that the youth eagerly sought the most trying initiations and submitted to them with a kind of fanatical joy. They knew exactly what they had to do and had a pretty clear idea of the why; and they were aware of exactly what they had to expect from either failure or success. They never dreamed of asking: "What's the use?" or of forming or setting up an individual judgment in the case. They took what was prescribed and liked it.

Is this nonsensical? Evidently not. It may have been crude and even cruel, to outward seeming, but it attained its end. And the youth did not find it gratuitous and repulsive, but natural and as matter-of-course as the rest of the settled mores. It invaded no rights of which they were aware. It was like a familiar feature of physical environment —present, inescapable as winter, and to be met with resolution when the time came.

Among savages there are, of course, only a few qualities to test. A boy goes on to do what all men do: maintain themselves, and procreate and maintain the next generation; and there are not many ways of doing that double job. By the time the young are a little beyond puberty, there is not much more to learn. But what there is is hammered in relentlessly, under an iron discipline calling for strict obedience.

It is possible to contend that the qualities tested by the initiation-ceremonies of savages have never ceased to be salient and, indeed, indispensable to society's life: courage, endurance, industry, responsibility, self-control, obedience. But no examination, certainly no universal and traditional one, is any longer set to demonstrate their presence or absence in the candidates for man's or woman's estate. No one wants to hang up all the young men by straps of their own flesh, or seat them in ant-hills to see whether an unmanly groan can be extracted from them, or to flog the girls or enter them upon a hoeing-marathon. If there were to be any re-introduction of the maturity tests, they would have to take some form reflecting the modern, not the primitive, societal organization. But do we test youth at all, even informally or indirectly, before we accord them the mature status, with its attendant rights, prerogatives, and duties?

If one runs over the tests applied to those who present themselves to be "made voters," as it is called in some places, we find the toll of years to be the actual dead-line. Beyond that there is a kind of intelligence- or information-test which is designed to eliminate congenital idiots and blank illiterates, and may do that. Property-qualification, once stressed, is out. National allegiance must be sworn to, at least in form, though an oath guaranteeing militant loyalty is regarded by not a few doctrinaires as an infringement of personal judgment and liberty. It is scarcely to be denied that we have welcomed into our society many persons who would have been summarily rejected by our distant predecessors. I cannot see that we have any test whatever, certainly no thorough or adequate one, of either manhood or womanhood, prior to our formal grant of the status of political maturity. In any case, examinations of any kind, whereby one must face a crises—come up to the scratch—seem to be out of favor among us.

The initiation-test among savages was a kind of culmination of education. It summed up all the boys and girls were supposed to have learned informally from their elders, plus a certain amount of deliberate instruction inculcated in bachelors' and maidens' houses and during the often protracted earlier stages of the initiation itself. Old men, sometimes equipped with paddles, enjoined the candidates: "You no tamper with other man's wife!" driving the injunction home with a resounding whack on the traditional impression-receiving area of the neophyte's anatomy. This polishing-off review of the moral code was enforced also by awe-inspiring mysteries and dire threats of ghostly vengeance. Observers have stated that the candidates were much subdued. The savages seem to have anticipated the Greek saying, which Goethe selected as the epigraph to his life-story: "He who is not flayed [literally, "skinned"] is not educated."

But if we do not and cannot test education by any such forthright methods, do we educate the youth with sound qualifications for their maturity in view? I cannot see that we do. And one of the reasons we do not is because we are not clear as to what those qualifications are, or should be. This is explicable, in part at least, by the fact that life is now so much less simple and the qualifications for social well-living so difficult to verify. Furthermore, the bearing of what we prescribe to youth to study is not evident to youth as is, for instance, the rationale of what the experienced savage hunter enjoined, or the precepts of the modern athletic coach.

A boy of even minimal intelligence sees very soon that if he approaches game down-wind, he loses his dinner; or that if he crowds the ball against the advice of the tennis coach, he loses games; but he cannot see why he should study Latin. The results are too remote and indirect. Hence, especially in this age, which encourages him to believe his own opinion as good as that of anybody else, he becomes skeptical and lethargic, or resistant. And if you tell him he must do what he is told by older and wiser persons, he is likely to become sulky and begin to declaim about rights and freedom. He admits the "older," especially as the term now means "more out of date," but not "wiser." Educationalists encourage his favorable opinion of his own innate rightness.

I might seem to some to be an unfriendly critic of Youth. I am not. I have lived my life in deep appreciation of the many young men who have sat in my classes. I shall return to that. But I am an unfriendly critic of the way Youth has been and is treated in home, school, and college. A good many graduates ought to get an engrossed apology at graduation, instead of a diploma—in addition to a personal apology, when they come of age, from their parents. I know some conscientious parents who, in all sincerity, have offered the latter.

One of Herbert Spencer's many trenchant passages has to do with the folly of trying to run a State on lines proper to the administration of a family. He is attacking paternalism and socialism. The upshot of the matter is that the family is a school that can and should progressively emancipate, or wean, its pupils from its own perfectly natural and defensible system, so that they are prepared for living usefully and less painfully outside the family system into which they were born. Children are like plants that need some hothousing, but must eventually live in the open air, if at all. It is no service to them to so accustom them to the greenhouse that they wilt and fade when they get out into an actual world to which they are unacclimatized.

It is merely common sense that the newly born infant must have the struggle for existence carried on for him by others. Paternalism is essential to his very existence. For a while he has all rights and no duties. He has no manners. No one expects him to have them, or morals either. He is not born a fit member of society. When grown men behave like infants, social chaos ensues, for there are no norms or codes of conduct at all. The trouble with home-preparation for life in society is that this infant-stage is prolonged by parents who, taking counsel only of their affection or alleged affection as an excuse for easy indulgence both of the children and themselves, "spoil" the former by teaching them the opposite of what they will need in the world outside the home.

There is about parenthood something ridiculous, which the humorists have not failed to seize upon; they have noted that young parents regard as unique in the world's history something that has been occurring every moment since life began, namely, birth—the "coming of a new soul into the world"; and that their vanity, or whatever else the sentiment may be, leads them to regard their own offspring as a miraculous combination of all that is beautiful, bright, and noble. This is, very likely, a sentiment implanted by Nature for her own ends, namely, the assurance that the mature generation shall focus attention, effort, and self-sacrifice the more sharply upon the generation that is to replace it; but, as is so often the case, that which is biologically expedient can be at hopeless odds with what is socially expedient.

In any case, wisdom is not conferred along with parenthood. Rather is it benumbed by that moving experience. A certain essayist once undertook a character-sketch of "The Hen." After reviewing at some length the list of her unbelievable inanities, he seemed to despair of exhausting the topic, for he suddenly wound up with the comprehensive summary: "The Hen is a Durned Fool." It would be unjustified to contend that the Parent was being symbolized in the Hen, but if anybody insisted upon that interpretation, one would know what he meant.

A tolerant and serene old gentleman who had been dean of a college for many years once remarked, in reply to an assertion that seventy-five per cent of the cases of college discipline would not exist had there been an adequate home-training: "More than that, Mr. Keller. Ninety per cent." School has to take up a good deal of slack left by the home. It will all be taken up eventually by that cold and inexorable schoolmaster, The World. And the taking up is exceedingly painful for those who are the products of parental slackness. Through indulgence to leave them exposed to the World's unsparing rod is no service to them. And it is a flagrant disservice to society.

It must not be forgotten, either, that the indulgence upon which parents pride themselves and accord appreciation to others—"he is at least an indulgent father"—is really self-indulgence. It is the easiest way. It is like the easy "generosity" that costs nothing, whereas genuine generosity involves self-denial. It is also the shortsighted way, that seeks instant satisfaction at the expense of future discomfort. If there were no future, there could be no fault found with absorption in the present. If a child were sure to die before nightfall, who would not let him eat anything he wanted or do anything whatever that he wished? There would be no point in teaching him manners or refusing to let him occupy the center of the stage which he is about to leave. But the older must assume not only that the young have a future to face but that they themselves will not be there to help. Those now young must face it alone.

Any other theory is prima facie absurd—unless, indeed, there is to be organized in society some duality of workers and loafers, the former charged with the duty of hothousing the latter throughout life, the latter endowed with all the rights there are. History has shown what happens to that kind of an arrangement. And experience is ready, at any time, to demonstrate the hard lot of the spoiled child who has never learned to keep his elbows in and otherwise to respect the rights of others. The unlicked cub is a misfit in the world, and he is never happy, for, knowing only Liberty and Rights, he has not made the acquaintance of Discipline and Duty—and the latter pair of traffic-cops stride up and down the ways of the world, from the dawn of man's creation until the very end. It is salutory to know them.

Does the home endow the candidates for the estate of maturity with proper equipment? Not often. Parents do indeed try to provide for their children's material welfare in obvious ways, but comparatively few of them, realizing that consequences are their best friends and that their inestimable privilege is to temper consequences, not to annul them, subordinate their children's and their own present comfort to the formers' long future interest. Much less do they take account of the interest of society. That calls for study and thought, which are the sour impositions of a conscientiousness that is itself a burden.

The public schools impose something in the way of discipline. It is significant that "discipline" meant originally "schooling" or "learning." There used to be a good deal of discipline in the schools. The old idea, as expressed by the seer of Archey Road, was that it made little difference what a boy studied so long as he did not like it. There is sense in that aphorism, for it is pulling against resistance that strengthens, and not muscular fiber alone but also mental and moral thews. Nowadays, under the spell of a liberty that runs out into license —a spell that has been muttered over art, literature, and all other aspects of society's life—the element of discipline in education seems to have entered eclipse. It will come out again from the penumbra, with renewed enlightenment as the result. It must; for Society needs it and will become chaotic in proportion as its light is dimmed.

There is one solace that, in his depression, one must not overlook. The schools afford a range of education for life in the world that is in no way dependent upon their curricula, however sound or freakish. The pupils discipline each other by standing up and asserting their real or fancied rights. Many a spoiled child has been rudely taught by his schoolmates that lack of sportsmanship is a disqualification for living endurably. The arrogant winner and the poor loser are alike made to feel the error of their ways. That means that, once bereft of the indulgence of the hothouse, the protected sprig must toughen up in fiber or be eliminated from the Gang, with its rough-and-ready code that is not so different from that of the savage. School life, especially in the public schools, is a kind of course in elementary folkways. It exposes the young to a kind of social selection that is natural in the sense of not being formally imposed. The public school has often straightened out the unlovely inclinations of the pampered youthful olive branch.

This may be taken to mean that the school, despite itself, educates for life. That is true enough, but it is no tribute to the educationalist. It does not ratify his Planning. It simply offers additional evidence that societal evolution, and especially societal selection, is typically unpremeditated and non-rational, being the result of the operation of forces that come into play automatically when human beings must live in proximity. As usual, the most rational procedure would be to identify those forces as we can, learn all we may about their nature and mode of operation, and adjust our conduct to them as to immutable life-conditions of society.

It cannot be said that the colleges, for all their talk about "service" to society, and with all their anxious effort to prove themselves no longer "academic," have succeeded very well, as yet, in putting on the finishing touches to education for life in society. Rather have they found yards and yards of slack to take up—slack left dangling by the slackness of home and school. Some colleges feel it beneath them to do such repair-work—even to remedy illiteracy of students who have never learned the rudiments of English style, much less to drill away the undisciplined stragglings of a truly awkward squad. They are intent upon constructing gambrels and seating gargoyles far up in the empyrean, assuming that the foundations have been soundly laid by groundlings of hypothetical efficiency—"schoolmasters" of somewhat plebeian tastes.

I have elsewhere[1] set down my impressions of contemporary college education. I cannot see that, with some notable exceptions, the college curricula make very strongly for a socially enlightened graduate body. But the college, like the school, has shown itself to be a kind of automatically acting instrumentality of education for life among one's fellows. It, like the school, is a kind of society in miniature—a kind of laboratory, if you will, where the atmosphere, at least, is not unlike that outside the pales that enclose the academic structure. And this despite the evident tendency of most colleges to follow the present line of least resistance: more ostentation, and greater acquisition of endowment and popularity by relaxation of discipline in favor of an equivocal freedom.

We have certainly not gone to school to the savage in this respect

1. "Educational Planning," *School and Society*, November 21 and 28, 1936.

of educating the next generation as regards the qualifications and responsibilities of maturity, not to mention examining them sternly and relentlessly prior to conferring upon them the status of manhood and womanhood. The reason the savage did that was because there was always upon him a pressure that he could not ignore. Civilization has removed many varieties of pressure from us. We live behind barriers which it has erected against Nature's realistic tests of survival or non-survival. Our sufferings, although referable at bottom to maladjustments like those into which the savage drifted, can be plausibly charged to any number of irrelevant or secondary factors which, in the fabric of our immensely complicated societal structure, have come to overlie and conceal the essential master strands upon which the whole is woven. It takes arduous labor and cold analysis to lay bare the master strands, whereas in the open work of a simpler structure they remained always visible.

You do not have to demonstrate to nature-man the paramount importance of work, thrift, capital, property, obedience, discipline, and the rest of the traditional social virtues. He is not taken in very long by economic utopias. Realities are too near. No matter, for instance, how pious he is, he is found dodging in some manner the burden of the cult. He has to. What he does is to interpret his religious theory or creed so that he can do what he has to: the daimons, he holds, have enjoyed the spiritual essence of the burnt offering—the smell of burning grease, and now he may without sin eat the de-spiritualized meat. We do something of the sort ourselves, say in the separation of Church and State; yet it is in a far less direct and realistic manner. It too belongs to the category of automatic adjustment.

But, however excusable we may be, we do not employ to any great extent, in the matter of fitting the Youth for Maturity, the rational and planful procedure upon which we are wont to plume ourselves.

I intimated, along back, that I am no unfriendly critic of Youth. I think that what I have said since is evidence of that fact. I do not blame flour for being gritty because it has been carelessly and clumsily ground. I blame the miller—or, it might be fairer to say, I do not share the self-complacency of the miller. Maybe he knows no better, and has inferior instrumentalities. The point is that if he put his mind upon it, he might do better. He is neither informed enough, nor serious enough, about his job. Indeed, he is not seldom unaware of what his job is. He thinks that intuition and an occasional bright idea are a complete equipment. I suppose it is not right to use the term "blame" in adjudging him. But I am sorry for him, sorry for his product, and sorry for Society. He, or it, may well be suffering under the racket so firmly established by the exponents of pedagogy.

Now, as to Youth, the product. No elderly man who remembers his own youth can take its self-evident follies very seriously, especially when he realizes that it has been egged on to be foolish by those in charge of it, who ought to have known better. You cannot often say that Youth ought to know better, for it lacks experience of its own and has not been very well instructed in that of others. At the present time, indeed, it is being taught from high places that experience does not count at all, or at least not in comparison with noble, wishful thinking.

Of late, certain whining old grandmothers have even been abasing themselves before the youth of the land, piling ashes upon their white or bald heads and beating their breasts, intoning the while: *"Nostra culpa! Nostra maxima culpa!"* Abjectly they have moaned: "Here! You take the world's destiny over into your unspoiled hands. We, alas! have failed you. Accept our apologies for having existed."

Others of us who are elderly have nothing of that sort to say. If we thought it worth while to bandy epithets, we should call such utterances "defeatism," rejecting the current connotation of that term according to which it is applied to any critic of any noble-sounding scheme who refuses to be stampeded into a credulity dressed up as "open-mindedness" or "liberalism." We are not abdicating yet awhile. Our word to youth is: "Let's see you do any better when your turn comes. And your turn will come when you have learned enough and have acquired a high enough degree of maturity to possess a right to an opinion."

It is a poetic thought that we come into the world trailing clouds of glory; but it is a fact that we enter life without knowledge, manners, or morals, and have to acquire all three by way of discipline. Wisdom does not vary inversely with the count of years. There are young fools as well as old ones, even though it be freely agreed that there is no fool like an old one—which is another way of stating that some kinds of foolishness, at least, are incongruous with maturity. If it is desirable to fix upon a quantity with which wisdom varies inversely, it is, of course, ignorance, especially an ignorance of which he who displays it is unaware—above all, a zealous ignorance, which Goethe—I quote him once again—called the most terrible thing in the world.

I myself have always found youth reasonable when treated sensibly.

If a young man of twenty is told by his elders that they have made a
horrible mess of things and now pass on, shamefacedly, to him the task
of rescuing humanity from its woes, hoping that from "our" gross
and pathetic blunders "you" may learn how not to do it, why should
he not become overconfident, iconoclastic, and even impertinent?[2]
Many cases of strenuous resistance have appeared in my own class-
room, where interested students have made a shocked first acquaintance with facts inconsistent with views hitherto unquestioningly held.
There was nothing to do to alleviate this natural and wholesome distress except to listen with sympathy to their emotional outcries and to
see that whatever facts they had were not overlooked, impatiently
rejected, or speciously explained away. The average college man needs
only to face a set of facts awhile—and he recognizes a fact when he
sees it—before he will square up to them unflinchingly, after letting
himself rage at them for a space. In short, the young American, as I
have known him, is intellectually honest and fearless. That is quite
a tribute to him. He has not yet made acquaintance with opportunism.

I shall make no attempt here to list or to weigh the qualities of age
and youth, with the idea of assigning superiority to either. Each has
its qualities. The paramount conclusion that can be arrived at by
aligning them is that, like the sex qualities, they are complementary.
That conclusion has substance, and also high value for the understanding. It is enlightening to note how the qualities of the ages, as of the
sexes, have cogged into one another throughout society's long
evolution.[3]

Any present-day comparison of the qualities of youth and age, however, no matter how dispassionate, will seem to favor Age. For Youth,
like Liberty, arouses enthusiasm, as Age, like Discipline, does not.
Youth is beautiful, interesting, and hopeful, as Age is not. "In the
youth who has perished in battle," mourns Priam,[4] "all is seemly, as
he lies there; all that is seen is fair, even in death." And he goes on to
contrast the "most pitiful" sight of the slain old man. There is always
a presumption in favor of youth. One writer of fiction[5] has put the
case as follows. A father has been discussing various matters with his
son, who has expressed differing and positive opinions. The father

2. "Youth States Its Case," letter in *New York Times,* April 27, 1936.
3. Keller, A. G., *Brass Tacks,* pp. 225 ff.
4. *Iliad,* XXII, 71–76.
5. Stewart Edward White, *Folded Hills,* p. 221.

"had a queer irrational feeling that their rôles had been reversed, that the austerities of judgment remained with" his son. This was the father's "first experience with the gloriously assured convictions of youth." The son "was absolutely certain"; the father was not. To the son, "for the moment that mere fact lent an illusory moral dominance."

Against so natural a prepossession as regards youth, any attempt at an impartial alignment of its colorful qualities with the somewhat worn and drab features of age, especially if the writer is elderly, is bound to seem to be an ex parte performance. That cannot be helped. I may state the fact, however, that I have had to do with youth, as my business in life, for forty-odd years, and in considerable numbers; and that relations with many young men have constituted the chief interest and compensation in my profession. In no sense have I ever esteemed them lightly, and in no case of any significance have I been treated by them otherwise than with considerateness, courtesy, and good will. The youth I have known have been a fine lot. This opinion that I hold of them has never prevented me from telling them home-truths when I thought I ought to do so, and will not soften anything I may be moved to set down about them at any time; but it may conduce to a truer appreciation of the attitude in which I am facing my subject.

Poor Richard[6] will be decried as a prejudiced old man when he states: "*Youth* is pert and positive, *age* modest and doubting: so ears of corn when young and light stand bolt upright, but hang their heads when weighty, full and ripe." Lincoln[7] is a little more tart concerning Youth: "He owns a large part of the world by right of possessing it, and all the rest by right of wanting it, and intending to have it. . . . His horror is for all that is old, particularly 'Old Fogy.'"

If I should ever seem to be making a brief for the generation to which I belong, that would be to some extent defensible as taking the part of the underdog. Age needs the stouter defense because of the elderly defeatists who are crying it down. Certainly the word "old" has been tagged in recent years with an uncomplimentary connotation. The easiest off-hand condemnation of almost anything is to call it "old," and all you have to do to attract immediate and favorable attention to anything or any project is to acclaim it as "new." One who seeks to hold the scales level between old and new, age and youth,

6. Franklin, B., *Poor Richard's Almanack*. Selections (N. Y., 1899), p. 137.
7. Sandburg, C., *Lincoln, the Prairie Years*, II, 240.

will seem to favor that one of the pair which occupies the beam-kicking pan. The writer, being aware of this situation, is resigned to the charge of special pleading, though spotlessly innocent of it.

No society is safe in the hands of either of the two indispensables, Youth or Age. It is secure only when there is a blend of the two, as of liberty and discipline, rights and duties, variation and tradition, liberalism and conservatism.

XVI

EVIDENCE.

THE EVIDENCE for a science of society, as for any other science, is to be found in experience. Experience must be past, or historic, in order to be experience. It must also be repeated, if it is to have any cogency. In the impossibility of experiment, the science of society must rely upon historic records rather than upon a laboratory, that is, upon records of processes set up neither under artificially established controls, nor with a scientific end in view. Out of a welter of accounts of human experience recorded for reasons irrelevant to science, it must seek to disengage the nature and workings of underlying forces that may reasonably be termed automatic, impersonal, unpremeditated, spontaneous, natural, original, universal. Nevertheless, scientific procedure within the social range involves no mysteries or revelations; it is the same old stock, reliable process whereby bodies of observed and verified facts of experience have been so handled as to express from them the inflexible nature and ways of the impersonal forces that have brought them to pass.

Observation of the way things are, that is, of facts, is the basis of all science. In dealing with material things, like rocks or wood, not only do observers commonly agree, but verification in case of disagreement is at hand. Nobody needs to rely on someone's say-so, for he can get his own original experience firsthand, and also be confident that the stone or wood he is experimenting with has not changed its character between observations. But with social facts the case is seldom or never so clean-cut, for a subjective element may enter into the most trivial observation and, in the impossibility of re-observation, reliance has to be reposed upon a comparison of many or, not seldom, a few say-so's. It may even occur that two contemporary observers of the same historic situation, now so long past as to be no longer re-observable, contradict each other. In that case, there is no evidence at all, unless there exists some reason, apart from the specific case, for trusting one observer rather than the other. In general, a science of society has to rest largely upon a comparison of say-so's. It lacks other means of verification.

Pareto is so impressed by the unreliability of the evidence from prehistory, or even history, that he proposes to start with the present, as something we know, and work back to explain the past, which he seems to think we cannot otherwise come to know. If that point of view is correct, the past would seem to many of us not worth bothering about except as a kind of antiquarian curiosity. Its records would be of no utility for the understanding of the present, for if the past can be understood only in the light of the present, it can hardly be thought that the present, for its understanding, needs the past at all. That point of view seems to me a mistaken one. I concur rather with those who hold that "the obscurest epoch is today." It is obscure as anything too near is obscure. We need the distance and detachment of perspective. Nor is it credible that the past, in its more general outlines, is so obscure as Pareto asserts—not even the chronological past, which alone he seems to have in mind, much less the evolutionary past, which seems not to have entered into his purview.

Pareto has no use for any other teacher of mankind than experience; only he has in mind merely that very recent experience which he calls "the present." But recent or "contemporary" experience, like new wine, lacks maturity and mellowness, the seasoned reliability embodied in the phrase "the verdict of history." No man of sense would wish to ignore the contemporaneous; the contention here is that for the understanding of the present there is need of the background and perspective provided by the past; that one has always to simplify the complex before he can comprehend it; and that the evolutionary past, whether it is or is not the chronological past, alone provides such simplification, in its portrayal of the lower terms of the complex quantities of the present.

The evolutionary past is portrayed in ethnography and history; in the latter there is also the element of chronology, though it is not nearly so important scientifically as has been supposed. I am coming, eventually, to the technically historical evidence; for the moment, I want to add a little to what is said in *The Science of Society* about the evidence to be derived out of ethnography, prehistory, legend, cultural anthropology, and other phases of history which the historian has ignored because they did not fit into traditional categories, especially the chronological, to which, true to its origin in chronicle, history has remained so partial.

The validity of ethnographical evidence, whatever "logical" objection may be made to it, has been demonstrated by those who have actually employed it, notably by Spencer. The basic adjustment-problems of all mankind have been, in kind, the same. All societies have faced the same broad life-conditions: the physical, social, and supernatural environments and bisexuality. There is no sharp cleft anywhere up the line from the most primitive to the most sophisticated forms of adjustment. The whole display is an evolutionary development of form out of form in a connected series, under the activity of variation, selection, and transmission. And, as one works up through the series, he acquires a perception of essentials that acts, like a kind of mental momentum, to carry him on an even keel into the debatable contemporary waters. The felt need of background, thus only to be correctly attained, has been recognized by writers on contemporary phenomena—for example, by those who have presented systems of economics or of social philosophy in general—in their rather shaky assumptions about what the primitive stages "must have been" but often were not. The crudest guesses of the sort have been those of the inventors of the "state of nature," the "noble savage," the "pure race," and similar gossamer phantasies. Less sweeping assumptions have been, in their degree, no less misleading.

And even those who have not ventured to formulate sheer guesses have labored under the impression that chronological sequences were essential. Pareto is willing, apparently, to go as far back as Homer because he thinks that there is an unbroken chronological sequence from that point. This is true enough, perhaps, culturally speaking; not racially, however, for only those who are under the illusion of the "pure race" can believe that the modern Greeks or Romans derive, without a metamorphosing intermixture destructive of identity, from the stocks represented by Achilles or Romulus. The history of any specific "people" is a short record. Indeed, history itself, if it is taken to derive from written records and established chronology—which is what the historians have seemed, through their own practices and their strictures on other types of evidence, to maintain—covers only a few millennia of the multimillennial life of mankind. And some historians would not go so far as Pareto; a very eminent one once pointed out the uselessness of the study of Homeric institutions because nothing could be dated.

If you insist upon chronology or upon the records of a single people, you cannot expect to uncover a very long sequence, much less one undisturbed by the entrance of distorting factors of all description. Relatively short, also, is the cultural sequence, which soon breaks down if you insist upon weaving it about a single racial or national strand.

Suppose you construct a cultural sequence, allowing yourself to start with Chaldaea and Egypt, as Pareto does not, then shift to Greece, then to Italy, then via various European paths down to the present— had, then, the Semitic stock no part in this sequence, even granted that the Oriental contribution, as a minor source, be ignored?

Sooner or later, in the search for social sequences and cultural perspective, the technically historic range is found to be a cramping one. This would be so, even if it were fully utilizable for that purpose, which it is not.

The truth is that chronological and racial sequences admit of no adequate perspective. The alternative presents itself of either abandoning perspective altogether or attaining it by some other means. The only other kind of sequence is the evolutionary series, which minimizes considerations of time, place, and identity of culture-carriers in favor of an arrangement of cultural phenomena on the criterion of their adjustmental characteristics. This is an approved method in science, for no science is limited either in time, race, or space. There can be no science of society under any such limitations, or in the absence of the comparative method. Science is nothing if not exempt from such taboos.

The criticism of the science of society that it gathers its evidence from different and widely separated places, times, and racial stocks is as pointless as it would be to find fault with an accepted organic series, that of the horse, for instance, because it is filled in from various times and places. If it could be shown, a posteriori, that you cannot get anywhere by constructing such sequences, instead of merely being alleged, a priori, that you cannot, that would be a crushing blow. As a matter of fact, the evolutionary sequence has turned out to be, in all ranges, including the societal, indefinitely enlightening. There is no apology called for, on the part either of those who have employed it or of those who intend to use it right along. Interest inheres in the evolution of society's institutions as adjustments to society's life-conditions; the where, the when, or the who in the case is of vanishing importance.

This being the fact of the matter, archaeological, prehistoric, and ethnographical evidence is wholly pertinent, and not to be looked askance upon because of logical quibbles or dicta from equivocal authority. All that is essential is the handling of this evidence in a genuinely scientific manner, that is, with a trained common sense.

I do not propose to describe that process. But the warning should be reiterated that all the materials which a science of society finds available as evidence are by nature more difficult to handle than those upon which the natural sciences have worked, and that the social scientist needs to be the more scrupulous in his manipulations just because he is new at it and the more exposed to the gibes and sneers of those who would like to see him make a fool of himself. He can take heart by reason of the much improved quality of his ethnographic evidence; for where once it was furnished casually by untrained observers with various types of bias, there has been for decades now a flow of data assembled by trained, objective minds. One should not condemn the old observers, as a body, for there were men of cold sense among them, nor yet swallow forthwith all the later reports, for new forms of bias have sometimes crept in, to produce novel types of distortion.

Except for the foregoing generalities, this essay addresses itself to the assessment of two types of evidence: that derivable from "pure literature" and that which is, as yet, only partially available in existing histories.

The former is a particular, technically unhistoric type of evidence that happened to enlist my interest at the outset of my professional studies and has held it ever since, namely, the evidence offered by literary materials. Since my predecessor was a strong advocate of putting to use what one already knew, he encouraged me to undertake the study of the cultural content of Homer. I expressed some misgiving as to what the classicists and historians might say to a study of that kind. "God knows what they will say!" replied Sumner; "but I will set you a theme to indicate what I want." The "Theme" follows:

Writers on the history of civilization, and on sociology, make references to Homer's poems for proof, illustration, etc. of generalizations affirmed by them. Such use of the poems may be fallacious, because the passages used may be isolated, fragmentary, selected, interpreted under bias, etc. It is required to make an exhaustive and unbiassed study of the poems, gathering under sociological categories whatever, and all, the product they offer for the use of the student of the history of civilization.

This was my introduction to pure literature, or belles-lettres, as a source of scientific evidence for society's evolution. What came of it, in the hands of a young and green student, is recorded in a small volume entitled *Homeric Society*. I had a good deal of trouble in determining what, in Homer, was evidence and what was not, but eventually worked out a general basis of discrimination. I do not want to trench upon what I shall have to say, a little later on, about Homeric evidence, but I shall, in this place, use Homer, as well as a few other authors, merely to point the broad distinction between evidence and non-evidence in literature.

In dealing with such materials, it is necessary to distinguish what may be called theme and setting. The theme is purposefully developed, the setting not. One must be much more critical of the former than of the latter. It is true that much can be learned from the study of the theme without at all accepting its validity, just as we can derive enlightenment from the history of any imaginative construction, like astrology or metaphysical speculation; for a strong light is shed by delusions upon the course of human thought. But the theme cannot be accepted forthwith as true, while the setting can. No one can believe that the plague, with which the *Iliad* opens, was caused by Apollo's arrows; but he can accept at once the theory of disease and the method of treatment revealed in the development of that episode. No one need credit Agamemnon's dream, but when the king awakens and puts on his garments, piece by piece, we have at least an objective picture of Homeric clothing.

The theme is something that the author is trying to "put across" by any means that seem to him effective; the setting is merely the background, taken out of ordinary life as lived at the time, with no idea of preserving a record of that life, in either veracious or ideal form, for the information or edification of future ages. The information is truly veracious because there is no object whatever in coloring it to produce effect. It is quite objective because there is no premeditation about it. It must be realistic in order to make the whole production plausible.

This sort of evidence ranks very high. Even the best type of ethnographer, being a purposeful observer from without, has to coach himself all the time to remain objective and to refrain from rationalizing. Even the conscious recorder of the mores of his own age is very likely to turn ethnocentric or patriotic or to engage in face-saving, that is, to become subjective. But the teller of tales, while he may become subjectively sinful as you like while developing his theme, is likely to be quite unconsciously and automatically objective in the matter of his setting. He must be so, I repeat, if he is going to lend verisimilitude to his enterprise; for fidelity to actuality in his background is one of his most effectual instrumentalities in securing for his theme an understanding reception.

I have held the substance of these views for many years,[1] having
had no occasion to modify them except in the direction of a strengthening of conviction. And not only that. I have come likewise to believe that later and more sophisticated literature contains considerably
more evidence for a science of society than has been accredited to it.

Since legend, as in the outstanding case of Homer, may be also literature of the highest grade, there is not so much of an abyss between
it and more sophisticated forms, not excluding the most modern, as
one might imagine at first sight. There is in all literature the same discrimination to be drawn between theme and setting, between the purposeful aim and the background in actual life before which exposition
takes place—a background portrayed not for itself at all but in the
interest of the theme. The theme may be designed purely to divert or
amuse; it may amount to the inculcation of some "lesson"; it may be
mere propaganda, religious, political, or other; but in no case can it
be suspended, unsupported, in thin air. And the ground it must rest
upon must be real, even though to some extent selected. It is true that,
as modern life is more complex than primitive existence, so too is modern literature more difficult to handle by reason of the entrance of
many factors, such as the didactic, which are represented not at all, or
in simpler and more obvious guise, in the older poems and tales.
Nevertheless it is maintained that there is, in all literature, a considerable residue of valuable evidence concerning the social life of its place
and time that can be extracted from the setting by the discriminating
student.

It is not that the theme is wholly and always under suspicion. Since
Schliemann's time we know that Homer used an historic setting, not
merely an imaginary one; and we might consider Shakespeare's use of
Holinshed and other chroniclers as a later parallel. Both needed a kind
of armature around which to apply the clay of their imaginative structure. Shakespeare was not particular about checking up on his sources,
and probably Homer was not. It is evident that the scientific student
must do that for himself before he accepts anything out of the theme
that may be purely impressionistic.

And even in the case of writers with the message—say, Tolstoi—it
is possible to effect, in varying degree, the elimination of the purposeful, thus leaving a residue of objectively portrayed setting. For even

1. Keller, "Sociology and the Epic," *American Journal of Sociology,* September,
1900; "Sociology and Homer," *American Journal of Sociology,* July, 1903.

the author who is most tendentious cannot color his whole setting to the hue of his sermonizing characters. Nevertheless, one must remain critical of all "themes."

Even a work presented as historical, such as Tolstoi's *War and Peace* or Carlyle's *French Revolution,* has to be handled with great caution. A reader of Tolstoi speedily realizes that he has to do with a preacher of doctrine, a teacher of "lessons," far removed from Shakespearean impersonality. This is the more evident if one reflects upon *Anna Karénina.* He thus acquires a sort of "yardstick" for Tolstoi. Nothing such is to be attained by the comprehensive reading of Shakespeare. Even more unmistakable is the emergence of a controlling dogmatic purpose in Dante's *Divina Commedia* or Milton's *Paradise Lost;* the opening lines of the latter announce its theme, indeed, in so many words. Tolstoi attempts a special interpretation of history; Dante and Milton a literary presentation of theological doctrine; no one of the three presents much in the way of setting that can be put to immediate scientific use. The Greek tragedies are pervaded by a kind of unexplicit doctrine—"Count no man happy till he is dead"— and even *Faust* works up to the broad "lesson" of life: *"Wer immer strebend sich bemüht, Den können wir erlösen";* but there is no specific "teaching" in either the Greeks or Goethe as there is in Dante and Milton.

Here are several scattering types of outstanding masterpieces to illustrate the degrees of dominance of themes over whole productions. The more dominant the theme, the less available the setting, for it will be sparse, selected, and colored in proportion to the degree of immersion of the author in his revelation, message, or mission. One who sets out to "justify the ways of God to man" is on a plane where science can hope to glean but few objective pickings.

There is yet another type of "truth" in literature that is neither theme nor setting. It might be called the flash of insight. It may be true. No reader of the classics of any literature is going to deny that the great writers have from time to time hit off a profound truth in an unforgettable epigram, couplet, or haunting phrase. So have the outstanding prose writers; and when they have done so, they are likely to be aligned with the poets because poets are the recognized specialists in that sort of thing. Any apt phrasing of condensed wisdom is likely to be denominated "Shakespearean" because, to English-speaking peoples, at least, Shakespeare is the exponent par excellence of the inevitable phrase. Such pungent pellets of wisdom are like proverbs in their appeal to corroboration by experience. But all such telling phrases demand critical assessment before acceptation; for there are also poetical pellets of anything but wisdom. They appeal solely to emotion or fancy, and may remain current for a long time despite their disharmony with experience. Many of Browning's optimisms are of this order, for instance the much quoted: "Grow old along with me; The best is yet to be." To accept that sentiment, one must realize that the author harbored a very special connotation of "best," a religious one, as the rest of the poem indicates. The appeal is to something else than all the facts; and it must not be overlooked that poetic universals, like other universals, are deflatable under the prick of even one sole adverse instance, one single refractory fact.

The truth is that poets and other exponents of the flash of insight or of intuition have emitted numbers of impressive sayings clothed in beautiful form, which may be truth, half-truth, or no truth at all. The only way to tell is to subject them to realistic test, the kind of verification that science specializes in. What the master of words can do, when he gets hold of a genuine truth, is to express it in concise, striking, inevitable, memorable form. He can beat all the rest of us at that game, and we are wise to adopt his version. The collections of the student or teacher of the science of society are much enriched by samples of his craft. An expert in language, like Kipling, or even, occasionally, some inferior fiction writer under the spell of composition, may coin a phrase—or, it may even be, pass off an unrecognized plagiarism— that is so much more graphic than anything encountered in treatises, that one hastens to reach for his tablets. A case in point is: "Quality prevents equality." Many another could be cited. It pays the scientist to read literature for the sake of such by-products and for the improvement of his usually deplorable style, even if he gets nothing else out of it. But—and this is the nub of the whole matter as regards the "flash of insight"—every such alluring piece of phraseology needs to be subjected to test on the facts, not accepted forthwith as truth. Phrase-makers are expositors, not investigators.

One might develop the topic of "the poet [or other artist] knows" under such query-headings as "What does he know?" "How does he know it?" "What of it?" These are the questions, as Sumner used to tell us, that should be asked about any proponent of alleged truth. They are the stock questions of science. It is scientific knowledge, not some strange and unearthly "epistemological" type, that this essay has solely in view. If one wants to center upon other kinds of "knowledge," that is his privilege; but it is no less a privilege to focus, as here, upon the kind of knowledge that can sustain test on the criteria of experience.

The truth is that all art is expository, not heuristic. The trouble is that telling exposition is readily mistaken for discovery or insight. One of the most effective instrumentalities of exposition is metaphor, along with other figures of speech, especially analogy. Professional expositors of pre-accepted theses, or dogma, have always doted upon such "verbal manifestations," as Pareto calls them. They all amount to elaboration of deduction, whereas science rests upon induction. Any deduction is valid enough if founded upon sound induction but not otherwise. Hence the reiterated warning against acceptation of any and all attractive generalizations or universals, even from the loftiest bard, without the application of Huxley's *"tätige Skepsis."*

Having considered the evidence derivable, provided the utmost caution is unremittingly exercised, from the literary theme and the sporadic flash of insight, let us now look further into the availability of the setting, realizing always, as has been stated, that theme and setting interpenetrate in a more or less close intimacy, so that sharp distinctions between them, as between any two interrelated evolutionary forms, cannot be expected. With full realization of this truth, however, it is yet possible to draw the type-distinctions, the species-distinctions, familiar to scientific procedure. There can be no absolute rules in the case. I shall confine myself to illustration, in the main, and in so doing shall not omit mention of the evidence derivable out of theme or flash of insight, where it occurs. It is understood that any setting presented by any literary work should be verified as thoroughly as possible before being utilized at all, but that the artist who is presenting his setting simply as such may bring to his portrayal of social phenomena a freshness of viewpoint, not blurred by theory or dulled by use, that in itself may offer much more than the formal recital of bare facts. His sketch may reveal something quite valid, over and above what a mere photograph can show; and, if it tells the truth, it will clothe its truth in a guise attractive to the reader. One might well prefer to show to the beginning student a slightly inaccurate picture—calling attention to its inaccuracies—than a painfully photographic but deathly uninteresting descriptive catalogue. There are perils in "going to fiction for the facts," but they are to be set off against the dangers of choking interest by impeccable dullness. I have used London's *Before Adam* in an elementary class in anthropology without noting any ill effects.

This feat of an outstanding artist, though faulty in certain inessential and easily identified particulars, is an incomparable and unforgettable picture, with an atmosphere that no learned treatise could generate. And the student has shown sense enough to take it for what it is worth.

In the following brief survey of literary products, authors are chosen rather arbitrarily, but not in the sense that any have been omitted because they have not appealed to my personal taste. Any layman's knowledge of literature is sure to be spotty; and I am limiting myself to what I have studied with attention to the original. In general, I am citing the works commonly regarded as masterpieces, excluding only the Bible and *Don Quixote*. There is a wealth of evidence in the Old Testament, and probably a good deal in Cervantes's classic; but I have the bias of a severe orthodox training as regards the former and have not as yet a close acquaintance with the latter. Familiarity with the original is not so important in the case of prose; when I touch upon the novel, I shall feel at liberty to cite from translations.

The first of the masterpieces of world-literature to be reviewed are the *Iliad* and the *Odyssey*. The Homeric poems afford the best case for the sort of evidence in question: there is more of them; they are more homogeneous, integrated, and consistent, not being so susceptible to critical anatomization on the basis of multiple authorship, or editorship, or time-strata; and there is in them no priestly or other distorting slant—not in the *Odyssey,* at any rate, where appears no dominating military or class bias. To establish these contentions, Homer may be compared with the Old Testament, the sacred books of the East, the Norse sagas, or other bodies of legend and tradition. What is true of the Homeric poems as offering evidential data is, however, true in varying degree of all such legendary literature.

The *Iliad* and *Odyssey* are the most naïvely objective large body of poetry extant. Neither conveys any lesson, gospel, or doctrine; there are a few comments on life which might be called generalizations, but they are conspicuous only by reason of their rarity. In short, Homer has a good, semi-historical story to tell, the details of which are already well known to his hearers, and he concentrates upon telling it in the plausible terms of common life as commonly lived.

He offers, consequently, materials concerning the life of his time that are comprehensive, unselected for any tendentious purpose, presented with simplicity and objectivity. He tells what men do rather than what they are supposed to think. Theme and setting are readily distinguishable. One need not believe that Achilles's horse spoke to him in Greek; he may be as skeptical as he likes concerning the credulity of Homer's audiences as regards such incidents; but when Odysseus is done recounting his adventures, you have learned something definite, important or not, about Homeric ships and navigation. Let me repeat, because Homer is my best and model case, that you can generally discriminate easily between what he has his eye on, consciously—what he is deliberately trying to "put over"—and what he uses, looking out of the corner of his eye, so to speak, as a proper and plausible setting. His only interest in the setting is to have it plausible because accurate; if it is not so, his major interest, in his story, is injured. For the setting must be taken in stride, as a matter of course, by the audience, which he can hold only by keeping it intent upon the story, not distracted by unfamiliar detail in the setting. No other of my cases is so simple and clear, demanding so little caution.

Out of Homer's wealth of setting there can be attained a remarkably full reconstruction of Homeric society and its institutions, economic life, property-system, government, religion, marriage and the family, and recreational practices. It is fair to say that, without the *Iliad* and the *Odyssey,* we should be much deeper in the dark concerning the earliest stages of Western culture. Homeric society is, so to speak, European society in its simplest recorded terms. And that it is an important link in the general evolutionary series of social organization, stretching from the primitive to the contemporary, is a truth familiar to all students of society's evolution.

Evidence that is set down by contemporary recorders with no purpose except to get it right and with little or no unconscious tendency to color it is, I make no apology for insisting, evidence second to none. This conviction, formed in my youth, has been confirmed by my experience since.

Homer may be styled the first member of a long series of Western literary productions that have become classics. Greek tragedy and comedy come next. I shall dismiss the comedies with brief mention, not alone because I am less familiar with them but also because their case is simpler. They are nearer the common life than the tragedies, and their settings, though selected, are richer. Satire is likely to handle its materials by way of exaggeration and distortion; at the same time, it is not likely to ascend beyond the common level of understanding. It makes fun of Aeschylus's big words or Euripides's stylistic habits, expecting to strike a chord that has already been vibrating in the perception of most of the auditors of the tragedians. Homely and familiar instances are its stock in trade. If allowance is made for the nature and object of comedy, the picking is pretty good and the gleanings are sound. The evidence-searcher can get a good deal out of Aristophanes.

The Greek tragedies offer nothing approaching a systematic or exhaustive survey of the folkways of their time; if they did, they would exhibit a purposeful quality saturated with subjectivity and lacking all the unconscious spontaneity that makes their evidence, such as it is, trustworthy. That is why I speak of "gleanings" rather than a harvest. In general, as in almost all of the literature to be cited, the available evidence occurs in small and unrelated pickings except where the theme as a whole appears as a datum developed throughout a play or set of plays—a phenomenon of tragedy rather than comedy.

The quantity and nature of the evidence derivable from Greek tragedy can be judged from the quotations and references scattered throughout *The Science of Society*. I ought to explain just how these were gathered. Previous to the composition of that book, the senior author had examined the body of Greek tragedy, in translation, deliberately seeking what he called its "sociological content." In a notebook of his, labelled "Subjects," in which he set down tasks for himself, occurs the following entry: "Collect from the Greek dramas of the 5" Cent. B.C. the expression of antagonism of the mores a) of that time and an earlier time; b) of that time and the mythology; c) of Greeks and barbarians." This was part of a wider survey of the sociological content of the dramas. A large number of excerpts had been copied out and filed under proper headings. The junior author had these to go on; he had also read a number of the plays in the original, years before he had become aware of the evidence they contained for the study he came later to pursue. Both of us had looked up passages from the Greek, as cited by authors such as Lippert, and found them correctly or incorrectly interpreted. Distrust of citations from Homer was one of the reasons why Sumner welcomed a systematic survey of the Homeric evidence. This was about the state of things when the junior author began work, in 1909, on the then collection of materials for *The Science of Society*.

For the sake of the record I think I should mention that, as I worked these materials over from year to year, I came to the conclusion that Sumner had used inaccurate verse-translations of the tragedies, and felt impelled to go to the original with every one of his excerpts.

Nearly all of those which were retained were re-translated. So far as I know, all passages from Greek tragedy that appear in *The Science of Society* are correctly translated and interpreted. This was all I had time to do prior to publication; the alternative to be faced was either to sacrifice further completeness, in this matter along with many another, or to run the risk of never finishing the enterprise as a whole.

I find myself obliged to enter, and even to penetrate farther, into such personal detail. I am going to state my lay qualifications for dealing with Greek tragedy as a whole. While the proofreading of the four volumes was in process, I undertook to realize a purpose of long standing, namely, to complete the reading of the whole body of Greek tragedy in the original. I had intended to specialize in Greek, while in college, and had kept it up to a sufficient extent to render the enterprise possible. During the summer of 1926 I read with care all but a few of the thirty-three plays with which I was not already familiar, and have since completed the list, by covering several of the plays of Euripides. I hardly think that I missed much of significance, though my incessant *coups de dictionnaire* may have distracted me, in my effort to determine the precise meaning of passages, from a comprehensiveness of vision over longer sections or over a particular play as a whole. My chief interest remained always that of the reader of literature, but I had also the conscious object of seeing what the dramas offered in the way of sociological content; and the science of society had been for so long my professional preoccupation that I think I recognized most of the evidence visible to a layman in Greek, as it came along.

I found the yield from the tragedies, in comparison with my hopes, a disappointing one. The reason inheres in the proportion of the elements of theme and setting. Those hopes had been raised, probably, by experience with the richness of Homer, and in the absence of a realization that one cannot look for so copious a yield from a sophisticated literature as from one that represents, in its simplicity and naïveté, the product of folk-accumulation. One comes, with experience of them, to sense that the tragedies are elevated above Mother Earth, with a sort of non-conducting stratum between. This is probably true of all or most later literary products, and is to be taken always into account. The way later literature, to judge by the Greek tragedies, gets into this upper region is by generalizing and moralizing upon cultural materials which the earlier literatures are merely assembling. Then it becomes natural and easy to fall into the juggling of ideas, by way of logic and dialectics, with occasional citation of selected facts by way of "proof" of pre-accepted generalizations or major premises. There results some message, revelation, or lesson for the like of which one may search Homer in vain. Thus emerges a theme of quite different stripe from that of the storyteller whose sole purpose is to divert.

The tragedies unite, explicitly or implicitly, in the warning that destiny is incalculable, so that no man can be considered happy until his account is closed by death. Again and again they record the fate of the suffering righteous and the visitation of the unintentional sins of fathers upon offspring tainted with an ancestral uncleanness that no righteousness of conduct can cleanse. The *Oedipus Tyrannus* is the greatest portrayal I know of the working of the aleatory element: how it intervenes between intent and consequence. The moral is sharply drawn in the majestic and melancholy passage that closes the play. The audience was evidently supposed to be worked up into a sentiment of "pathos" by the graphic rehearsal of the ills that might well overtake any one of its members, no matter how blameless his intentions, in this his mortal life. Even the gods were helpless before unpredictable Chance, or Fate. This "lesson" was pure truth, is still, and always will be; but the preoccupation of the tragedian with the enforcement of it upon his audience limits his freedom to touch life at all points and controls to some degree his approach to whatever facts he cites.

Further, the tragedies are written around legendary characters, including divinities as well as heroes, and thus demand a certain deference to tradition and religion and in particular to miracle. They illustrate the truth that, to secure an atmosphere of dignity and solemnity, it is necessary to reproduce the old, and especially the discarded old, that is to say, the survivalistic. It is difficult to decide, as regards the allusions in the plays to religious matters, just what is real to the audience and what merely survivalistic—as difficult as it would be to assess what is in the minds of a modern congregation listening to the reading of the Scriptures or to a sermon drawing analogies between the contemporary and some incident in the Bible; for there always enters the element of conventionalization or rationalization.

No one denies that there is evidence in such presentations—vivid portrayals of a prevailing way of looking at life which no other form of exposition could convey. But whatever we learn from them remains in that elevated and rarefied stratum, far above the mundane level of functioning institutions. It is of secondary rather than primary intention. It belongs to the theme-foreground rather than to the back-drop of setting which displays actions performed in daily living. We learn a good deal about what the thinkers have thought, but not much about what the common men, who carry the mores, have done. This is not the kind of thing we are looking for. What is found in such explicit profusion in Homer is no more than assumed in the tragedies.

The dramas contain long passages that are little more than word-play or trivial exercises in logic. About all they tell is that Athenian audiences liked such tricks, which, though a piece of real evidence, is not of much more significance to one interested in institutional development than the cat's-cradles of the savage. Equally unproductive are the wailing passages and the display of artistic ingenuity in gradually and plausibly precipitating a tragic climax. The artistically matchless technique of the *Oedipus* contributes about as little evidence apt to our purpose as do the propositions of Euclid. Of the utmost significance to the playwright or mathematician, or to culture in general, they offer very little to the purpose in hand. That that purpose may seem a very lowly one to the precious is both true and also irrelevant.

Here are some of the reasons for the comparative barrenness, for the social scientist, of a tremendous literature. Broadly speaking, tragedy feels no need of the lowly and factual setting to which Homer naturally gravitates. One derives broad conceptions of a somewhat vague order, plus incidental and isolated allusions to life as lived. Particularly in the utterances of the chorus, which, elaborating on the obvious, so often check up the actors' doings or sentiments upon the prevailing code of the mores, may we derive information as to that code and its items. Very often the function of the chorus seems to be no more than the vocalization of the reactions to be expected of the audience.

My own reading of the tragedies did not materially add to the relatively scanty collection represented by scattered references in *The Science of Society*. It would be impossible to gather out of the plays any mass of *Realien* comparable to Buchholz's *Homerische Realien* or to Seymour's *Life in the Homeric Age*.

After the foregoing general inspection, there might be listed briefly samples of the kind of evidence, in addition to the portrayal of the aleatory element, which one encounters, always in the vividness of supreme artistry, in the tragedies. The Oedipus plays spread a convincing canvas of the horrors of incest and of parenticide. Again, the mind of the student of family-evolution turns to the alleged collision of mother-family and patriarchate which Bachofen thought he saw in the

Orestes episodes. That much of this was real in the minds of the audience, and not merely productive of an occasion to enjoy the logical quibble, is doubtful; but there was in the legendary situation at least a survivalistic conjuncture that allowed the staging of that particular quibble. That there was not much reality in the case seems clear enough from the farcical handling of the no-longer-terrible Eumenides in the comedy-finale of the Aeschylean series. The brother-sister relation is strikingly portrayed in the several plays that present Orestes, Antigone, Electra, and Iphigeneia. Euripides deals graphically with the bacchic mania and with various human relations, as in the *Medea,* the *Hippolytos,* the *Alcestis,* the *Andromache,* the *Trojan Women,* and the *Phoenician Women.* Special religious beliefs are thematic in *Prometheus, Philoctetes, Iphigeneia in Aulis, Iphigeneia in Tauris,* and *Alcestis.* The madness of *Heracles* and *Aias* is convincing. The very spirit of war pervades the *Seven against Thebes,* as its author is reported to have boasted.

There is no question but that out of the study of the tragedies there can be derived broad impressions of the Greek spirit that cannot be acquired otherwise; nevertheless, the dominant reason for reading them must remain· æsthetic and general rather than scientific and special. At any rate, that is the conviction at which I have arrived. The hopes once entertained of a large yield of materials from the body of Greek tragedy were unwarranted.

If one were endeavoring to cover literature exhaustively he could not omit Hesiod, Theocritus, Vergil in his bucolic phase, nor yet the Latin comedies. All of these offer settings that promise a restricted yield. The same cannot be said of the *Aeneid,* which is so largely an artificialized version of Homer. Some interest inheres in the Roman coloring lent to the Homeric incidents, for instance in the contrasting attitudes taken toward Helen's culpability. But both Vergil and Horace, as court poets, occupy and portray a social stratum of a special order, sophisticated and aristocratic. I have been under the necessity of re-reading a good part of the *Aeneid* a number of times since my interest in a science of society was aroused but have not hit upon much along my line; and I am not recalled to Horace by any expectation, based upon what I have read or on references encountered, that he has much that is worth while for me. He has a certain typical philosophy of life, as has Lucretius, that interests me mildly but to no specific end. There is a good deal more in the comedies, however unattractive otherwise to individual taste; and the same may be said about the satirical poems. But Latin Prose rather than poetry seems to me, as historic evidence, practically our only important source, and a very reliable one—a situation quite different from that encountered in the case of Greek literature. Personal distaste for the Latin poets, so far as I know them, except Horace and Catullus, may enter into this judgment; I have not been attracted to read or re-read them.

The *Divina Commedia,* to add one other item to a foregoing characterization, is not only an unrivalled presentation of Catholic doctrine; it is likewise, in a number of its episodes, a partisan document of a rather petty political order. In that latter aspect, it is of little utility to a general science: its stage is too narrow and its tone too passionate; and too much antiquarian research, as exemplified in the indispensability of learned apparatus, is necessary for the visualization of even that restricted stage. With some exaggeration, it might be said that, where Homer is all setting and no theme, Dante and Milton are all theme and no setting. In the *Divina Commedia,* which is taken here to be "Dante," as *Paradise Lost* and *Paradise Regained* are "Milton," there is, in a momentous sense, no human setting at all: the medium of the poem is not human but superhuman, and science cannot investigate or verify that variety, at any rate, of the subjective. There is no evidence to speak of about economic life, property, and the other institutional forms portrayed so objectively by Homer. There is very little about what men have done; the interest is focussed upon and nearly confined to what certain men have thought. The element of tendency prevails. The *Commedia* is an elaborate display of religious doctrine, together with a good deal of philosophical speculation, both clothed in highly poetic form. And that is about all there is. Sophistication has elbowed out all simple objectivity, as in Homer.

An elaboration of fine-spun dogma is no evidence as to what men do; it is not even a display of what the common run of men believe. To weave history upon dogma as a frame is much more hazardous even than to write it around codes of enacted law. As evidence, Dante is comparable with Thomas Aquinas or other non-poetical elaborators of dogma. If we had records of the obscure priests' confessionals, we should be getting down to the life and actual doings of the masses; but the dogmas and philosophies are a tenuous and often highly misleading mirage of earthy actualities. Moreover, they are far from being original factors. They are always secondary, amounting to rationalizations upon the mores already existent as automatic adjustments to actual life-conditions—rationalizations attempted by wishful thinkers who yearn to place the facts of living upon some Procrustean bed, that they may be mutilated into conformity with some preconceived pattern more appealing to the heart's desire.

No one wishes to deny that unearthly beliefs have entered into the parallelogram of social forces. But they float far aloft in a kind of stratosphere, touching the earth not at all or casually and briefly, at long intervals. You can cull out of Dante's cantos examples of cultural survivals, employed for literary effect rather than otherwise, such as the absence of weight or shadow in the case of the disembodied spirit. Occasionally you encounter a profound truth clothed in majestic verse, to us the more imposing, doubtless, in its foreign dress:

> *"Le vostre cose tutt' hanno lor morte*
> *Si come voi; ma celasi in alcuna*
> *Che dura molto, e le vite son corte."*[2]

But the profit from reading the *Commedia* for any human setting to its theme is a vanishing quantity.

It would be a lengthy and ambitious task to try to cover what Shakespeare reveals as to the mores of his place and time; but even the lay reader knows that there is a good deal. The historical pegs upon which he chooses to hang his plots do not matter much; he sketches a gesture, often quite perfunctory, in the direction of historical plausibility: he labels a scene, or hangs up a signboard on the stage, announcing: "Forest of Arden," "Battlements of Elsinore," and goes ahead with human beings as he knows them. He is interested in persons rather than things. That makes him a good hunting-ground for the psychologist, as the acrimonious disputes about the states of mind of his characters witness. But the profusion of those characters, all the way from grave-diggers to kings, and of his scenes, ranging from inns to palaces, is bound to call for a number of those inimitable identifying setting-touches for which he has always been noted. He has the power also of generating atmosphere, subtly, in a few words, both for a whole play and for constituent scenes: "The night is bitter cold and I am sick at heart"; "In sooth, I know not why I am so sad." Here is setting in its gossamer aspects.

Shakespeare, like many another creator of world-literature, is quite innocent of any other aim than to divert, evoke sympathy, or otherwise to appeal to the emotions. "Lessons" have been read into his plays

2. *Paradiso*, XVI, 79–81.

by sentimentalists, but any person of perception knows that he was not trying to teach anything. He puts into the mouths of his characters, not his own views, which nobody knows, but the kind of utterance that the character in question would make: lofty sentiments are ad-credited to the sententious and senile Polonius, as one instance among many. Shakespeare is always doing what he advises the Players in *Hamlet* to do: holding a mirror up to Nature—and not to physical nature alone but also to human nature, to the nature of both individual and society. There is about him no theory or "ideology" to look out for. If he is not objective, no great author ever was.

This preoccupation with the immediately observable is witnessed to by his indifference to anachronism: the clock in *Julius Caesar,* for an obvious case. Shakespeare was no antiquarian, seeking a technically accurate reconstruction of a Roman or other background. That he was not can be judged by comparing his Greek and Roman scenes with the dull, footnoted exactitude of Becker's *Charicles* or *Gallus.* No student of English mores need make allowance for the foreign loca-tion of a Shakespearean scene.

If, with some exaggeration, Dante is said to be all theme and no setting, Shakespeare, as well as Homer, might be described as all setting and no theme. His plays are, for that reason, a better hunting-ground for the scientist. No social scientist, so far as I know, has ever examined them at all exhaustively, to determine their sociological content. Sum-ner uses passages from *Hamlet* and *Coriolanus* on the title page of *Folkways;* and Spencer may introduce Shakespearean allusions; even a layman has noted the titles of articles on Shakespeare's acquaintance with law or some other branch of knowledge; but there has been no systematic exploration of his output as a record of the mores of his time. No one can say beforehand what the product of such an enter-prise would be; but the foregoing considerations amount to favorable auspices.

So many of Shakespeare's phrases have become all but proverbial that they have come to share in the authenticity of the proverb, which is conferred by the fact that it has been found good under the test of wide and protracted appeal to experience. That makes of Shakespeare's lines, at any rate, a treasure-house of the flash of insight and the apt expression. At his least, he can help those who have cultivated him to tell what they know; and the chances are good that he can also furnish them with something to tell.

A few concrete illustrations may serve as samples out of Shakespeare's record of his age. The *Merchant of Venice* may be whimsical as regards its law, but it reveals the prevailing attitude toward the Jew, much as *Othello* depicts the popular impression of the Moor. Concessions to the Pit amount to recognition of the popular level in matters of propriety, decency, conventionality, morality, and other details of the mores. There is significance in the fact that the German, in translating *Macbeth,* not sensing the need of relief from agonies piled up to the toppling-point, replaced the maudlin Porter's fuddlings with an angel's song. The low life that centers around Falstaff shows clearly enough through any and all humorous exaggerations; that which is, so to speak, taken for granted, as a setting familiar and recognizable to all is not so difficult to isolate. Court scenes contain a similar conventional content. The normal behavior of members of the various social classes, both to one another and to outsiders, involving the distribution of rights and duties, is presented in what might be termed the living picture, as contrasted with dead description. Shakespeare is strong on human relationships, not alone as between individuals but also as they take on the nature of mass phenomena.

"Wer vieles bringt, wird manchem etwas bringen."

I do not intend to consider secondary poets, or my list would become unwieldy; but there is a group of English poets of the nineteenth century that will, if not world-poets, repay a paragraph or two. They are essentially subjective, romantic, and mystical. One could not look for much in the way of factual setting in Coleridge, Keats, Shelley, or Byron; and, despite his interest in "commonalty," no more than a small and insubstantial yield can be expected from the pedestrian stretches of Wordsworth. I recall, from unsystematic reading of these poets, few instances of insight into social life; I remain of the impression that pleasure is the only, though very strong, reason for any future re-readings. They are graphic and eloquent expositors of selected types of beauty or of selected moods in the individual. I shall remain always under deep obligation to the man who first introduced me to them. But they seem to me to be embroiderers of life, with small interest in its main fabric, in the world that "is too much with us." It is a charming sentiment that "beauty is truth, truth beauty," but that that is "all we need to know on earth" is evidently a poetical flight. No one contends that we live by bread alone; but that we do not live, to make verses or to yearn, long without it is no less true than trite.

Science cannot expect to discover much of its kind of truth in what such subjective and in-the-void-suspended authors have to offer. They too have a theme that is not so dissimilar from Dante's or Milton's. That is nothing against them, any more than against those two; but it renders them less available for the purpose under consideration. It is a historic datum that such a group of poets has existed and has attained to a well-deserved high rating on criteria that are wholly valid. The same might be said of Plato or Aquinas, whose productions are similarly irrelevant to our purpose. What we are seeking may be belittled as no more than lowly and vulgar facts bereft of all sparkle; but it is generally conceded that someone ought to be assembling that kind of evidence, wherever encountered; and if one's taste, or sense of duty, impels him in that direction, those who pursue only the "higher things"ought to be relieved, and neither contemptuous nor vituperative.

Browning and Tennyson seem to occupy a firmer and less unearthly footing. Though the latter is most closely identified with the *Idylls* and other romantic subjects, the body of his poetry might yield a rather valuable set of snapshots of the society of his time. I speak with considerable diffidence, however. Browning I know rather better; and I do not see how anyone can read *The Ring and the Book* without profit along the lines of social understanding.

Browning is something of a dual personality. His exactitude, not seldom painful, as in his translation of the *Agamemnon,* is no less than astonishing; it is so faithful and painstaking that his personal choice of readings of certain passages can be identified. He is so meticulous as to render certain portions of that translation questionable in the matter of their English—as muddy as some of his careless, awkward, and unintelligible lines elsewhere in his poems. No one can doubt his erudition in the matter of historical detail, nor his capacity in putting life into his settings.

The other side of the man is his didacticism, or his message, or the reflection of his moods of optimism. He has a kind of religion, though it is not a formal exposition of dogma. It leads him into extravagancies, into the enthusiastic enunciation of universals on the basis of selected, subjective, non-comprehensive criteria. He is strong on prophecy, which so many are wont to accept as evidence. If you already believe as he does, he is a source of deep satisfaction; but if you are critical of his exuberance, you are as if in the presence of an eloquent expositor of half-truths, or of something less. In general, this side of Browning is less likely to appeal to experience than to youth.

If one is able to make and to hold this distinction between the two irreconcilable aspects of Browning, he can derive more than a little from his poetic product. When Browning gets some social relation straight, he is likely to hit it off in as unforgettable a form as does Goethe. In another mood he will proclaim that only the poet "knows," which is manifest nonsense. Again, he will solemnly enunciate the unintelligible—unintelligible, it is said, even to himself, once the mood had receded. It seems to me that he becomes, at times, as recklessly careless as he is scrupulously careful in his rendering of his Greek. But I think this soaring mood so readily recognizable that he puts up, as it were, his own warning, which reads, to me, at least: "Not to be taken too seriously."

One more world-poet remains: Goethe. He has been described as "cosmic." The scope of his interests is reflected in all his major and most of his minor works. And no great poet is more self-revelatory. He is, in this respect, almost the antithesis of Shakespeare. But his subjectivity is of a special order; it might almost be called objective. He wrote love-songs when he was in love and would not write hate-songs when he did not hate. No other of the great poets, and very few other human beings, have led so self-scrutinized and self-directed an existence. And yet his writings, while self-centered, are not tendentious. He had no doctrines to promulgate, no major premises to defend. I have never been able to see where his egocentrism, if it be so called, has shortened his perspective or distorted his accuracy of observation or judiciousness of conclusion. His scattered epigrammatic summations of human experience, his clear flashes of insight, rank him among the wisest men who have ever lived, and there are enough such passages in his poems to accord him a place among the foremost seers of all time.

If Goethe has any theme at all, it is to be found in *Faust,* a work that lay before him for almost six decades. Faust has had revealed to him, by sample, "the little, then the great world."[3] To no actual experience can he, at any time, say: "Stay! thou art so fair!" Only in envisaging the homely lot of laborious and self-reliant folk—only in the consciousness of having done something tangible and useful—does he pronounce that fateful phrase which delivers his soul into the hand of the tempter. But his immortal part is rescued by white spirits who chant:

> *"Wer immer strebend sich bemüht*
> *Den können wir erlösen."*[4]

3. *Faust,* I, 2052.
4. *Faust,* II, 7323–7324.

If a "lesson" is thus conveyed, it is one far removed from religious dogma or metaphysical speculation. The religious phraseology is incidental; and Goethe had no use for metaphysics.

> *"Ich sag' es dir: ein Kerl der speculiert,*
> *Ist wie ein Thier, auf dürrer Heide*
> *Von einem bösen Geist im Kreis herum geführt,*
> *Und rings umher liegt schöne grüne Weide."*[5]

One need recall only the irritation of the metaphysicians at Goethe's general attitude. The "lesson" of *Faust* is of a realistic and practical nature, taking into account the welfare of society as well as the salvation of the individual. It enforces the indispensability of the social virtues of industry, thrift, self-denial, and self-control:

> *"Nicht sicher zwar, doch thätig-frei zu wohnen. . . .*
> *Ja! diesem Sinne bin ich ganz ergeben,*
> *Das ist der Weisheit letzter Schluss:*
> *Nur der verdient sich Freiheit wie das Leben,*
> *Der täglich sie erobern muss.*
> *Und so verbringt, umrungen von Gefahr*
> *Hier Kindheit, Mann und Greis sein tüchtig Jahr."*[6]

The incidents throughout the work exhibit the futility of magical means in the governance of society, which is a datum of experience, not at all a utopian sentiment out of wishful thinking of pure "inspiration."

The satanic comment of Faust's tempter over his worn-out body runs:

> *"Den letzten, schlechten, leeren Augenblick,*
> *Der Arme wünscht ihn festzuhalten."*[7]

I do not care to go on with this theme, or synthesis, so different from other grand-scale poetic "arguments," except to state my conviction that no student of society can afford to ignore its development under a master hand in the service of a master intelligence engaged in synthesizing human experience. Goethe exhibits a penetrating insight into realities, and he is practically free of the various prepossessions whose presence casts doubt upon the objectivity of most poets. What

5. *Faust*, I, 1830–1833.
6. *Faust*, II, 6951, 6960–6965.
7. *Faust*, II, 6976–6977.

he says in incomparable phraseology about individual and societal life regularly survives verification upon scientific criteria. That is because he observes life, as does Shakespeare, closely and through no distorting medium of wishfulness, and with, in addition, a curiosity as to cause and effect not visible in Shakespeare—who may well be the more nearly perfect artist just because he confines himself to holding up the mirror. But Goethe's inquiring spirit, brooding from young manhood to advanced age upon an almost unrivalled wealth of experience, provides a "cumulative impression,"[8]—something very like a scientific generalization.

It does not seem out of place to record here the lifelong counsel which the individual, in the matter of his own private living, can derive from Goethe—who is as one who has passed over the whole course of life before you. He has been young, middle-aged, and old; and he has recorded the features of each stage, while traversing it, with such insight that one recognizes immediately, as he reaches one stage after the other, that a master surveyor has preceded him. What has seemed incomprehensible, as read in youth, becomes clear and inevitably true as one attains the stage of life through which Goethe was passing as he observed and recorded. Collections of Goethe's *Weisheit* confer upon him a high place among the many-sided thoughtful, beginning with Solomon. *"Freudvoll und leidvoll, gedankenvoll sein." "Entbehren sollst du, sollst entbehren." "Warum ins Unendlich' schweifen? Sieh', das Gute liegt so nah."*

There are certain feats of Goethe's which witness to his ability to seize upon the spirit of that which he portrays. The mood of youth—emotional, impatient, pitiful—was what lent to *Die Leiden des jungen Werthers* its remarkable contemporary appeal, and also what rendered it painful to its author after he had once rid himself of that fever. *Wilhelm Meister* is another such characterization of a nautilus-chamber from which the poet had emerged. *Götz von Berlichingen* reproduces the mood of a period, as does Schiller's contemporary *Räuber. Iphigenie auf Tauris* furnishes an ancient play with modern, more sophisticated motives and emotions, in this respect being alignable with Browning's *Balaustion's Adventure. Tasso* has a formal Italian setting, but the interpretation is of the universal type; and the same is true of *Egmont,* in another setting. Perhaps the most remarkable case of all is that of *Hermann und Dorothea,* which, in my opinion, is the closest approach ever made, in form and spirit, to Homer—not that there is any re-

8. See Essay on this topic below.

construction of Homeric life, however, for the setting is purely German. This ability to shift the universal into selected settings is displayed in many of the shorter and detached poems: *Heidenröslein, König im Thule, Erlkönig,* and many another, as well as in the several, often loosely attached episodes in *Faust: Hexenküche, Walpurgisnacht, Auerbachs Keller,* and the classical episodes in Part II.

Goethe thought that his reputation might come to rest upon his *Farbenlehre,* an illustration of how the master in one line of human endeavor may overestimate his accomplishment in another. Nevertheless, the poet had caught hold of scientific method, at least by its fringes, and of the scientific attitude with a much stronger grip. He was enough of a biologist to receive prominent mention in *The Origin of Species* as a forerunner of the evolution theory—and not because he had hinted vaguely, as many another had done, at some developmental sequence, but because of actual observations, no matter how limited and therefore inconclusive, as indicated in his two poems on the metamorphosis of plant and animal. Throughout his writings, he manifests an habitual objectivity and a tendency to keep his feet on the ground of verified experience. His geological collections witness to his interest in specimens rather than in speculation. His avocations as critic of literature and art, as lawyer, as theater-director, finance-minister, draughtsman, and sculptor reveal the many-sidedness of his actual experience. *Aus meinem Leben* is a record of an insatiable intellectual interest in things as well as ideas; for a similar universality and versatility one has to look to a Da Vinci. No other man whose main claim to genius lay in his poetry has had so many seriously pursued avocations as Goethe. It is likely that no other man who ever lived touched life at so many points.

Goethe has a richness of setting that is surpassed by few. But, despite his ability to shift into a convincing milieu of another place and time, and although his genuinely synthetic mind, which habitually employs the scientifically authentic method of comparison, his persisting background is German. He started out, he tells us, to learn to write German; and, while he was a world-citizen and no provincial, and not patriotic in the popular sense—indeed, strongly averse to Prussianism, he represents the best of Germany as does no other writer before or since. Out of his works, were all others lost, one could derive an intelligible and valid conception of the mores and institutions of the Germany of his time—one not too generalized by his cosmopolitan outlook to lose focus on local and national life. His "sociological content" may not yield as rich a store of raw data as that of some of the rest; but the essential objectivity of his generalizations furnishes an altogether unique wealth of materials that might be called data of secondary intention.

For all the reasons, explicit and implicit, in the foregoing sketch, I am of the opinion that no student of society's evolution can afford not to make a close acquaintance, and in the original, with Goethe. I am sure, in a greater degree, to a degree that lifts year by year, that anyone who aspires to see life, individual or social, whole, had better make that acquaintance early in life and not allow it to lapse as the years go by. For here is a supremely able and wise man who, with unparalleled candor and absence of reservation, offers the almost daily record of his wide and varied experience through a long lifetime. That his offering is presented in a poetic medium of the highest quality adds much to its value to mankind.

That the novel, an almost modern development, is an effective instrument for the transmission of culture is undoubted. Several times in his book of "Subjects" Sumner set down the topic: "Novels as Agents of Uniformity of Ideas throughout a Culture Area." This characterization would seem to befit the novel of contemporary manners rather than the historical novel. Let us set aside the latter for the moment.

Evidence recorded with fidelity by observers of the social phenomena of their own times is, of course, of high historic value. Historians prize diaries like those of Pepys, making due allowance, however, for whatever personal bias or party spirit the author exhibits. In the case of the novel, we face again the question of the theme and setting in an often aggravated form. If a storyteller sets out to write mere romance, he is interested in representing things as they are not; and his readers are attracted in proportion as he makes life appear, if only for the moment, more closely in accord with the heart's desire. Any storyteller who can divert his readers, even when they know what he is about, by dispelling their boredom with the actual, has his uses and will receive his reward; but there is little in this service that is of use to science. He cares not at all for the accuracy of his setting.

Novels of pure romance are proverbially untrustworthy. They have been charged with responsibility for many of the vagaries of romantic youth. Such are the "love-stories," which represent love as a kind of convulsion, irresistible or not-to-be-resisted. Then there are the wild

stories of a Verne, a Haggard, a Doyle, a Bellamy—the edifyingly unbelievable, despite the prophetic strain that runs through some of their
phantasies about what is to come or what has been. The hypnotized
Trilby or the superhuman sleuth are for entertainment, pure and
simple, with the unreal or highly improbable. And where the wonder
tale fails to offer much but iridescent froth, a painful and often merely
exhibitionist realism digs up sour, repulsive, and no less misrepresenta-
tive dregs. Doctrinal realism and fidelity to life are two different
things. The idea of the former is often solely to shock. For a time,
even the discreet may become victims of some dismal Ibsen or Dostoievsky, with their insistence, amounting to misrepresentation, upon
pathological aspects—"Little did Dostoievsky dream that one day he
would be the mainstay of foreign writers unable to understand or explain events in Bolshevik Russia!"[9]—but presently the lopsided exaggerations pall upon taste and common sense. It is well for the searcher
for evidence as to life in literature to be sure about his literature. Has
it, or has it not, the "verdict of history" behind it?

That the element of romance must always remain strong is evidenced by the sparseness of popular stories that do not play up the
love-interest; but even that once wholly romantic motif has been
twisted in the direction of realism, so as to be presented as a kind of
sensual or even clinical relation, highly offensive to many. Such fiction
is represented as "frank," "courageous," "sincere," whereas, as a matter
of fact, its "realism" is about as unreal as the romanticism it replaces.

I do not intend to consider the swayings of popular taste except
to note that the student must not mistake for the genuine popular
taste the passing predilection of a talkative small minority of the
"emancipated," even though they delude or hypnotize an ovine following into feeling that it must appreciate as it is told. That would be
another case of mistaking a variation for an adjustment.[10]

Plainly, the sociological content of fiction needs to be identified and
extracted with the utmost critical caution. I am in no position to offer
a manual of procedure for the investigator, but I can mention in illustration several types of fiction as produced by authors of high
repute. Presumably, of all fiction-writers the historical novelist can be
checked up most readily, for we can go to his recorded sources. Some
historical tales are nothing but treatises thinly coated with a pallid

9. Lyons, E., *Assignment in Utopia*, p. 217.
10. See accompanying essay on *The Variation and the Adjustment*.

wash of awkwardly applied human interest. Their fidelity to sources may even be attested by learned footnotes. They are not literature at all and should be classed with the plain treatises. At the other end of the series of gradations, starting with this zero-line of artistry, is the trilogy of Henryk Sienkiewicz, let us say, which, in addition to its accuracy, fulfills the definition of a good novel as "a good story, well told." On a somewhat lower plane, to some readers, are the Sienkiewicz of *Quo Vadis?*, Walter Scott, and a number of contemporary historical novelists—for example, John Buchan. One can fill in the series to suit himself, if he keeps in mind as a controlling criterion the question: To what degree has the writer under consideration produced a vivid, and, at the same time, veracious characterization of the historic period which he treats? It is difficult to draw the line between the historical novel and fiction like that of Thackeray. It is unnecessary to do so in any formal manner. There is an atmosphere of tolerant calm about Thackeray which is confidence-inspiring. He knows plenty of the facts of life, views them with insight, records them with restraint, and does no essential violence to them by reason of harboring some thesis to maintain or mission to discharge. The novel which combines objectivity with historical sense and insight, however it may be classed, is the one that offers material to science.

The opposite type is the tendentious novel, the one with a "message." The horrible example here is the "Sunday-school book." When I was young, "novels" were tabooed, but not the pious, debilitating stuff perpetrated by one E. P. Roe. On a higher artistic plane, Dickens, Tolstoi, Mrs. Stowe, London, and other high-class propagandists have produced stories of this general tendentious type. Utility for our purposes, in the works of such authors, inheres only in passages where the writer has temporarily forgotten his mission in his artistry, or through a painstaking calculation, which is not likely to repay the effort, as to where and in what degree, in view of the author's predisposition, discount should be made. The difficulty of that calculation removes this type of fiction from profitable consideration for the present purpose. The theme is, again, too pervasive of the setting. To winnow out the grains of truth in, say, *Uncle Tom's Cabin,* is an almost impossible labor.

Here emerges a pretty good rule for the social scientist in search of evidence in literature: always to distinguish cautiously between a temporary fad and a virtual permanency; between, again, a variation on trial and a settled adjustment. The latter is what has endured under protracted selection because it has been found by generations to be true to life. The new and startling must always pick up and bear that burden of proof which the time-honored has long sustained.

The foregoing might be regarded as a series of warnings about the dangers incurred in trying to extract any evidence at all from fiction. For the novel is young and most novels, no doubt, ephemeral. There is in fiction so often some personal slant of the writer, some unconsciously, unpremeditatedly occupied viewpoint. Turgenev is criticized as an unreliable portrayer of Russian mores because, as an exile, he described only the Russian exile and, at that, saw him, in the main, as he looked to the Frenchman or German. And one has to approach with the utmost caution the satirist or caricaturist who is always under temptation to lay on color incontinently.

The same writer may well produce works in diverse styles. I once had a student who was much interested in Chambers, especially in his set of stories dealing with the Long House of the Iroquois and the wars in which the Six Nations took part. He undertook to check up on Chambers's ethnological and historical accuracy and, after considerable study, was able to give him a substantially clean slate. Yet any reader of this author knows that some of his novels revel in the sheerest of unchecked fancy. Lewis's *Arrowsmith* reveals a genuine objectivity, while his *Elmer Gantry* is a hasty, hostile caricature.

Nothing is less reliable as evidence about the mores than the novel of "emancipation": the "frank, brave, and sincere" portrayal of the whimsies of a useless, posturing, and sensual clique of mutually admiring "advanced thinkers." At best, such fiction represents merely a variation on the literary stock, an abnormal budding that will presently rot and drop off. It may seem, for the moment, to have won popular acclaim because of the din-producing powers of its claque; but the masses who carry the mores are sublimely unconscious of it. Even as literature, many a much-touted production, once excitedly hailed as immortal and even as setting a new and altogether emancipating mode, has presently fallen by the wayside and been forgotten by all except the doctoral embalmers and resurrectionists. It is always incumbent upon him who embarks upon the risky search for the residue of fact in fiction to post over his desk the aforesaid warning: Do not confuse the variation with the adjustment! Nor should he repine if he finds that many a piece of literature that has survived the assaults of literary criticism cannot measure up to the criteria of utility to science.

Even from so inadequate a survey as the foregoing I think it must

appear that the novel will come to be a source of considerable significance to social science, as time goes on, for it generally presents a view
of the mores, fragmentary or more complete, as a setting for its action.
After making proper allowance for the nature and variety of fiction,
one has in the end a residue of unpurposefully presented information
about social phenomena, together with flashes of insight into their
nature and working that are often highly instructive and suggestive.
And it is no drawback that whatever evidence the searcher can gather,
even from a minor artist, is likely to be couched in terms neither form-
less nor void. The literary artist, it may be reiterated, who is intent
professionally upon clarity and vividness of exposition, is more than
likely to express truths in such manner as to relieve them of that in-
visibility of the obvious or conventional which permits mankind to
pass them by without realization of their significance. If truth were as
vividly presented as error has always been, instead of being clothed
upon with learned dullness, there would be a much heightened prospect of general enlightenment.

The main reasons why those who have been interested in developing
a science of society have shied away from the range of history, leaving
a gap in the stream of evidence between the primitive and the contemporary, are set forth in *The Science of Society*.[11] To rehearse them,
by way of a start-off, they are as follows: History, as a descriptive art,
true to its origin in chronicle, is written around chronology, paying but
slight and somewhat condescending attention to materials unsuscep-
tible of being dated, as these exist in ethnography, prehistory, legend,
and folklore; it has centered its interest in agency, particularly in the
Great Man, rather than in cause; it has ignored other aspects of social
life in favor of the military, political, and, to a considerable extent, the
religious and philosophical phenomena, affording but slight and inadequate information about the economic organization, property-
systems, and, above all, about marriage, the family, and population;
and, finally, historians cannot seem to agree with one another, as
chemists, for example, can. It is manifest that the student of society
must, as a rule, get his historical data out of concordant secondary
sources; if they are not concordant, he runs a grave risk in pinning
his trust to particular authors.

Sociologists, beginning with Spencer, who have attempted to use
historical evidence, have straightway encountered the criticism, gen-

11. § 457.

erally patronizing, that their history is all wrong. They used to be regarded, indeed, as interlopers and almost as thieving encroachers upon a preëmpted domain. The historians are not to be censured overmuch for their intolerance, considering the reckless use that irresponsible "sociologists" have made of what they took to be history. It is human enough, especially under irritation, to condemn a whole profession—the Money Lenders, Wall Street—for the flagrant misbehavior of the few; though, in the present case, one is bound to admit that that formula does not apply precisely, for it is the many, not the few, sociologists who have misbehaved, so that injustice has been done by the historians to the discreet few rather than to the venturesome many. There is no getting away from the fact that "sociology" is a kind of jocular term, as compared, say, with "geology." It started clothed in respectability, with Spencer, but is now faced with the need of reconquering that attribute, if it can, after the corruption of its good manners by frivolous associations. I have thought sometimes that if it desires to lead a new life, it had better, because of these associations, change its name or adopt an alias.

The gap in evidence between the primitive and the contemporary, the lack of evidence from the historic period, is perhaps the chief reproach encountered by *The Science of Society*. Scoffers seize upon that break in continuity to flout, gibe, and sneer: "Do you want to know about morals? Go to the Hottentot!" As a matter of fact, the aforesaid gap, or hiatus, is not nearly so serious a defect as represented by enemies or as admitted by the faint of heart. Hiati in series are an experience common to all scientists; Darwin enlarges upon the incompleteness of the geological record in *The Origin of Species*. And the gap between prehistory and the present, say, of ten thousand years, is relatively small in the long course of men's life on earth, which is the course of society's evolution—not over five per cent, at the highest estimate, of the length of that course at its lowest figure. In rebuttal of that contention, it is alleged that ten thousand years multiplied into its pace of development equals a much larger degree of import assignable to the historic period than the time-element alone would indicate. One is instructed to the effect that the last century, or even the last decade, outweighs in significance all preceding eras put together.

There is only one reply to that type of assertion: that a difference in degree does not carry with it a difference in kind. The historic period of society's evolution is immensely more complex and difficult to handle than what went before; but there is nothing new in it, any more than there is in the organic or inorganic realm. Lyell's principle goes for every science: the forces at work now are those at work then and vice versa. Evolution is continuous, not catastrophic. The past still remains the key to the present and future.

The gap is not so deplorable, I say, as has been asserted. No one who knows the ethnographical evidence, even sketchily, fails to have it dawn on him that continuity exists between the primitive and the present, that is, across the gap. Even the youths in elementary classes sense that continuity, without having their attention called to it. It leaps to the mind. No serious student of the subject can have the slightest doubt that transitional forms extend across the historic range, for he can see enough of them to infer the existence of the rest.

Nevertheless, he does not want to rest upon inference if demonstration is possible, any more than an anthropologist is content with an inferred missing link if an actual one can be unearthed. He remains entirely ready to be convinced, by actual evidence to the contrary, that organic or social evolution is broken, discontinuous, catastrophic, but he is going to hold to his strong inference that it is not until that position is proved untenable. The evolutionist, organic or social, with all the evidence he now possesses countenancing and rendering inevitable the inference of continuity, is more eager for justification, or the reverse, in the fact than anybody else can be. In the societal range, he deplores the lack of materials, and, perhaps of the ability to handle them if he had them, much more deeply than any layman can.

Which brings us to a crucial double question: can (1) the historical data, and (2) the technique be made available, even in a partial and defective degree, for the bridging of the gap under consideration? Let us take these two desirables in reverse order: assuming the availability of the data, have we the technique to handle them? Would different investigators be likely to arrive at reasonably concordant conclusions?

Given a body of data in the range of ethnography, it can be expected, on the basis of actual demonstration, that a substantial unanimity of conclusion will emerge. It is true that, despite the relative detachment natural to the handling of such non-emotion-rousing materials, subjective elements have appeared to cause divergence of interpretation. In the face of that fact, and before illustrating it, one needs to bear in mind Darwin's saying that errors in theory do not matter—only errors in observation. Theoretical vagaries eventually correct themselves.

There have been plenty of them. Not alone has the missionary's prepossession caused him to see the facts in a light different from that of the scientist, but among professional scientists there have appeared quasi-dogmatic slants productive of similar divergences. Take the issue of diffusion versus parallelism: prior conviction as to the rôles of the two have had an effect, at any rate in the interpretation of borderline cases. Then there are certain anthropologists who make it a kind of tenet never to generalize at all. Nevertheless, taking the scientists alone, they all repudiate the dogmas of the mere deducers; and they can agree pretty well up to a point, beyond which, after all, their disagreements do not seriously count. What matter if there is a dispute about some item of the mores, as to whether it is borrowed or independently developed? It becomes, or does not become, an adjustment, whether it arose from local variation or appeared first as a result of diffusion; for, to all intents, transmission of novelties amounts to the presentation of variations before the local bar of selection. And any science, even the laboratory disciplines, always has its highly theoretical fringes surrounding on all sides and hanging from a solid and verified fabric of the undisputed. It is only those who ignore the main yardage of durable cloth, while fixing their attention upon the abstract or even metaphysical frayings, who try to tell us that the whole construction is unstable and of chameleonlike changefulness. Such allegations serve only to betray the kind of mind—excitable, narrow, credulous, unscientific—of those who make them.

Within the range of the ethnographic and other evidence, an at least passable scientific technique has become available. The question is as to whether that technique is capable of handling the more complicated and confused materials of recorded history. The answer is that no one can tell until those materials are available in a much more workable form than at present. In other ranges, men have managed to handle higher complexities as they have come to face and realize them. They have grown up to them. When calculus was needed, it was developed. This proves nothing; but it offers a certain hopeful probability as against an antecedent despair.

In any case, the impression that scientific method involves profound and esoteric mystery is a mistaken one. It has been disseminated by writers on social science, chiefly "sociology," who, because of their own sterility, or of revulsion at the hard labor and obscure solitude demanded of the genuine researcher, have sought the prestige they hanker after by assuming a sort of directorship over others. They have developed a pretentiously elaborate "methodology"—a ghastly term.

They illustrate a favorite anecdote of Sumner's, related by him to a convocation of teachers who were under the spell of "educational methodology." The story was of a college mate who had various theories about the way to study—sitting, lying, standing on one leg. He tried them all out, but in the end flunked the examination because he had not studied at all. "The way to learn a language," Sumner used to say, "is to sit down and learn it"—a "method" which he demonstrated to the full.

Scientific method is not at all esoteric or mysterious. Science is "trained and organized common sense," with few or no tricks about it.[12] Probably the evidence from the historic period can be handled by the scientist, even though it is more complex, tangled, refractory, and slippery, when it once becomes available to him.

When one hears the heralds of some New Dispensation, who want to reject all experience, as "past" or "old," proclaim that "the only thing to be learned from history is that nothing can be learned from history," he is obliged to believe that the historians have been at fault in the matter of technique, viewpoint, or exposition. At any rate, no discreet sociologist dares, in view of the experience of his predecessors, to depend upon history, as yet written, for the original assembling and ordering of the basic historic facts.

There is here not a shadow of adherence to the imbecile claim of certain spacious "arrangers of things" that sociology is a science of sciences to which all other workers in the societal range are bound, in servile meekness, to bring their results as tribute, thereafter to await, humbly, "methodological" orders as to what to do next. That is the attitude of philosophy, and is offensive to all science. The desirable attitude is one of coöperation between equals, not a feudal relation between lord and vassal. If the smelter does not coöperate—for his own advantage, not at some behest from above—by producing the needed metal, how can further processing go on? There is no censure here, expressed or implied, of the smelter, or of the historian, for pursuing his interest as he sees it. There is simply the statement of fact, that the historian has not yet seen fit to develop an interest and technique capable of producing results usable by the social scientist. When the latter tries to utilize what the historian offers, he gets nowhere but only encounters the jeers of some historian for his naïveté in reposing confidence in some other historian. That is to say, there is no substantial unanimity among the historians—which means that they have

12. See essay on "Common Sense," above.

attained no such technique as have the concordant scientists. Evidently, then, there is no chance, as yet, for the social scientists to develop a technique for handling the offerings of historians when there is no consistent body of such offerings to handle. Therefore the question about the possibility of developing a sociological technique capable of dealing with historical materials can be answered, as above: "We do not know. Maybe what we have will do. Maybe we shall need something else or a refinement on what we have. No test is yet possible."

History, says Thackeray,[13] speaking of the early decades of the eighteenth century,

in our age busies herself with the affairs only of kings; waiting on them obsequiously and stately, as if she were but a mistress of court ceremonies, and had nothing to do with the registering of the affairs of the common people. . . . I wonder shall History ever pull off her periwig and cease to be court-ridden? . . . In a word, I would have history familiar rather than heroic: and think that Mr. Hogarth and Mr. Fielding will give our children a much better idea of the manners of the present age in England than the *Court Gazette* and the newspapers which we get thence.

This passage speaks also for the evidential value of fiction.

It is a matter of observation, however, that historians are now writing history from a viewpoint somewhat shifted from that of aforetime. I recall, once more, the remark of Dr. G. B. Adams concerning the responsibility of Spencer for that shift.[14] Today histories are much more "social" than they used to be: they pay more attention to cause as contrasted with agency, and to aspects of the life of society other than the military and political. One historian has caustically remarked that, where they used to center on the trumpet and drum, they have come to focus upon the strumpet and the bum. The stricture is not fair but it illustrates, by way of exaggeration or caricature, the shift toward the writing of "social history," toward the record of low life as well as high, toward the life of the masses as well as of the classes, toward interest in impersonal movements as well as in those formerly referred to various Great Men, or, farther back, to demigods.

History has been laying claim, for some time now, to the attribute "scientific." The evidence cited in substantiation has had to do, however, almost wholly with the routine handling of original sources, wherein has been sought an approach to the objectivity of the labora-

13. Thackeray, W. M., *The History of Henry Esmond, Esq., a Colonel in the Service of Her Majesty Queen Anne, written by Himself*, pp. 1, 2.
14. P. 5, above.

tory. That is very desirable, so far as it goes. It is, indeed, indispensable if history is going in for exactitude rather than romance. But if there is to be any adequate understanding of the materials thus scientifically assembled, it must needs come by way of a scientific handling of them *after* they have been scientifically assembled. No science is present where there has been developed merely a scientific technique in the collection of data. All that is no more than preliminary. When it has been accomplished as a *sine qua non,* the treatment of the results still remains to be done before enlightenment dawns. Indeed, in the collection itself there is need of orientation attainable only by way of taking a more comprehensive view of human society than the historian has done in the past—a view that science alone can open up. Former gropings toward such a perspective, on the part of historians, have resulted in what has been called the "philosophy of history." That term is almost exactly descriptive of what was attained; and then the short-sighted historians have plunged into an incontinent identification of their newly christened find with "sociology," or the science of society—which has demonstrated merely their lack of acquaintance with science. Nevertheless, history, in these gropings, was really after unifying principles, or laws.

No historian groped more wistfully than Henry Adams,[15] and no one of them seems to have been more scientifically myopic and yet at the same time more disillusioned as to the availability, as a unifying element, of some metaphysical abstraction. But Adams got hold of at least one item of scientific procedure, namely, that of comparison. His *Mont St. Michel and Chartres* is a kind of desperate *tour de force* in the application of the comparative method. It is a great book. Nevertheless, he never attained the object of his ardent quest.

It may be that there is no unifying of history; but if there is, it must come, to judge by experience, by way of the establishment of social laws; and laws have never been discovered otherwise than by the handling of masses of facts in accordance with inductive scientific method. Laws need to be discovered, if possible. Otherwise, as Cardozo expressed it, we must "acquiesce in incoherence," reject experience as a teacher, and flounder about, without any bearings, in an ocean of wishful thinking, under the impulsive pilotage of those who jeer at all lessons from history. History needs the coöperation of a science of society as much as that study requires the coöperation of history. That is what is meant by parity between the two disciplines, as against any

15. In his *Education of Henry Adams.*

alleged dominance of one over the other. The desirable coöperation between them seems to be on its way; and the sooner it arrives, the better for all concerned. And all are concerned, and deeply, in the development of a better understanding of the social medium in which we live, move, and have our being.

Returning specifically to the matter of evidence on the historic period available to a science of society, what do we lack, and what can we do with what we have? We need, I repeat, an understanding of society, not a mere recording of the past; but the recording must come first, an adequate and comprehensive recording that takes account of all the aspects of society's life, not merely of a few selected ones. That is what we do not have. Let me come down to particulars.

It happens that I studied, in 1894–95, a widely heralded work on *Civilization during the Middle Ages,* by the same George B. Adams whom I have quoted above. Some twenty-five years later, having been drafted to teach a division of Freshman history, I found the same volume in use. I have no word of criticism of the author. He was my colleague and neighbor. He had a right to study what he chose and to take whatever point of view he pleased. His slant was legal, as is indicated by his notable work on the English Constitution. In any case, he had produced a stock historic volume. And it outdid most histories of its period in its attention to the social aspects of its field, as is indicated by its title. Much more was to be expected of it, for the use of a man like myself, than from the more formal, chronologically arranged histories. But what was there in it for me, in the way of evidence for a science of society?

It is not unfair to judge a book by its summary, and, with any skilled writer, his last paragraph is likely to be a summary of summaries. At any rate, let me quote that paragraph in its entirety.

The catalogue is not long of those things in which the first years of the sixteenth century surpassed those of the fifth. The great change was in the new race, the new spirit, which now entered into the possession of the results of the past. New impulses were felt by every man, and the promise of a wider future. New forces were opening the way in every direction. Humanity was entering upon another great era of the rapid conquest of nature and of truth.

"The purpose of this book," says the author, in his Preface, "is not to teach the facts of history themselves. It assumes that they are known. If not, the uninformed reader is referred to Duruy's *Middle Ages* or Fisher's *Outlines of Universal History.*" Evidently, Adams's volume

ought to offer ideal evidence for the social scientist because it constitutes a set of conclusions drawn directly from the facts by an acknowledged authority. But let us follow Adams's suggestion to the uninformed and take a look at Duruy. Says Adams, in his Editor's Preface
to the translation of Duruy:

It is generally considered that the most successful textbook on mediaeval
history in any language is M. Victor Duruy's *Histoire du Moyen Age*. Its
great merit consists in the fact that while it gives a very clear conception of
the great currents of the period, it also gives a sufficient number of the facts
and details of the history to furnish a solid basis for such general views. . . .
The reader can hardly fail to gain a clear conception of the general life and
growth of the race during this time, and of the relation of the several lines
of progress to one another, and yet these general views are continually an-
chored to the facts and given fixed and definite place.

Here, then, is a prize for the scientist: a kind of synthesis of which
Adams's book is a further refinement. Now, what does Duruy have to
say for himself?

The important facts to be noted are:
    The decline of the Roman Empire and the successful accomplishment
of the two invasions; the transient brilliancy of the Arabian civilization.
    The attempted organization of a new Empire by Charlemagne, and its
dissolution.
    The rise and prevalence of feudalism.
    The successive Crusades.
    The contest between the Pope and the Emperor for the sovereignty of
the world. . . .
    Humanity, that tireless traveller, advances unceasingly, over vale and
hill, to-day on the heights, in the light of day, to-morrow in the valley, in
darkness and danger, but always advancing, and attaining by slow degrees
and weary efforts some broad plateau, where he pauses a moment to rest
and take breath.
    These pauses, during which society assumes a form which suits it for the
moment, are organic periods. The intervals which separate them may be
called inorganic periods or times of transformation. On these lines we may
divide the ten centuries of the Middle Ages into three sections: from the
fifth to the tenth century, the destruction of the past and the transition to a
new form; from the tenth to the fourteenth, feudal society with its customs,
its institution, its arts, and its literature. This is one of the organic periods
in the life of the world. Then the tireless traveller starts again: this time he
again descends to depths of misery to reach, on the other side, a country
free from brambles and thorns. When the fourteenth and fifteenth centuries

are crossed we already perceive from afar the glorious forms of Raphael, Copernicus, and Christopher Columbus, in the dawn of a new world.

Overlooking the once-edifying "fine writing," it is readily to be inferred from the above summaries that Duruy's slant at the Middle Ages affords little promise of evidence for a science of society. Examination of his text confirms the inference. His pages bristle with proper names of places and persons, and his index must have been exhausting to the upper case of any font. I am not criticizing anyone for writing as he thought best, I repeat; I am trying to state what is lacking in Duruy's pages for the use of the social scientist. The prevalence of proper names witnesses to his preoccupation with the prominent individual and the specific location; this, together with the thick sprinkling of dates, reveals the stock historical restriction as to place and time. Biographical passages and historical anecdotes abound. Battles occupy much space, as do treaties and other formal arrangements. One would get the impression that history is nothing much but the doings of individuals, governments, and armies. The moral judgment is ubiquitous. Some things are "bad," others "good"; the status of the slave is "frightful." "From every point of view that we have taken, the reign of Justinian is worthy of praise. It is contemptible, if we consider the inner factions, the bloodthirsty quarrels"—etc., etc. After forty-five years, I find Duruy as dull and confusing as I found him while I was trying to keep awake over his pages in the preparation of the next day's lesson. There is almost as little that is unifying, to my mind, now as there was then.

Most of the "facts" are irrelevant to any scientific purpose and the interpretation put upon them rouses suspicion of antecedent selection. In any case, they constitute, as a whole, a lopsided collection. Here and there are passages that afford a brief glimpse of the life of the masses, but such almost incidental side-views, all told, are so out of the general focus of interest as to be of a penumbral dimness. And, even in the penumbra, one fails to descry anything at all, or worth while, about certain of the aspects of social life—say, about marriage and the family—which the student of society's evolution regards as of commanding significance.

What Professor Adams used to do in his lectures was to enlarge upon Duruy; and his own book is, in substance, that enlargement. He once told me that Professor Sumner had come near to diverting him, during student days, into anthropology; and I think that *Civilization during the Middle Ages* reveals some little echo of Sumner—which means that it takes some little account of the slant of the social scientist. Nevertheless, this volume is distinctly of the Duruy type, as was inevitable, and is of practically the same utility to the social scientist as is Duruy's. Adams's index is not so peppered with capitals nor his text with dates. He omits the battles and anecdotes. There is more of the impersonal cause and less of the individual agency.

But the moral judgment is not absent: "Konrad was a brave and earnest man who had a high conception of the duties and rights of his office and strove manfully to realize that conception." This shadow of the moral judgment broods rather dismally over a number of stretches, especially when religion and allied topics are touched upon. The "one decisive cause of the crusades" was "the ascetic feeling." "The occasion of the crusades was Mohammedanism." One misses a number of other elements that have been present in the "Drang nach Osten" which culminated in the Discoveries, in which the East was sought both directly and also via the West. Again, the "long and general preparation for the Reformation" is labelled as "religious, intellectual, and political." The "first step," which was the "great step" in the Reformation was "the formation of a clearer theory of justification by faith as the confident and satisfactory answer to the need of personal reconciliation with God." Luther was admittedly preoccupied with that theoretical question, but was it in the minds of the masses, or even in that of Henry VIII?

Here is an historical publication which has come to be a kind of classic—one which professes by its title to be a history of civilization during an extended period, and by its subtitle to view that civilization "especially in relation to modern civilization"—one which was written by a man who had no sneers for Spencer, no matter how critical of sociology after Spencer—and yet it is of little value, as historical evidence, for the student of societal evolution. Perchance Adams and Duruy were altogether right in conceiving of history exactly as they did; maybe a science of society is forever out of the question; but, even granted that those who are trying to work out such a science are on a wild-goose chase, Adams does not help us appreciably on our way. His forays into the range of "social history" are too tentative and timid, not to say partial in both senses of the word, to amount to much. If he has more for us than the rest, it is not much more, nor of a distinctly different quality. His interest is still so confined to the, to us, superficial aspects of society's evolution—persons, philosophies, creeds, politics—that we miss not only relevant materials but also somewhat distrust the attitude that leads him to his omissions as probably conducive to the distortion of what he does give.

We are interested in mass-phenomena interpreted by use of the comparative method. We want to center, not upon the individual, however "great," nor upon the "classes." We desire to know what men did, not what they, much less a few of them, thought. We want to know about the mass economic life as basic to all the other mores, and about the family life as second only to the economic. If the two grand natural functions of all life; self-maintenance and self-perpetuation, are not deserving of attention, we do not know what is of significance. We want to know about that perennial human interest, property. Compared with such information, the records of what all the Pippins, or even the Napoleons, thought and fought and arranged is of vanishing moment. We want to know about the law, not Justinian, and about its impact, not merely its functionaries. We care little about what the Planners thought or tried to do, or how they squabbled over tenuous theories and utopian schemes. It is nothing that a writer thinks this or that "good" or "bad," progressive or retrogressive, according to his private capacity for rationalization.

If I have not made clear by example that the scientist has not much to hope for in the way of materials from what may be called "straight history," then I ought probably to give up the effort. What chance is there that this absence of coöperation may pass?

I know that Duruy and Adams will be labelled "old," and the citation of them aligned with the attack on a straw man. I know that there have been sound historians who have adopted a more modern manner—Andrews, for instance—together with a number of unsound ones beside whom Adams is Hyperion to a squad of satyrs. In general, it would seem that there is a kind of vicious circle here: the historian will not furnish the evidence needed by a science of society until he has apprehended what that science is and needs; but he will not apprehend these matters until he has seen it employ historic data productively. You can't have a chicken till you have an egg, nor yet an egg until you have a hen. And yet this impasse, like many another logical impossibility, seems to me in process of resolution in the fact. For I think what the social scientist has worked out of what materials he has had available, even though incomplete or faulty, has amounted to a demonstration that his chase is not that of the wild goose.

No one can blame the historian, I say, for steering clear of what has gone by the name of "sociology." Historians know, and the genuine social scientist knows, though the historians do not know as well as they might that he knows, what an ocean of balderdash has left in its ebb on the strand called "sociology." But responsible scholars in other ranges are coming to a point of discrimination where all sociologists do not look alike to them. Nor do all historians look alike to the discriminating worker on the foundations of what may sometime become a genuine science of society. Let the sociologist demonstrate his respectability, instead of talking about his nobility, and he will be respected by the honest historian, who is at present by far the more respectable of the twain. And eventually the twain may meet and join forces. That forecast is not mere divination. It is offered on the basis of anticipated recurrence.

No matter about forecasting. The situation will work itself out or it will not. The immediate question for the science of society is that of evidence available as things now stand. The case as above presented looks rather hopeless. But if it is not as yet practicable to exploit the whole range of history, or history in large sections, is it not possible to make raids upon outlying parts?

For a good many years I have thought it possible to drive a thin edge into the block of history by way of an investigation of frontier institutions. A colonial or frontier society is composed of a relatively small number of immigrants who are subjecting themselves to a set of conditions that might be called primitive. They have moved out of complexity into relative simplicity. Adjustment to such simplicity results in a simplified code of mores. After a while, however, such societies have practically caught up with the older societies. The course of that evolution amounts to a kind of rapid recapitulation of the stages through which the parent countries have slowly passed. The evidence offered to societal evolution is comparable to that provided, for the organic process, by embryology. A frontier society is a kind of experiment under isolation from certain factors, a simplification of complexity, a removal of some of the causes that make up the confusing multiplicity of causes.

Several studies have now been made from this point of attack. Another peripheral opening into the historic range is by way of the study of communities isolated by geographical factors: Iceland, for instance, or Ireland; or, on a minute scale, Pitcairn Island. Any form of isolation, whether geographical or other, results in an elimination of certain influences, with consequent simplification. Within an enclosing society, groups that seek isolation, generally to nurse up some pet code, allow of special study: religious sects, communistic utopians. They naturally seek geographical, as well as other isolation, as did the Mormons. Any case of simplification—ethnography, or ancient as contrasted with modern history—has its possibilities. If institutions cannot be found in lowest terms, they can be discovered in lower terms.

Further, amidst the stretches of the historic record that are sterile so far as our special purpose goes, occur scattered oases that repay cultivation. There are works that have been described as culture-history (*Kulturgeschichte*) or historical anthropology. Their range extends beyond the limits of ethnography, as that term is commonly used; it includes even the contemporary. Examples are Rossbach, *Römische Ehe;* Lecky, *European Morals;* Weinhold, *Die Deutschen Frauen in dem Mittelalter;* Stern, *Die öffentliche Sittlichkeit in Russland;* Molmenti, *La Storia di Venezia nella vite private*—treatises, it must be acknowledged, which cover isolated reaches and lack any placement of their subjects within the inclusive social setting, much less within the general evolutionary series. But they fall into a series, when put together by the comparative method. If we had enough of them, even such as they are, the gap between the primitive and the contemporary would yawn much less formidably. Sets of detail studies made by enthusiasts, with no inkling of the evolutionary significance of their efforts were prime materials for Darwin to draw upon. It is not to be expected that authors of special studies, much less the mere hobbyists, shall have any conception of the services they are performing toward the development of future syntheses, unless, perchance, the wider bearing of those services is gradually apprehended as the result of even partial demonstration by synthesists.

Such a widening of outlook is not likely to happen until there is generated within the social range some such general atmosphere as envelops the organic, whereby practically all investigators breathe the spirit of synthesis infused by Darwin and others. The hospitality of historians and other established professionals to social science, and their willingness to coöperate, will be directly proportionate to the discretion and trustworthy conduct of sociologists in the use of such historic evidence as is already at their disposal. It must never be lost to sight, I reiterate, that the burden of proof always rests upon the new. A historian must needs be superhumanly tolerant if he is going to make the effort to extract the scanty grains of wheat out of the bushels of whirling chaff deposited by the winds of empty sociological theorizing. It is small wonder that he refuses to discriminate between sociologists. Nevertheless, he limits his own grasp if he lumps a Spencer with an H. G. Wells—though, in fact, he can learn something even from the latter swashbuckler, with all his self-confident blatancy and pet theories, for he is at least intent upon the evolutionary perspective which the historian generally misses. No matter about the Wells type, and worse—the historian defeats himself who eschews the Sumners, Spencers, Lipperts, or Paretos because of the company they cannot avoid.

It is futile for the sociologist to complain, to make "demands" for recognition, or to seek to dazzle, shame, or bully the other scientists or the historians. Sociology will get recognition when it comes to deserve it, after a bad let-down, by actual demonstration along scientific lines; and not from the other specialists alone, but from the sensible layman. Genuine, durable, matter-of-fact recognition comes slowly. It is one of those desirables, like character or culture, which cannot be won by direct frontal assault, with trumpets blaring, but arrives as a by-product of performing the next inconspicuous duty or learning unostentatiously the next little piece of knowledge about society's life. What the sociologist needs to do is to quit proposing resolutions of confidence in himself and to cultivate what garden he has in such manner as to win confidence in him and his results. Let him reflect upon the Parable of the Talents.

XVII

THE AUTHORITY OF THE CUMULATIVE IMPRESSION.

THIS TOPIC was thrust into view under the following circumstances. When I was an undergraduate I entered a course on Homer, given by the late Thomas D. Seymour, in which he took up the "Homeric Question." With great care and in considerable detail he presented to us the views concerning the single or multiple authorship of the poems held by Lachmann, Kirchhoff, and Von Willemowitz-Möllendorf. We became presently aweary of the type of "those conscientious bits of work in which the reviewer points out that the author has erred in rendering an obscure text, 'I, the King, have built six temples for my glory,' and that the proper translation would rather be, 'I, the King, have bestowed six oxen on my daughters (nieces?)' "[1] We floundered about in a maze, expecting, youthfulwise, some "answer" to the Question. The course was about to end without any gratification of our curiosity.

One of us, as a delegate, approached Professor Seymour, to ask: "What do you yourself believe?" He began to quote the Germans again, aligning their positions. The youth persisted: "Yes, but what do you yourself think?" and at length elicited the reply: "The poems seem to me to bear the impress of a single mind." "Thank you," replied the youth. "That is what we wanted to know."

We were aware that Seymour had read the *Iliad* and the *Odyssey* many times. It was said that he re-read them every year, in addition to his intensive teaching of parts of them. We knew that he had a keen mind of wide scope. He knew other literatures besides the Greek. He knew music and art. In short, we respected his intellect and equipment; and any judgments he might have arrived at through the accumulation of impressions received during many years of close acquaintance with the Homeric text had weight with us. We did not care whether or not he could cite chapter and verse for his opinion as to single or multiple authorship. We wanted to know what the upshot of his impressions was. We thought that he had earned the right to

1. Strunsky, S., *Professor Latimer's Progress*, p. 6.

say what he thought, and we wanted much more to hear that than to know whether this or that verse was corrupt or interpolated, according to some German student on whose opinions, in fact, we realized we were incompetent to pass judgment. Of course we knew that Seymour might be wrong; but we knew him experienced, competent, and honest.

This instance raises the question of "Authority." No scientist can believe in the authority of revelation—not as a scientist, that is. He cannot even believe a thing because it is accepted by "everybody." Too many errors have been accepted by great numbers—the witchcraft delusion, for one example. He does not believe anything merely because he is told that "it stands to reason"—which he knows to be merely an attention-diverting phrase analogous to the prestidigitateur's sudden ejaculations or pistol-firing at the psychological moment. He never believes anything because, say, Aristotle said it, such credulity being of a piece with the uncritical frame of mind demanded of the receiver of revelation.

But, with all his suspicion of error quite alive, and always guarding himself against uncritical acceptance, any scientist is willing to give certain masters of science at least the benefit of the doubt. Especially when he is familiar with the mind and character of such eminences, and knows that their results have been proved correct, over and over again, by other investigators, is he willing to concede to them a certain authority. Even such a concession has its dangers—Darwin himself made certain inexplicable errors, not in theorizing alone but actually in straight observation. The trust reposed in him is indicated by the wonderment of his admirers at his lapse and the comment: "What could have been the matter with him that day?"

The scientist will be careful not to confuse this evidence from accumulated impression with "intuition" or any other figment of the imagination. He will realize that, given time to recall them, a large number of the perhaps unconsciously stamped impressions could be traced back to concrete experience. I have no doubt that Professor Seymour, had he set out to collect the verses, or sets of verses, which to him revealed the influence of a single mind, could have made a pretty convincing display. Also, as any student knows, the significance of instances previously scanned more or less mechanically has a way of breaking over the mind suddenly, so that one marvels that he has hitherto been blind to it. He can recall that there was much evidence in his reading, perhaps for years back, for some new point of view;

but, since he did not while reading recognize its significance, he has made no record of that evidence. It is virtually lost, for he cannot go back and do all his reading over again. Once in a while he can recall where he encountered what he now wishes he had at hand but, unless his reading has been much restricted, that is exceptional. For example, one student of anthropology became suddenly aware of the significance in culture-history of the smith and his social function. No sooner had he received the suggestion than he realized that he had had the evidence before him, without focussing on it, during years of reading ethnography. He had had the solution in his beaker but not the precipitate. In any case, he had not experienced the precipitating jog.

The point I am stressing is that such a student's accumulation of unidentifiable evidence, evidence for which he can give no original source, is not worthless. It is like the impression a veteran doctor gathers from the general aspect of a patient. It depends altogether upon the kind of man that student has proved himself to be; upon whether he has the authority of accuracy and honesty as verified elsewhere in his work and life. That there is a subjective element in the case is good reason for the utmost caution, but not for instant and final rejection. Seymour, who was a stickler for chapter and verse, was very reluctant to state his private impressions, even in private. It is a pity that he felt he must cleave so tenaciously to his principles in his *Life in the Homeric Age,* for, as a result, that book of his life lacks life. He once intimated that he meant to state his net impressions later; but his life was cut short. He should have written chapters of accumulated impression. He had the right—I had almost said that he had the duty. He had the authority, not The Authority of revelation or enthusiasm, but of the diligent, intelligent, discriminating, conscientious, teachable mind that has been disinterestedly immersed in its materials over a long time. He knew all that anyone else had written about Homer. That was clear enough—too clear—to us students. What we wanted, though, was the upshot of his own impressions. That was good enough for us—and I am constrained to believe that our scent for the significant did not play us false.

This is a ticklish topic, but the reader has not lacked warnings to that effect as he has gone along.

However, an accumulated impression is something else than pure guesswork. A guess has been defined as an hypothesis without the facts. The net impression here in mind involves conclusions upon the basis of facts than can no longer be cited. As one grows older and finds himself personally convinced about this and that, though he has no time, strength, or patience to go back over his course and pick up what he has dropped, it is perhaps pardonable for him to venture some guesses that are not wholly guesswork, because they rest upon what, uncouthly expressed, he has encountered and forgotten. Provided he does not present his conclusions for any more than they are worth, he is deceiving and harming nobody by stating, without taking himself too seriously, the residual deposits which a long acquaintance with facts of experience has left upon his mind.

XVIII

OUTSTANDING SOCIOLOGISTS AND SOME OTHERS.

To ONE who has read the preceding pages, the conviction of the present writer that Herbert Spencer was the first genuine sociologist could not have been mistaken. Those who hold that great analytic mind cheap merely reveal their own intellectual triviality. If the succeeding pages seem to concentrate upon criticism of the work of Spencer, Lippert, or Pareto, that implies no lack of respect for their achievements. It is time that social scientists should speak their minds about each other's work; there has been too much spineless deference in assessing slight and unscientific production far above merit, as well as in minimizing or ignoring the weak spots in works that, as wholes, deserve to rank in the forefront. No science can get very far ahead until there is developed in its cultivators a relentlessness in intelligent criticism which shall be both approved and desired by all, especially by its victims. It should be impossible to insult or to be insulted professionally by fault-finding whereby faults are found, not merely imputed. On the contrary, a true scientist is always avid of criticism that enables him to correct his errors; he wants his faults to be found, even though he prefers to find them for himself. Any serious scientist will keep in mind the model attitude of Darwin in this respect, as in all others.

The only genuine type of criticism is that of those who have won the right to an opinion. The conquest of the right to judge is the result of one kind of campaign, and one only, namely, the acquisition of scientific knowledge concerning, in this case, the evolution and life of human society. The critic who is armed merely with logic or rhetoric or expertness in word-juggling, with mere rancor, is to be dismissed forthwith and without ceremony. No busy man can afford the time and effort to listen to him, much less to debate and rebut. The horrible faces that such a fault-finder makes will not distract if the back be turned upon the first of them. The serious student of society must cultivate indifference to irrelevancies, whether they are things, persons, or ideas. He will find it quite easy if he abjures vanity, keeps his eye on the ball, and does not take himself too seriously. What sense is there, for one who is trying to devote the whole of his short human life to the search for truth, in paying any attention whatsoever to strictures from persons who have no right to an opinion? The only reply possible, if one is vouchsafed to that kind of a critic, is: "Go and learn something, and then you can answer your own carpings or you will find out that they are too foolish to demand an answer." There is a cheap and captious kind of criticism that should always be ignored, as well as a precious variety, eagerly to be sought and appropriated.

It is the fashion to decry Spencer as "out of date." But truth is never out of date; and Spencer set forth a number of truths. As is the way with such discoveries, they pass into the body of accepted knowledge, gradually losing the fading label or signature of their authorship, and becoming, often enough, "self-evident" to the sons of those who had strenuously and even with horror denied them any validity whatsoever. There is here no attempt to deal with that aspect of Spencer's case, by seeking to identify his forgotten contribution to accepted knowledge and accredit him with it. There is here no "constructive" criticism, which is contradiction in terms, but almost solely "fault-finding"; for if criticism is not destructive and correctional, it is merely commendation and new construction.

Spencer's *Principles of Sociology,* despite the fact that he was forced, in the production of this one work, to accumulate original data and deal with them inductively on a scale far more extensive than in any other of his treatises, is injured by reason of constituting a section of his *Synthetic Philosophy.* It is corrupted in its scientific good manners by its philosophical evil communications. Spencer had a formula which, being philosophical, had to be universal. To be universal it had to be spread very thin, like too little butter on too much bread. This made it vague and of indefinite outline. His formula, stated at the outset, in *First Principles,*[1] doubtless with an extraordinary scope of vision over many ranges, worked out to nothing very illuminative in its application to any specific range. That evolution proceeds from an indefinite, incoherent homogeneity toward a definite, coherent heterogeneity may be true enough, but it is very difficult for a biologist or a scientific student of society to make any conclusive answer to a highly pertinent query concerning the formula: What of it? The formula does not keep suggesting itself to him, as he studies and works along; it does not emit recurrent flashes of illumination; it is somewhat like an overcast firmament—a "low ceiling"—that is in no way favorable to the getting and keeping of bearings. Indeed, in no fruitful respect does

1. § 145.

it serve Spencer himself, as he wends his way through the three volumes of the *Principles,* though he now and then lugs it in by the ears in deference to his grand evolutionary thesis. Every passage in which he does that could be deleted without loss to, probably to the advantage of, his *Sociology.* This general defect of the work is, of course, merely another piece of evidence as to the futility of mixing philosophy, or something pretty near to it, with science. The two are birds of a quite different feather that do not profit by flocking together; the metaphysical one is likely to lay its cuckoo eggs in the other's nest.

However subtly he may disguise the fact or however stoutly deny it, evidently Spencer has a pre-chosen thesis to prove: the formula of "Spencerian evolution." The essential differences between evolution of the Spencerian and of the Darwinian type are recorded elsewhere.[2] This a priori procedure of Spencer's, together with the tendency toward "diabolical dialectics" that goes naturally with it, has alienated many scientists. It constitutes the chief general defect of the *Principles of Sociology* as a section of the *Synthetic Philosophy.* And because Spencer had a weakness for thesis-defending, he was the more readily tempted by analogies, which have always been a favorite stock in trade of metaphysicians and preachers.

The "biological analogy" has been sufficiently considered by a number of critics; but it is impossible not to wonder, from time to time, whether there is not a mechanical analogy also in the offing of Spencer's horizon—a mirage readily understandable when we reflect upon his youthful preoccupation with engineering and also upon the title of his earliest book, *Social Statics.* Of course this mechanical analogy and its biological fellow were strongly suggested by the necessity of covering the inorganic realm as well as the organic under an inclusive formula. Encouragement of a tendency to confuse analogy and identity arose also from the fact that identity is capable of pulling the various exhibitions of evolution in the several ranges of phenomena together much more tightly than is analogy: "Society *is* an organism" is far more useful to that end than is "Society *is like* an organism." In any case it is prudent for the reader of Spencer to scrutinize pretty carefully his mechanics-derived terminology—"motion," "equilibrium," and the rest—in order to be sure whether it is or is not being employed metaphorically; and it must always be realized while so doing that Spencer is cautious, agile, and subtle, never falling flat upon his face in the

2. Keller, *Societal Evolution,* chap. ii (revised ed.).

entanglements of analogy, as does Ward, for example, in his *Pure Sociology*.

Moving from the general toward the particular, there is, as regards the *Principles,* exception to be taken to Spencer's order of presentation. From his line of approach it is logical enough to begin, as he does, with "Super-organic Evolution" and the original external and internal factors behind social phenomena—however dubious or irrelevant his generalizations concerning primitive man's physical and mental qualities may be. But, despite the admissions and justifications of the author at the beginning of the chapter (XXVII) on the "Scope of Sociology" (where the treatise really begins), I believe that nearly half of Volume I, dealing as it does with "Primitive Ideas," is out of place. That half is practically all of a religious character and seems to belong at the outset of Part VI, "Ecclesiastical Institutions." Its presence in a position where it seems to steal some of the legitimate thunder from Part VI and to produce an impression of broken sequence or even of repetition, is ill-advised. There is really no place where primitive religious ideas end and another type begins; and there seems to be no more reason for singling them out as a "preparation" for what is to come than for trying to identify and list at the outset the primitive economic, domestic, or political ideas in preparation for the later treatment of economic, domestic, or political institutions. And why this one section should be called "The Data of Sociology," in view of the many facts later cited, is beyond understanding. Possibly the initial prominence accorded these primitive religious notions is a kind of measure of Spencer's growing appreciation of their relevancy and significance, as he came to know them more intimately.

I have a feeling that Spencer's idea of evolution, which seems always to be tinged with a tendency to make evolution mean "progress," is somehow responsible for this arrangement.

As for the order in which the institutions of society are treated (Part III, Domestic Institutions; Part IV, Ceremonial Institutions; Part V, Political Institutions; Part VI, Ecclesiastical Institutions; Part VII, Professional Institutions; Part VIII, Industrial Institutions), it seems to me to be no order at all. But first let us consider items IV and VII. What right have they to figure as "institutions" in a classification whose other categories contain Marriage and the Family (III), the Regulative System (V), Religion (VI), and the Industrial Organization, with Property (VIII)? All institutions are ceremonial; if one wants to cover ceremonial, he ought to do that, as Sumner did, in a preceding book or section. Every one of Spencer's chapters under Part IV could go under some other one of his rubrics, or under one not represented (Gratification), or under some truly "preparatory" section on what Sumner called "Folkways." It has always seemed to me that in Part IV Spencer was feeling for what Sumner fully develops in his *Folkways*. In any case, to make a separate item of Ceremonies, at the same time dignifying them as institutions, seems to me unjustifiable and also damaging to the continuity of presentation.

Somewhat the same is to be said of "Professional Institutions" (VII). On the basis of Spencer's own theory about their priestly origin, they could readily be classified under the Religious Organization. In any case, the poet, painter, or sculptor, names which head his chapters in Part VII, are not institutions; nor is "Poetry" or "Painting" or "Sculpture." And, though one differs from Spencer's theory as to the origin of all these professions in the priesthood, he finds no trouble at all in classifying them under the several admittedly master categories (III, V, VI, VIII), plus Gratification.

These major categories show undoubted interrelations; it is the way of evolutionary things to merge across zones of transition. Bodily mutilations, for example, are sometimes purely religious, sometimes purely decorative, sometimes both at once. But they are seldom purely ceremonial. Behind ceremonial there is almost always something of a denser and more solid texture. Neither "ceremonial" nor "professional" is a good rubric, for neither is a term of primary intention. "Industry," "Religion," "Government," are primary, for each has a core of its own. Ceremonies and professions are attachable to them all as secondary manifestations.

Aside from reservation as to the admission of these two items, the order of the remaining four groups of institutions—Domestic (III), Political (V), Ecclesiastical (VI), Industrial (VIII)—is not convincing or clarifying. To judge by Spencer's preliminary emphasis upon "Primitive Ideas," we should think that he ought to have begun with the Religious. "Ecclesiastical" looks like an attempt to distinguish the indistinguishable, so as to account for the break between the "Primitive Ideas" and the resumption of the same topic in Part VI. But, setting that impression aside, upon what possible criterion could the Industrial Institutions be stationed in the rear, behind all the rest? Surely the prime activity of any society, as of any organism, is self-maintenance— in the case of society by industry and the accumulation of capital, distributed as property. There is only one other prime function of society, again as of organisms: self-perpetuation. This would assign the Domestic Institutions to second place in order of importance.

The only quarrel I should have with any classification-placement chosen by Spencer or anyone else, when these two primary sets of institutions had been recognized as such, would be over a non-recognition of the fact that Government and Religion are to be connected with primary self-maintenance, and that some category or additional overflow should be provided for social practices that are motived as a whole or in part by impulses toward self-gratification—impulses solely of pleasure-seeking, catering to the senses or to the all-pervading sentiment of vanity. Naturally, I prefer the classification adopted in *The Science of Society;* but I believe that my preference has not blinded me to virtues in Spencer's order so that I could not see them if they were there.

Of the sections into which Spencer divides his treatise, that entitled "Domestic Institutions" seems to me by far the most defective. There is a story, good enough to be true, that, in the myopic self-absorption of the confirmed bachelor, he had omitted marriage and the family in his original prospectus of the *Principles*—an omission pointed out to him, somewhat jeeringly, by George Eliot. In any case, this section on *Domestic Institutions* contains little of value, being taken up largely by an arid controversy, conducted in the manner of the schoolman rather than of the scientist. The author pounds away at McLennan's theory of exogamy, later to shift over to an attack upon the ideas of Sir Henry Maine about the family. Whatever may be the truth about Spencer's original attitude toward this section of the *Principles,* its chapters certainly give the impression of haste, incompleteness, lack of insight and perhaps of interest, and certainly of disproportion; they might well suggest afterthought and a retreat, in order to cover manifest haste, into logical but sterile "reasoning"—the abandonment, in good part, of induction in favor of concept-juggling.

It should never be lost to sight, along with the fact that Spencer was engaged in formulating a philosophy, that his earliest interest in society lay in the questions of government. Witness his *Social Statics* and *Man Versus the State.* This may help to account for the length and prolixity of Part V (Political Institutions) and for the end position of Part VIII (Industrial Institutions), which winds up with such questions of the day as "Trade-Unionism" and "Socialism"; possibly also for the subordination of "Property" to a score of pages under Part V (Political

Institutions). Recurring for a moment to the former of these two interests, it is possible for one to infer that the arrangement of the topics
in the *Principles* was dictated by the exigencies of the *Synthetic Philosophy* as well as by those of this one of its parts; for the whole series
of volumes was working up toward the *Principles of Ethics,* which was
to be the crown of the edifice and, in a sense, the "lesson" to be learned
from the whole series, from *First Principles* through the *Principles of
Biology, Principles of Psychology,* and *Principles of Sociology.* When
a man starts out early in life to write a set of ten volumes covering
everything and winding up with what might be called a life-philosophy,
there is always a suspicion in the offing that the character of the several
components of the series will be subordinated to the covering interest
of the whole. The tendency of the author to such subordination may
have been less marked in *The Principles of Sociology* because that
study was forced toward induction from facts that had to be collected;
nevertheless even the categories provided by the author for the collabo-
rators in the *Descriptive Sociology* had to be laid down beforehand,
and that could scarcely have been done in detachment from the grand
principles upon which the whole *Synthetic Philosophy* had been
planned. It seems to me, therefore, that *The Principles of Sociology* has
been damaged, often in indirect and subtle ways, as well as directly,
by its relation to and inclusion in the enveloping grandiose life-enter-
prise, the *Synthetic Philosophy.* There was too much Planning in the
case.

There is at least one thing that Spencer could do that most other
sociologists cannot, namely, express himself clearly and flawlessly in
the matter of language and style. The only criticism of that style is its
monotony and, occasionally, its verbosity. I lay this in some degree to
his formal and consciously "logical," often ambitiously syllogistic, presentation, but chiefly to the fact that he always dictated, except for his
Social Statics. Dictation invites mannerism and wordiness, and the
wonder is that Spencer was able to resist to the degree he did. Though
the style is clear, it does not seem to me admirable in other respects; so
I cannot share the lament of Sumner that he was not able to "write as
well as Mr. Spencer." Maybe he was not when, old and ill, he labored
on *Folkways;* but his style in his maturity was to Spencer's as a
broken country, with relieving roughnesses and contrasts, is to the
almost featureless monotony of a flat plain. Spencer, to me, is too
smooth and self-conscious in his writing; too calmly superior; too
serenely didactic. I like to see a writer struggle with his medium, even

as poor Darwin had to do it—Darwin who, he himself says, always fell naturally and first into the most awkward expression there was, but, as is clear to any reader of him, not seldom wrought so persistently to get out of the trap that he eventually emerged with an unforgettable phrase or even passage.

One of the criticisms of the *Sociology* has been its employment of inaccurate history. Insofar as that criticism is apt, it simply registers, once more, the peril to the science of society of utilizing historical evidence.

The Study of Sociology should not be passed over, though it was a species of afterthought transformed by a publisher's forethought, it is said, into an introduction to the *Principles*. I have elsewhere[3] expressed my view about the relevancy of the "preparation in biology" and the "preparation in psychology," which are the titles of two chapters of the *Study;* and I think the shadow of the *Synthetic Philosophy* impends over them. But I should never regard a student as well-grounded in the science who had not soaked his mind in the ever-timely wisdom of the other chapters of this remarkable little book. I do not know of any presentation of the need for and the difficulties confronting the development of a science of society, nor of the biases that the human mind is heir to, that surpasses Spencer's in this *Study*. It makes me think of Sumner and Pareto at their best. Though somewhat more urbane, Spencer is equally mordant in his destructiveness of the shams and his disclosures of the hypocrisies that are always with us. He is, perhaps, as compared with the other two, a little cattish; but he attains the same clearing of the air; and every beginner in the subject needs that kind of service in the dispelling of the mephitic if he is to avoid giddiness and nausea. Spencer, Sumner, and Pareto are a trio of relentless fumigators.

I do not like to leave Spencer without reiterating my deep respect and even reverence for his work. I should dislike very much to be numbered among those who sneer at him. He has no need of excuses, for he accomplished a great and important labor; and one cannot in justice fail to take into account his poverty and his long invalidism. He could not gather his own materials, and his deputies largely broke down and failed him. Though he was not the scientist or the man that Darwin was, he was scarcely less heroic; and he was poor and alone where Darwin was comparatively wealthy in a material way and humanly rich in his devoted wife and family. Spencer may not be the

3. Essay on "The Scientific Study of Society," above.

loftiest intellect and character among the great men of his time, but there are few indeed, of his day or any other, who deserve to be ranked above him. Sociology has every reason to take pride in its founder; and it has not yet gone so far beyond him that it can ignore his labors as of merely historical significance.

Julius Lippert's services in the development of a science of society have not been recognized in proportion to their deserts. It is easy enough, on reading his truly pathetic autobiographical sketch, to understand why he was underestimated in Germany: he was a mere schoolmaster and popular lecturer, belonging in no way to the *Professorenstand;* he remained for most of his life both poor and obscure. It is possibly due to his effort to make an impression upon learned academic circles that he evolved another handicap to his success abroad, namely, a style of such tortuous unloveliness that even Germans have been staggered by it. What remains inexplicable is the fact that, having acquired such an enviable instrumentality, he did not attain to that academic renown which has often been accorded by an impressed, though bewildered German scientific Sanhedrin. That this monstrous manner was not natural self-expression seems to be proved by Lippert's popular edition of the *Kulturgeschichte* and by other writings of his. Unquestionably his ponderous exposition, as exhibited in his great work, has discouraged and repelled many who would have valued him highly had he been less inaccessible. The best of that work is now available in an abridged English translation, of a style extraordinarily lucid and attractive.[4]

The defects of Lippert's *Kulturgeschichte* are due to his poverty and unremitting efforts to make a living. I have no doubt that we have in him an illustration of the stunting of a high talent, approaching genius, by the circumstances of life. So far as can be seen, he seized and improved every slight opportunity that came his way, denying himself even the simplest pleasures in his burning desire to utilize in study every moment of his scant leisure. The *Kulturgeschichte* was written mainly during a two-year period when, by exception, he was moderately free of his life's long grind. The marvel remains that he did so much with so little; he could not have done what he did had not his health been rugged.

The chief criticism of Lippert is that he generalizes, in his main treatise, from too few facts. It was, with him, that or nothing. Further,

4. Murdock, G. P., translator and editor; Lippert, *Evolution of Culture.*

the data also upon which he relies are of uneven distribution and authenticity; he knows a good deal about Hebrew history and tradition, and not a little about the local records and mythology of his native region; but he is not widely read in general ethnography and history. Naturally, then, he leans rather heavily upon secondary sources, not always well chosen. Furthermore, he was no linguist; in his latter days, writes his daughter, he was struggling slowly, though with great interest, through Sumner's *Folkways*. And, in addition to all this, he does not seem to possess more than a superficial knowledge of economics or biology or, indeed, of any other science remotely or closely related to his main interest. Even his references to the classics seem to be taken secondhand; they appear to be chance cases that have come his way, very likely after having passed through several hands, and they include inaccuracies. In short, Lippert was inadequately equipped to make the most of his natural gifts and of his industry, which were very great; that he accomplished what he did, I repeat, is a lasting wonder.

Before I come to the criticisms which must be passed however readily Lippert's faults may be explained—not excused, for he is not in need of excuse any more than was Spencer, I wish to set down briefly the superiorities of his work on the basis of which some of us rank him among the few great figures in the development of a science of society. Lippert was, so to speak, as inductive as he could be: tireless in gathering facts during every fraction of time that he could save from his daily breadwinning. But his industry would have been put forth and his small harvest gleaned in vain, had he not possessed a sanity and an insight into the handling of his scanty materials which enabled him, in general, to make the most he legitimately could of them while avoiding the temptation to universalize not cautiously but too widely, a temptation to which many lesser men have unresistingly yielded.

I do not say that Lippert had "intuition," for I do not believe that the untutored have ever accomplished anything reliable. There is no question whatever that he would have made a much greater name for himself if he had had the chance to assemble a richer store of materials. But he used what he had with such an intensity and intelligence, tempered with so rare a combination of objectivity and controlled imagination, that his conclusions were largely sound and always suggestive. It is something to be full of suggestion in general, when actually wrong in particular; there are plenty of the "hodmen of science" who, meticulously accurate, thorough, and dry in the matter of detail, yet reveal no scope and are able to open up no interesting vistas. Lippert's active imagination was generally bitted by his common sense; he did not generalize baselessly or wishfully, nor did he run off into that unproductive, even though highsounding, speculation which is the inviting refuge of him who has too few facts because he is too lazy to gather them; in the main, not even Tyndall could have found great fault with Lippert's enacted version of the scientific use of the imagination. Lippert's chances were not of the ten-talent description; but he made the most of what he had and only now and then more than they would bear.

Of a consequence, his critical reader has a comparatively simple task. Equipped with a knowledge of facts that Lippert lacked, it is not difficult to detect the instances where he generalized too boldly. It is not as if the critic had to pass upon an abstract and speculative structure; either Lippert has taken enough materials into account or he has not; his generalizations upon scanty materials do or do not cover the case when tried out against a richer store of facts. He is not a writer who "has something to prove." Because he is honest, the chaff shows up readily and the wheat can be winnowed out without much trouble. And it is good grain.

Dr. Murdock has eliminated most of the less valuable portions of the *Kulturgeschichte* in his translated and edited version, a service to science which will be more deeply appreciated as time goes on. I need not list his omissions here, for the interested student can readily compare the *Evolution of Culture* with the original. Dr. Murdock has relieved Lippert of his two most damaging short-comings: his formidable German style and his serious lapses. Nevertheless, this author is always to be read critically, in the light of the multitude of cases which he could not know. The student who preserves that attitude in approaching him is bound to emerge with a very high respect for his scope, grasp, and suggestiveness.

Spencer has been criticized for the pronounced unevenness of his presentation. The same cannot be said of Lippert. Fault is perhaps to be found with him for overstressing religion and the family, to the understressing of the industrial organization, property, and government; in Dr. Murdock's version, out of fourteen chapters five have to do with religion and four with the family; nevertheless, all the primary institutions are there, and their interrelations are traced adequately and with high ingenuity and insight.

Perhaps out of the caution heretofore recommended, Lippert confines himself, in the main, to evidence other than historical.

There are those who might object to the inclusion of Lippert among the sociologists, and especially to the assignment of him to so high a place among them. The reply is that, in the judgment of the writer, no one except Spencer and Sumner has contributed so many enlightening ideas and positive points of attack to the scientific student of society's evolution. That Lippert did not entitle his volumes "Soziologie" is irrelevant. At any rate, they are no mere history of culture, for they record sequences, whether or not chronological, and reach out toward general societal laws.

Pareto completes the trio—Spencer, Lippert, Pareto—of the outstanding scientists of society other than Sumner. His *Trattato di Sociologia Generale* is so different from the other comprehensive works on the subject that it is, very likely, not fair to estimate it upon the same criteria. For Pareto makes no attempt to treat of the institutions, major or minor, of society. His analysis is one of underlying factors, as illustrated in classical history and in that of a limited portion of Europe, chiefly Italy. He stops deliberately at 1912 or thereabouts, regarding the subsequent years of war and its sequels as, in a sense, abnormal. He evidently regards ethnography as invalid evidence, and evolution as a false guide. While he decides that mathematics cannot be employed upon non-quantitative social phenomena, he seems to have a kind of leaning, recalling that of Spencer, toward a terminology suggested by the mechanics and physics upon the study of which his, and Spencer's, early profession, engineering, rested. He does not seem to have paid much, or any, attention to other sociological writings, but to have struck off alone and wholly independent—indeed, with a kind of scornful intolerance—upon a self-chosen path leading, he hopes, toward a genuine understanding of the nature of society and of the motive power behind history. The thought recurs over and over, while reading him, that Henry Adams and he are kindred souls, though the wistful uncertainty of Adams is replaced, in the harder-fibered Pareto, by positiveness, irony, and a kind of mordant disdain.

Much foolishness was printed about Pareto prior to the publication of the English translation of the *Trattato*. Excited heralds of a new prophet made proclamations on the basis of slight understanding, or hearsay, that would have inspired their seer to outdo his notable suc-

cesses in pouring scorn upon pretentiousness and sentimentalism in
the service of self-advertisement. For if Pareto is anything he is
"tough," as his proclaimed disciples soon found when they attempted
actually to read him. No book of the sort ever had a more copious pre-
publication publicity; but when some of the rhapsodists had broken
their teeth over it, they ceased their chorusing. Than their discomfiture
nothing would have pleased Pareto more. For he was not looking for
applause, much less notoriety. He was, he says, simply taking his shot
at making a science of society; and he remarked to a student that the
sooner the *Sociologia* reached the top shelf, the better pleased he would
be, for that would show that someone else had advanced farther. He is
after no more than "successive approximations to the truth." If anyone thinks that he is pleasuring the shade of Pareto by announcing his
apotheosis in dithyrambs, he is in error. The last thing Pareto coveted
was worship by Americans, for whom he had little liking in any case.
His shade must be enraged at the trivial sacrilege of entitling his
austere treatise, in translation, "The Mind and Society"!

Even if he be exempted from the criteria by which other sociologists
have been measured, and excused for not having produced a system,
Pareto has his faults. A very evident and also damnable one is his habit
of intricate classification. No one can carry in his head the endless labels
this author devises; it is necessary to make one's self a key, or he will
be under the necessity of incessantly turning back. Pareto's topics, sub-
topics, sub-sub-topics, and so on, are not so much an exposition as an
imposition. They are doubtless a reflection out of the profundities of the
author's mathematics, but they remain a challenge to patience and are
a real disfigurement of a great work. Many of the saltant greeters of
the *Trattato* broke down promptly when it came to digging their way
through the difficulties of their new 1900-page scripture. And it is a
safe bet that Pareto knew what would be irritating to the reader and
put it in anyhow. He shows absolutely no deference or reverence for
anybody or anything. The reader may take the *Trattato* as it is or leave
it. Pareto does not care a whoop which he does.

It is in order to present a bird's-eye view of these inexorably mar-
shalled ranks and files. Pareto's first volume begins with a distinction
between "logical-experimental" and "non-logical-experimental" actions.
Here is in reality a treatise on scientific and non-scientific method,
which is applicable to any field. These two terms are about synonymous
with "inductive" and "deductive." Actions of the first kind are those
dictated by positive, inductively acquired, verified knowledge, as in a

laboratory. As such, they are very rare anywhere and absent within the social field, or nearly so. That is about all we hear of them in this work. Of the second type of actions which rest on deduction in the main, some are dictated by "Residues," basic drives that vary little, and others by "Derivations," which, as covering reasons for all sorts of actions that call for a respectable or noble motive behind them, vary much. Residues are real reasons; Derivations are good reasons.

The Residues are classed as (1) the "instinct of combinations"; (2) the "persistence of the aggregate"; (3) the "need of the manifestation of sentiments by external acts"; (4) "residues in relation with sociality"; (5) "integrity of the individual and of his attachments"; (6) "sexual residues." The analysis of them covers 385 pages. The Derivations, analyzed through 547 pages, are (1) "affirmations"; (2) "authority"; (3) "accord with sentiments, or with principles"; (4) "verbal proofs." In general, the Residues are the primary and genuine sentiments or motives, the Derivations a set of pretty rationalizations and camouflagings. The stripping of Derivations to the skin is, perhaps, Pareto's most congenial exercise, and he does it with a thoroughness, ruthlessness, and jeering mockery which appeal very strongly to a robust taste.

The development of these categories leads into a maze of Roman and Arabic numerals, spiced up with the Greek alphabet: $I\beta_5$; $IV\gamma_3$; $V\delta_2$; and so on. The application of the analysis narrows down, in the end, to the relative effectiveness, in any society, of the first two Residues: the combination-tendency and the persistence-tendency, as exhibited by a "circulating" Élite. The former amounts to a preponderance of variation, progressiveness, new combinations, while the latter represents conservatism and traditionalism. History, Pareto holds, is a matter of the "undulatory movement," away from equilibrium between the two types and back toward it. A good many illustrations are presented, many of them incapable of checking by the non-professional student of the Italian peninsula's history.

This sketch of Pareto's analysis does not pretend to completeness or even to exactitude. The way to know Pareto is to read Pareto, not somebody else's version of him. It is very difficult to thread one's way through his jungle of classification in such manner as to retain any adequate perspective of the ground covered, as a whole; but this sketch will do to hang certain comments upon.

In his "undulatory theory" of history, Pareto had no idea that he had produced a magic formula applicable to all situations. The fact

is that his Residues of Classes I and II—he does not say much about
the others—are much too general, unmeasurable, and indeterminable
to be of practical utility. They resemble Spencer's evolutionary formula:
probably true, broadly though mistily illuminative, but of little value as
actual instrumentalities. Roughly speaking, they seem to say that if enterprise and regard for experience are happily united in a folk-disposi-
tion, the people in question are going to prosper; if not, they do not.
This is by no means the whole of the matter, but it is the gist of it.
There is nothing startling, that is to say, in Pareto's theory of history.
It is only to be feared that the worshipful will use his terminology as a
shamanistic jargon.

To one of Pareto's principles I find myself in stark opposition. He
advises the study of the contemporary first, as better known, thence to
work back to the earlier stages. The contrasting position holds, as
previously stated, that the present is the more obscure epoch and also
the one toward the understanding of which it is needful to work up
through what precedes. Indeed, to me the study of the past would be
of merely curious interest, had it no bearing upon the understanding
of the present and the forecasting of the future. If the present were
understandable without the study of the primitive and historic, many
of us would not bother about the past; for, despite all the accusations
levelled at the method we profess, as cold and hard and indifferent to
improvement and uplift, we have always subscribed, despite the self-
conceit of its context, to the sentiment of the Roman orator quoted at
the beginning of this volume. Our course is as straight and direct toward improvement as we can make it, consistently with the verdict of
experience. The criticism of it, that it is not precipitate, headlong, ob-
stacle-ignoring, we shall have to sustain as best we can.

Pareto, of course, is not alignable with the critics who pant to "do
something" at once; he repeatedly warns the student of society that he
must keep his eye off immediate applications. He is for pure science
as eagerly as anyone else—by way, indeed, of a colder, more indifferent,
even more cynical, detachment than any other eminent writer on
sociology. It is evidence of his thoroughgoing objectivity and indifference to any considerations of improvement that he proposes the
present as a key to the past instead of vice versa. But, with him, we
take issue with this attitude of impatience and eagerness to do something at once in that we contemplate, or at least hope and work for, a
science of society that may issue eventually in practical applications and

more expedient adjustments. Otherwise, we should be studying something else.

And, theoretically, we regard the past as the sole key to the comprehension of the present, believing that the study of institutions in their lower and simpler terms is the only way to apprehend their essential nature—the core of them, now overlaid by so many concretions that it is next to impossible to dissect it out. We work from the simple toward the complex. And we hold that, to an evolutionist, which Pareto is not, the historical sequence upon which Pareto lays such weight is of no sole significance. Clinging to the adjustment-idea, to us chronological sequence is a matter of some indifference compared with evolutionary sequence and series. The former seems to afford a lineal relation which fits better into our traditional conception, derived from history, that the time-element is basic; but with the alterations through the history of any people, however, say of the Greeks, in environmental conditions and racial character, it is not so clear that we have in that record anything unquestionably superior to a set of ethnographical descriptions of the status of different and even widely separated societies.

In any case, as elsewhere[5] stated, and although we mean to cultivate historic and even contemporary evidence so fast as it is available to us, we do not venture to rely very confidently upon history as it has been written. There is a strong suspicion, resting upon the fate of Spencer and other eminent students of society who have tried to use history, that the historians will pick all sorts of flaws in Pareto's interpretations of the Greek, Roman, and Italian past. They will say that he has got his history all wrong, despite his learned efforts to draw from original sources. And when he analyzes the present, which he thinks better known, he offers himself to an even sharper and less refutable criticism. In short, he opens himself to attack within a range where, as yet and probably for a very long time ahead, defense behind the earthworks of piled-up, verified facts is impossible. His effort, like that of Henry Adams, is likely to be regarded as a kind of literary, genial feat, not as a scientific demonstration.

If one were obliged to reply in one unqualified word to the query: Is Pareto's approach biological, psychological, or philosophical? he would have to call it psychological. It is not biological, and Pareto's often expressed contempt for philosophy is such that to call his work metaphysical would be to offend his manes. It is hard to call to mind

5. *Science of Society,* III, § 457; also essay on "Evidence," above.

any other critic who has nailed more hides of social philosophers, like Rousseau, to the barn door. He is evidently, however, no friend of psychology. The fact is that he constantly goes back to mentality—to what has been called "folk-psychology," perhaps, though there exists nothing such except metaphorically—but he does so with no deference whatever to the "schools" of psychology that succeed each other so rapidly and whimsically. His is another case where an author can by violence be classed as psychological because he takes human mental action for his start. Similarly has Sumner been classed as a psychologist and *Folkways* as "social psychology." Such pilferings are not worth the calling in of the police.

If the plumber who uses his head in the making of an admirable wiped joint is a psychological practitioner, then Pareto is one. So is each one of us a chemist and a physicist and a biologist.

This attempted extension of "psychological" to mean "mental" involves a *reductio ad absurdum*. Enough of it! If Pareto speaks of the "instinct of combinations," there is no call for a powwow over the exact meaning of "instinct"; any reader of sense knows well enough what the author means and no critic can confute his usage out of a dictionary. That Pareto did not adhere to somebody's pet and arbitrary definition is wholly immaterial and irrelevant, and any criticism of him for not doing so is gratuitous.

The value of Pareto's work does not lie in his theory of history, but in his analysis of the motives to group-action; and it does not inhere so much in that analysis as a whole as it does in his detail characterizations. The clean-cut distinction between the scientific and the non-scientific with which he begins, together with his illustrations as drawn from mankind's behavior, is a fine thing; but it is an overture to a science of society—a suggestion of a methodological order, if you will —not an integral part of a systematic "treatise on general sociology." It might well head a volume on anthropology, or economics, or, indeed, on any science whatsoever. It is a characterization of scientific method with special application to the social sciences, and as such it has few or no equals. It retires all other utterances upon "methodology" in social study, except, perhaps, the one in J. S. Mill's *Logic,* into an inglorious obscurity.

It is evident, even from a passing inspection of Pareto's various major categories, that one is going to have his troubles because of the high abstraction of the terms employed. "Residues" and "Derivations" are perhaps clear enough, but the rest do not, for the most part, impress one with their inevitableness. He experiences the feeling, all along, that he is following in the wake of a very subtle mind that has its own and rather peculiar way of looking at things and is not at all solicitous about blazing the trail so that those who trudge along after him shall lose no time in reading his markings. There is in Pareto a trait of arrogance which makes a reader feel that his own abilities are held in rather light esteem—that unless he can follow the author with ease—which he cannot—he had better drop out, and good riddance! One feels at times that the only person who could follow Pareto immediately and without effort would be someone who had duplicated the author's life, mental and spiritual, and his studies, so that his mind would act identically upon an identical content. This exaggeration may convey the impression it magnifies.

The upshot of Pareto's analysis, stated impressionistically, it may be, runs somewhat as follows: There are in society constituent groups or classes that exhibit certain basic and comparatively unvarying sentiments or attitudes, called Residues. They are at one time alert to seize upon new combinations; again, they hold back from innovations that might imperil the persistence of society. They are now progressive, now conservative. All of them project their sentiments upon the external world in the form of instruments, ritual, institutions, and the like. They exhibit attitudes harmonious with "sociality": social as distinguished from antisocial sentiments. They combine to attain and defend the integrity of the individual guaranty of rights. And, finally they all exhibit profoundly buttressed sexual sentiments. All these can be relied upon as a species of rock bottom.

But they are overlaid with a protective and often deceptive stratum of Derivations: empty "affirmations"; accepted, untested "authority"; persuasions that accord or seem to accord with sentiments, or principles that have been embraced as the result of wishful thinking; verbal "proofs" attained by word-juggling. These Derivations have no real substance or permanent color, but are light and chameleon-like. They are like the painted cheesecloth of camouflage. They are always present, for the mind delights in them; but beyond the constant feature of their presence they have no constancy, and they so obscure the vision toward reality that they must be torn away by calamitous social crises, or by the inexorably analyzing mind, before the underlying residues, the supporting realities, can be apprehended. To one who is accustomed to regard hunger, sex love, vanity, and fear of the supernatural as the basic socializing forces, Pareto's analysis appears as a kind of spectral, tenuous classification of the ways in which people feel and behave under the actions of these forces. It might be regarded as a kind of cross-classification of the folkways from a special, selected point of view—from that of one, let us say, who is primarily interested in the limits of rational action under the mores. If I do Pareto an injustice by this interpretation, I am sorry; but I cannot see the matter in any clarity otherwise. He is certainly interested primarily in the distinction between the logical (rational) and the non-logical (irrational) actions and, secondarily, between two types of what might be called automatic (irrational) response to society's life-conditions. Indeed, he sometimes seems to be bent upon demonstrating as his main thesis the essentially automatic nature of all social action.

In brief, his success in accomplishing that demonstration seems to me to be his outstanding feat in the service of the truth. It is, therefore, not his theory of history, nor his tortuous classification, as such, but his learned, comprehensive, and acute detail-analysis of societal phenomena, that leads me to class him as one of the greatest writers on human society. He has no system that deserves the name; he renders us no account of the evolution of society in the evolution of its institutions. His work is, in more than one respect, similar to that of Sumner in *Folkways;* it is not for nothing that a student of Sumner's, later of Pareto's, remarked that Pareto was unmistakably of the Sumner type in his approach to and manner of handling social phenomena. Sumner might well have written certain of the mordant passages in the *Sociologia,* and Pareto certain of the vitriolic paragraphs in Sumner's *Essays.* That same sardonic grimness seems to have characterized the expository style of both and the same deep loathing of shams and sentimentalism. "O, yes!" remarked Pareto, of the soft type of "sociology," "the kind that should be given in a cathedral, with a little music now and then"—in his own words, *"avec un peu de musique de temps en temps."*

No one should set out to read Pareto's volumes in the original unless he is prepared to brush up his Latin, and even his Greek, for the author assumes such linguistic attainments in his readers. He himself was ready to lecture in Latin. And this suggests again a certain indifference in Pareto to his readers' comfort, an absence of any intention of smoothing the way. The *Sociologia* is, as a piece of exposition, disfigured by the bulk of its footnotes, all in rather small type; and it is in these notes that his long excerpts, chiefly in Latin, occur. But one cannot afford to neglect them. The experience of the present writer, whose eyes are far from tireless, may be in point. Having decided that I must read a certain proportion of the footnotes, in order to sample them, I wound up by having to read them all. Over and over again, a passing glance at what was below the line caught attention and rendered the intended omission out of the question. Much of Pareto's best material and comment occurs outside his main text. Here is some pretty good, though unsought, evidence that a great deal of Pareto's most valuable and suggestive work lies in his detail rather than in his generalities.

It is probable that not a little of Pareto's testiness was due to his in-different health. He suffered always from insomnia and has himself described the writing of the *Trattato* as a race with death. The original Italian text is followed by pages of errata. The author must have been much astonished to find himself still living after the work had been in print for several years.

I do not wish to leave the slightest impression of derogation as re-gards Pareto. If I did not rate him very high, he would not be among the few sociologists first to be mentioned. No student of the science of society can afford to neglect him, if for no other reason than in the interest of his own critical sense. That can be said of scarcely any other writers on the general science. Pareto's treatise stands forth as one of the classics of the subject.

For reasons that need not be cited here, the name of Sumner, who is regarded by the present writer as the greatest of all students of human society, appears only incidentally in this survey.

As compared with Sumner, Spencer, Lippert, and Pareto, the rest of the sociologists fall into a distinctly secondary group. I shall not attempt to subdivide this group, which includes at one end some very meritorious writers and at the other a rabble of experts in "verbal manifestations" and not a few equivocal prophets and exhorters. I shall select a few names, chiefly of those who have attained a certain prom-inence, for brief characterization. (It is to be noted that I am always speaking of the generalizers and system-makers rather than of the "practical" sociologists or demologists. I am for the present interested solely in the theoretical or "pure-science" writers, with no disparage-ment of the devoted practitioners of "applied sociology" intended.)

Gumplowicz, to begin with, can hardly be reckoned as a student of the evolution and life of society as a whole. But he is, nevertheless, a considerable figure in the development of a genuine science of society.

There is in him a fire and positiveness that have endeared him to many a reader, in addition to their effectiveness in underscoring his dominant idea of *Rassenkampf* and *Klassenkampf* in the evolution of the State.

Political science has a right to claim him, on the ground that, whatever he called his books, they were all treatises on the State. Unquestionably, the environmental conditions of a writer on the social life of Austria-Hungary could not have left him cold to politics; they surrounded him with an atmosphere of race-struggle. The fact is that he never got very far away from it except as he wrote what might be considered a series of short essays on the conception of sociology and on its relations with the other social sciences, to statistics, history, and so on, in his *Soziologie und Politik*. That these essays are crisp and brilliant needs not to be recalled to anyone who has read them. Gumplowicz writes more like a Frenchman than a German. Nevertheless, not even by putting together all that he has written do we emerge with anything that can be called a systematic science of society. It may be said that, within the range of his interest, Gumplowicz was an unique contributor toward such a science.

The manner of death of Gumplowicz affords a key to his habits of thought. The press of August 22, 1909 carried a notice of the double suicide of himself and his aged, blind wife, to whom, in his retirement, he read aloud daily. He and she were old and poor. He discovered that he had cancer of the tongue. To a pupil, he said: "I should have shot myself long, long ago, had it not been for my wife, whose only protector I am." The aged pair discussed the situation and decided to die together by taking poison. Gumplowicz left a statement explaining that they preferred death to prolonged, hopeless, poverty-stricken suffering. Needless to say, sentimentalists all over the civilized world seized upon the occasion to express horror over this assumption of the right to die. That right was defended by an eminent American judge who was also a pillar of his church.

Gumplowicz brought to his writing on society the same fearless realism that led to that assumption of right. His exposition of the nature of rights should be familiar to every student of society.

It is not my main object, as I have noted, to enlarge upon the contributions of the several authors here treated; rather is it to record the shortcomings of their attempts at the construction of a science of society. It is fair to reply that Gumplowicz never aimed at any such large-scale construction. That he calls one of his books *Grundriss der*

Soziologie is, however, a fact which perhaps lends occasion for a brief account of what he did not do.

He has practically no historical evidence to cite, as his analysis deals almost wholly with the contemporary; and he seems to know no ethnography beyond a few chance pick-ups. His biology also is haphazard and his economics inconsiderable. In short, he presents a restricted background. And when it comes to treatment of the evolution of institutions, there is nothing to speak of upon the industrial organization, religion, marriage and the family, or the gratification-mores. He himself calls his "sociological investigations," mentioning the *Rassenkampf,* "modest opening-tones [*Anfangslaute*] to a great science of the future."

As for the essays mentioned, they are clarifying upon certain general and specific considerations and relations interesting to the sociologist; and in their brevity, style, and clarity form a startlingly agreeable contrast to most German sociological writings; but the author no more than plays around a possible science. He is surveying the land in a manner singularly keen, attractive, and even arresting; but he does no cultivating of an inductive order.

Some of us have always had a soft spot in our hearts for Letourneau, the chief cause of which has been, perhaps, that he had so many interesting and pat cases upon which we, in our early scantiness of materials, could draw. The best recourse, in a case where one recalls an apt instance but cannot place it, has so often been to look up Letoureau. And it remains true that his *Sociologie d'après l'Ethnographie* is spread upon a wide canvas. In fact, he has gone out, rather undiscriminatingly, after all varieties of social phenomena, and captured a considerable bag of them all; then he has arranged them under obvious and simple categories. Out of them has come also a series of small, separate volumes on the evolution of war, trade, marriage, education, and so on. If there ever was an industrious and tireless human ant, it was Letourneau, and his hill is worth knowing about.

It has been valuable less to him than to others; for Letourneau was unable to perform any induction of significance upon his materials. He could not rise to syntheses of consequence. In fact, he was naïf in his mental operations when it came to anything more than accumulation and classification into obvious categories. His conception of sociology was loose and vague enough for him to rate Plato and Aristotle, together with their imitators and followers, as sociologists. In brief, Letourneau was not possessed of—at any rate, did not display—any maturity of judgment, discrimination, or insight. If he had confined himself to setting down his instances in case-book fashion, under the least subtle of categories, not much would have been lost to the world. It is difficult to recall a single fructifying idea of his origination; if one thinks he has found such a treasure-trove, he suspects that further investigation will reveal that Letourneau derived it from someone else and did not comprehend it very well at that. Letourneau might be called a "hodman"—a mighty good hodman—of social science; or an exceedingly enthusiastic and industrious collector of valuable data. He was neither a builder, to use his own bricks and mortar, nor an original mind capable of extracting new truths from his rich materials.

It was the original intention to confine these estimates of authors to men no longer living, but I think Thurnwald, by reason chiefly of his inductive soundness, deserves mention above all the other names which follow. A field-observer with much data of his own, he has also read copiously in ethnographical literature. His eye has been trained to the microscopic view, at which he is an expert.

He feels the urge to synthesize but succeeds only moderately in his effort to do so. His several volumes make a kind of case-book, ineffectively digested. His attempts at generalization are unconvincing; they are really feeble and fumbling. His field-man's short perspective stands in his way. He is a kind of Letourneau, minus the Frenchman's sprightliness and plus a much more critical handling of his cases.

Thurnwald's opening volume of representative cases, while it witnesses to his preoccupation with induction, is but an ineffectual device, insofar as its bearing upon what follows is concerned. It might as well not be there; the rest would be as clear and cogent without it. It is a gesture toward induction rather than a demonstration of it.

There is no "red thread" running through the volumes. The classification of institutions is rough and somewhat vague. Thurnwald distinguishes the industrial and regulative organizations and marriage and the family. Religion appears as a set of unsystematic references to magic, and nothing much is done with property or with the mores of gratification. The political organizataion seems to stand on a par with the industrial.

The distinction between evolution and progress is blurred; the author's term, "irreversability" is apt for the case of adjustments in mechanical techniques but its general use witnesses to the aforesaid lack of distinction. Moral judgments are interspersed through the text. There is some little kowtowing to psychology, but it is verbal and tactical rather than substantial.

The exposition, even upon so invertebrate a classificatory structure, is heavy, plodding, vague, repetitious, platitudinous. The style is pedestrian; exasperating, yet soporific.

The work, so far as I have had the patience to read and scan it, is that of a very honest, laborious, inarticulate artisan, with no flashes of sweeping insight or even a gleam of humor. It would be as unendurable to read the whole, word for word, as to peruse the dictionary; there is about as much "plot" in one as in the other. I know that Thurnwald is not metaphysical or sentimental and that he has collected much raw material. But I think him devoid of what Tyndall calls "the scientific imagination."

Constantly irritating and boring is his reiteration of solemn admonition and small-caliber generalization. His chief interest seems recurrently to reside in petty, detail fault-finding with any attempt at generalization by others. If sociological generalization were conceived ever to cover more than a high percentage of the cases—if anyone of sense ever fell into the delusion that such generalization could be one hundred per cent correct—then the citation of petty exceptions might be serviceable to upset unwarranted universals. It is the way of the field-man, apparently, to condemn all generalizations, for to any one of them he happens, naturally enough, to know exceptions.

Thurnwald has something of dignity, and it is not by any means all "the dignity of dullness."

It seems hardly fair, having given space to Thurnwald, to omit such names as those of Tylor and Wilken. They rate very high indeed with anyone who has tried to write on the science of society. But they and other anthropologists have, and make, and have had made for them, no claim to the dubious title of "sociologist"; and the line must be drawn, arbitrarily, somewhere. If I include a word on other writers who have far less title, it is because they have had a claim staked out for them by indiscreet, if enthusiastic, partisans.

If L. F. Ward is to be judged by his *Pure Sociology,* in combination with his *Applied Sociology,* as he seems to have wished, the verdict is certain, and unfavorable. If it came to a choice, it seems to me that

Ward would have done well to rest his case upon his *Dynamic Sociology* rather than risk it upon the later pair of volumes. Nevertheless, the earlier work was taken up into the later, after many years of grievance because the former had been neglected by everyone; and it was with a kind of jubilation and sense of vindication that the amiable and childlike old gentleman imbibed the temporary popularity of *Pure Sociology*—dedicated grandiosely "To the Twentieth Century, on the first day of which it was begun." A simpler, kindlier, more unworldly, more childishly and inoffensively egotistical soul than Ward is seldom to be encountered. No one could begrudge him the delight of his latter days in the recognition that came to him. But the truth is that, scientifically speaking, he had better have stuck to his palaeobotany.

That Ward is saturated with analogical "reasoning" appears unmistakably in his topical headings: "Social Mechanics," "Social Statistics," "Social Dynamics," "Social Karyokinesis," "The Ontogenetic Forces," "The Phylogenetic Forces," "The Sociogenetic Forces." He has also a kind of metaphysical terminology: Parts I, II, and III of the *Pure Sociology* are headed, respectively: "Taxis," "Genesis," and "Telesis." Moreover, he dabbles constantly in psychology of a sort. His volumes are a naïve display of *Gelehrtheit*. This welter of terminology contributes in no way to exactitude or clarity.

There is no body of original materials upon which to test his generalizations. His treatment gives no unmistakable impression of induction. "The basis of method," he writes, "is logic, and the basis of logic is the sufficient reason or law of causation." The chaos of history can be made into a "cosmos" only "by using the data furnished by all the special social sciences, including the great scientific trunks of psychology, biology, and cosmology, and generalizing and coördinating the facts and groups of facts until unity is attained." A rather imposing order, and a vague; but Ward strives faithfully to honor it: he gropes out *con amore* into the "cosmos" (his autobiography, in six volumes—out of a planned twelve—is entitled *Glimpses of the Cosmos*) and retrieves all sorts of materials, the bearing of which upon the science he professes is revealed to his unearthly vision alone. There is no question about the wideness of Ward's reading and information; he is full of allusion; very many of his observations are true enough, or even striking; but I see no science of society here. In fact, though I get glimpses of many scientific facts and even of the "cosmos," I see no science at all.

Whatever Ward may be in the studies of his earlier days, he strikes me as a wishful thinker and special pleader in both his *Pure Sociology* and his *Applied Sociology*. I do not believe that a genuine scientist could have written the section in the former work entitled "The Gynaecocentric Theory" nor yet the two chapters in the latter volume on "Opportunity," in which, relying mainly upon Odin's *Genèse des Grands Hommes,* Ward proves to his own satisfaction, on very questionable evidence, that genius, existing in all classes of society, is released only under favoring circumstances or privilege. I do not see scientific dispassion present in either of these attempted demonstrations; I see merely a defense of a pre-accepted thesis set forth with a show of much random learning, so that, no matter with what conclusions the defender emerges, I should regard them with the deepest suspicion. Either of these two cases would be enough to shake any youthful belief I may once have had in Ward as a trustworthy scientist in the societal range.

One can account for the ex parte quality of his treatment of opportunity, though what his experiences with women were, beyond the hysterical adulation accorded him by certain female admirers, to motive his ridiculous gynaecocentrism, I have never been interested enough to search out. Ward was an absurdly self-centered and naïvely vain man who, almost all his life seems to have bitterly resented or agonized over the lack of recognition accorded him as an authority on society. He certainly regarded himself as an outstanding intellect; witness his autobiography. Furthermore, he was always poor and generally out of luck, and had struggled desperately for what education he could get. Is it any wonder that he saw genius always under repression by reason of lack of opportunity: of leisure and, above all, of education? He is skeptical of the "alleged self-made men," and moans over the power of circumstance. He can readily believe that the biography of the great men is "a form of history," and conclude that their number can be indefinitely increased by an extension of opportunity. This is why his whole line of thesis-defense abuts into the needs of education by the "socialization of human achievement."

I do not know the lingo of modern psychology, so as to dress up the foregoing simple and commonplace estimate of Ward with a pretentious jargon of "fixations," "aggressions," "inhibitions," "compensations," and so on. I merely offer my own homely explanation of why he, for all his learning and despite his occasional flashes of insight, was not capable of taking a scientific attitude when he entered the societal range, no matter what excellence he may have exhibited as a palaeobotanist. He had not even learned to know his own biases. He remained to the end a juvenile-minded sentimentalist and wishful thinker. What lends him a certain interest as a person, especially when combined with his paternal amiability, totally destroys confidence in him as a scientist.

In idle moments, while reflecting upon books like Ward's as possible class-texts, I have wondered what possible questions, based on an assignment of twenty or thirty of their pages, one could set to a class. That one could be nonplussed in such fashion is certainly an indication of the nature of the book he has in mind. The same uncertainty has come over me when reflecting upon Giddings's *Principles of Sociology:* I have never understood its once wide sale as a text-book, except on the grounds that it stood, for some time, alone in the field.

Giddings, like Ward, is another writer in regard to whom a critic who knew him must, lest he be disarmed in advance, seek to exclude remembrance of an appealing personality—only that Giddings was a sound, unself-conscious, witty man of the world. It is easy to see why his students cherished him in their respect and affection long after they had forgotten or discarded his specific sociological teachings. Apart from his personal appeal, the only outstanding result of his sociological thinking seems to me to be his pet formula, "the consciousness of kind." That, he once stated to me, came out of his early experience as a reporter; he had come to note the bonds between "We-folks"; that "birds of a feather flock together." There is nothing very startling about that discovery, especially as it is proverbial; but Giddings succeeded in building up a quite consistent little structure upon it and in tracing a number of social phenomena more or less plausibly to it as an underlying sentiment.

The evidence upon which Giddings based his conclusions was primarily historical, as distinguished from ethnographic; and he had many an exchange of words both wingèd and witty with the historians over their charges against him of historical inaccuracy. Into these exchanges he entered with blithe spirit, asserting against the charge that all that was valuable in sociology was history, the counter-charge that all that was worth while in history was sociology.

Even if his history was libelled, it was of no great wealth or scope. Giddings was interested in the practical, contemporary phenomena of the life of society, which he pursued with never-decreasing gusto, rather than in pure science. I cannot see that he developed anything approaching a system in the sense of Spencer or Lippert or even Pareto.

The "consciousness of kind" is too slender a base to support any such structure. He was a man of affairs rather than a scientist: a useful, sane, keen-witted, fearless critic of the contemporary. Despite my long-standing friendship with him, I have never been able to see him as a synthesist of consequence. As a teacher, however, he outranked nearly all his generation.

As regards Small, I always used to feel about him as he professed to feel about Sumner: I never understood what he was really trying to do. His name recalls to me a pleasant gentleman who, it seemed to me, was thrashing out, amidst a pale and acrid dust, over and over again, bundles of split-straws—a performance that he somewhat pompously referred to as "methodology." He was always explaining, rather didactically, just what sociology is and exactly how it must be pursued—getting elaborately and somewhat fussily ready to do something which has never come off.

Small's *General Sociology* is "an exposition of the main development in sociological theory from Spencer to Ratzenhofer." He calls it a "syllabus." His thesis is that "the central line in the path of methodological progress, from Spencer to Ratzenhofer, is marked by gradual shifting of effect from analogical representation of social structures to real analysis of social processes." By sociology, Small means a discipline whose subject-matter is *"the process of human association."* He thinks that "there is more in common between the scattered forces of sociology than can easily be made to appear. Differences of emphasis create illusions of separateness, and even antagonism, where there is only division of labor." Evidently, then, the object of this *General Sociology* is to fit a large number of separately evolved conceptions into a general pattern. So the author chips away at them, commending and deprecating, in a mood that runs benevolently but admonishingly all the way from pained surprise at density of apprehension to joyful elation over exhibitions of what he takes to be insight. He himself realizes that there are not a few "verbal manifestations" in his product: "one cannot have made the foregoing argument in ignorance that to most minds it must seem a mere churning of words. It affects even rather mature students of social science, and almost invariably specialists in other departments, as a species of speculation for which one can have no serious respect," for they regard sociology of this order "as a profitless refinement of academic trifles." And then, with quadrupled excitement, as indicated by his punctuation: "To this state of mind we must cheerfully respond: If sociology is profitless, by all means let it alone. Wisdom is justified of her children!!!!"

It is evident enough, out of the author's own mouth, that we have here something like an attempt to fix upon the greatest common divisor or core of many separately originated quantities. What stands forth pretty clearly is that the chippings make a pile that nearly fills the shop, dwarfing the common core, if any, to something like indistinguishability. About all that remains common, in the end, is that all the sociologists have been concerned with reasoning and theorizing, rather abstractly, over social phenomena. The general wind-up of the whole book is to the effect that "to do the right thing, except by accident, in any social situation, we must rightly think the situation. We must think it not merely in itself, but in all its connections." To be sure, "the philosopher may find so many things to think of that he can choose nothing to do," but not if he acquires a sweeping insight by adding cubit after cubit to his intellectual stature. "Sociology aims to become the lens through which such an insight may be possible"; it is evidently, or rather it "must be," a kind of synthesis of all the sciences. There is an almost evangelistic fervor about the writings of Small; but his evangel differs from the traditional one in that it has not been imparted in terms other than those of pious hope.

As a matter of fact, *General Sociology* is yet another treatise on methodology—how things should be done—not a system of sociology, as the author warns, "but merely an argument to indicate the line of action which may ultimately work out a credible system." It is anxiously placating rather than judgmatic; it is one of those hopeless attempts to be "constructively" critical—hopeless because they strive to mix oil and water, destruction and construction. It is a "logical juggling" of concepts of a prevailingly abstract order, emerging into conclusions vaguer than Spencer's evolution formula. There is no "feel" of science about it; its quality is soft rather than firm, idealistic rather than realistic, moralistic rather than objective, earnest rather than austere. Small is overeager to do something upon the basis of some grand theory which he hopes to distill by theory-juggling; for the slow inductive process he has no patience—indeed, no eye for it at all.

There are a number of names that have got themselves connected with the science of society in such manner that historians of the subject have felt it necessary to accord them some attention. An example is Wundt, whose *Völkerpsychologie* was once recommended vociferously to younger students of society both by psychologists who sought to instruct their inferiors and also by sociologists who ought to have known better. Wundt is not so blatant as Freud or so venturesome in his raids into country unknown to him, but he has the same self-complacence and confidence in his own empty guess-work. Whatever he may have been in psychology, he discards even the appearance of scientific accuracy and caution when he seeks to pontificate as to anthropology and the science of society. Within a very few pages he relieves the reader of the *Völkerpsychologie* of all confidence in his pronouncements. I do not propose even to illustrate. I have said already what I have to say about the so-called "psychological approach" to social science; and shall add only this: that when a man who feels himself a master of one discipline enters a field with whose details he is not familiar, with the idea of straightening everything out, he generally makes a bigger fool of himself than the veriest layman. Thinking he hears the "Macedonian cry," he rushes in with the mien of Coeur de Lion supported by the less than moderate equipment of a Don Quixote.

Resentment of mock-heroic invasions like Wundt's does not extend to non-pretentious border-line studies made by proved scientists in whatever line. The student of the science of society may profit greatly by cultivating Buckle, Tylor, Bagehot, and many another specialist who attempts no "sociology" as such, nor yet seeks to instruct or correct or admonish. Take as an illustration *Energetische Grundlagen der Kulturwissenschaft* by the eminent chemist, Wilhelm Ostwald. To his widely ranging mind the idea has been suggested that at the basis of human social life has lain the appropriation out of nature of various types of energy: physical, chemical, electric, and so on. He sets the idea forth in a small, unpretentious, gracefully written volume. The idea is sound enough, and the exposition which presents it is the more convincing by reason of the special knowledge—not of human society, but of physics and chemistry—that the author can draw upon. Studies of this order are full of suggestion to the student of society, especially as he is himself unlikely to be versed in the physical sciences. It makes all the difference in the world whether the outside specialist offers his ideas for what they may be worth or whether he enters the field as a kind of self-appointed liberator. Certain biologists who have seen themselves as emancipators of the social sciences have made unlovely spectacles of themselves in that heroic rôle.

All of the criticisms offered in connection with the foregoing names are applicable to a great number of other writers who denominate themselves sociologists but whose output is, as regards quality, insignificant. Spencer of the "biological analogy" is out-Spencered by Schäffle and Lilienfeld; Pareto as a classifier is outdone by the abstract Von Wiese and others who have not the acumen that reveals itself in Pareto's category-making and challenges the inquiring mind to follow him into whatever labyrinths he may choose to stray. There are a number of competitors, along with Simmel, for the palm of psychological and philosophical obscurity and irrelevance. Defects which are minor flaws in Spencer and other writers of first rank have been embraced and earnestly raised to the status of disqualifying weaknesses by lesser men.

As the title of this essay is "Outstanding Sociologists and Some Others," I do not hesitate to wander a little from my main topic. I have mentioned several authors who are not systematic sociologists, partly by way of throwing into relief the figures of those who are. And now I want to devote a few pages to what I call "slanters." All of us are to some degree slanters; several of the names I have cited might well come under that category; but I think the category itself needs some little attention.

Nobody doubts that objects show different aspects when viewed from different angles. It is proverbial that a shield has two sides; but the same side may take on reflections for the beholder who stands far off at an angle which he who directly faces it may not observe at all. Hence the precept that one who wants to see anything as it is must circle about it, so as to scan it from all angles—see it whole.

As elsewhere noted in these essays, there is a constant danger, particularly for the beginning student, of rationalizing the life of the masses by importing into it what he sees from the narrow angle of his own personal experience as a member of his native interest-group.

It is a somewhat similar rationalization when an author pre-selects some hitherto unoccupied or unnoticed point of view and insists upon its validity as the only answer to the ancient *pou sto*. And if the glint is a new and iridescent gleam, we are apt to flock to him and join him in his rhapsodies. We are dazzled by the bright idea and do not stop to inquire whether it is not of the *ignis fatuus* order. The older aspects seem dull and pallid beside the new one, and we straightway fall for the ancient assumption that it is gold alone that glitters.

Here is no disparagement of the sudden enlightenment that has dawned upon the mind of a Darwin, as the significance of the Malthusian conclusions for his own studies has all at once stood forth; nor even of the "accidental" discovery of a Goodyear. But too much has been made of the element of luck in such cases. It is not unreasonable to believe that opportunity lurks at many a door that remains hermetically sealed upon the sleep or sloth within. The Wedding Feast was for those Virgins who had their lamps trimmed and ready. What we call "pure luck" certainly determines many an outcome, but there is such a thing as putting one's self into or out of its field of action.

Many a man gets a slant at truth by what might be termed accident: by reason of his inborn temperament, let us say, or his life-experience; by reason of his heredity or his environment. Recall Gumplowicz, who saw the social process as a *Rassenkampf;* and why not, living as he did in old Austria-Hungary? Consider Tarde, a criminal judge who, noting that crimes arrive in waves, evolved his Laws of Imitation; Ward, who, having struggled all his life against odds, saw in education the panacea of all social ailments; Giddings, who used to say that what called his attention to "consciousness of kind" was his experience as a reporter. Nobody can help having a slant.

The slant, like many another personal peculiarity, does no harm, provided it is self-recognized, bridled, and assigned its due place. The trouble is that it is commonly ridden wildly forth into the range of the universal. It is taken too seriously. That leads to lopsidedness. The antidote is scope. If a man has that, his pet idea is going to be hitched in with team-mates, to do its proper hauling along with the rest. For scope makes for perspective and weakens the human hankering after a single cause. And multiple causation is a kind of axiom to the genuine social scientist.

Scope, breadth of outlook, is the issue of wide experience. It is well if that experience can be personal; but, in practice, for the scholar, personal experience is bound to be limited. The professional field-worker is generally a failure at synthesis. He becomes microscopical and parochial, and is likely to sneer at the inevitable injury to exactitude done by the operator in the "arm-chair"—just as the photographer might belittle the painter or the meticulous anatomist be horrified at certain of the larger effects attained by a Michelangelo—who knew all about anatomy but, with his vast scope, refused to be confined to any formula.

For the scholar, scope arrives with the wide knowledge of historic, recorded experience. Whoever has that is in a position comparable to that of the great inventors: his lightning-rod is up and ready to catch the flash of luck. Also, he is convincing. What persuaded the unimaginative specialists, Huxley's "hodmen of science," to accept Darwin's views was their conviction that Darwin knew about as much along the lines of their special interests as they themselves did. He had scope. He knew all the slants—not meaning, however, in this case, all the bright ideas set afloat by irresponsibles but all the kinds of evidence that were embodied in large accumulations of verified experience.

The slants which I have in mind are of another sort. They are occupied by men of narrow experience and interests. Their proponents are incapable of assigning them their due place. It is their hearers who have to do that, if it is done at all. But the bulk of such a prophet's exhortees will not be critical; they will like what he offers, or will dislike it, emotionally, welcoming or rejecting it accordingly.

It is useless to proclaim that the slanter must be his own prime critic. That would make him a real scientist. But what he yearns for is notoriety or some other personal advantage; or he may be, honestly enough, intoxicated by the vision or revelation which, in his naïveté, he believes to have been accorded to him. In either case, he becomes emotional. So he devotes himself to special pleading. His simple-minded audience is entranced by his eloquence, inspired by his catchwords, and pelts along after him toward some New Jerusalem. Thereafter, criticism becomes the sour, ungracious, and envious function of those who, few in number, have kept their heads.

The critics do not deny that the slant of such a prophet may reveal a ray of truth; they want only to assign that slant-aspect its proper place in the panoramic view. But they regard it as a perversion of the truth to proclaim any such restricted view as the only correct and "progressive" one. Even though the slant-view may be correct enough within its limitations, and also necessary to the panoramic one, yet it becomes, in its exaggeration, sheer illusion. It is not even a half-truth; and all fractional truth, when elevated into universality, straightway becomes the opposite of truth.

It is time to illustrate, and I am going to cite a name that is on the lips of worshipful adorers: Veblen.[6] His slant was very narrow—not nearly so wide as that of Marx, for instance; narrower than that of most of the sociological writers alluded to in preceding paragraphs.

6. H. L. Mencken (*Prejudices,* first series, pp. 59 ff.) pays his edged respects to Veblen. He performs the kind of skinning operation that should be executed on all birds of the species.

He is a first-class example of the restricted slant portrayed in such manner as to appeal to prejudice at just the favorable juncture—that is, a little before a lot of malcontents are ready to be told their grievances and equipped with good reason for their envy. The panacea gets its best chance in periods of maladjustment, when discomfort impels people to reject the givings of experience because they do not provide an immediate solution—as if any human theories or their applications could be forthwith and one hundred per cent comprehensive and effective. The expectation of such perfection in the quick molding of circumstances to the heart's desire is humanly juvenile.

A while ago, certain enthusiasts wanted to raise money contributions in honor of Veblen. He was represented as a great sociologist who had vitally influenced the whole trend of sociology. I do not recall the name of any reputable student of the science of society on the roster of sponsors of that enterprise. The truth is that the writers who have any title to the kind of service accredited to Veblen are, as this essay contends, very few indeed. I cannot see that Veblen has contributed anything whatsoever of importance to science. He could not very well do so, being no scientist himself. He is not in the same class with, say, Gumplowicz, whose slant-view has emphasized the importance of certain aspects of societal evolution that had been well enough known but assessed at less than their real significance. The value of slants has been directly proportionate to the degree of scope of their proponents, not to eloquence or other irrelevant qualities in their authors.

That last point calls for a word of elaboration. How was it that Gumplowicz managed to insert his conquest-theory of state-formation into the body of accepted or, at least, unrejected social theory? By some sort of appeal to emotion and prejudice? By representing it as a "message"? Not at all. It was because Gumplowicz, despite his obvious limitations, had scope enough to set his conclusions—results arrived at, it goes without the saying, by obviously inductive processes —in some relation with those of others which had been arrived at by the same methods. He inspired the confidence of the scientifically minded because he gave evidence of being himself so minded. He was not trying to appeal to popular discontent but was untheatrically after the truth.

The same might be said of many another investigator who has made minor additions to the body of social theory. Take two or three more cases. The rôle of the secret society was known but not fully appreciated prior to Webster's scholarly volume; Frazer shed light upon many an issue of a religious order, without himself being much of a synthesist; Ratzel succeeded, despite his prolixity, in rendering much more impressive the influence of geographical environment upon social structure. No one of these men was propagandizing for some bright idea or redeeming gospel; all were toilfully examining masses of facts to see what generalizations could be extracted from them. And one and all of them had scope enough to realize that what they had to offer must needs be fitted into a composite.

Veblen had no scope or background to speak of. Compared with these other slanters, he was raw and ignorant. He was highly emotional and naturally seized upon an emotional issue. He had a thesis to establish, not a field to investigate. His *Theory of the Leisure Classes* is no theory at all in any scientific understanding of the term. It is a partisan pamphlet, not a documented treatise. It belongs with Jack London's *Iron Heel* and the fiction-clothed "investigations" of Upton Sinclair rather than with scientific studies of the mores of interest-groups. One needs to be on his guard all the time, in reading Veblen, against his tendentious bias. He inspires no confidence in the reader that what he cites as facts, provided the reader does not know them from other evidence to be true, are facts at all. In a word, Veblen is impressionistic, which is no quality for the scientist. It is possible to extract grains of wheat from the chaff, but that is a highly hazardous process, yielding a small and dubious product.

Veblen's angle of observation is clear off to the left, from which station he seldom circulates far. He seems to have no idea of how the "leisure class" looks from other slants. Probably his temperament and life-experience rendered him incapable of occupying any other point of view; certainly what training he had did not perceptibly increase his mobility. He seems to have hankered after personal notoriety, not after the establishment of truth irrespective of its bearing upon his individual destiny or that of the "class" with which he obviously identified himself.

He gets a welcome glint from a selected point of view. Emotionalists hurry to see whether they can perceive it. They do, since they wish to. Then the whole set-up of society is viewed by them, henceforth and forever, from that side angle. That is the way "schools" of sociology are formed: the Marxian, the Paretan (before reading Pareto). Why not, then, "clinical sociology," "endocrine sociology," "Christian sociology," and so on? All such adjectives advertise the narrow slant of some petty and shaky seer.

A man with that sort of slant is evidently no scientist; much less is he capable of exercising a vital influence upon any science, no matter how undeveloped. He is an expositor, perhaps a rather vivid one, of a pre-selected thesis. That is why he becomes a kind of idol, for the time being, to those who like his slant and revere his "message." They too are wishful thinkers, and part of their wishfulness is exhibited in their bestowal on him of an acclaim to which he has won no title.

The outstanding figures first reviewed show how, the lesser ones how not, to do it. I am going to concentrate for a time on the "how not." Many writers there are who cannot even tell what they think they have got; they cannot answer even the first of the classic questions: *What is it?* There are more who can make no scientifically acceptable answer to the second test-question: *How do you know it?* They usually know it with their "whole humane totality," a faculty not readily communicable. And there are cohorts of those who have no convincing reply to the third and most devastating query: *What of it?* Generally, however, those who can pass on the second question have little trouble with the third.

It is not so much that candidates for the title of "sociologist" cannot express themselves, or that they spend toil upon investigation the results of which are trivial; the main difficulty is with the question: How do you know it? They conceive that knowledge is attainable by some process of reasoning, either from a swelling major premise or from a few selected instances. They consult their predispositions as a preliminary to suggesting revolutionary changes in the economic system or marriage or religion. They Plan under the influence of emotion. Their eyes are upon the present rather than the past, and upon the future rather than the present. Instead of working, they talk; and they are strong on rationalization. Above all else, they yearn to tell the rest what to do.

It is worth reiterating that when a man is found spending a lot of time on methodology, he usually means that he has opened no vein for digging or has mined out whatever lode he has found. Did anyone ever catch Darwin in a state of preoccupation with methodology?

There are models enough for him who wants to work, in any field; but such models never have had the time to explain their methods, even to themselves. If they had to give counsel, it would be very simple: Get to work and use common sense. And who wants advice from those who have never demonstrated? The method of science is not very recondite; it is the getting to work and sticking to it, especially to the hack-phases of it, that is hard.

There are novelists who are doing work in the social range far surpassing that of many a sociologist, and there are sociologists whose books resemble fifth-rate novels. Can anyone fail to divine why that hard-headed group of Japanese Elder Statesmen wrote privately to consult Spencer, and no one else, upon a question of their national policy? And can anyone be much surprised that the solutions volunteered by many a modern sociologist are curtly ignored as "academic"? Could Theodore Roosevelt have roguishly appointed a representative of labor to the Anthracite Commission of 1902 because he could call him a sociologist without demur on the part of the operators or anyone else, had all the sociologists been of the quality of Spencer? Men of affairs are not altogether fools; they know what a chemist or a geologist is, and know how to find, and are quite willing to trust, and to pay, a good one. There is no use bemoaning the fact that sociologists have not been called upon for leadership when they inspire in the discreet no confidence in their knowledge of facts or how to handle them. No one wants to know their visions about "reconstructing" religion or the family, or, even more ambitiously, "human nature." The young want their fairy tales to be of a less dismal type, and the mature have outgrown a juvenile credulity in preposterous utopias. The fact that candidates for scientific prestige handle a pretentious terminology recommends them to no person of discretion. And when they are actually called in by persons of discretion, their results would be laughable if they were not also deplorable, as is demonstrated by the noble experiments of recent years.

There has been a flood of wrangling among sociologists, in convention assembled, about "concepts." Beginning students in the subject must, we learn, become acquainted with "at least" sixty-two of them, including "attitude," "crowd," "group," "instinct," "personality," "social distance," "social process," and "values." Now, where do these concepts come from? There are a few, like "mores," that represent necessary distinguishing labels of bodies of accumulated and classified phenomena. They have been arrived at by such protracted labor as led to the designations "species," "atom," and the rest of the authentic scientific terms. They are objective. By contrast, a scientist in any other field has no trouble in recognizing out of his own experience that a great many of the items in any list of "sociological concepts," are, by contrast, merely gratuitous and pedantic terminology, where common terms that are well enough understood are either replaced by mysterious substitutes or exotically defined amidst hair-splittings productive of shapes and sights unholy. A large number of the proposed basic "concepts" are still worse in that they are subjective and metaphysical. To expect beginners to appropriate them is to propose a cruel and unusual ordeal. Naturally, they can all be loosely illustrated, especially by drawing upon analogy, as in philosophy and ethical exhortation. The process of their genesis seems to have been that of "free meditation" over a few facts hastily scanned under some emotional spell.

"Consciousness of kind" is not represented in this list. I do not regard that "concept" as world-shaking, but it was at least the outcome of a long-accumulated set of impressions upon an alert and honest mind. It is cited here as in attractive contrast to a number of the abstractions and pointless distinctions with which it is proposed to clutter up the minds of beginners. The more faithfully an earnest student strives to appropriate such sets of concepts, the worse for him. To propose to start him off in this manner reveals an ignorance, I do not say of "pedagogy" or educational theory, but of the practical art of teaching. Beginners need something with substance, to "chew on." Masticating froth cannot fail to make them flatulent and colicky. Even their milk teeth cannot be cut on dough.

What is called for, to produce a germ of confidence in sociology, is not a pseudo-impressive parade of abstractions, nor self-recommendation in any of its forms, nor mutual recrimination over matters so far removed from general experience and vocabulary as to be incomprehensible to a well-educated layman. Who cares whether A forces a fancy terminology on B or vice versa? What is needed is substance of some sort: actual work to show, actual learning, actual experience, actual demonstration. Any student of society who is prepared to offer a product of industry in assembling cases, together with modest and understandable inferences as to their meaning—comparable in quality, no matter how humble, with Darwin's volumes on barnacles or to Spencer's *Descriptive Sociology*—will look impressive enough. He has foils aplenty before whom to appear like a colossus.

The need of the present and of a considerable stretch of the future, if there is ever to be a science of society in anything but the name, is a long series of thorough, factual detail studies. Only thus have syntheses been made possible that have had assured prestige. It is a safe bet that any productive synthesis in the social realm will arrive only after a similar preparation. There is no legitimate call for shovelling together a tangle of random "concepts" and utopian yearnings. If, prior to Darwin's time, naturalists had merely composed dithyrambic orations and adjurations about plant and animal life, panting with divine compassion after a "reconstruction" of Nature ("red of tooth and claw") to the heart's desire, there would have been no *Origin of Species*.

Before Darwin came there had been many humble investigators of nature who were not aiming at any generalizations whatever. There were the practical plant-breeders who had as little background in comprehensive science as Luther Burbank. Then there were the unworldly artists, again like Burbank, who, stimulated by no thought of gain, pursued through life some hobby, often a very narrow one. Collectors of butterflies described the minutiae of their coloration and structure; pigeon-fanciers had their own publications through which to inform and counsel one another as to the details of the art in which they had a common and consuming interest. The Dutch tulip-mania had its parallels, over and over again, on a smaller scale and humbly and obscurely recorded. In brief, for a long time men had been interested in observing and recording with anxious exactitude and in leaving behind them myriads of facts about plant and animal life. Their interest was microscopic, specific, unoriented; it was that purely of the collector whose mania was for comprehensiveness and exactitude within a narrowly circumscribed area. Thus came into being many thousands of monographs of a nature drily objective and practically innocent of imagination and insight.

And then duly appeared the famous invalid with his fabulous capacity for labor, his ever-growing sagacity in experimentation, his incredible scientific scope, his transparent honesty, and his mind keyed to comprehensiveness.

If there is ever to be a Darwin of the social sciences, he will need just the kind of objective, descriptive, preliminary detail-studies without which the historic Darwin, despite all his personal qualifications, could not have achieved the ordering of the world's knowledge and thought for which he is acclaimed.

The beginner in sociology confronts a situation more difficult than does the apprentice in other lines. First of all, there is the multiplicity of eager guides who besiege him as the European traveller is pulled about by rival porters. And he must usually face, as he starts out on his teaching, the necessity of conforming to some locally esteemed "school," of dealing with the practical or applied aspects of the subject —indeed, he is quite likely to be required to give instruction in economics, ethics, or some other longer-established discipline. This is not bad for him, for it is of a piece with the "general practice" admittedly wholesome for the would-be specialist. In the older days the newest college instructor was expected to teach the subjects his superiors liked least. Sumner began his career by teaching geometry and Greek. It did not hurt him. He was not like the narrow specialist who was capable of teaching only the last fifteen minutes of Louis XIV's reign.

An indispensable requirement for the beginner in social science, undergraduate or graduate student, is to make himself intimately acquainted with the life and work of Darwin, or some other genuine scientist, as a model to be kept ever before the eye. Then he will have acquired for mere "concepts" a distaste which will exempt him somewhat from the temptation to conceal or pad out his little store of real knowledge by a camouflage of bright ideas or a stuffing of east wind.

The pull of that temptation is, for a graduate student, very formidable indeed. He cannot yet know very much; nevertheless he is presently a beginning teacher who must make a showing somehow. He must hold his classes and at the same time impress older colleagues in whose hands his destiny lies; and both classes and colleagues are apt to be more immediately susceptible to show than to substance. From the standpoint of science, it is a pity that this is so; one hesitates to say it, but it would be a good thing for the science of society if it could number among its devotees more men in comfortable private circumstances, upon whom would impinge fewer of the forcing processes that weigh upon the impecunious and anxious teacher. And I hasten to say that fellowships granted by educational foundations do not seem to me ever likely to take the place of unsupervised private means. The trouble is that *"Wer den (Geld-) Pantoffel führt, gebietet,"* while there is nothing more individualistic than scientific research and discovery. To do his best, the scientist should be his own master. Free individual initiative exercised in solitude is the only thing that ever produced variation and new adjustment. There is far too much weight attached in these days to collectivism. It usually amounts to interference by the incompetent with the precious initiative of the competent.

I do not say that teaching is bad for the scholar, or poverty good; I suggest only that teaching may have its unfavorable influence. So may wealth; there seems to have existed a kind of affinity between poverty of material resource and successful scientific achievement. I do not need to cite cases; consider only the proverb covering the mother-child relation between necessity and invention.

The tendency now seems to be to rebel against teaching. A young man is sorry for himself if he has to do much of it; and others are sorry enough for him to endow escapes into research. But every serious instructor knows how much he is learning while he teaches. The necessity of exposition gets his facts and ideas into both definiteness and order, if he is capable of developing those essentials, and he picks up an endless gleaning of criticism, not only from his hearers but from listening, more or less subconsciously, to himself. He says something striking and perhaps the class responds, but "Risky!" is the verdict of the inner monitor. And then, by contrast, he coins out something that strikes him at the instant as apt and true—and too often, alas! he cannot recall it when the lecture is done.

The truth is, as regards teaching, that the self-critical instructor, once realizing the situation, can use it for what it is worth and guard against the perils lurking in it. If he has sense enough to do that, I am confident that it is better to do some teaching along with one's study than not to do any. And, in general, most human beings need, for very discipline's sake, to have duties imposed from without. Self-direction, though theoretically very desirable and even noble, is a stance difficult to hold. It is hard on the nerves. Man being what he is, it is, after all, good to have a "job."

There are enough books on human society nowadays that are capable of being used as texts for beginners—I mean books with plenty of facts in them, from which the beginner, student or teacher, can draw modest inductions of worth. If the young teacher restrains his tendency or aspiration to evolve cosmic theories, he will get along well enough. The facts of anthropology and of societal evolution in general are human and interesting to most young people around the age of twenty. They will retain their interest even if they are not encouraged to out-Bertrand Russell. And it is as sure as shooting that keeping close to the facts will succeed where the parade of a host of "concepts" corresponding to nothing in student-experience can evoke only confusion and boredom.

It seems to me that no particular preparation is needed for the professional study of sociology beyond interest enough to drive one through the toil of collecting and classifying materials. The assertion that some sort of a priori exercises are indispensable as preliminaries to that activity has always left me cold. One must always, crows the metaphysician, select his evidence upon some "philosophical criteria." Of course one has to decide what he will collect. Anybody who intends to study geology must naturally plan to collect rocks, not postage stamps. If that is to "select evidence," then nobody ought to feel misgivings if some specialist in eternal verities accuses him of that misdemeanor. The trouble with the accuser who lodges this stale charge is that he is so accustomed to select his "evidence," through his skillful or clumsy recourses to analogy, that he cannot conceive how anyone could be innocent of his own weakness (any more than some primitives can believe in a liceless man). Furthermore, he is intent upon proving that "some philosophy" must underlie all science, a sentiment which flatters both himself and his subject. That, too, is why he does his buzzing on the theme of "What do you *mean* by 'facts'?" or some other melody adapted to his type of *chanson,* his paean on philosophy as the master science. He cannot believe that a priori assumptions, his *deliciae,* can be revolting to any intelligent human being.

He mouths the phrase, "Man does not live by bread alone," neglecting to add that he cannot exist without it. He repeats what he has been told, that nothing is so dull and arid as a mere collection of facts. Everyone knows that facts by themselves are sterile. To harp on that truism is like insisting that two and two are four—a common practice of those to whom "God has revealed himself in the form of platitudes." Facts must be illuminated; it is only a question of how. And the scientist rejects the *ignis fatuus,* with its ambiguous waverings, in favor of the kind of glow from within outward that lights things up, and also heats the raw material into incandescence. He lets the facts light themselves up by induction. He lets them, to change the metaphor, tell their own story instead of having insubstantial imaginings thrust upon them.

The objector, for one more instance of his operations, cries out for "open-mindedness," meaning really "credulity." That is what the uplifter with a message means when he exhorts to open-mindedness and inveighs against "dogmatism," that latter term being applied by most accusers of the type before us to any firm conviction won arduously by the scientific method. To certain specimens of the microcephalous, it is dogmatic to assert that faith has never moved a mountain nor absent treatment set a broken leg. "Open-mindedness" means to more people than one likes to think no more than a suppression of the critical faculty, a lack of fortitude in standing by conviction. An exhortation to open-mindedness in that common-enough sense of the term is nothing else than an encouragement to intellectual cowardliness and treachery to the truth. The conquests of culture have never been attributable to soft and mean spirits.

No one has a divine right to say what "sociology" means. All that even the dictionaries can do is to record usage. Even Spencer, who put the term "sociology" into current usage, has no right to say what it means nowadays. The respectability of "sociology under Spencer's hand has been tarnished under those of unworthy successors, just as John Smith's good manners may have been corrupted by evil communications; nevertheless, John Smith is not thereby made into James Brown, but, even in his diminished repute, keeps his designation still. It might conceivably be more expedient for John to re-name himself, if he gets religion and desires to lead a new life. It might be better for the peace of mind of a young fellow not to bear the name John Smith, on account of its associations, just as a certain American citizen recently repudiated his family name of "Hitler" because, he said, everyone jeered at him and called out "Heil!" when he hove in sight. It might be better to drop the term "sociology" as perverted beyond hope of redemption. Some such consideration lay behind Sumner's attempt to replace it. The other alternative is to labor with John Smith, urging him to regain his respectability through bringing forth fruits meet for repentance. It all depends upon how hopeless John's status is thought to be.

Although no one has the right to say what sociology shall be, in common usage, he has the privilege of deciding for himself that his own studies, whatever they may be called, shall be directed toward the development, within the societal range, of an authentic science. That is a clean-cut objective, whether or not it is ever to be realized, whether or not, indeed, it is realizable. He can repudiate, for himself, all speculative philosophizing about society, all easy manipulation of "concepts," all "bright ideas," all efforts to crash the limelight by pleasantly shocking people or by toadying to their prepossessions. He can struggle against the temptation to say things that will evoke an arch squeal: "Oh, Professor!" from his auditors as he addresses some woman's Saturday morning club, or otherwise to exhibit himself as a devil of a fellow. It is not necessary to be clapped into jail for soapbox tactics, or to figure in a divorce scandal, or to get up risqué questionnaires, in order to prove one's self a scientific sociologist. By restricting one's ambitions to his desk he is relieved, even though he sacrifices publicity, of cutting stagy pigeon-wings of any description. It is a quiet kind of life, distasteful to certain temperaments, but there is in it some hope of durable achievement in helping to erect a science where one is desperately needed, even though the materials one manages by a lifetime's diligence to furnish are eventually buried in the foundation masonry so as no longer to emblazon his name.

INDEX

Adams, G. B., 5, 288, 290ff.
Adams, Henry, 289, 313, 317
Adjustment Idea, the, chap. V; and variation, chap. VI
Adversity, 185; see also Aleatory Element
Aeschylus, 264, 269
Agency vs. Cause, 5, 6, 36, 115ff.; see also Arrangers of Things
Agnosticism, 7, 164ff., 186, 187
Aleatory Element, 50, 55, 140, 154ff., 176, 185ff.
Analogy, 14ff.; biological, 304
Anarchism. See -Isms
Anthropology, 286
Arrangers of Things, 52, 82ff.; of sex relations, 237ff.
"As if," 23
Authority, 25, 53, 77, 147ff., 299ff.
Automatic Forces, 48, 50ff., 109, 114ff., 126, 208, and passim; see also Evolution

Bible, the, 136ff.
Big Medicine, 159; see also Planning
Biology, 14ff., 309
Birth Rate, 119ff., 133ff.; control of, see Prudential Restraint
Bisexuality, 55, 204, 218, 240; see also Sex Differences
Bismarck, O., 131
Browning, R., 261, 274, 275
Builders of Delusion, 3, 153

Capitalism, 95, 96
Cardozo, B., 29, 289
Chambers, R. W., 282
Chance, 13, 78; see also Aleatory Element
Children, 223ff., 234ff.
"Christian Gentleman," 144ff.; see also Lincoln
Church, 32
Civilization, 157; benefits the weaker, 201ff.; see also Culture
Classics, 136, 137
Clean Sweep, 66, 67, 163; see also "New Level"; Planning
Clergy, 146ff.
Common Sense, chap. II, 85

Communism, 57, 180, 231; see also -Isms
Concepts, 338ff.
Conservatism, 60, 69, 74ff., 98, 108; see also Permanencies
Continuity. See Clean Sweep; Zones of Transition
Contraception, 134ff., 221, 222; see also Prudential Restraint
Coöperation, 53, 101; antagonistic, 64
Coördination, 53
Cost, 92ff.
Credulity, 85; see also Open-mindedness
Criticism, 91, 302ff.; see also Pareto
Culture, 79
Cumulative Impression, chap. XVII

Dante, 260, 270, 271
Darwin, C., 3, 4, 14ff., 20, 21, 35, 166, 168, 192, 284, 285, 296, 299, 302, 308, 309, 337, 339ff.
Death, fear of, chap. XII
Deduction, 3, 22; see also Wishful Thinking; Logic
Deity, anthropomorphic, 141
Dialectics. See Philosophy
Dictatorship, 94, 95; see also -Isms
Discards, 57, 58
Discipline, 100ff., 180ff., 218, 219, 241ff., 246
Discussion, 32
Divorce, 219, 220
Doers of Things, 82ff., 146, 147; see also Arrangers of Things
Dogmas. See Theology
Doing vs. Thinking, 12, 13, 70, 143
Dual Standard, 221
Duruy, V., 291ff.
Duties, 77, 246; and rights, 107ff.

Economy of Abundance, 126; planned, see Planning
Education, 29ff., 184, 185, 212ff., 246ff.; see also Youth
Emergency, 23
Emotionalism. See Planning; Science; Utopia
Environment, 55; see also Life-conditions

Index

347

"Man, the Master," 48, 49; "the Oppressor," 203, 213; *see also* Arrangers of Things

"Man-made World," 203

Marriage, for alliances, 226; alternatives to, 219ff.; for sake of offspring, 223ff.; companionate, 237; as economic partnership, 227ff.; idealization of, 231, 232; modern motives, chap. XIV; of romance, 227; for ostentation, 226

Masses, the, 27ff., 143, 153, 158; *see also* Public Opinion

Maturity Tests, 241ff.; *see also* Discipline; Youth

Metchnikoff, E., 188

"Methodology," 286, 287, 318, 337; *see also* Small, A. W.

Milton, J., 260, 270

Moral Judgment, 292, 293, 294

Morale, 173ff.

Morals, 59, 60

Mores, 14ff., 33ff., 50, 100, 204, 219, and *passim*

Murdock, G. P., 310, 312

"New": Deal, 71; Dispensation, 287; Level, chap. VII, 54, 201ff., 224; Jerusalem, 80, 209; Social Order, 93, 94

Novel, as evidence, 279ff.; historical, 280ff.; romantic, 279, 280

Novus Ordo Seclorum, 55, 71; *see also* "New"

Numbers, chap. X; limitation of, 126ff.; mania for, 124ff.; *see also* Standard of Living

Oath, 62, 63

Obvious, the. *See* Common Sense; Proverbs

"Old," 251; *see also* "New"; Planning; Utopia

"Old-fashioned Continence," 129

Open-mindedness, 343; *see also* Credulity

Opportunity, woman's, 208ff.; *see also* Education

Origin of Species, The, 3, 16, 45, 278

Ostwald, W., 331

Overpopulation. *See* Population; Numbers

Parenthood, 244, 245

Pareto, V., 104, 120, 253, 254, 255, 262, 309, 313, 336

Partisanship. *See* Planning

Past, the chronological *vs.* the evolutionary, 254ff.

Paternalism, 244

Peace, the trend toward, 130ff.; of mind, 175; *see also* Religion

Permanencies, the, 36ff., 55, 59ff., 66, 139, 233, 234, 240; *see also* Adjustment; Variation; Institution

Persistence. *See* Permanencies

Perversion by Oversimplification, 27ff.

Philosophy, 7ff., 25, 44, 45, 59; *see also* Spencer

Plans and Planning, chap. VIII, 25ff., 51, 77, 247, 337; *see also* Methodology

Poets, 45, 46, 261; English, of nineteenth century, 273; poets' guesses, 3; *see also* Evidence

Popularization of Social Science, chap. III

Population, chap. X; Law of, 121

Positivism, 165

Prayer, 177ff.

Prehistory, 283; *see also* Ethnography

Press, the, 31ff.

Probability, 58

Proof, 16

Property, 60; *see also* Institution

Prophecy, as argument, 209; as evidence, 198ff.; scientific, 214

Prostitution, 219ff.

Proverbs, 34, 35, 65, 73, 87, 272

Prudential Control, Restraint, 122ff., 195; *see also* Contraception; Malthus; Standard of Living

Psychology, 10ff., 116, 130, 222, 225, 317, 318, 327; *see also* Wundt

Public Opinion, 59, 63ff., 72, 111, 112, 126ff.; *see also* Popularization; Social Virtues; Permanencies

Purposes and Consequences, 50, 117, 134; *see also* Wishful Thinking

Radio, 33

Rationality, 35, 36, 118; Ante- and Post-rationality, 65; *see also* Science

Rationalization, 73, 153ff., 191, 218

Realism, 94, 280; *see also* Science

Rearguard Action, 129

Relativity, 53ff.

Religion, what is happening to, chap. XI; nature of, 136ff., 149, 150; as "opiate of the people," 175, 177; and numbers, 123ff., 128ff.; of the scientist, 165ff.; services and survival value of, 173ff., 196, 197